Protestant Thought in the Nineteenth Century

❧❧❧❧❧❧❧❧❧❧❧❧❧❧❧❧❧❧❧❧❧❧❧❧❧❧❧❧❧❧❧❧❧❧❧

Protestant Thought in the Nineteenth Century

Volume 1, 1799-1870

❧❧❧❧❧❧❧❧❧❧❧❧❧❧❧❧❧❧❧❧❧❧❧❧❧❧❧❧❧❧❧❧❧❧❧

by

Claude Welch

New Haven and London

Yale University Press

Designed by John O. C. McCrillis
and set in Baskerville type.
Printed in the United States of America by
The Murray Printing Co., Forge Village, Mass.

Published in Great Britain, Europe, and Africa by
Yale University Press, Ltd., London.
Distributed in Latin America by Kaiman & Polon,
Inc., New York City; in Australasia and Southeast
Asia by John Wiley & Sons Australasia Pty. Ltd.,
Sydney; in India by UBS Publishers' Distributors
Pvt., Ltd., Delhi; in Japan by John Weatherhill,
Inc., Tokyo.

Contents

Preface   ix

1   The Problem of a History of Nineteenth-Century Theology   1
    Historiographical Note   8

2   The Eighteenth-Century Background   22
    Pietism and Evangelical Revival   22
    Enlightenment and Rationalism   30
    Romanticism   52

Part I   1799–1835 The Possibility of Theology   57

3   Schleiermacher's Theological Program   59
    The Nature of Religion   64
    The Structure of Theology   68
    The Naming of God   76
    Theology and History   81

4   Religious Truth in Image and Concept: Hegel and the
    Speculative Theology   86
    Dynamics of a System   88
    The Place of Religion   91
    The Nature of Christianity   99
    Issues and Consequences   104

5   Reasoning Faith and Faithful Reason: Coleridge
    and the Struggle against the Eighteenth Century   108
    The Rational Character of Faith   113
    The Idea of God   120
    Church and Nation   121
    The Authority of Scripture   123

6   God's Moral Government or Man's Goodness: Taylor
    and Channing   127

Part II   1835–1870 The Possibility of Christology   139

    Introduction: The Shapes of the Problem   141

7   The Claim of History   147
    David Friedrich Strauss   147
    Ferdinand Christian Baur   155
    Alois Emanuel Biedermann   160
    Essays and Reviews   167

8   Humanism, Religion, and Culture   170
    The Celebration of Man: Ludwig Feuerbach   170
    The Divinity of Man: Emerson and the
        Transcendentalists   177
    Religion, Culture, and Man: Comte, Mill, Carlyle,
        and the Arnolds   183

9   Strategies for Restoration and Conservation   190
    Confessionalism, Repristination, and Biblicism   194
        The Idea of the Confessional Church in German
            Lutheranism   194
        "Biblical Realism": Johann Tobias Beck   198
        The Princeton Theology   200
        The "Absolute Divinity" of Jesus Christ: H. P. Liddon   204
    Confession and Catholicity: The Struggle for Creative
        Theologies of the Church   207
        Newman and the Oxford Movement   207
        The Erlangen Theology   218
        The Mercersburg Theology   227
    The New Venture in Kenotic Christology   233

10 Toward a Critical Orthodoxy: Frederick Denison Maurice   241
    The Method   243
    The Kingship of Christ   247
    The Knowledge of God   253

11 Toward a Critical Orthodoxy: Horace Bushnell   258
    Theological Language and a Right Sensibility   258
    Organic Solidarity in Sin and Redemption   263
    Symbols of Incarnation and Atonement   265

12 Mediation, Speculation, and Criticism   269
    The Program of Mediation   269
    The Incarnation as Progressive: Isaak August Dorner   273
    Speculation, Criticism, and Secularity: Richard Rothe   282

13 Subjectivity as Truth and Untruth. Søren Kierkegaard   292
       Christianity versus Christendom   295
       Away from the Aesthetic!   299
       Away from the System: Thought and Existence   303
       Away from the System: Truth Is Subjectivity   306
       Subjectivity as Untruth   310

    Index   315

Preface

This volume had its origin nearly twenty-five years ago, when I first began to lecture at Princeton University on religious thought since 1800. Thus to many graduate and undergraduate students at Princeton, Yale, and Pennsylvania, as well as to faculty, I owe a great debt for encouragement and criticism in projecting and shaping the work. Among the faculty colleagues, however, Professors H. Richard Niebuhr and Hans W. Frei of Yale, Professor Wolfhart Pannenberg of the University of Munich, and Professors Van A. Harvey and Robert F. Evans of Pennsylvania deserve special words of gratitude for continuing counsel and debate. Professor Frei, in particular, has critically reviewed various drafts of the entire manuscript. The University of Pennsylvania granted me a leave of absence in 1968, when large portions of the text were prepared as lectures at the University of Mainz—doubtless a reason for some of the Germanisms that remain in the text.

The problems involved in writing a history of nineteenth-century Protestant thought are discussed at some length in chapter 1. I need add here only that I am keenly aware of the extent to which this volume represents a series of compromises. The state of scholarship concerning the nineteenth century calls for a work which will be useful both to the mature interpreter and to the nontheologian, and which will also be of value for readers on the Continent and in Great Britain as well as in the United States. Since Americans, even those with considerable theological sophistication, are often ill-informed about large segments of nineteenth-century European theology, while continental readers are often quite unaware of British or American developments, the task of mutual interpretation is important. To this end I have tried to strike a balance between locating major figures in the context of broad trends and themes and being faithful to the primary distinctive theological intentions of the thinkers themselves.

In every case I have sought to give a fresh reading of the original sources and to advance the state of discussion by redrawing the map of nineteenth-century theology. Yet the final result must also be considered a general introduction, designed to encourage the reader to go farther. Hence a modest bibliographical apparatus has been provided.

It is painfully obvious that in this work I have not been able to deal in any adequate way with Protestant thought in France, in the Netherlands, or in Scandinavia. This is a fundamental shortcoming, but in the interest of trying to hold together at least the German, British, and American patterns of thought, it was another compromise that had to be made.

Chapter 1 has been published in a slightly different form in the *Journal of Religion* 52, no. 1 (January 1972): 1–21, by mutual agreement of the Bross Foundation, the Yale University Press, and the University of Chicago Press.

In due course I expect to proceed to the writing of volume 2, which will treat the last third of the nineteenth century, that is, from 1870 to the beginning of World War I.

C. W.

Berkeley, California
1972

1

The Problem of a History of
Nineteenth-Century Theology

The student of religious thought in the nineteenth century is confronted by a curious puzzle. It has long been agreed that between the publication of Friedrich Schleiermacher's *Speeches on Religion, to the Cultured among Its Despisers* (1799) and the outbreak of World War I there occurred dramatic and far-reaching changes in the patterns and styles of Protestant theology. These may be saluted as creative breakthroughs or they may be put down as dangerous though finally only temporary detours from the true line of development, or they may even be combated as the expressions of infidelity and apostasy. But that there occurred theological events of decisive importance, few will deny. Further, it is at least a defensible thesis that the theological situation of the twentieth century is peculiarly dependent on the developments of the nineteenth century. That is, not only do the same problems continue to bedevil and to fascinate, but the shapes which those questions still bear are essentially derivative from the forms they were given in the nineteenth century. This is one of the reasons why in the present generation we see an impressive renewal of study of nineteenth-century theology, not only of the few giants whose names have always been familiar, though whose work may actually have been as much hidden as disclosed by well-worn clichés, but also of many other thinkers whose significance has been less well attended to.

In spite of that, a general history of nineteenth-century Protestant theology has not yet appeared.[1] Works which have passed for this

---

1. It would be too much to ask for a combined study of Protestant and Roman Catholic thought—to say nothing of religious thought in general in the West. Attempts can be made to identify the common influences on the theological trends of the century from the French Revolution on, but the responses of Roman Catholic and Protestant thinkers were sufficiently diverse (and the areas of theological concern even more so) that it would be artificial to try to combine them in a common scheme of interpretation. There were important points of contact, to be sure, and these will be appropriately noted. But I shall be content in this volume to focus on the Protestant

have in fact turned out to be something else, usually histories of theology simply in Germany, or in Britain, or in America. (See the appended historiographical note for a detailed discussion of the literature and of this problem.) It is my intention in this volume to help remedy that defect, for I believe that the common practice has been badly wanting.

I propose, therefore, to take a new look at Protestant theology in the nineteenth century, and to view it as nearly as possible as a whole, at least with respect to the German, British, and American scenes. The full dimensions and heuristic value of such an interpretation can naturally be seen only in the detailed elaboration of the chapters that follow, but the bare outlines can be sketched briefly.

It can be assumed that the century, defined as extending from the publication of Schleiermacher's *Speeches* in 1799 to World War I, is a significant chronological span. This is a judgment not likely to require extensive defense. Though it would be foolish to suppose that beginnings and endings are absolute or that tendencies everywhere follow precisely the same time scale, not many will dispute that the work of Schleiermacher marks a crucial turning in Protestant theology. His friends and foes alike have judged him to be the founder of an epoch, though obviously he does not stand alone as a sign and source of transition into a new century. Nor will it often be denied that World War I is a more significant landmark in theological history than is the year 1900. Just what sort of theological beginnings, endings, and crises these chronological points of reference may indicate, and whether they necessarily denote a single epoch in Protestant thought, are questions for investigation; but that these are useful reference points we may take for granted.

In the interest of moving away from the scheme of national history and of seeking valid perspectives from which theological efforts on the Continent, in Britain, and in the United States may be viewed together, we may divide the century into three segments: 1799 to 1835, 1835 to 1870, and 1870 to 1914.[2] The validity of this periodization can be established only by the whole of the study, but it is a scheme that seems to me almost inescapable.

The first of these periods was dominated politically and socially

---

side of the developments. For a general study of Roman Catholic theology, see Edgar Hocedez, S.J., *Histoire de la théologie au XIXe siècle*, 3 vols. (Brussels, 1947–52).

2. A similar pattern is adopted by Hocedez for 19th-century Roman Catholic theology in *Histoire de la théologie.*

by the repercussions of revolution—by the French Revolution followed by the Napoleonic wars and the Restoration, or by the American Revolution and the consequent attempt to build a new nation. In literature, the romantic movement was at its peak. Theologically, the era was most significantly represented by Schleiermacher and Hegel, by Coleridge and Bentham, and by Taylor and Channing. The deaths of Hegel in 1830, Bentham and Goethe in 1832, and Coleridge and Schleiermacher in 1834 made the early 1830s a definite terminus.

The beginning of the second third of the century may appropriately be symbolized by the publication in 1835 of David Friedrich Strauss's *Life of Jesus*—though in Britain the Reform Bill of 1832 and the launching of the Oxford Movement were equally significant. The 1830s in Germany were marked by a sense of great change. Revolution broke out anew. The collapse of idealism, which had been born out of the Protestant spirit, was experienced as a collapse of Christianity itself; and the influence of the mixture of inherited Christianity with *Aufklärung* and idealism was weakened. That the 1830s marked a decisive turn in religious thought in America is less immediately evident, yet one recalls Emerson's famous Divinity School Address of 1838, a manifesto of the Transcendentalist movement.

On every hand emerge indications that the period from the 1830s to about 1870 forms an intelligible segment of theological history. To note only a few: this is precisely the span that may most usefully be called the "Victorian era"; [3] it is the time "between Schleiermacher and Ritschl"; it nicely encompasses both the Transcendentalist era and the development of the confessionalist Princeton theology by Charles Hodge; it embraces the active careers of such thinkers as F. D. Maurice (1805–72), Horace Bushnell (1802–76), Ludwig Feuerbach (1804–72), Gottfried Thomasius (1802–75) and J. C. K. von Hoffman (1810–77)—to say nothing of the many others (including Kierkegaard) whose primary work falls within this time. All in all the period is singularly rich and diverse in theology (perhaps its complexity is one of the reasons it so often tends to be passed over in the surveys of theology as one hastens to get from Schleiermacher to Ritschl). The 1840s in particular stand out as a lively and fertile theological era; and through the revolutions of 1848 and the Chartist

3. See Walter E. Houghton, *The Victorian Frame of Mind, 1830–1870* (New Haven, 1957).

and Christian Socialist movements, this decade also provided the political and social axis for Europe. The year 1846 has been called the "year of decision" for America (by Bernard De Voto), even though 1860 might be a better analogue to 1848 in Europe, since American energies for social reform were focused on the slavery issue.

Finally, then, the years 1870 to 1914 remain as a feasible unit for theological as well as for political and social history. This is the period between the Franco-Prussian War of 1871 (or in America, the Civil War) and World War I—a time in which "Victorianism was dying, and a new frame of mind was emerging," [4] a time of growing industrialism and urbanization, a flourishing of that bourgeois mood that Tillich has called "self-sufficient finitude," a period of imperialism and heightened national self-consciousness. Theologically, the landmarks may be less clear-cut than at some other points in history, but the most appropriate sign for the beginning of the era is surely the publication of the first volume of Albrecht Ritschl's *Justification and Reconciliation* in 1870, since Ritschl proves to be the most "representative" theological man of the period, the thinker in whom many of its characteristic concerns and tendencies are brought together. To say this, of course, is not to deny the great impact of Darwin's *Origin of Species* (1859) or the storm in England over *Essays and Review* (1860), which broke open the biblical question.

A fresh approach to the history of nineteenth-century theology will also involve asking, not primarily about the relation of theologians to the development of particular schools or parties, but how the individual thinkers, schools, and programs alike reflect the presence of dominating theological concerns, tendencies, and problems, through which the character of the century as a whole may be more adequately understood.

It is not profitable, in my judgment, to seek a single center for the great array of theological efforts in the century—nor to view its three epochs as successive stages in movement toward a single outcome—but it does seem possible to identify three interweaving themes, or questions, that appear in shifting focus and fluctuating intensity as major preoccupations of theologians throughout the century, without respect to national boundaries. These I shall formulate as (1) the question of the possibility of theology, (2) the question of the possibility of Christology, and (3) the question of Christianity

4. Ibid., p. xv.

and culture. Each of these areas of concern led to radical questioning and profound change, and in each it becomes strikingly plain how the theological problems of the twentieth century are continuous with those of the nineteenth. Each focus of interest is present at all stages of the century's development, since each necessarily involves the others, and any one of the themes could usefully be used to organize a discussion of the whole century. Yet in each of the three periods one seems to predominate over the other two.

The "possibility" of theology means both the question of the inner logic or rationale of the theological enterprise and the question whether theology is possible at all. It is the problem of theological method as well as the constellation of problems that could later be summed up as the question of "God-talk" or of the nature of religious assertions. Other labels calling attention to different aspects or elements might also be used, for example, the problem of the knowability of God, or reason and revelation, or the meaning of revelation, or the relation of religious knowing (or believing) to science's way(s) of knowing, or the right of theology to exist alongside other *Wissenschaften,* or the nature and authority of the Bible as an organ of revelation, or the nature of religion. This area of questioning could be said to dominate Protestant thought in the whole of the nineteenth century (or even from the Enlightenment to the present). But it was especially the problem of the first third of the century, the center of the efforts of Schleiermacher, Hegel, and Coleridge (all, of course, against the background of Kant), and in a different way of Channing. And out of the work notably of Schleiermacher and Coleridge emerged new directions for understanding the nature of religious truth and the theological enterprise as a whole, requiring new recognitions of the uncertainties of theological language, and of the role of the religious subject in every view of the "object" of religious belief. As has often been remarked, the question after 1800 was no longer primarily whether revelation was to be affirmed or denied, but first of all what the very idea of revelation meant.

The questions of the nature of religious truth were not at all left behind in the middle segment of the nineteenth century. Indeed, they were complicated by the further development of historical understanding. But for the most part the thinkers of the middle period were engaged in building upon (or attacking) the new sorts of foundations laid by Schleiermacher or Coleridge or Hegel, though the problems of Christianity and culture were not ignored, as both the Oxford Movement and Christian Socialism testify in Britain. In the United States the slavery question was a major concern for the churches. And in Germany the reactions to 1848 ranged from the confessionalist's "throne and altar" to Rothe's secular Christianity.

But what is striking about the theology of the mid-nineteenth century is the way in which the christological problem claimed attention and took on new dimensions—both as a historical problem, put at the beginning of the era by David Friedrich Strauss, of whether and how the historical figure of Jesus could be available as an object for faith, and as a problem of developing a Christology genuinely *von unten nach oben*. Thence the whole of the nineteenth century may be seen as a struggle to affirm the humanity of Jesus. Roots of the christological concern can be found in Schleiermacher's call for a christocentric principle, that is, for everything in theology to be directly related to the redemption accomplished in Jesus of Nazareth, and in Hegel's claim to have recovered and exalted the truth of the concept of the incarnation. But a new preoccupation was evident in many ways. There was the sudden flourishing of kenotic theories and the spirited controversy that ensued in German theology. The question of Christ also lay at the heart of the work of the most seminal theological minds in Britain and America: F. D. Maurice and Horace Bushnell. In quite another vein, and at the same time, the Christ of orthodoxy was being rejected by the emerging Unitarianism and Transcendentalism (see Emerson's Divinity School Address). And for Kierkegaard the paradox of the God-man and the absolute qualitative distinction which it embodies was the essential counter to the "System's" confusion of time and eternity and its abolition of Christianity; and no less critical was the problem of contemporaneity with Christ.

Toward the close of the nineteenth century the question of Christianity and culture, or church and society, came to flower. The christological question was still acute in the last third of the century, of course, especially as a historical problem (and the international and interdenominational character of the theological enterprise is here well illustrated by the common inquiry into the origins of the Christian community). The question of religious knowing also recurred with increased intensity, for example, in the attempt to relate personal faith to sociological and psychological analyses of religion as well as to historical inquiries. But these interests were also shaped by a new concern for the social interpretation of Christianity—in its origins, its historical expressions, and its relevance to modern society. A revived ethical emphasis and interpretation stressed the practical nature of religion, supporting even a "muscular" Christianity. More explicitly, there was the "social gospel," including in its European as well as its American expressions the concepts of a social ethic and a social redemption. On the other side, there was a new sociological view of religion. The attempt to justify Christianity in modern society blended into *Kulturprotestantismus*. Yet the concentration of interest must not be overstated, for it was also characteristic of the last part of the nineteenth century that no real synthesis or principle of unity appeared. Social and ethical interests were in tension with other main motifs of the period, the stress on personal religion, for example, often viewed quite individualistically, or the culmination (and breakdown?) of the quest for the historical Jesus, or the attempts at scientific study of religion. And the latter motifs generated other conflicts as well.

The first two of these three periods of theological history will be covered in the present volume. The third will be dealt with separately in a second volume. But one further judgment on the character of the century as a whole must still be offered in a preliminary way. There was a movement throughout the century toward radicalization within the theological house. This was not, as I have said, a development in three stages toward a single or simple outcome; but it is, in relation to all the three themes we have mentioned, a real revolutionary process appearing in transnational forms.

The beginning of the century was marked by decisively new starts. In midcentury there was a strong conservative churchly reaction, but there was at the same time even more radical questioning—in Strauss and Bruno Bauer, in Feuerbach and Emerson, in Kierkegaard and Rothe, and later in Ritschl. It may even be contended that the real theological struggle with the churchly conservatives was won in the middle of the nineteenth century; the later "fundamentalist" controversies, and even the post-Darwinian science and religion debates, largely reflected a journalistic level of theologizing through which positions established earlier in the century became more widely accepted (thus the characteristic appeal of twentieth-century fundamentalism has been to mid-nineteenth-century formulations).

The culmination of the process in the early decades of the twentieth century was both a greater international commonality in the structure of the theological problems than in either of the preceding periods and also the intensification of historical, social, and psychological questioning by Schweitzer and Troeltsch, by James and Freud, and by the "New Theologies" in Britain and America. This was to be followed by post–World War I reaction and revival of a dramatic sort (for example, in Tillich, Barth, and the Niebuhrs) and then again by a new turn to secularity in theology.

HISTORIOGRAPHICAL NOTE

There is no want of books whose titles suggest that they are inclusive histories of nineteenth-century Protestant thought. To mention, for the moment, only some of the more interesting studies, there is above all Karl Barth's *Die protestantische Theologie im 19. Jahrhundert, ihre Vorgeschichte und ihre Geschichte*,[5] a book of great power and insight, and within its limits the most provocative of all the works one could cite. More recently, and partly as a consequence of the revived interest in the nineteenth century, we have also the lectures of Martin Kähler, *Geschichte der protestantischen Dogmatik im 19. Jahrhundert* (Munich, 1962, based on lectures from 1898). One thinks too, going back to the time to which Kähler's work really belongs, of Gustav Frank's concluding volume in his *Geschichte der protestantischen Theologie* (vol. 4, *Die Theologie des neunzehnten Jahrhunderts*, published posthumously, Leipzig, 1905).

But even the most casual inspection of these books reveals that they are not histories of Protestant theology but histories of *German* Protestant theology. To be sure, H. L. Martensen is treated briefly by Kähler—though Kierkegaard is nowhere in view—and the names of Wesley and Whitefield are mentioned (in the exposition of the Erlangen theologian F. H. R. Frank!). It is also true that in Barth's interpretation of the prior history, Rousseau has an important place, but in his treatment of the nineteenth century no non-German thinker, not even Kierkegaard, seems to merit anything more than the most incidental reference, and even these total only a half dozen. Nor can this restriction be explained by the fact that Barth's history was unfinished, for there is no suggestion in his remarks on this point that he intended the scope of the study to go beyond Germany (see *Die protestantische Theologie*, p. v.). The same observations apply to the work of Gustav Frank.

5. First published in Zurich in 1946, but containing lectures from 1932–33. The English translation by R. Gregor Smith, *From Rousseau to Ritschl* (London, 1959), unfortunately contains only about half the essays from the original.

In short, these works called histories of "protestant" or "evangelical" theology are not essentially different from volumes with more modest titles, like the excellent text by Horst Stephan and Martin Schmidt, *Geschichte der deutschen evangelischen Theologie seit dem deutschen Idealismus* (2d ed. Berlin, 1960), or Ferdinand Kattenbusch's *Die deutsche evangelische Theologie seit Schleiermacher* (Giessen, 1924), or F. A. Lichtenberger's *History of German Theology in the 19th Century* (Edinburgh, 1889).[6]

The apparent identification of nineteenth-century Protestant theology with German theology in that century is not peculiar to those who write in German. One thinks immediately of what is undoubtedly the most widely read history of modern theology in English, published in 1937 by the Scottish theologian Hugh Ross Mackintosh, under the title *Types of Modern Theology*. The "modern theologians" dealt with by Mackintosh are precisely the major nineteenth- and twentieth-century German thinkers, plus Søren Kierkegaard (who after all has a certain right to be considered among the Germans).[7] And one may even mention the publication of tape-recorded lectures by Paul Tillich, *Perspectives on Nineteenth- and Twentieth-Century Protestant Theology* (New York, 1967, from lectures delivered in 1962–63). Out of respect for the memory of Tillich, one would not want to refer to that book, which is so obviously from Tillich's old age and is filled with uninformative reminiscences, were it not for the remarkable fact that after thirty years of teaching in the United States Tillich could still find it possible to survey the nineteenth century in theology without any reference to British and American thinkers, except for a misleading comment about Walter Rauschenbusch and a passing mention of Unitarianism.

The two volumes just mentioned might indicate that we encounter here the common prejudice that all good theological things come from Germany, a prejudice that has often been shared by British (or at least Scottish) and American theologians. But something more is at stake: the almost universal tendency to treat theological history in

6. The same restricted focus of attention characterizes most of the "programmatic" interpretations by German authors, such as the first volume of Erich Schaeder, *Theozentrische Theologie, Erster, geschichtlicher Teil: Der anthropozentrische Zug in der dogmatischen Theologie seit Schleiermacher* (Leipzig, 1909; 2d ed., 1916), or F. H. R. Frank, *Geschichte und Kritik der neuern Theologie* (1894), or the brilliant analysis by Ernst Troeltsch in his "Rückblick auf ein halbes Jahrhundert der theologischen Wissenschaft" (1908; see *Gesammelte Schriften*, 4 vols. [Tübingen, 1913], 2 : 193 ff.).

7. There are a few scattered references to non-Germans, but without expansion.

the nineteenth century as a form of national history, a tendency that has been present also in the interpretations of British and American thought, though with the acknowledgment of German influence.

Among the histories of nineteenth-century theological movements in the Anglo-Saxon world, there is on the one side a series of more or less inclusive studies of British theology. The most interesting and informative of these works (though others could be mentioned to establish the same point) are those of Tulloch, Storr, Elliot-Binns, Webb, Willey, and most recently Reardon.[8]

In American theological historiography the situation is similar, though nearly all of the useful writing on nineteenth-century theology has taken the form of relatively specialized studies.[9] To view the century as a whole, one must look to such inclusive surveys as H. R. Niebuhr's *Kingdom of God in America* (New York, 1937), or *Theology in America: The Major Protestant Voices from Puritanism to*

8. Bernard Reardon, *From Coleridge to Gore: A History of Nineteenth-Century Religious Thought in Britain* (London, 1971). John Tulloch, *Movements of Religious Thought in Britain during the Nineteenth Century* (New York, 1885), is a relatively full and still useful survey of both English and Scottish theology down to 1860, with a few remarks on subsequent developments. The work begun by V. F. Storr in *The Development of English Theology in the Nineteenth Century, 1800–1860* (London, 1913), is continued by L. E. Elliot-Binns, *The Development of English Theology in the Later Nineteenth Century* (New York, 1952), and especially *English Thought, 1860–1900: The Theological Aspect* (Greenwich, Conn., 1956). Elliot-Binns's other volume, *Religion in the Victorian Era* (London, 1936), is important. See also C. C. J. Webb, *A Study of Religious Thought in England from 1850* (Oxford, 1933); M. B. Reckitt, *Maurice to Temple* (London, 1947); and especially Basil Willey, *Nineteenth Century Studies, Coleridge to Matthew Arnold* (London, 1949), which, though it makes no attempt at a connected account of the development of ideas but consists of studies of individuals, is surely the most penetrating and illuminating volume of its scope. Willey's *More Nineteenth Century Studies: A Group of Honest Doubters* (London, 1956) is also useful. One may also note more general works, such as Houghton's *Victorian Frame of Mind*, a truly excellent study of an unusual sort; H. V. Routh, *Towards the Twentieth Century: Essays in the Spiritual History of the Nineteenth* (New York and Cambridge, 1937); and D. C. Somervell, *English Thought in the Nineteenth Century* (London, 1929). But these take us beyond the limits of our immediate concern.

9. Not to mention works on individual thinkers, there are, for example, works on the "New England theology," such as F. H. Foster, *A Genetic History of the New England Theology* (Chicago, 1907), which remains the only volume treating the tradition of Jonathan Edwards as an organic whole, reaching down to the early 19th century; and Joseph Haroutunian, *Piety versus Moralism: The Passing of the New England Theology* (New York, 1932). Among the histories of 19th-century liberal theologies should be cited F. H. Foster, *The Modern Movement in American Theology* (New York, 1939) continuing his earlier work; John W. Buckham, *Progressive Religious Thought in America* (Boston, 1919); and D. D. Williams, *The Andover Liberals: A Study in American Theology* (New York, 1941).

Neo-Orthodoxy, edited by Sydney E. Ahlstrom (New York, 1967), or perhaps to a work like H. Shelton Smith's *Changing Conceptions of Original Sin: A Study in American Theology since 1750* (New York, 1955).[10] Or one must turn to the more general histories of religion in America, though even these large works often tell us relatively little of theological development.[11]

In the account given so far of the historiography of nineteenth-century theology we have left aside three works that in quite different ways are among the most interesting and important ones to be considered and that at first glance might seem exceptions to the pattern we have observed. One of these is the classic work by Otto Pfleiderer, *The Development of Theology in Germany since Kant, and Its Progress in Great Britain since 1825* (London, 1890), which was first published in English, having been written at the request of a British publisher, and which has had a profound effect on British and American views of nineteenth-century theology.[12] The second is the important and most helpful book by Emanuel Hirsch, *Geschichte der neuern evangelischen Theologie, im Zusammenhang mit den allgemeinen Bewegungen des europäischen Denkens,* particularly the second part, which treats the middle of the eighteenth to the second third of the nineteenth century (vols. 3, 4, and 5, 2d ed., Gütersloh, 1960). Third is a volume of a quite different sort by Bernard M. G. Reardon, *Religious Thought in the Nineteenth Century, Illustrated from Writers of the Period* (Cambridge, 1966). For the most part this book comprises selections from important nineteenth-century thinkers, though with useful introductions by the editor.

But do we actually have exceptions here? No. For as even the title

10. Niebuhr's volume is still in my judgment the most illuminating study of American religious thought that has been produced. Ahlstrom's work consists mainly of well-chosen documents but also contains a brief useful account of the development.

11. E.g. the four volumes on *Religion in American Life,* edited by James W. Smith and A. Leland Jamison (Princeton, 1961); or the two volumes edited by H. Shelton Smith, Robert T. Handy, and Lefferts A. Loetscher, *American Christianity: An Historical Interpretation with Representative Documents* (New York, 1960, 1963). Both of these works contain excellent bibliographies. Neither here nor elsewhere in this discussion of the literature of the 19th century have I intended to provide a full bibliographical account—though the number of specific histories of 19th-century theology is so small that I have tried at least to mention those I consider important.

12. Including Pfleiderer's omission of such figures as Menken, Tholuck, Beck, Vilmar, Kohlbrügge, and Blumhart—all of whom Barth sought to recover. Pfleiderer's work was later published in Germany as *Die Entwicklung der protestantischen Theologie in Deutschland seit Kant und in Grossbritannien seit 1825* (Freiburg, 1891).

of Pfleiderer's book makes clear, this is not a common history of German and British theology, but a history of German theology to which has been appended a sketch of the important moments of British thought. It is noteworthy that the author is not quite so much under the influence of the assumption that all significant theological thinking takes place in Germany or in essential dependence on German thought. He is also quite conscious of the geographical limitation as a defect, apologizing that he has included only one theologian from the Netherlands.[13]

What then shall we say of those five volumes by Emanuel Hirsch that propose to give an account of modern Protestant theology from 1648 until the middle of the nineteenth century? First of all, particularly in view of the paucity of histories of post-Reformation theology, this work must be judged a masterful achievement, truly impressive in the range of material covered and in its detailed interpretation of individual thinkers, as well as in its tracing of the development of ideas.[14] Further, Hirsch's study is genuinely international in scope. Though understandably he devotes most attention to German theologians, Hirsch is by no means unaware of British and American thinkers, and he seeks to be responsible to movements of thought in the Anglo-Saxon world. That is a remarkable achievement, and one must take special note of Hirsch's extensive treatment of British Enlightenment thought from Herbert of Cherbury and John Locke through the deists to David Hume (see especially chaps. 3, 13–17, 27). Yet it is evident that Hirsch is much more successful in escaping the pattern of national theological history when he is dealing with the

13. E. C. Moore's popular work, *An Outline of the History of Christian Thought since Kant* (London, 1912), is quite similar. He begins by surveying the German development and then, although in a chapter on the natural and social sciences he introduces British thinkers, he concludes with a special chapter on "The English-Speaking Peoples; Action and Reaction"—with attention to both British and American theologians.

One should also mention here the recent work by James C. Livingston, *Modern Christian Thought: From the Enlightenment to Vatican II* (New York, 1971). A useful textbook for introduction to a number of the important figures, the work is still conventional in its approach and selections, concentrating almost entirely on the well-known thinkers and problems. Scant attention is paid to the important conservative theological movements of the 19th century, to the critically orthodox, or to the American scene.

14. In comparison with this massive history, in which more than a large volume is given over to the theology of only the first half of the 19th century, our own sketch can claim merely to indicate the possibility of a different perspective and to suggest other approaches.

seventeenth and eighteenth centuries than when he comes to the nineteenth century. After treating in general "the spiritual and religious-historical influences of the French Revolution," the "ideas and aims of restoration," and "the beginnings of agnosticism, positivism, and socialism in Western Europe"—all in a quite transnational vein—he goes on to describe what he sees explicitly as a splintering of Western European theology into opposing directions in England, in Scotland, in Switzerland, and in the Netherlands. But then he is content to conclude his third volume with two quite separate (though genuinely perceptive) chapters on nineteenth-century theology in England and in the United States: "Theological New Departures in the Anglican Church," and "History of North American Theology to the Civil War." In the former, we view events in England from Coleridge and the Oxford Movement to the Cambridge triumvirate and *Lux Mundi* (1889). In the latter chapter, Hirsch seeks to treat the development of theology in America from Jonathan Edwards to Horace Bushnell and Ralph Waldo Emerson in thirty pages! Then Hirsch is able, one suspects almost with a sigh of relief, to return in two large volumes to the course of German thought from Semler and Lessing to Ritschl and Kierkegaard.

About Reardon's *Religious Thought in the Nineteenth Century* we need say only a word. In the selection of texts the volume is remarkable for its comprehensiveness of Continental, British, and American thought (including also the French Protestant Sabatier, the Catholic Lamennais, and the Orthodox Solovyov), yet in the organization of the material the threefold pattern of European/British /American is deemed sufficient, nor is there any effort in the introduction to suggest other possibilities for ordering and interpretation.

In short, these works are also, in the end, examples of the writing of nineteenth-century theological history by nations. For a significant exception to this procedure, one would have to turn to such a work as the small volume by J. M. Creed, *The Divinity of Jesus Christ: A Study in the History of Christian Doctrine since Kant* (Cambridge, 1938). Creed, though focusing on the development in Christology, gives a connected account of several aspects of the modern theological situation in which at least both German and British thinkers and movements are seen from a common perspective. Or one might recall A. C. McGiffert's *Rise of Modern Religious Ideas* (New York, 1915), a most useful treatment of themes that is genuinely an exception to the pattern of national history. For example, in his chapter "The Rehabilitation of Faith," McGiffert deals with Wesley, Jacobi, Coleridge, Hare, James, Kant, Ritschl, Rousseau, and Hamann. But nearly all the specialized studies in nineteenth-century theology, whether of men or movements or problems, fall into the usual circumscription by national boundaries.[15]

We shall need to reflect on other tendencies that have appeared, with varying intensity and breadth, in the writing of the history of nineteenth-century theology. But before identifying these, we may consider in a preliminary way the fundamental question now forcefully put before us. In view of the almost universal attempt to interpret Protestant theology in the nineteenth century through the categories of theology in Germany, theology in Britain, and theology in America, is it not perhaps true that this is the way the history of nineteenth-century theology must be written, that the theological situations were so different that the developments in these countries are most naturally considered in independence from one another, that the theologians did in fact work within intellectual horizons roughly coincident with national boundaries, or at least that they brought to theological expression a strong national consciousness?

This is a question to be faced honestly, and while I shall argue for another viewpoint, I would not want to deny that much can be said on behalf of an affirmative answer. It is surely not indifferent to the actual intellectual and theological situation that in interpreting the eighteenth century, Emanuel Hirsch can move back and forth relatively freely among Continental Europe, Britain, and America, whereas he does not try to do this for the nineteenth century. Nor can the peculiar locus within his volumes of the surveys of British

---

15. Several illustrations of this tendency we have already mentioned in connection with the histories of American theology. Analyses of such phenomena as the Oxford Movement or the Erlangen theology (e.g. F. W. Kantzenbach, *Die Erlanger Theologie*, Munich, 1960) will quite naturally also exhibit similar characteristics. So do such works as A. W. Benn, *The History of English Rationalism in the Nineteenth Century* (London, 1920); Janet E. Courtney, *Freethinkers of the Nineteenth Century* (London, 1920); John M. Robertson, *A History of Freethought in the Nineteenth Century*, 2 vols. (London, 1929); W. L. Knox and Alec Vidler, *The Development of Modern Catholicism* (London, 1933); and Ernst Günther, *Entwicklung der Lehre von der Person Christi im 19. Jahrhundert* (Tübingen, 191:). Strikingly, this was not at all true of I. A. Dorner's earlier great work, *Entwicklungsgeschichte der Lehre von der Person Christi*, 4 vols., 2d ed. (Stuttgart, 1846–56), nor was the same writer's *Geschichte der protestantischen Theologie*, 2 vols. (Munich, 1867) restricted to the German development.

and American thought in the latter century be ascribed simply to lack of information or interest on Hirsch's part. Similarly, it is neither wholly from ignorance nor mere caprice that when Karl Barth treats the eighteenth century he takes serious account of what went on in France and Britain, but when he looks at nineteenth-century theology his view does not include those nations. No, the thought of the Enlightenment did have a genuinely international character, such that Frenchmen, Germans, Englishmen, Scots, and American colonials can all be called *philosophes,* participating in a common experience and program.[16] The characteristic forms of Enlightenment religious thought had no respect for national boundaries, and there was steady intellectual commerce across the Atlantic as well as across the English Channel. Similarly, eighteenth-century German pietism, the Wesleyan revival in England, and the Great Awakening in America were not only contemporary but interrelated.

By the beginning of the nineteenth century, however, especially following the French and American revolutions and their aftermaths, the intellectual community was obviously not the same; and a certain national "distancing" and self-consciousness can be observed in the religious thinking of the period. Certainly some of the most important religious and theological movements of the nineteenth century were bound up with national experiences. The Luther revival of 1817 and the years following in Germany was at the same time a celebration of Luther as a national hero. There were strong tendencies to interpret Lutheranism as the distinctively German form of Christianity and to promote the national church idea. The early century marked the birth of political nationalism in Germany, and both Schleiermacher and Hegel were conscious of sharing in the rebuilding of German cultural life after the Napoleonic conquests. Schleiermacher in particular was a passionate patriot who pressed for moral and educational regeneration as a way to patriotism and nationalism. In England the Oxford Movement is hardly intelligible apart from the peculiar situation and condition of the Anglican church in 1833. And quite readily one senses in the American churches, as well as in American life generally at the beginning of the nineteenth century, a new spirit of independence that was willing and even eager to be free from the intellectual influence (or domination) of the Old World. Thus in surveying theology in the nine-

16. Cf., e.g., Peter Gay, *The Enlightenment, an Interpretation: The Rise of Modern Paganism* (New York, 1966).

teenth century one must allow for orientations that reflect more general expressions of national self-consciousness.

Further, one may not overlook or minimize the singular burst of scholarly and theological energy in nineteenth-century Germany. It is true that in critical areas of theological, historical, and biblical study, German scholarship shaped the issues, and theology elsewhere often followed along or reacted. There was much influence from Germany, but little influence on Germany from Britain or America (in sharp contrast, for example, to the earlier influence of the British deists). And it is also true that German theology in the nineteenth century is often fascinating in its own right as technical theology of the highest order, whereas American and English theology become especially interesting when viewed as factors in a given culture (which means, for the nineteenth century, largely a national culture). Yet this is only part of the truth. It is wrong to suppose that the history of nineteenth-century theology can be competently or fairly interpreted by identifying the seminal German thinkers and then tracing out their influence, or by asserting that all important developments elsewhere were essentially dependent on progress east of the Rhine. And it would also be wrong to suppose that theological development in any country can adequately be considered in isolation.

Thus we return to the basic question, put now the other way. Granted that there were forces in the nineteenth century making for national self-consciousness and distinctiveness in theology as elsewhere, granted that there was, with notable exceptions (e.g. Coleridge, Dorner, Schaff, Nevin, Hare), much provincialism, were there not important unities in the Protestant theological scene as a whole? Were there not common elements in the situations of the Christian communities and in their theological responses to them? And were there not common problems being dealt with, or common directions being taken? Would it not at least be worthwhile to ask these questions seriously by arguing the thesis that Protestant theology in the nineteenth century can best be understood from a point of view in which national or language boundaries are not the primary grids in our examining screens? Perhaps the national histories of theology reflect a habit of looking which is as characteristic of the twentieth century as of the nineteenth century theological situation itself, and which therefore conceals as much as it discloses.

It seems reasonable to suggest that a different scheme will at least have heuristic value, that it will provide another and possibly corrective bias, that it will illumine other important dimensions of the history. And perhaps a truer picture will emerge when we recognize that the theological conflicts, renewals, and reactions of the nineteenth century are fundamentally not functions of national boundaries, and when we attempt to hold at least the Continental, the British, and the American developments in a common focus.

I hinted earlier that there have been other features in the historiography of nineteenth-century theology about which questions need to be raised. I mention three areas. The first is that penchant of which Karl Barth complains so eloquently (and rightly) in his own discussion of the task of a history of modern theology, namely, the desire to show that all the developments of the nineteenth century lead up, either positively or negatively, to the particular systematic program that an author has to propose.[17] To be sure, the task of writing the history of nineteenth-century theology is not one of passing in review with utter indifference and "objectivity" the thinkers and movements of the nineteenth century as if the present century were not involved in them, as if they were all to be lined up in cages in a zoo, properly sorted out and safely separated from us for our casual observation, or as if, on the other hand, we were able to enter secretly into their natural habitats and inspect their lives without our presence being in any way an influence. That would not be historical study. We are properly interested in what they have to say to us and how our situation is to be illumined, and conversely in how our theological understanding and questions can provide significant perspectives for viewing the past. This is especially important in dealing with the nineteenth century, which just because of its nearness may be most difficult for us to reckon with, and which, at the same time, remains most important for us to understand because of the way in which it has shaped our most disturbing questions. Yet on the other hand, and for the same purpose, we must avoid reducing the theological efforts of the nineteenth century to precursors, either negative or positive, of more recent programs, and thus we must constantly listen to what the thinkers themselves understood to be *their* theological intentions.

A second tendency in the more or less inclusive works on the nineteenth century is to rely largely on one of two patterns for interpretation: either the individual theologian or the theological school or

17. Barth, *Die Protestantische Theologie*, pp. 6–7.

party.[18] The two single most interesting volumes on German and British developments respectively, by Karl Barth and Basil Willey, consist of independent essays on particular major figures. The excellence of these works may not be unrelated to that method, for the historian of theology is concerned with actual theologizing and not just with products or ideas or systems, and thus he is finally responsible to men thinking in the concreteness of their own situations. One would hardly want to deny the viability of such a procedure. Yet from it one gets only with difficulty a sense for the whole, for its pervasive problems and its dominant directions.

The alternate pattern, especially prominent in some of the German historians, stresses the clash and succession of schools. In Pfleiderer, for example, we have, as the forms of the "development of dogmatic theology under the influence of idealistic philosophy," the "school of Kant" and the "school of Schleiermacher," to which are added "speculative theology" and an assortment of "eclectic theologians." One also commonly finds the Ritschlian school, the Erlangen school (or the Erlangen theology), and the "history of religions" school. In Kattenbusch there are, for the mid-nineteenth century, the liberal, confessional, and mediating schools; and in Kähler the mediating theology is divided into three kinds (he does not use the term "school" in this connection): the speculative, the ecclesiastically and pietistically determined, and the humanistic (*humanitaristische*) or anthropocentric mediating theologies. The difficulty here is not that these and comparable designations have no correspondence to reality. Certain aspects of theological development, notably in Germany, can be so understood. But the notion of the theological "school" is much less useful for interpreting events outside Germany, and it tends to restrict attention to the professional theologian. Furthermore, we find here a common failure to recognize the need for a *plurality* of categories and levels of interpretation.[19] The concept of a theological "school" is indeed not a simple notion at all, as can be seen by juxtaposing "Chicago school," "Ritschlian school," "Hegelian school," and *religionsgeschichtliche Schule*. Even at the risk of being overly precise about terms to be applied to diffuse entities, I would suggest that the category "school of thought" may most naturally and properly be used to refer to relationships of historical dependence, whether in the

18. Emanuel Hirsch is a major exception.

19. For a fuller statement of the argument that follows, see my article "On Theological Typology," *Theology Today* 22, no. 2 (July 1965): 176 ff.

sense of the dominant or crystallizing influence of a particular individual on those who are more or less disciples (e.g. Ritschl and the Ritschlians), or in the sense of the continuance of an established tradition of a particular theological complex (e.g. the Erlangen theology). The term itself is of doubtful explanatory value. Yet the kind of historical interconnection suggested in reference either to the immediate spheres of influence of seminal thinkers or to broader theological traditions is indispensable as one tool of interpretation.

From this more limited category, then, one might be able to distinguish the theological "program" or "movement." Were it feasible, we might even differentiate between those two terms, reserving the latter for the broader, vaguer developments (e.g. "liberal Catholicism" as a movement in the tradition of the *Lux Mundi* program), but the habits of usage are against us (the "Oxford Movement" is an excellent example of a theological program, though one might also say it was a program that became a movement). Candidates for designation as programs will certainly be the kenotic Christology in Germany in the 1840s and 1850s, some of the confessionalist theological revivals, proposals for "a theology for the social gospel," and so forth. In these cases we have points at which theological development has obviously come to a definite focus (often classically stated by a few individuals or even by one). There is a self-conscious and deliberate community in aim and method, through which the endeavors of several (or even many) thinkers can well be interpreted. But patently this is no adequate tool for describing a whole period, and many of the most important thinkers cannot be understood by being assigned to schools or programs.

The virtues and deficiencies of interpretation by definable programs are like those which attend an effort to describe a theological era by focusing on its special controversies. (And of course a controversy is in fact often simply the obverse, or the result, of a program.) The scope of interpretation is necessarily restricted to only a part of the whole (even though one might believe it to be the most significant part). The value of allowing the dimensions of a single problem to determine the approach to the work of many thinkers and thereby illuminating certain facets of their thought as well as the fortunes of a theme or an idea is counterbalanced by the inevitable abstraction from other issues and (as one seeks to be more and more inclusive) from the chief interests of a good number of the thinkers involved. Thus the levels of interpretation represented by individual

studies and by schools, programs, and movements must be complemented by other and more inclusive patterns of typology or schematism, for example, by the appeal to such notions as theological strategy
or stance and theological mood and temper. Granted, these are dis-
tressingly vague categories for theological analysis. Yet within a given
epoch the term "strategy" at least helps to specify a level above that
of the tactics of a particular program or school or position, and denotes something more than just theological method in the technical
sense. In speaking of mood and temper we can often express lines of
affinity that are just as important as adherence to a specific movement.
The heuristic role and value is like that which attaches to the characterization, on a larger scale, of the "spirit" (e.g. "rationalism" or
"romanticism") of an age.

Whether it is possible to identify such theological strategies or
stances for periods within the nineteenth century is a question that
can only be dealt with later. Yet we may offer a brief warning against
a common schematism which is often but by no means exclusively
used in conjunction with the concept of schools. This is the tendency
to classify as "conservative," "mediating," or "liberal"—an adjunct
of which is the typology of theological "right" and "left," which
comes to much the same thing except that it is even more dangerous.[20] These schemata are not meaningless. Though the notion of
"mediating" theology frequently becomes a mere catchall, the vague
contrast of "liberal" and "conservative" is commonly recognized, and
there are varieties of perspectives to which such terms have relevance,
for example, as describing maximum versus minimum accommodation to the world, or desire for "reform." But in general the terms are
not illuminating, and they are usually misleading. This scheme is
misleading because whether we are interpreting the theological scene
as a whole, or only sorting out the parties on a single theological issue,
the assumption is implicit that there is a one-dimensional spectrum or
a continuum on which all the theologies or positions can be ranged.
This is always a distortion. The encounter of actual theologies is
never so simple that, even on a single issue, it can be reduced to a
direct and unambiguous collision on a one-track line (except as one
constructs ideal types). Equally serious is the failure of this "spectrum view" to illuminate the characteristic intention of any theology.
No significant theological program is *as such* an attempt to be liberal
or conservative, to go left or right (or to stay in the center). Theolo-

20. See also below, the introduction to Part II, pp. 141–43.

gizing is not finally concerned with whether, or how much, to interpret and adjust, but rather seeks rules to govern reformulation and tools to be used in refashioning. Thus again the question is one of responsibility to the actual theological intentions of the thinkers themselves.

A third feature of many studies of nineteenth-century theology is their fixing on philosophical influences and relations as the all-important clues to theological development. Pfleiderer is a useful illustration. His organizing theme for viewing systematic theological endeavors in Germany is specifically their relation to idealistic philosophy, so that we have in Book I, "The Basis of Modern Theology in German Idealistic Philosophy," and in Book II, "The Development of Dogmatic Theology under the Influence of Idealistic Philosophy." A similar pattern dominates the interpretation of British thought in Book IV. Pfleiderer quite candidly writes off the importance of such things as involvement in the practical life of the church when he says of F. D. Maurice and I. A. Dorner that they exhibited "the same waste of power on the endless frictions of the actual world" (*Development of Theology*, p. 374). There the question is in the open. Of course it is true that some of the crises of nineteenth- and twentieth-century theology result from the claim that the truth of the Gospel is universal and therefore must be integrally related to all other possible sources of truth. But it may also be true that theological efforts are powered and shaped as much by the theologian's situation within the Christian community and its concerns, or by his social and economic setting, as by the influences of philosophy or science. Thus Schleiermacher's more than thirty years of preaching in the Trinity Church in Berlin are just as important for understanding his theology as is his view of *Dialektik*. Horace Bushnell forged his theology in sermons to his congregation in Hartford, Connecticut. Coleridge's literary connections and his struggle with opium were as significant as Kant or the Cambridge Platonists for his view of sin and salvation and his conception of how to validate religious truth. F. D. Maurice's interest in the working class was as relevant to his theology as was his "platonism." For many thinkers of the century, pietist and revival influences were stronger than those of technical philosophy. Hence we will do well to be on guard against the bias which assumes that the fundamental determinants of theology are always to be sought in philosophical presuppositions or influences or, similarly, in conflicts with science.

2

The Eighteenth-Century Background

The immediate background of Protestant theology in the nineteenth century must be described by reference to at least three broad movements of thought, commonly labeled pietism, rationalism, and romanticism. These were the influences from the religious thinking and attitudes of the preceding era that played most strongly upon the theologians of the early nineteenth century, the "near background" against which we may understand their peculiarities in personal history and intellectual influence, as well as the contrasts in their religio-theological situations. Other trends might well be distinguished as important for particular thinkers and contexts, for example neo-Spinozism, neoclassicism, and cosmopolitanism for early nineteenth-century German thought; but those tendencies were clearly less pervasive in influence. Here we can offer only a brief interpretation of the more extensive movements as they bore on the course of religious thought. This cannot be a full statement of their varieties, nor should we try to incorporate them into aspects of one grand characterization of man in the eighteenth century.[1] Rather, we shall be better served by a relatively unsystematic, even impressionistic, portrait of multiple tendencies of thought and attitude as they came to expression in the eighteenth century and as they continued to be present to and in the minds of the thinkers of the early nineteenth century.[2]

PIETISM AND EVANGELICAL REVIVAL

The word pietism (like rationalism and romanticism) is notoriously vague, being sometimes used so inclusively as to include the

1. As e.g. Karl Barth seems to do in his provocative depiction of the absolutism of the human will to form (see his *Protestantische Theologie* [Zurich, 1946], chap. 2, especially pp. 19–20, 44; in R. Gregor Smith's English translation, *From Rousseau to Ritschl* [London, 1959], pp. 14–15, 41). In subsequent references to the *Protestantische Theologie*, page numbers in Smith's translation are set in brackets following the German citation.

2. It must also be clear that I am not attempting here a *new* interpretation of the 18th century, but only a short recollection and summary of the features most important in the background for the early 19th century.

whole ethos of Puritanism.[3] However, while allowing for the obvious close relation with both Puritanism (cf. especially the influence of William Ames in New England and the Netherlands) and Dutch precisianism, we may best allow the term to designate in the first instance the German Lutheran development identified with Philipp Jakob Spener (1635–1705), August Hermann Francke (1663–1727), and Graf Nicholas Zinzendorf (1700–60). But then we must immediately associate with this movement the Wesleyan revival in England and the so-called Great Awakening in America (1740 and following). Whether we call them all manifestations of "pietism" or speak of pietism and evangelicalism, it is evident that these were closely related phenomena, so similar and interwoven that interpreters can speak of "a curious uniformity" or even a single evangelical revival sweeping Protestant Europe, Great Britain, and the New World in the height of the Enlightenment. Some of the ardor and vitality of these pietist movements had waned by the end of the eighteenth century, but their influence on some of the decisive thinkers was strong, and the early nineteenth century was to bring a renewal of pietist and revival tendencies.

The pietism of Spener and his followers, classically expressed in *Pia Desideria* (1675), arose against the background of the Thirty Years' War, Lutheran scholasticism, and the territorial church system. In part a renewal of the mystical spiritual tradition mediated to Spener especially by Johann Arndt's *Wahres Christenthum* (he was influenced also by Leger and Labadie in Switzerland and by Puritan devotional works), this movement had in view particularly the evils of laxity, indifference, and immorality, and of absorption in learned theological sophistry and polemic, "theology which, while it preserves the foundation of faith from the Scriptures, builds on it with so much wood, hay, and stubble of human inquisitiveness that the gold can no longer be seen." [4] Spener's proposed remedy was a recovery of "apostolic simplicity" and concern for active faith (the *fides qua creditur*) in contrast to articles of belief (the *fides quae creditur*). He asserted that "our entire Christianity consists in the inner or new man, and its soul is faith." This faith expressed itself distinctively in small groups, the *collegia pietatis,* centers for biblical devotional study and the cultivation of the inner religious life. In spite of con-

3. E.g. by Ernst Troeltsch, *Social Teachings of the Christian Churches* (New York, 1950), pp. 678 ff.

4. Spener, *Pia Desideria*, ed. and trans. T. G. Tappert (Philadelphia, 1964), p. 56.

flict with the ecclesiastical and theological establishment, but aided greatly by the asylum offered by Frederick III in Brandenberg, the movement had, before the death of Francke, become the dominant force in German religious life, exerting its influence especially through the University of Halle. The Halle stream had nearly dried up by the mid-eighteenth century, as rationalism dominated the theological faculty itself at least from the appointment of J. S. Semler (1753) until the coming of August Tholuck (1826). But pietism lived on intensively in the so-called Württemberg pietism, which was more "domesticated" into the parish system and whose most distinguished proponent was J. A. Bengel, and in the separate Moravian brotherhood of Graf Zinzendorf, through which Schleiermacher was deeply formed. With these continuing influences and others "underground" in church life generally we can connect the late eighteenth- and early nineteenth-century neopietism expressed, for example, in Gottfried Menken (1768–1831) and in the Berlin circle of Baron von Kottwitz, who was of great importance not only for Tholuck, but also for Julius Müller, Richard Rothe, and Hermann Olshausen.

The influence of Moravian pietism upon John Wesley and the Birtish evangelical movement is well known—perhaps too well. Wesley was deeply impressed by the spirit of his Moravian companions on the voyage to America, and he visited the communities at Herrnhut and Marienborn during the summer of 1738 (though his reactions were mixed). It was Peter Böhler who during the spring of 1738 had kept pressing upon him the need for inner assurance, the "sure trust and confidence" in God that Wesley knew he lacked. And it seems that at the outset Wesley even expected to join his move to existent Anglican-Moravian groups.[5] But this tie should not be exaggerated. Other roots were important, going back at least to Wesley's much earlier Oxford "conversion" under the influence of Jeremy Taylor's *Rules and Exercises of Holy Living and Dying,* Thomas a Kempis's *Christian Patterns,* and William Law's *Christian Perfection* and *Serious Call.* Well before the specific Moravian influences, Wesley's concept of the nature of faith and the need for inward assurance had been shaped. By the end of the Georgia mission his theological *ideas* were, in fact, nearly in final form, though he himself was still convinced by inward feeling only of sin, not of grace. It is also noteworthy that Wesley was much impressed by Edwards's report of the revivals in Northampton, Massachusetts, and

5. See Albert C. Outler, ed., *John Wesley* (New York, 1964), p. 353.

published parts of it, as well as of Edwards's treatise on the religious affections. Outler concludes that "It is not too much to say that one of the effectual causes of the Wesleyan revival in England was the Great Awakening in New England." [6]

Theologically, the context for Wesley's work was not set by scholastic orthodoxy, as in the case of German pietism, but by the rationalist thought then dominating the Church of England. Hence in Wesley and in evangelicalism generally there was an emphasis, not found in German pietism, on the recovery of doctrines that were being minimized or abandoned, for example, the doctrines of the Fall, of Atonement, and of grace, as well as the doctrines of the inner testimony of the Spirit and of scriptural holiness which Wesley thought it a peculiar mission of the Methodists to recover. One consequence of this—even though for Wesley it was the whole doctrinal tradition of the Thirty-Nine Articles and the Book of Common Prayer that was to be revitalized—has been that later British and American evangelicalism came to focus rather narrowly on such doctrines as Atonement and the deity of Christ, to such an extent that these were regarded as peculiarly the doctrines of the "evangelicals." Similarly, in the later evangelicals, the Bible became more and more the authoritative book of revelation certifying the orthodox faith, whereas the early pietists, though they had no interest in denying the inspiration of the Scriptures, were interested more in the content than in the formal authority, and for them the Bible was primarily a devotional book. German neopietism, as represented by Menken, for example, also tended to become more "biblicist," though the Herrnhut tradition (as reappearing in Tholuck) remained closer to the original attitudes.

But the way to recover the doctrinal tradition, and the purpose in doing so, was for Wesley to experience the truth of it inwardly. All was to be translated into living experience. This did not mean that theology was founded on experience; it was rather established on Scripture and confirmed by experience, that is, by the inner and direct testimony of the Holy Spirit, the "inward impression on the soul, whereby the Spirit of God immediately and directly witnesses to my spirit, that I am a child of God; that Jesus Christ hath loved me, and given himself for me; that all my sins are blotted out, and I, even I, am reconciled to God." Thus the internalization of the truth was finally decisive.

6. Ibid., p. 16.

Evangelical revival in eighteenth-century America was directly connected with British movements through the work of Whitefield (who made seven trips to the colonies) and the Wesleyan group. But it also had independent roots in the Puritan tradition. Early American Puritanism had assumed the necessity of individual conversion experiences (hence the need for the institution of the Half-Way Covenant in 1662, permitting the baptism of children of those who had not had the crisis experience but were willing to "own the covenant"). Periodic revivals had taken place, including one in Jonathan Edwards's church in 1735, and Edwards, writing in 1739, could associate that event with the revival of religion in Germany through the work of August Francke, as signs of a glorious new upsurge of Christ's work. Thus the "Great Awakening" of 1740 and following had both direct and indirect relations to other manifestations of the pietist spirit.

Jonathan Edwards (1703–58) was not the most characteristic figure in American evangelicalism, for the main revival stream flowed more directly from the tradition of Whitefield and the Methodists. His special theological struggle was with Arminianism. Deism and rationalism were more distant, even incidental problems, though they had begun to trouble the American scene. As in England, revival was more often a reaction to unbelief and indifference than to "sterile orthodoxy." Edwards's own understanding of conversion, furthermore, was deeply informed by Lockean psychology and epistemology. But just because of these factors, as well as because of his stature as America's greatest theologian, Edwards is the most useful American representative to recall. He had lit the fuse of revival in New England before the arrival there of Whitefield (in the middle of the latter's second trip to the colonies). The concept of the "religious affections" which Edwards formulated more acutely than any other thinker prior (at least) to Schleiermacher, was to have a strong influence even on mid-nineteenth-century Transcendentalism, supporting romanticist influences.[7] Finally, both Calvinist and Arminian-oriented churches were swept up in the revivals of the first decade of the nineteenth century, though it was indeed the theology of revival that was close to the center of debate in Nathaniel William Taylor's turn away from strict Edwardseanism.

Clearly, pietism was no system of thought. Were it possible, one

7. "True religion, in great part, consists in holy affections" (Jonathan Edwards, *A Treatise Concerning Religious Affections*, ed. John E. Smith [New Haven, 1959], p. 95).

might speak rather of a system of feeling, or of a theological mood and stance as well as a religious revival, in which all attention was centered on the heartfelt character of true religion, on inner conviction and peace, on the intensity of feeling, on the affective and the emotional elements in experience. The religion of the heart stood in contrast both to the intellectualism of orthodox polemics, which seemed irrelevant to the practical issue in faith and love, and to the intellectualism of an arid rationalism. Whether in validation of accepted doctrine, or in defense against unbelief, the central thrust of the pietist movements was toward the *interiorization* of the Christian truth. "The principal thing," Spener had said, is to know that Christianity wholly consists of "the inner man or the new man." The Word must "penetrate to our heart," so that we "feel the sealing of the Spirit with vibrant emotion and comfort." [8] Though he vigorously rejected the idea of irresistible grace, Wesley as much as the Calvinist Whitefield insisted on the doctrine of Original Sin and the entire corruption of man (here, said Wesley in his sermon on Original Sin, is the fundamental point of distinction between Christianity and heathenism), and Whitefield spoke for both when he located the obstacle to conversion in men's lack of "the sense" of depravity, thus their need "to be pricked to the heart with a lively sense of their natural corruption." Correlatively, it was the inner experience of grace, the sure confidence in forgiveness and reconciliation, the full reliance on the blood of Christ, that was to be sought. Without the experience of assurance, the "inward impression on the soul," there is not yet true faith. "The most infallible of proofs," Wesley wrote, is "inward feeling" (*Journal*, 8 January 1738). Thus a young Schleiermacher could write home in distress from the Moravian School at Niesky that he was fully convinced by experience of man's corruption, but still sought in vain the inner certitude of grace, "the supernatural experience of communion with Jesus."

Illustrations of the pietist demand for internalizing the truth and of the characteristic turn to introspection and to reliance on feeling and emotion can easily be multiplied, but it hardly seems necessary. Nowhere is this better seen than in the hymns, prayers, and letters of the period, probably the most useful documents for sensing the spirit of the movement. The language was most extreme in Zinzendorf and the Moravians. It was less strained in the British and American movements (but see some of Charles Wesley's hymns and White-

8. *Pia Desideria*, pp. 116–17.

field's renowned emotionalism in preaching). Yet Edwards, utterly
dry and cold in manner, deliberately and almost scientifically in accord with his Lockean psychology, constructed the most vivid of images as the way to the emotions and thus to the springs of action.[9]

Yet certainly an intellectual content was implied in pietism and
evangelical revival, and distinctive motifs can be identified, some of
which reveal that pietist and rationalist conceptions of religion were
by no means altogether antithetical. One characteristic tendency that
seems most clearly related to the call to inwardness was toward individualism. This was not, as Barth would have it,[10] the *leitmotiv* of
original pietism; that would be interiorization, which is not the
same thing as individualism. Yet undoubtedly the concentration was
on the individual self and its experience. The sense of sin was sharply
personalized: it is I who am a lost soul, sinful and defiled, in need
of cleansing and renewal. And so for the other dimensions of the
faith. The drama of the race—of Creation, Fall and Redemption—is
to be reenacted in each life. The historical and the socially inclusive
are subordinated to the individual existential challenge. The true
birth of Christ is his birth in our hearts, his true death is in that
dying within us, his true resurrection is in the triumph in our faith.
Or, to put it another way, Christ deals with men one by one.

A second characteristic theme was the principle of religious fellowship (different from the inclusive or territorial church principle)
which came to expression most clearly in the *collegia pietatis,* in the
Herrnhut community, and in Wesley's societies and bands (even "select bands"). The principle was one of voluntary association in groups
that both expressed and supported the new religious disposition and
attitude—though also with the hope that these smaller communities
would leaven the whole life of the church. The missionary impulse
was especially strong among the Moravians, where the pietist outlook was closer to the sectarian and spiritualist motifs of the radical
Reformation.[11] The *collegia pietatis* and their parallels well embodied aspects of the pietist and evangelical renewals: the internalization and introversion of religious life, the turn from external authority and the lack of concern for institutional expression,[12] the lay
orientation, the tendency to locate the center of Christian existence

9. See Perry Miller, *Jonathan Edwards* (New York, 1959), pp. 141–47.

10. *Protestantische Theologie,* p. 93.

11. Though it is not correct to identify pietism with the sect ideal, as Troeltsch
almost does (see *Social Teachings,* p. 714).

12. Though Wesley, obviously, was not wanting in organizational interest or talent.

in the new life in Christ rather than in forgiveness, and the emphasis on transformation of character.

It is only seemingly paradoxical that pietism's interiorization should have been accompanied by a moralizing of Christianity and even an emphasis on the outward shape of the good life that had much in common with the Enlightenment's desire to identify religion with morality. Christianity was not doctrine but life. And though there were quietists among the Moravians, the dominant pietist-evangelical stream insisted that the inner religion of the heart be expressed in an outward and visible quality and shape of existence: Christianity consists rather in practice than in knowledge, as Spener had said, and specifically the practice of love. The true Christian community is less a fellowship of sinners than a brotherhood in transformed life. Conversion overcomes depravity, as the coming of the Kingdom is already being realized, leaving only remnants of sin. Thus the doctrine of sanctification moved nearer to the center of interest, as indeed denoting the chief task of the Christian. And while both Spener and Wesley understood Christian perfection as an inner movement and process of growth in love that would go on throughout life, both also found it possible to insist that the believer could be free of outward sin. The power as well as the guilt and fear of sin is broken, said Wesley, and the "being" of sin that remains *can* be resisted (this was not to deny, of course, the continuing results of ignorance and error, or the likelihood of involuntary transgressions). Spener had felt that perfection could be required of the church in the sense that Christians "should be free of manifest offenses, that nobody who is afflicted with such failings should be allowed to remain in the church without fitting reproof and ultimately exclusion, and that the true members of the church should be richly filled with many fruits of their faith." [13] Such views were roots of the legalism and moralism that later came increasingly to characterize the revival and neopietist movements.

Finally, there was a tendency, especially among the Moravian pietists (much less in the Wesleyans, in spite of some of Charles Wesley's hymns, and not at all in a man like Edwards), to rely wholly on Jesus as the savior and object of devotion. With all the talk of the Spirit-filled life, it was the Jesus-experience that dominated, and sometimes in the extreme form of what H. Richard Niebuhr has called a "unitarianism of the Second Person of the Trinity," that is,

13. *Pia Desideria*, p. 81.

a Jesus-cult in which all attention is taken up by the Redeemer-Savior figure, to the virtual exclusion of the Creator and the Spirit.

Though pietism has been called a phenomenon of church life rather than of theology, its importance in the reorganization of Protestant thought in the eighteenth and nineteenth centuries must not be underestimated. If the doctrinal forms were not much altered, at least the basis, manner, and method of theology were deeply affected. Particularly in the "theologies of religious experience," pietist influence showed in the tendency to separate out the "religious" as only one among other aspects of life. Men as diverse as Kant, Herder, and Schleiermacher, though they revolted, never escaped the force of pietism. (Nor did Ritschl, in spite of his attack in the *Geschichte des Pietismus*.) In Britain, in the first third of the nineteenth century, the evangelicals formed one of the most influential church groups in the renewal of church life, although they constituted a minority and had no major theologian (William Wilberforce was perhaps their most prominent leader). And in both Germany and America the early decades of the nineteenth century were marked by a resurgence of pietism and revival.

ENLIGHTENMENT AND RATIONALISM

Facets of Rationalism

If *rationalism* can be used at all as a catchword for the Enlightenment, it must be taken in a sense capable of embracing a complex of themes and tendencies. One of its characteristics was a call for "reasonableness" in religion. Here first of all *reason* designates that faculty which seeks clear and distinct ideas and which, in religion, is therefore concerned with the precise examination and accrediting of those religious propositions to which the mind may legitimately give assent. In Locke's classic formulations, such propositions may come to us "by the deductions of reason" or they may be recommended by some proponent as "coming from God in some extraordinary way of communication," that is, as revelation (and therefore to be received in the assent called *faith*). In either case, it is both our necessity and our duty to assess their credentials by clear principles of reason:

Reason must be our last judge and guide in everything. I do not mean that we must consult reason, and examine whether a proposi-

tion revealed from God can be made out by natural principles, and
if it cannot, that then we must reject it; but consult it we must, and
by it examine whether it be a revelation from God or no; and if
reason finds it to be revealed from God, reason then declares for it,
as much as for any other truth, and makes it one of her dictates." [14]

Reasonableness in religion could also refer, however, to a much
broader spirit present in the seventeenth and eighteenth centuries:
the antidogmatic, antienthusiastic temper of an age tired and dis-
gusted with religious controversies, persecutions, and wars. Through
the long history of disputes, the splintering into sects, all the points
of belief had been called into doubt and reduced to the level of
controversy. Christianity, it was claimed, was based on revelation,
but no one seemed to know what in fact was revealed—or rather,
everyone knew his own version to be the correct one. Anthony Collins only reiterated a common complaint in his *Discourse of Freethinking* (1713) when he noted that while the Bible might be divinely inspired, this had not prevented its official interpreters from
disagreeing on all the fundamentals. The man of the Enlightenment
wanted no part of that sort of confusion and dogmatism run wild.
On the one hand, this rejection sprang from the judgment that
dogma is as much the enemy of faith as of knowledge, because it is
superstition, ignorance claiming to be truth; whereas reason, freely
exercised, could lead to agreement on essential matters of belief
(from this we get one sort of plea for tolerance). On the other hand,
antidogmatic "reasonableness" could reflect the general tendency to
the secular and the bourgeois in eighteenth-century life, the desire
to settle down to relative security and a life governed by "good common sense," as one well-satisfied with his lot (the lot, that is, of an
educated and financially secure Englishman in a mercantile culture),
not thinking too highly or too humbly of oneself, but seeing oneself
as a pretty decent sort of fellow, entitled to some pursuit of self-
interest, and certainly not to be preoccupied either with the joys of
heaven or the torments of hell. This attitude led easily to a tolerance of indifference and of *ennui* in the Franklinesque blithe secu-
larism.

The "reason" of the Enlightenment, further, was a reason made
confident by great scientific advances. Through mathematics, astronomy, and the physical sciences, the world was opening itself to

14. John Locke, *An Essay Concerning Human Understanding*, bk. 4, chap. 19, par.
14; cf. also chaps. 17, 18.

man's rational quest, disclosing itself as most intricately and har-
moniously ordered. The man who had been made so small by the
Copernican revolution was precisely the one with the gift of reason
able to discover this great new truth and to comprehend the laws of
the universe, and thus to rise ever to new heights of accomplishment.
Yet the *philosophes* of the Enlightenment were not generally characterized by claims for an all-encompassing power of reason, either
as the sole proper ground of human action or as the ability to comprehend all the mysteries of the world. The principle of the Enlightenment was not the omnipotence of reason. Rather one might speak
(to use Peter Gay's phrase) of a claim for the "omnicompetence of
criticism," [15] understood as the assertion that everything is properly
subject to rational criticism, that is, as the "political demand for the
right to question everything," in the confidence that in such criticism reason will recognize and mark its own limits, thus finally showing its competence and certainties. This principle of free critical
examination is laid down in Bayle's *Dictionnaire historique et critique,* from which the *philosophes* mined so much, and it is expressed in Kant's classic definition of Enlightenment:

> Enlightenment is man's exodus from his self-incurred tutelage. Tute-
> lage is the inability to use one's understanding without the guidance
> of another person. This tutelage is self-incurred if its cause lies not
> in any weakness of the understanding, but in indecision and lack of
> courage to use the mind without the guidance of another. "Dare to
> know" (*sapere aude*)! Have the courage to use your own understand-
> ing; this is the motto of the Enlightenment.[16]

That principle of criticism was, further, at the center of the Enlightenment's philosophical justification of tolerance in religion,
from Locke through the English deists, and from Bayle through Voltaire and Lessing. Toleration did not mean for the important thinkers a commendation of indifference to religious questions, nor did it
spring primarily from a judgment about human fallibility in matters
capable of neither proof nor disproof; it was more deeply a positive
principle of freedom in faith and conscience springing from confidence in the possibilities of inquiry, from the morality demanded in
rational inquiry, and from the hope for a more comprehensive awareness of God.

15. Gay, *The Enlightenment, an Interpretation: The Rise of Modern Paganism*
(New York, 1966), pp. 141 ff.
16. *Immanuel Kants Werke,* 11 vols. (Berlin, 1912–18), 4 : 169.

What reason in science seemed to be discovering in the eighteenth
century was a benign and friendly if not a divinized nature. Everywhere design, order, and law were being revealed where hitherto
had been if not chaos at least mystery and uncertainty. Nature's laws
appeared to have the clarity, authority, and universal acceptability
of laws of reason and the axioms of mathematics. At least at first,
moreover, it seemed that the order disclosed could be readily fused
with the presuppositions inherited from Christianity.

> Whether one contemplated the infinitely great through the optic
> glass of the Tuscan artist, or the infinitely little through the micro-
> scope of Malpighi, one received at every turn new assurance that all
> was "according to the Ordainer of order and the mystical mathe-
> matics of the city of heaven." Biology had as yet revealed no disturb-
> ing ancestries, and man was still unassailed by anthropology and psy-
> choanalysis. Materialism itself could scarcely dispense with a divine
> hypothesis (though this soon followed): the Great Machine pre-
> supposed the Divine Mechanic.[17]

God's first revelation, in nature, was now being received in its fullness. Alexander Pope could exult:

> Nature and Nature's laws lay hid in night:
> God said, *Let Newton be!* and all was light!

And in Addison's famous hymn "The Spacious Firmament" (1712)
the heavens, sun, moon, stars, and planets all in turn were summoned
to display the Creator's power. Some of the glory was gone, since "no
real voice or sound" was heard from these witnesses; yet no matter, for

> In reason's ear they all rejoice,
> And utter forth a glorious voice;
> Forever singing, as they shine,
> "The hand that made us is divine."

Even after the teleological and cosmological arguments were destroyed by Hume and Kant, the inference of the great Creator from
the vast design of the cosmos continued strong in its appeal, in Paley's
famous *Natural Theology,* for example.

The zeal for the natural was also directed to the "natural man"
(except by Thomas Hobbes). Rationalists as well as romanticists
could find the good and the unspoiled at the bottom of man's nature. To be sure, the ambiguity in the meaning of "natural" lay

17. Basil Willey, *The Eighteenth Century Background* (London, 1940), p. 5.

closest to the surface here—what finally is natural about man? But for the most part rationalism rejected with special intensity the conception of original sin (hence the scandal of Kant's notion of radical evil) and found the laws of God and nature inscribed on the heart. Natural religion reached God not only through the starry heavens above but also through the moral law within.

Secularization, understood as a redirection of attention or a shift in the center of gravity in which religious institutions and theological interpretations no longer occupy the dominant place in life and other fields of knowledge develop without concern for legitimation in theology, was plainly taking place, though slowly, in the eighteenth century. But a still more inclusive aspect of rationalism was its utilitarianism, that is, its desire to regard all things as ordered teleologically for the benefit of man. This could be a "secular," this-worldly utilitarianism in which all is directed to the state of happiness achievable here. Or it could be a supernatural utilitarianism, in which our aim in life is to use the present existence in such a way as to reach our eternal destiny—and so things have been well arranged by God. Both forms were popular in the eighteenth century.

Finally, the rationalism of the Enlightenment was characterized by a deep and pervasive moralism. This meant both moral passion exhibited in the quest for truth and the application of criticism, and the conviction that, finally, morality is the better part, the final meaning and content of religion. At the latter point, deism and "reasonable" Christianity could make common cause with the moralism of pietism. Religious beliefs point us to the moral life. Matthew Tindal could argue not only that natural and revealed religion do not differ in substance, and that the worth of the latter consists in its agreement with the former, but that the republication of the law of nature occurs precisely in the knowledge of morality. Religion is the acknowledgment of moral duties as divine commands. Tillotson held that the only value of religion, both natural and revealed, is the provision of divine sanctions for morality. Further, ethical principles became the criteria for theological and biblical criticism. And as the cosmological argument was undercut by Hume, the moralism was further intensified, so that for Kant the struggle of religious belief itself was to be validated by the practical reason.

From Christianity to Natural Religion

The rationalism of the eighteenth century was not antireligious in nature. To be sure, one can argue that in the seventeenth century

the leading thought was still essentially Christian in orientation, that
it was Pascal, Newton, and the Cambridge Platonists (rather than
Hobbes, who was regularly denounced as an atheist) who characteristically expressed its sense of harmony between science and Christianity, whereas in the eighteenth century the inherited Christian
tradition came fundamentally into question, and supernaturalism
and its defenses were destroyed (a destruction that in the nineteenth
century was to be internalized in theology). Yet eighteenth-century
rationalism was itself deeply religious—only its commitment was to
a new form of faith and religion, to a search for an identity of religions beneath all the phenomena (including the Oriental religions,
which began to demand recognition), and thus to a religion finally
to be distinguished from all "positive" religions. The common name
for the object of this quest was "natural religion," the substance of
which had been given classic definition as early as Lord Herbert of
Cherbury's *De Veritate* (1624), in the five doctrines he held to be
essential in all religions: that there is a Supreme Being, that he ought
to be worshiped, that virtue joined with piety is the chief part of
worship, that vices and crimes should be expiated by repentance, and
that there are divine rewards and punishments in both this life and
the next.

The variations on the theme of natural religion may be summed
up under three heads, which suggest a dialectical development, not
unfolding in any clear chronological progression but nonetheless
leading up to the destruction of natural religion in Hume and Kant
and thus to the necessity for new beginnings. The first stage was admirably expressed by John Locke (1632–1704) and by Christian
Wolff (1679–1754), the popularizer of Leibnizian philosophy.[18] The
principle was that announced in the title of Locke's book, *The Reasonableness of Christianity* (1695). Essential Christianity, though its
content transcends what reason alone is able to discover, is harmonious with natural religion. In both Locke and Wolff there is the
familiar distinction between truths that can be derived (as Locke
put it) by "natural deduction" simply from "those ideas we have
from sensation and reflection"—such truths as the existence of God
and his nature as the most perfect being, creator and governor of
the world—and the truths that are "above reason" in the sense that
they have to be supplied by revelation and may yet involve some
mystery—including, according to Wolff, the Trinity, Christology,
grace, and atonement. But obviously no truths contrary to reason are

18. See Wolff's *Theologia Naturalis* (1736).

to be admitted (and relative simplicity is required by Locke, since Christianity is a religion for the plain man). Thus reason specifies the criteria by which the essential and genuine elements in purported revelation are to be recognized: they must, for example, be worthy of God and needful for man to know for his salvation, as well as not in conflict with any necessary truths (miracles, said Wolff, conflicted at most with accidental truths). Further, as Locke asserted, it is reason that accredits those great evidences for the redemption and revelation in Christ, the performance of miracles and the fulfillment of prophecies about the Messiah. Thus the evidential value of miracles can be accepted.

The general view of Christianity as a reasonable and necessary supplement to natural religion continued in the Wolffian and in the "transitional" German theologians (e.g. Mosheim, Canz, Carpov, and especially Baumgarten). It endured in the English scene in the "theology of evidences" from Samuel Clarke (1675–1729) to William Paley. (To the intellectual power of Clarke even Voltaire paid tribute, though Anthony Collins quipped that nobody had doubted the existence of God until Dr. Clarke tried to prove it.) It was also represented in a slightly different form by Joseph Butler in the *Analogy of Religion, Natural and Revealed, to the Constitution and Course of Nature* (1736). In reply to the deists who affirmed natural religion but denied Christianity, Butler sought to show that those who found evidences of divine activity in nature could not deny a similar significance to Christian revelation, for the kinds of difficulties attributed to the biblical records and Christian doctrines are of the same sort as those found in the arguments of natural religion: both involve uncertainties and rest on probabilities; and the relations within one area of argument are similar to those in the other.

The second stage in the dialectic of natural religion was characterized by the assertion that Christianity (insofar as it is acceptable) does not transcend natural religion but is an instance of it. At no point may Christianity go beyond reason. In the year after Locke's *Reasonableness of Christianity*, this view had been set forth in John Toland's *Christianity not Mysterious* (1696). The essence of Christianity, he said, is the same as natural religion; there is nothing mysterious or above reason in the Gospel.[19] We are not called upon to

19. The so-called mysteries of the Gospel "were certain things in their own nature intelligible enough, but called mysteries by reason of the veil under which they were formerly hid [under the Mosaic dispensation]. . . . Under the Gospel this veil is

adore what we cannot comprehend. "Revelation" is of use to inform
us, but the same is true of every matter of fact, whereas it is the evidence of the subject that persuades us. The title of Matthew Tindal's
book, *Christianity as Old as Creation; or, The Gospel a Republication of the Religion of Nature* (1730), indicates the point sharply:
genuine Christianity is identical with the religion of nature; natural
religion is a perfect thing, and "additions" are both unnecessary and
false. The goal of religion is morality.[20]

The same basic motif appeared in Germany, where the writings of
the English freethinkers were widely read. The shift away from
Wolff's position, which had kept room for a unique content of revealed truth, took place notably in the *Neologen,* in the work of
A. F. W. Sack (1703–86), J. F. W. Jerusalem (1709–89), J. J. Spalding
(1714–1804), who translated Butler's *Analogy,* J. S. Semler (1725–91),
J. A. Ernesti (1708–81), and J. D. Michaelis (1717–91), for whom
nothing could be allowed in the content of revelation except what
experience found reasonable. For Semler, as for Tindal, the center
of religion is the moral law, and so the genuine elements in the
Bible are the moral truths taught by Christ. Revelation is throughout a reconfirmation of reason. Two further points are important
concerning these views. First, the concept of revelation as a divine
disclosure of truths remained unchanged; only the content of the
disclosure was restricted to what is in keeping with reason; consequently, nothing new could be revealed.[21] Second, "reason" for the
Neologen tended to mean not so much formal deduction from first
principles or from empirical observation, but a broad reasonableness, that which makes practical sense, which is comprehensible to

---

wholly removed. From which [it] follows—that such doctrines cannot now properly
deserve the name of mysteries" (Toland, *Christianity not Mysterious; or, a treatise
showing that there is nothing in the Gospel contrary to reason, nor above it: and that
no Christian doctrine can properly be called a mystery,* 2d ed. [London, 1702], p. 94).

20. Even the more conservative archbishop John Tillotson could also say, "All
the duties of the Christian religion, which respect God, are no other but what
natural light prompts men to, excepting the two sacraments, and praying to God in
the name and by the mediation of Jesus Christ" (*Works,* ed. T. Birch, 10 vols. [London,
1820], 1 : 450).

21. Lessing well summarized the Neologians' position in his comments on the first
of the *Wolfenbüttel* fragments: "All revealed religion is nothing but a reconfirmation
of the religion of reason. Either it has no mysteries, or, if it does, it is indifferent
whether the Christian combines them with one idea or another, or with none at all."
And he asked: "What is a revelation that reveals nothing?" ("Gegensätze des Heraus-
gebers," *Sämtliche Schriften,* ed. Lachmann and Muncker [Leipzig, 1897], 12 : 431–32).

the reasoning self, or which springs from inner certainties. This was not strictly an "intellectualist" system. Thus Jerusalem could appeal to inner experience as a principle of religious certainty—"my experience is my proof"—in a kind of theology of religious experience that had been anticipated by the Cambridge Platonists.[22]

Already in this second stage, the real primacy of natural religion is apparent.[23] It was only a short step to the declaration that revealed religion was wholly unnecessary, or even opposed to the true religion of reason. This was the step taken by the thoroughgoing rationalist Hermann Reimarus (1694–1768), whose *Apology for the Rational Worshipers of God* was published by Lessing in the so-called *Wolfenbüttel Fragments*. For Reimarus, religion wants no revelation, because it rests on sound natural reason. Reason and claims to revelation are indeed in opposition, and the reasonable worshiper of God must return to the purely natural religion which alone is true and capable of bringing the race to permanent improvement and happiness, and which forms the basis of every historical, positive, and allegedly revealed religion, though it has been tragically corrupted by them. God, freedom, immortality, virtue—especially virtue and the moral conviction based on one's own insight and certainty instead of faith-prescribed doctrines—form the content of rational religion. Reimarus's case was argued most strikingly in his biblical criticism (Schweitzer put him at the beginning of the quest for the historical Jesus), leading, for example, to a sharp distinction between the purpose of Jesus, which remained within the orbit of ordinary Jewish thought, and the new universalized program of his disciples with its heavenly kingdom and consequent revisions of the story of Jesus' life.

Reimarus was much influenced by radical English deism, in which the opposition of natural religion and Christianity had long been proclaimed by men like Anthony Collins (1676–1729), who severely attacked the evidential value of prophecy, which he held to be the only "proof" of the divine origin of Christianity, and without which all Christian claims collapsed; Thomas Woolston (1670–1733), who precipitated a controversy over the historicity of the New Testament miracles and suggested that the resurrection was a fraud; and Peter

22. See Ernst Cassirer, *The Platonic Renaissance in England*, trans. J. P. Pettegrove (Edinburgh, 1953), pp. 30–34.

23. Locke had very early been charged with direct responsibility for Tindal, and Voltaire put down in his English notebook that "Mr. Locke's reasonableness of Christian religion is really a new religion" (quoted in Gay, *The Enlightenment*, p. 321).

Annet (1693–1769), who vigorously stated the frequent complaint over the moral inadequacy of scriptural (especially Old Testament) religion. In this radical strain of deism there was deep suspicion of all actual religion. The church was commonly seen as filled with superstition, pious fraud, and invention, the constructs of priestcraft. At this point English and German rationalism approached the attitude of the more revolutionary and anticlerical French rationalism of Voltaire.

The Burning Questions of Rational Religion

Three special problems continually recurred in the literature of the Enlightenment. One was the question of miracle. Perhaps one should call this a problem only for the apologists rather than for the *philosophes* or the deists; for the defenders of "revealed religion" miracle became more and more a millstone around the neck. The world of the rationalists, while not devoid of wonder and awe, was a demythologized or naturalized world. As such a natural world, it might be filled with marvels (Voltaire noted that originally a miracle means "something admirable"),[24] and the wonderful orderliness of the universe with its unbreakable laws could well be called a miracle by the deists. But this was the only miracle that could be allowed. There could be no violation of the laws of nature. The rejection of the theology of miraculous evidences, given classic statement in Hume's famous *Essay on Miracles* (1748), was as sharply expressed by Diderot: "I should believe, without hesitation, a single honest man who announced that 'His Majesty has just won a complete victory over the allies'; but all Paris could assure me that a dead man had just been resurrected at Passy, and I would not believe a word of it."[25] And Reimarus went patiently through the Gospels, giving naturalistic explanations for the reported miracles, for they all had to be understood as either fictitious accounts or events scientifically explicable.

A second special theological problem for the Enlightenment was theodicy; on this question, so it was thought, hung the fate of religion and philosophy alike. More precisely, the conflict was between a renewed humanism and the dogma of original sin. Polemic against the latter was a constantly recurring theme, and Pascal's formulations in the *Pensées* were particularly the object of attention from

24. "Miracles," *Philosophical Dictionary*, ed. and trans Peter Gay, 2 vols. (New York), 2 : 392.
25. Quoted in Gay, *The Enlightenment*, p. 146.

the French *philosophes,* including Voltaire's throughout his career. Moral evil is undeniable (and great natural evil, too, as the Lisbon earthquake made clear), and it may even be said to be inevitable in human life as it is. But to account for this by an original sin whose consequences were visited on all later generations was absurd—to Voltaire, to Rousseau, to the deists, and to the *Neologen.*

It can hardly be said that the eighteenth century made much headway in its consideration of the problem of evil. For the most part the discussion was carried on within the orbit of Leibniz's ideas. A really new approach came only with Rousseau, who transferred the problem from the realm of theology to that of law and society. Rousseau did not deny the decadence of man's present state, his inner poverty, any more than Pascal had, but he refused to account for human degeneration by an original fall or innate radical evil. The conflict in man is rather between *l'homme naturel* and *l'homme artificiel,* "natural man" and "civilized man." Man in the state of nature, as he leaves the hands of the Creator, is not characterized by sin and guilt; "all degenerates in the hands of man," and specifically of man in society. This alone is responsible for "selfish love." Thus Rousseau began to change the terms of the problem of evil from the theological-metaphysical formulations of the seventeenth century to forms independent of the question of God.[26]

The problems of miracle and of sin engage us in the Enlightenment's broadest considerations of the structure of the world and the nature of man. They also called into question the truth of the Bible, a question at least as revolutionary for theology as the metaphysical problem. The Bible was the special point at which eighteenth-century rationalism concerned itself with the problem of history. Earlier, Hobbes in the *Leviathan* (1651) had outlined aims and methods for critical study of the Old Testament, suggesting that the date of biblical writings was to be determined by exegetical study of traditional opinion and concluding that Moses wrote only parts of the Pentateuch and that much of the Old Testament was post-Exilic. Richard Simon (whose *Histoire critique du vieux Testament* appeared in 1678), in the interest of furthering Catholic claims by showing the untenability of Protestant reliance on Scripture alone, had proposed hypotheses about the authenticity and development of the books of

26. On this topic, see Ernst Cassirer, *The Philosophy of the Enlightenment* (Boston, 1955), pp. 137–60.

the Bible that were highly dangerous to orthodoxy. Spinoza (in the *Tractatus theologico-politicus,* 1670) had stated a philosophical foundation for biblical criticism and out of it had developed the idea of the "historicity" of the Bible, due to the impossibility in his system of allowing the Scriptures a privileged place in thought. The Bible, he held, is a part of nature and subject to its laws, and it must therefore be interpreted by a method "almost the same" as that used to interpret nature.

But it was the second half of the eighteenth century that saw the most influential development of the principles of "grammatico-historical" interpretation, and then more against the background of Erasmus and Hugo Grotius than of Spinoza. Jean Astruc (in *Conjectures,* 1753), while accepting the Mosaic authorship of the Pentateuch in contradiction of Spinoza and Simon, approached the study of Genesis from a new angle, noting the stylistic peculiarities and especially the use of divine names as clues to documents within the text. This evidence was taken up by Eichorn in his *Introduction to the Old Testament* (1781). Semler developed a view of the basic Jewishness of the Synoptics and the Greek character of John. Reimarus insisted on searching for historical causes that might account for the recorded events. Lessing applied an evolutionary idea to criticism, which was to be concerned with origin and end, to become genetic and historical, seeking the laws of growth of the subject. Herder (in *The Spirit of Hebrew Poetry,* 1782) brought the Bible still more definitely into the sphere of literature and history, calling attention to the character of early Hebrew literature, with its elements of myth and poetry, and emphasizing the way in which religious literature reflects the mind of particular nations and their special traditions.

With such developments as these in biblical criticism, we have evidently come far beyond the questions of the detailed fulfillment of prophecy and the historicity of miracles. (And in Lessing, the recognition of the "historicity" of the sources was no longer, as for so many of the rationalists, a subverting of the claims of revealed religion—but this is a sign of his movement away from the mainstream; see below, pp. 49–51. The question has become, at the deepest level, the most inclusive problem of the basis and nature of religious belief, that is, of the possibility of theology at all, and that is the question that eighteenth-century rationalism handed over to the nineteenth-century.

The Destruction of Natural Religion

David Hume (1711–76) was not taken as seriously by most of his contemporaries as he was by Kant (or by the twentieth century), but he needs to be viewed with Kant as a terminal figure in eighteenth-century rationalist religion, and also as a vigorous and often scornful critic of evangelical doctrine, of the "enthusiastic" concentration on experience, and of the latitudinarian defense of the established church as a bulwark against moral chaos.

Several elements in Hume's critique are of particular importance. The first, which dissected the theology of evidences, was his attack on the evidential value of miracles.[27] Hume did not, in that essay, deny the possibility of miracles (though one can hardly suppose that he wished to affirm any); indeed, he concluded the discussion with an assertion that "the Christian religion not only was at first attended with miracles, but even at this day cannot be believed by any reasonable person without one," and thus "mere reason is insufficient to convince us of its veracity: and whoever is moved by *faith* to assent to it, is conscious of a continued miracle in his own person, which subverts all the principles of his understanding, and gives him a determination to believe what is most contrary to custom and experience."

This seeming affirmation was pure irony and actually restated the principle of the argument: Verification is by appeal to experience, and to try to prove something by what is contrary to experience is absurd. Earlier, Hume had made his point succinctly: "A miracle is a violation of the laws of nature; and as a firm and unalterable experience has established these laws, the proof against a miracle, from the very nature of the fact, is as entire as any argument from experience can possibly be imagined." The "plain consequence" can be laid down as "a general maxim . . . that no testimony is sufficient to establish a miracle, unless the testimony be of such a kind, that its falsehood would be more miraculous, than the fact, which it endeavors to establish." Obviously, no such testimonies are to be found.[28]

For Hume, the problem of miracle was one on which revealed re-

27. In the essay on miracles, incorporated into the *Inquiry Concerning Human Understanding* (1748) as chap. 10.

28. While many of the replies to Hume misunderstood his specific aim, the attack actually proved so effective as to produce a major shift in supernaturalist apologetics, such that (e.g. in Paley) an attempt was made to show the "antecedent credibility" of miracles and the "probability" of their accompanying divine revelation.

ligion foundered. But his skepticism was hardly less directed toward natural religion, and it was he rather than the orthodox theologians who brought the deist movement in Britain to an end. In the delightful *Dialogues Concerning Natural Religion*,[29] consisting of conversations among Philo the skeptic, Cleanthes the defender of rational religion, and Demea the "orthodox" believer (who often joins with Philo's skepticism because of the incomprehensibility of God) Hume wove a subtle and compelling pattern of criticism of the received forms of the argument from "design" (with some incidental, though substantial, attack on the cosmological, so-called a priori argument as well). No valid conclusions about the whole of the natural order can be drawn from our knowledge of only a part; the causal sequences we know are all within nature and provide no basis for affirming a causal relation between God and the whole of nature (if it is a whole); why not an infinite series of causes, including one for the supposed author of nature? Random occurrence is a possible explanation for the emergence of the order we know; the universe may as well be likened to a cabbage, or the product of an act of generation, as to the work of a designer; at most, the argument could provide us an architect rather than a creator. How could one show the infinity or unity or infallibility of a creative mind? And how especially could one *prove* the goodness of deity from the very mixed phenomena we observe—that is, in the face of the positive evil in the world?

Far more inclusive than even the sustained arguments of the *Dialogues* was another element of Hume's attack which came directly from his epistemological position developed in the *Treatise* and the *Inquiry,* and which if valid would rule out any sort of argumentation to God, namely, his critique of the idea of causality (and also of the self, whose continuity we cannot establish). The concept of cause is neither a priori necessary nor required by an immediate evidence. Immediate impressions may provide contiguity and succession in the relation of events, but they cannot supply us with any necessary connection or causal force. The so-called principle of causality is not a principle but a custom or habit of mind, an acquired disposition that is very useful but without philosophical justification.

From another direction, in his brief *Natural History of Religion* (1757), Hume's conclusions cut against both natural and historical

---

29. For obvious reasons, Hume was reluctant to publish the dialogues; they appeared three years after his death.

religion. By later standards, the *Natural History* was not a very adequate account of the origins of religion, but it was sufficient to destroy belief in the historical development of actual religions out of
any universal natural substratum of rational religion. The real beginnings are to be found in polytheism rather than in monotheism,
and the "progress" of religion is marked by a kind of "flux and re-
flux," men having "a natural tendency to rise from idolatry to theism,
and to sink again from theism into idolatry." Therein also is disclosed the real psychological sources of religion, in man's fears and
hopes, not in "speculative curiosity" or "love of truth," but in "the
ordinary affections of human life" in primitive man: "the anxious
concern for happiness, the dread of future misery, the terror of death,
the thirst for revenge, the appetite for food and other necessaries."
Nor for Hume was revealed religion exempt from this explanation
or from the continuation of superstition, albeit in more subtle forms:

> Examine the religious principles, which have, in fact, prevailed in
> the world. You will scarcely be persuaded, that they are any thing
> but sick men's dreams: Or perhaps will regard them more as the
> playsome whimsies of monkies in human shape, than the serious,
> positive, dogmatical asseverations of a being, who dignifies himself
> with the name of rational. . . . No theological absurdities so glaring
> that they have not, sometimes, been embraced by men of the greatest
> and most cultivated understanding. No religious precepts so rigorous
> that they have not been adopted by the most voluptuous and most
> abandoned of men. . . . The whole is a riddle, an enigma, an in-
> explicable mystery. Doubt, uncertainty, suspense of judgment appear
> the only result of our most accurate scrutiny, concerning this subject.
> But such is the frailty of human reason, and such the irresistible
> contagion of opinion, that even this deliberate doubt could scarcely
> be upheld; did we not enlarge our view, and opposing one species
> of superstition to another, set them a quarreling; while we ourselves,
> during their fury and contention, happily make our escape into the
> calm, though obscure, regions of philosophy.[30]

Finally, Hume's investigation into the basis of morals (*An Inquiry
Concerning the Principles of Morals*, 1751) struck at the familiar defense of the church as a necessary support and advocate of moral
principles. Here again, in Hume's concentration on sentiment and

30. David Hume, *Natural History of Religion*, ed. H. E. Root (London, 1956), pp.
46–47, 28, 75–76.

feeling, one can see both his empiricism and, in a certain way, his anticipation of a theme of romanticism.

But it was Immanuel Kant (1724–1804) who stood at the end of the broad road of rational religion, both as *terminus* and as *telos,* and who more than any other single thinker cast his shadow over theology in the nineteenth century. How and why this was so, we cannot here hope to trace out in detail; at best, we can suggest the areas of his importance for subsequent theology.

First of all, Kant represented the culmination of the Enlightenment's confidence in reason, a culmination precisely because of critical reason's humility, because reason knows how to set its limits and can therefore be sure of its sureties. The general Enlightenment principle of criticism therefore took on more exact focus in Kant. When he said, "Our age is the authentic age of criticism, to which everything must submit," [31] he meant to inaugurate a new kind of critique, namely, a critique of knowledge itself and as such, which would not be skeptical but by which in fact *certain* knowledge could be established, and the ideas of law and necessary connection, so essential to natural science and philosophy and ethics, could be rescued from the danger posed by Hume.

But precisely in the establishment of the certainties of theoretical knowledge, the boundaries were also fixed. Theoretical knowledge, with its transcendental principles, is limited to phenomena, to objects as objects of experience, and it does not extend to the noumenal, the "thing-in-itself." God, freedom, and immortality are not possible objects of our theoretical knowledge. They are not given to us in the concrete unity of intuition and concept which is actual empirical knowledge. Nor could they possibly be established by using principles whose validity is wholly restricted to the realm of possible experience. Antinomies, irresolvable conflicts resulting from the equal possibility of proving opposite conclusions (e.g. that the world has a beginning in time and that it has no beginning, or that there is freedom in the world and that there is no freedom) arise as soon as these ideas are treated as if they were objects of theoretical knowledge. Kant reviewed in detail the arguments for the existence of God, showing their fatal defects. The ontological argument fails because the proof rests on a confusion between the logical necessity of thought

31. *Kritik der reinen Vernunft,* 1st ed., preface, p. v. See the English translation by Smith, *Immanuel Kant's Critique of Pure Reason* (London, 1964), p. 9.

and the ontological necessity of existence, and because existence is never a predicate in the sense that it can alter the idea of a thing (the idea of a nonexistent hundred dollars is just as perfect as an actual hundred dollars). The cosmological argument, by seeking a cause for the whole, goes by definition beyond all possible experience, thus misusing the categories. The teleological argument, even if it were possible for it to have the persuasive force which an observation of design in the whole of nature could provide, would only show an architect and not a creator, hence the cosmological and ontological arguments have always to be smuggled in.[32] In short, natural theology, as it has traditionally been conceived, is at an end, and the idea of God, within the realm of pure reason, can be only a "formal condition of thought," an "ideal only," a "regulative principle," by which the speculative reason is led to view the order of the world as if it were based on a necessary unitary cause; but the principle does not involve the assertion of an existence necessary by itself.

But Kant had not said all he wanted to say about religion in the *Critique of Pure Reason,* for the same reason also acts; it is also (even primarily) the practical reason. Here man is laid hold of directly by the moral law, by the universally valid categorical imperative, by duty, by the reverence for law which alone is the finally good motive for action, by the will for the highest good. But now further assertions can be made. Freedom is the universal and necessary presupposition of morality: If I ought, I can. This is not an affirmation of theoretical knowledge; no explanation is to be given in terms of the phenomenal order of causality; but the reality of freedom must be asserted, that is, postulated or presupposed. And the will for the highest good, in which moral perfection is joined by complete satisfaction, requires two further postulates of the pure practical reason: the immortality of the soul, as providing opportunity for the self to approach the highest good, and the existence of God, as the ground of the unity of virtue and happiness, duty and desire. Thus while the basis for any knowledge of God through theoretical reason has been destroyed, a new possibility for theology has been found, a moral proof for God.

It is evident that Kant's way of viewing religion and the possibilities of theology was still thoroughly within the orbit of rationalism. That was made explicit in his *Religion within the Limits of Reason*

---

32. The teleological argument was also treated extensively and sympathetically in the *Critique of Judgment,* but with the same conclusion as to its insufficiency.

Alone (1793) and in *Der Streit der Fakultäten* (1798). To be sure, it is possible to see in the doctrine of radical evil developed in the former work a "foreign" intrusion into an otherwise rationalist perspective, and Karl Barth finds at the border of Kant's conceptions of the church, of evil, and of atonement a recognition of possibilities for theology on other premises: the Bible, historical revelation, Christology, grace, and the Church.[33] But it is highly dubious that Kant had any interest in promoting (for himself or for others) any theological option save the thoroughly rational one (any more than Hume's acknowledgment of the possibility of a faith that subverts the understanding is to be taken as his recommendation of it). The typical rationalist conception of religion as a duality of beliefs and morality reigns throughout, with the emphasis on the moral to the point of theological utilitarianism. In *Religion within the Limits of Reason Alone,* Kant's Jesus is wholly the ideal of moral perfection and the founder of a moral community; his discussion of the features of specific religions is inevitably oriented to translation into the terms of rational moral religion. Kant can also say, in words identical to those of the English deists, that religion, subjectively considered, is "the recognition of all duties as divine commands" [34] and that man's morality is the essential thing in all worship of God. But even more, the rationally permissible belief structure now explicitly rests on the self-certifying moral experience. Beyond this in the moralization of theology it is hardly possible to go.

Kant, we said, was above all the philosopher with whom the nineteenth-century theologians had to reckon. After him, four possible routes for theology may be distinguished, all of which were traveled to a greater or lesser extent. One was to question the validity of the first critique's restriction of theoretical knowledge or cognition, either (as in the idealistic philosophy) by "more consistently" and "courageously" following out Kant's speculative principle and overcoming the phenomenal–noumenal "dualism," or by some revised program of natural theology that would take account of Kant's work (e.g. in more recent neo-Thomism). The second, a minor stream in the nineteenth century which was renewed in the twentieth by Karl Barth, was the acceptance of reason's criticism of its limits and thereby the denial of reason's right to establish the point of depar-

√33. See Barth's *Protestantische Theologie,* pp. 260 ff. [176 ff.].

34. *Religion within the Limits of Reason Alone,* trans. Theodore M. Greene and Hoyt H. Hudson (New York, 1960), p. 142.

ture for theology. This raised the possibility "that theology would be content to stand on its own feet vis-à-vis philosophy, that it would recognize its methodological point of departure as defined in revelation." [35] The third, which was to be taken up most dramatically in the Ritschlian school, was the full acceptance of both the Kantian critique of theoretical reason and the adoption of the moral as the basis for proceeding. The fourth, by far the most widely followed, was to enlarge the category of direct experience by turning to *Gefühl* (Schleiermacher) or *Ahnung* (de Wette), or by finding in a fuller "reason" the possibility of knowing the spiritual order (Coleridge). In all of these ways, however, there was to be reflected a Socratic turn to the role of the subject in faith and knowledge, a turn which had its epistemological expression in Kant's analysis in the *Critique of Pure Reason*.

The Edge of Rationalism: Rousseau and Lessing

In the thought of Jean Jacques Rousseau (1712–78) and Gotthold Ephraim Lessing (1729–81) we move within the orbit of the Enlightenment, and yet in such a way as to be led quite beyond its rationalism in the direction of romanticism and of a new age generally. Rousseau was above all the man of the French Enlightenment to influence German thought (notably from Lessing to Fichte). His own "creed," set forth most fully in the "Confession of Faith of a Savoyard Vicar" (in the fourth book of *Emile*, 1762) sounded nearly all the characteristic themes of the representatives of natural religion in the preceding century. Reason is the necessary judge of truth: the testimony of others "can add nothing new to the natural means of knowing truth which God has given me." [36] The proper guide in testing revealed religion is the book of nature, which is open to all as a source for the knowledge of God, and which leads us to the knowledge of God and of his providential ordering of the world so that human life can be fulfilled. Original sin as an account of moral evil is wholly to be rejected (though here Rousseau begins to look in a new direction, as we noticed above). The destiny of man is eternal life. Prayer as praise and adoration is appropriate and to be

35. Barth, *Protestantische Theologie*, p. 274 [191]. Barth notes the second, third, and fourth of the directions suggested here, though with a slightly different version of the fourth.

36. *Emile,* trans. Barbara Foxley (New York, 1925), p. 261. And "The God whom I adore is not the God of darkness, he has not given me understanding in order to forbid me to use it; to tell me to submit my reason is to insult the giver of reason. The minister of truth does not tyrannize over my reason, he enlightens it" (p. 264).

cultivated, but not prayer as petition. Divine providence has already provided all that is needful for the pursuit of man's goal, and one could not wish the order of the world to be torn by miraculous acts. Finally, Rousseau did argue for religious toleration.

Yet all this was stated in a new way, deriving from Rousseau's discovery of a new "inner" world—new to the intellectualism prevalent in the Enlightenment, though not new to the pietism by which Rousseau had also been influenced—the world of the self as centered in the heart and the feelings. The beginning point was not "I think, therefore I am" but "I exist, I sense, I feel—therefore I am." This was Rousseau's anthropological discovery, the heart and soul which was simply himself existing; and it was exhibited both in the whole course of his life and in his reflections on religion. Thus the nature whose wonder he apprehended was quite different from the nature of Locke or Kant or Wolff (or Addison!). It was a nature echoing immediately the inner voice of the heart, to which he appropriately responded with an intense lyricism. As a consequence, his proof of God from the order of the universe was not quite the same as deism's. Thus also he saw differently the "good" nature of man as he came forth from the hand of the Creator; man in whom the voice of the soul continues to express itself as the voice called conscience in feeling for truth, justice, and goodness; man also caught in the tensions and evils of society. For Rousseau, individualism took a new shape. The final religious and ethical measure was to be the individual's own thought and feeling insofar as it truly originates in his own heart, without the determination of tradition and foreign *Raisonnement*. Perhaps most importantly, the concept of reason was expanded by Rousseau's recognition that reasoning and reflection are dependent on the voice of the heart.

Gotthold Ephraim Lessing was in another way a transition from the Enlightenment. In his writings of the early 1760s (before he became the librarian at Wolfenbüttel), it is clear that Lessing was a genuine follower of natural religion and essentially deistic in his position. Even in *Nathan the Wise* (1779) and *The Education of the Human Race* (1780), as well as in his publication of the *Wolfenbüttel Fragments* (by Reimarus) in 1774–78, he has been alleged to be a devotee of rationalist religion.[37] Surely, Lessing was committed

37. Peter Gay, for example, will let him be nothing but this (see *The Enlightenment*, pp. 331–35). And Henry Chadwick, in his introduction to *Lessing's Theological Writings* (London, 1956), tends to the same conclusion. But see Barth, *Protestantische*

throughout his life to examining the claims of religion by free rational criticism. The Enlightenment's devotion to the moral as the heart of religion was strong in him. And in *Nathan* the great religious traditions (personified in the characters—a Jew, a Muslim, a Christian) were stages in man's development toward an inclusive rational moral religion that is the goal of human history; and to that religion alone did man finally have any "duty." Toleration, cosmopolitanism, and brotherhood were the virtues of Nathan:

> I have never wished to find
> The same bark growing on every tree.
>   [Act IV, scene 4]

No more than Reimarus or Semler could Lessing accept the idea of an exclusive revelation. His criticism of the *Neologen* was not on behalf of orthodoxy, but for the sake of more radical change than this compromise represented.

But Lessing's was not merely a wider and deeper rationalism, less polemical in its attitude to the historical religions (or more subtle in its critique of them). It also marked the genuine engagement of the Enlightenment with history, a turn to historical ways of understanding and a recognition of the historicity of religion, not as a refutation or an establishment of its truth, nor as a mine for illustrations of nonhistorical (especially moral) truths, but in the sense that particular historical process is an essential ingredient in religion. Thus the width of the famous "wide, ugly ditch" over which Lessing said he could not leap, however hard he tried: "Accidental truths of history can never become the proof of necessary truths of reason." [38] The quest for rationality and universality in religion is not to be given up, but neither is the involvement of belief in historical par-

---

Theologie, Cassirer, *Philosophy of the Enlightenment,* and especially Henry E. Allison, *Lessing and the Enlightenment* (Ann Arbor, 1966). Allison argues convincingly that an important shift in Lessing's thought took place after the move to Wolfenbüttel in 1770 and that Lessing's interest in Leibniz is a key to his later position. Helmut Thielicke, on the other hand, tries to make the Lessing of *The Education of the Human Race* into a transcendental theist in *Offenbarung, Vernunft, und Existenz: Studien zur Religionsphilosophie Lessings* (Gütersloh, 1957); and Otto Mann would even see him as a believing Christian (*Lessing, Sein und Leistung,* 2d ed. [Hamburg, 1961]).

38. "The Proof of the Spirit and of Power" (1777); cf. Chadwick, ed., *Lessing's Theological Writings,* p. 53. At one level, of course, this saying could be simply the familiar rejection of proofs from miracle and prophecy. It could also mean that the question of the historical facticity of any particular revelation is irrelevant to the question of its truth (see Allison, *Lessing and the Enlightenment,* pp. 101 ff.).

ticularity to be rejected.[39] Lessing's biggest step toward reconciling these two seemingly irreconcilable demands of religion was taken in *The Education of the Human Race,* where he moved toward a synthesis of the historical and the rational. Whether or not he himself conceived of a real reconciliation or synthesis, at least many in the nineteenth century understood his work as a move to overcome the antithesis. Human history, said Lessing, is to be viewed as a teleological process of development in which the infinite is manifested in the finite, that is, in which the revelation of God is given immanently in the history of religion, so that the moral and religious development of human life is at one and the same time a natural and a divine activity, in which mankind moves (is led) toward the fullness of truth.

Thus positive religion is positively valued, and Lessing could join (with and yet against Reimarus) the attack on Protestant biblicism on behalf of a positive principle of divine disclosure in biblical religion. Revelation is actual in the Jewish-Christian history, and it has not been improved upon by the rational religion of the *Neologen,* though also it is not yet finished. The positive religions are not distortions of some original or non-historical religion of mankind, but strivings toward an ideal that they will never completely realize. As he put it in the famous parable of the three rings in *Nathan the Wise,* from the judgment seat of reason none of the three religions can definitely be claimed true, in the sense that they fully express the ideal for humanity of virtue and piety, yet each *may be* in the process of becoming true, moving toward an actualization that lies always in the bosom of the future (but will not thereby cease to be historical). In this sense Lessing could insist that "the development of revealed truths into truths of reason is absolutely necessary, if the human race is to be assisted by them." [40] And to this should be added his other, most famous saying: "If God were holding all the truth that exists in his right hand, and in his left just the one ever-active impulse toward truth, even if with the condition that I should always and eternally err, and said to me, 'Choose!' I should humbly fall on his left hand and say, 'Father, give! The pure truth is surely for thee alone!' " [41]

---

39. Thus the scorn of Lessing's question to the *Neologen:* "What is a revelation that reveals nothing?" See above, p. 37.

40. *Education of the Human Race,* paragraph 76.

41. *Eine Duplik* (1778), *Sämtliche Schriften,* 13 : 24.

ROMANTICISM

The work of Kant marked the end of a theological era, and already in Rousseau and Lessing we see beginning a definite movement away from rationalism's view of religion toward new ways of understanding theology that would be distinct from those of both orthodoxy and rationalism. This tendency was accelerated and carried farther by the new intellectual and spiritual climate of romanticism. The word "romanticism" has been used so freely, unfortunately, that it has little explanatory value. Here we mean above all the movement beginning in Germany in the 1790s which gave itself this name. Some of the ideas of this movement had been announced in Rousseau and Lessing; for its nurture Herder and Schiller, along with the *Sturm und Drang* movement, were of special importance; it came to full flower in literature and as a *Weltanschauung* in Novalis and the Schlegels (especially Friedrich Schlegel), Schleiermacher and Fichte, Görres and Adam Müller, Tieck and Wackenroder. Schleiermacher's *Speeches* and *Soliloquies* have been called its two chief manifestos in the realm of religion, but this romanticism (along with the closely related movements in other countries) was also of importance for theology in Hegel and Schelling, in Coleridge, in Emerson and the Transcendentalists, in Newman and the Oxford Movement, and in the Mercersburg theology.

One facet of the romanticist outlook was its protest, in the name of freedom and dynamism, against formalism and structure—whether the formalism of neoclassicism; or that of a rationalism whose ideal was simplicity, self-evidence, and universality in conceptualization; or that which saw uniformity in the law of nature; or that of the moral asceticism and discipline that could characterize men as widely different as Immanuel Kant, John Wesley, Jonathan Edwards, and Benjamin Franklin. Against all such imposition of form, romanticism sought a new freedom and spontaneity instead of the mechanical perfection of a wholly ordered universe. It emphasized the storm and thrust of life, power rather than pattern, the impulse to fullness of content, even to play, in contrast to purity of form.

Immediately related to this motif was the romantic stress on individuality, the near worship at times of originality and genius. Friedrich Schlegel wrote: "It is precisely individuality that is the original and eternal thing in men. . . . The cultivation and development of this individuality, as one's highest vocation, would be a divine egoism." [42] And in the *Soliloquies*, Schleiermacher, too, set forth the manifestation of uniqueness as the true goal for persons (and also for such entities as nations and families):

> Thus there dawned upon me what is now my highest intuition. I saw clearly that each man is meant to represent humanity in his own way, combining its elements uniquely, so that it may reveal itself in every mode, and all that can issue from its womb be made actual in the fullness of unending space and time.[43]

Of course, romanticism did not discover the individual for the first time. Not only pietism but also strains of rationalist thought were close in the background. Yet where the dominating quest of the Enlightenment had been for the *universal* beyond the individual, or for the participation of the individual in the universal, romanticism self-consciously and enthusiastically turned in the other direction.

Romanticism turned to the individual, furthermore, with a different sense of the nature of the self. Following Rousseau, romanticism exalted the immediacy of feeling—in the self, for humanity, and for the world. The fundamental relation of man to the world is not through the dignified structure of reason, with its objectifying categories, but in the direct relation of the whole man in his inner heart and in "sensuous impulse" to the vitality and flux of life. Even philosophy is originally feeling, dreaming, said Novalis. The romanticist took an aesthetic rather than a utilitarian approach to the world, and aesthetic in a sense quite different from what is implied by the neoclassic search for universal form. In Paul Tillich's language, this was an "aesthetic-meditative" rather than a "scientific-analytical" or "technical-controlling" attitude. The world is to be appreciated as worthy of wonder, as an object of delight, and thus as symbolic of a mysterious power behind.[44]

---

42. *Athenaeum,* 3 : 15.
43. *Schleiermacher's Soliloquies,* trans. Horace L. Friess (Chicago, 1957), p. 31.
44. Cf. Wordsworth:

> If indeed there be
> An all-pervading Spirit, upon whom
> Our dark foundations rest, could he design
> That this magnificent effect of power,
> The earth we tread, the sky that we behold
> By day, and all the pomp which night reveals;
> That these—and that superior mystery
> Our vital frame, so fearfully devised,
> And the dread soul within it—should exist
> Only to be examined, pondered, searched,
> Proved, vexed and criticised?
> [*The Excursion,* Book 4]

A fourth facet of romanticism, interwoven with all of the others and of no less importance for theology, was its concern and feeling for history. The most important man in the background here was Johann Gottfried Herder (1744–1803). With Lessing and Goethe, Herder had helped to recover Spinoza from the false picture given by Bayle and from the darkness to which Wolff had consigned him; he helped to make Spinoza a fruitful source of inspiration to the late eighteenth and early nineteenth centuries, no longer as the "atheist" and "fatalist" but as the "God-intoxicated man," the "arch-theist." [45] Like Lessing, Herder spoke for the discovery of God *within* living human experience. Religion is, indeed, "the highest humanity of man." And more vigorously and deeply than Lessing, he located religion in historical process, complaining against rationalism's lack of historical sense and writing a philosophy of history. The history of humanity is the history of revelation: "Facts are the basis of all the divine in religion, and religion can only be set forth in history, indeed it must itself continually become living history." [46] To this theory of history is related Herder's conception of biblical interpretation, in which the divine is discovered not in opposition to the human, but in correspondence with the human: the more fully the truly human character of Scripture is discerned, the more fully the living divine spirit may be recognized. Herder's is not a history susceptible to uniform characterization, but history as the continual birth of individual forms and new creatures, of many peoples and ages, each to be understood in its peculiar value and place. At this point Herder, even more than Lessing, broke with the Enlightenment and laid the basis for romanticism's historical sense.

Finally, romanticism may be described by the dominance of what Lovejoy has called the principle of plenitude—or rather, by the twin principles of plenitude and diversity: diversity in contrast to uniformity and simplicity, and plenitude in contrast to the restriction of content by formal rules.[47] "Every kind of perfection must attain existence in the fullness of the world," said Schiller. Aesthetic appreciation must be catholic enough to embrace the inexhaustible fullness of life, and for the creative artist (or in any aspect of human

45. See Herder, *God, Some Conversations.*
46. *Briefe, Herders Werke,* ed. Bernhard Suphan, 33 vols. (Berlin, 1877–1913), 10 : 257.
47. Arthur O. Lovejoy, *The Great Chain of Being* (Cambridge, Mass., 1936), chap. 10. Lovejoy makes the point that the principle of plenitude had always been there, e.g. in the Enlightenment, but as subordinate to the principle of uniformity; in romanticism it burst free of this restriction.

life) diversity is as such an excellence. The whole range of human experience and imagination seeks expression. Thus Schleiermacher, in the second of the *Speeches,* celebrated the diversity in humanity:

> What would the uniform repetition of even a highest ideal be? Mankind, time and circumstances excepted, would be everywhere identical. They would be the same formula with a different coefficient. What would it be in comparison with the endless variety which humanity *does* manifest? Take any element of humanity and you will find it in almost every possible condition. You will not find it quite by itself, nor quite combined with all other elements, but you will find all possible mixtures between, in every odd and unusual combination. And if you could think of combinations you do not see, this gap would be a negative revelation of the universe, an indication that, in the present temperature of the world, this mixture is not possible, in the requisite degree.[48]

A living nature everywhere aims at diversity and individuality. And so Schleiermacher in the fifth speech drew the consequence for religion:

> You must abandon the vain and foolish wish that there should only be one religion; you must lay aside all repugnance to its multiplicity; as candidly as possible you must approach everything that has ever, in the changing shapes of humanity, been developed in its advancing career, from the ever fruitful bosom of the spiritual life. . . . Nor can these different manifestations of religion be mere component parts, differing only in number and size, and forming, when combined, a uniform whole. . . . I therefore find that multiplicity of the religions is based on the nature of religion. . . . We must assume and we must search for an endless mass of distinct forms. . . . The whole of religion is nothing but the sum of all relations of man to God, apprehended in all the possible ways in which any man can be immediately conscious in his life. . . . You are wrong, therefore, with your universal religion that is natural to all, for no one will have his own true and right religion, if it is the same for all. As long as we occupy a place there must be in these relations of man to the whole a nearer and a farther, which will necessarily determine each feeling differently in each life. . . . No single relation can accord to every feeling its due. . . . Hence, the whole of religion can be present only when all those different views of every relation are actually given.[49]

48. Schleiermacher, *On Religion: Speeches to Its Cultured Despisers,* trans. John Oman from the 3d ed. (1821) (New York, 1958), pp. 74–75. Hereafter cited as *Speeches.*
49. Ibid., pp. 214–18.

PART I

1799–1835

The Possibility of Theology

3

Schleiermacher's Theological Program

At the beginning of the nineteenth century the theological problem was, simply, "How is theology possible?" This was a question of both rationale and method, and included, at least implicitly, the question whether theology is possible at all. Of course, this had been a question in every age, but now it emerged with new strength and in a special configuration provided by the eighteenth century. The theologies of orthodoxy were still present, but fundamentally they were fighting rearguard actions as they retreated steadily before the forces of Enlightenment into the backwaters of intellectual and cultural isolation.[1] The quickenings of religious life in pietism and the revival movements had brought no fresh theological vision. Except for the tentative but still unexploited suggestions made by Lessing and Herder, the historical or positive religions were viewed with suspicion. The historical reliability, apologetic value, and even moral authority of the Scriptures had come under heavy attack, and the possibility (or even the desirability) of revelation was in doubt. With Hume and Kant, natural theology also reached the end of the line, and the older metaphysics was destroyed.

How then is theology possible? What basis can it have and what claims can it make to "truth"? This was the constant question for the Protestant thinkers of the early nineteenth century. Those who proposed the newest and most creative solutions were Friedrich Daniel Ernst Schleiermacher (1768–1834), Georg Wilhelm Friedrich Hegel (1770–1831), and Samuel Taylor Coleridge (1772–1834).

In the work of Schleiermacher and Coleridge particularly (though Hegel also illustrates the point in another way), we see a decisive Socratic turn to the self, to an understanding of religious truth that may rightly be called "existentialist." Theology now had to start

1. The supranaturalism of G. C. Storr (1746–1805), who sought to combat rationalism by a sharp separation of theology and philosophy, or of F. Reinhard (1753–1812), as later of E. Sartorius (1797–1859), who was a forerunner of nineteenth-century repristination, or the more rationalist supranaturalism of K. L. Nitzsch (1751–1831) et al., can hardly be said to be exceptions.

from, to articulate, and to interpret a subjective view of the religious object. That is, any significant speech about God had to be talk in which the self was concerned, talk about God as the object of devotion, or of utter dependence, or of passionate concern and fidelity.

In this insistence, the Protestant thinkers of the nineteenth century were in part continuing (or recovering) a basic theme of Luther and Calvin, of pietism and of Pascal: that God and faith belong together, that God is to be described only as he is apprehended in faith. But Schleiermacher's proposal to develop theological statements as implications of the religious self-consciousness, and Coleridge's conception of a Reason (the "organ of the supersensuous") that at its highest is an act of will, a venturing forth and throwing of oneself into the act of apprehension, also represented a new way of taking the believing self into the theological program. Consciousness of the truth was peculiarly one with self-consciousness. The religious subject—his point of view, his cognitive limitations, his "interest," his willing and choosing—had to be self-consciously and systematically recognized as ineradicably present in that with which Christian theological reflection begins. This theme is the foundation for a striking community of interest and effort in the whole course of Protestant theology in the nineteenth century, and it qualifies its concern for "subjectivity" as clearly distinct from those of the Reformation or of pietism or of rationalism.[2] Consequently, the idea of "revelation" had to be fundamentally reinterpreted, and the former kinds of confidence in its truths were dissolved.

The self's involvement in theological assertions was to be expressed in many other ways later in the nineteenth century: in F. D. Maurice's insistence on the partiality of every apprehension of the headship of Christ; in Horace Bushnell's theory of religious language; in Albrecht Ritschl's idea that religious knowledge consists simply in "judgments of value"; in William James's account of the will to believe; in the Erlangen school's effort to develop and confirm the theology of the Lutheran confessions from the "deep inner grounds and life roots" of Christian experience; in Isaak Dorner's effort to show the coincidence of the interests of piety and speculative science;

2. Thus Schleiermacher's theology could also be regularly interpreted (e.g. by F. C. Baur) as a return to the "objective." The emphasis on subjective viewing was for the sake of a critical and therefore sound development of statements about the object of faith. I.e. it was intended to be genuinely a viewing of the theological object from the standpoint of the religious subject.

in J. H. Newman's "illative sense"; and of course in Kierkegaard's idea of truth as subjectivity.[3]

With Schleiermacher and Hegel particularly in mind, we may also say, in the language of a much later controversy, that the nineteenth century began with the demythologizing of theology. That is, the demand for a self-conscious translation into a new idiom, and especially for a reconsideration of the status and reference of theological assertions, was a determining element in the new views of religious truth that emerged in Schleiermacher and Hegel.[4] From the standpoint of the succeeding generation, Schleiermacher and Hegel could be looked upon as great mediators or synthesizers. And that they were, as they tried to unite theology and science, religion and culture. But they were at the same time epochal demythologizers within theology.

Rationalist criticism during the Enlightenment had identified biblical history and its world view, and with it theological orthodoxy, as "mythical," that is, as belonging to the genre of religious mythology, of man's stories of the gods and their dealings with men, and of the world's beginnings and endings. Christian stories and belief systems could claim no exemption by virtue of a unique origin or a wholly different character, even in the sophisticated versions of the philosophical theologians. The eighteenth-century Enlightenment thus attacked the Christian myth and destroyed it, or at least dethroned it from the position it had attained in the Middle Ages as the motive power and bearer of the deepest energies of civilization.

In the nineteenth century, of course, there were "liberals" who continued the rationalist attack, rejecting mythical and supernaturalist forms altogether and seeking to eliminate all such elements from religious faith. There were also "confessionalists" and "repristina-

3. See the discussions of these thinkers below. The point is not that their views are the same, or even that they are all consistent with one another, but just that in their varying ways they testify to a new recognition of the place the believing subject occupies in the sphere of religious truth.

4. I do not, of course, use the term demythologizing in Rudolf Bultmann's specific sense, with his particular definitions of mythological conceptuality or with his idea of "existential" interpretation. But I use it deliberately to suggest that the decisive shift to new modes of theological conception did not take place with Bultmann, nor with those whom he calls the "older liberals" who sought to "eliminate" mythology (cf. especially Bultmann, *Kerygma and Myth* [New York, 1961], pp. 12–13) but rather at the beginning of the 19th century. And indeed, for Hegel the philosophical task was not the elimination of religious "representation" but the articulation of the true content that is present in it.

tors'" (see chap. 9, below). But in Hegel and Schleiermacher (and in Coleridge in a different way), the recognition of the mythological nature of much of Christian orthodoxy was *internalized* in theology, that is, it was taken up in new and constructive views of the nature, the truth value, the limitations, and the possibilities of theological assertions.

The paths that Schleiermacher, Coleridge and Hegel followed were, of course, quite different. For Schleiermacher, the new way could be found by locating "religion" in the realm of "feeling" (*Gefühl*) or immediate self-consciousness, and by understanding that "Christian doctrines are accounts of the Christian religious affections set forth in speech."[5] Theology was both possible and necessary, though not the theology of rationalist orthodoxy or supernaturalism. "It is obvious," Schleiermacher wrote, "that the textbooks of the seventeenth century can no longer serve the same purpose as they did then, but now in large measure belong merely to the realm of historical presentation; and that in the present day it is only different dogmatic presentations that can have the same ecclesiastical value which these then had" (*CF*, § 19.2). Nor could the nonhistorical theology of the seventeenth and eighteenth centuries be accepted. For Schleiermacher, Kant had destroyed the older metaphysics and the basis of Enlightenment natural religion. But Schleiermacher refused to follow Kant in basing God and immortality on moral experience. Here his upbringing in Moravian pietism was of great influence. Theology must be grounded in historical Christianity and an end put to the putative conflict between historical religion and natural religion. A new mapping of theology's place in the intellectual terrain was required, since for Schleiermacher the only possible Christian theology was a "public" theology, one whose warrants could be made clear and whose statements would be intelligible outside the bounds of the believing community. Those statements must also not be in conflict with other, nontheological claims to truth.

Schleiermacher's program thus called for a "cultural" theology (not to be confused with what later generations called *Kulturprotestantismus*, a Protestantism that had become simply an expression of the prevailing culture). At the beginning of his theological authorship stands the significant title *Ueber die Religion, Reden an die*

5. *Der christliche Glaube*, § 15. (*The Christian Faith*, ed. and trans. H. R. Mackintosh and J. S. Stewart [Edinburgh, 1928; reprinted, New York, 1948, 1963]). Hereafter cited as *CF*, with section and subsection numbers. Translations are my own unless otherwise specified, from the Berlin edition of 1861.

Gebildeten unter ihren Verächtern (*Speeches on Religion, to the Cultured among its Despisers,* 1799).[6] When he laid out his conception of the whole theological curriculum at the outset of his theological professorship in Berlin in 1810, he described the ideal of a "prince of the church" as combining "both religious interest and scientific spirit in the highest degree and in the best possible balance for theory and practice alike." [7] And toward the end of Schleiermacher's career, writing to his friend Lücke in 1829 about the forthcoming second edition of *The Christian Faith,* he put the now famous question: "Is the tangle of history to be unravelled by linking Christianity with barbarism and science with unbelief?" He went on to speak of his aim (which was also that of the Reformation) "to create an eternal covenant between the living Christian faith and an independent and freely working science, a covenant by the terms of which science is not hindered and faith not excluded." [8]

The last clause is of critical importance. On the one hand, the final independence and integrity of religion and theology must be defended. (This was not, therefore, Hegel's synthesis.) Theological assertions are distinct and have their own basis. Thus, as Schleiermacher went on to say to Lücke, he had striven in his *Glaubenslehre* to the end "that every dogma which actually represents an element of our Christian consciousness can be so formulated that it leaves us unentangled with science." [9] But the independence of religion and its assertions could not mean unrelatedness to *Wissenschaft,* that is, to the whole range of scholarship and organized knowledge. Quite the contrary, Schleiermacher's decision to retain the structure of the *Glaubenslehre* was an expression of his insistence that the language of theology should not be merely private and esoteric. Religion, further, was to be understood as grounded in the structure of human existence, as the exaltation (and transformation) of life, individual and social, in the most comprehensive sense. And thus Schleiermacher himself, because he was a Christian, had to participate in the philosophy, the politics, the art, and the social life of the time.[10]

6. The fullest bibliography of Schleiermacher's works and the literature from 1800–1964 is Terrence N. Tice, *Schleiermacher Bibliography* (Princeton, 1966).

7. *Kurze Darstellung des theologischen Studiums* (1810, 2d ed., 1830; critical ed. H. Scholz [Leipzig, 1910]), § 9. (The *Kurze Darstellung* has been translated by Terrence N. Tice under the title *Brief Outline of the Study of Theology* [Philadelphia, 1966]). Cited below as *KD.* Translations are my own.

8. *Sendschreiben an Dr. Lücke,* ed. Hermann Mulert (Giessen, 1908), pp. 37, 40.

9. Ibid., p. 40; see also pp. 21, 24–25, 34, 66.

10. See Jerry F. Dawson, *Friedrich Schleiermacher: The Evolution of a Nationalist* (Austin, Tex., 1966).

Schleiermacher began in 1811 to offer lectures on *Dialektik* because he found no philosophical structures available that were suitable to his own view of the independence yet partnership of theology and philosophy, or of the relation of theology and culture generally. Certainly the ideas of his Berlin colleagues Fichte (until 1814) and Hegel (1818–31) were not satisfactory.[11] He did not seek a higher synthesis that would take up and transcend the assertions of theology, nor did he propose that philosophy could establish the truth of Christianity. Rather, Schleiermacher sought to develop a view of thought that would be *compatible* with theology's assertions, and that in this sense would allow theology freedom.[12]

Yet neither the argument of the *Dialektik* nor the particular place in the domain of Ethics where Schleiermacher located religion was the primary element in his reconception of the theological enterprise. Nor was it that he called for a "theology of culture"; all theology that is not mere repetition of past formulations (and thus dead) is fashioned in living relation to a contemporary world; the question is only one of the rules and tools by which that relation is worked out. The most important step was rather Schleiermacher's effort to find a basis for theology in a more profound view of religion and his resulting view of the nature of theological assertions.

THE NATURE OF RELIGION

What is the locus of religion in human experience, the nature of *homo religiosus,* the fundamental character of religion, piety, faith (terms that Schleiermacher sometimes used interchangeably)? From

11. In dialectic, or "speculative philosophy" as Schleiermacher also called it (though he rejected both "pure speculation" and "pure empiricism") one dealt with the highest level of methodological generalizations, i.e. with the theoretical foundations of all processes of knowing (in the two great realms of physics, or the intellectual study of the principles of predominantly natural being, and ethics, the science of history). Dialectic discloses the polarities and relativities inherent in knowledge, the interrelation of identity and difference, or the omnipresent relativity of polar duality (not absolute antithesis), which leads us to the *formal* principle of a transcendental ground of being and knowing. But this has an entirely presuppositional character, and while Schleiermacher was willing to apply the term "God" to it, he had great difficulty in trying to move to a "living conception" of God (see the study of the *Dialektik* by Gerhard Spiegler, *The Eternal Covenant* [New York, 1967], especially chap. 4). At best, he formulated two limiting canons: "The world is not without God, and God is not without the world"; and "the two ideas are not identical." But it is not the task of dialectic to provide (or justify) the Christian conception of God. What is given, in the idea of the formal transcendental ground—and this reflects the independence and coequal partnership of theology and philosophy—is an appropriate parallel to the Whence of the Christianly determined feeling of utter dependence.

12. See also *CF,* § 28.

the first edition of the *Speeches* to the second edition of *The Christian Faith* (1830), Schleiermacher emphasized the distinction of religion from metaphysics and morality, from knowing and doing. Religion is neither a kind of belief nor a kind of moral activity, nor is it a combination of the two. "Piety cannot be an instinct craving for a mess of metaphysical and ethical crumbs." [13] Thus Schleiermacher set himself firmly against the most characteristic idea of the Enlightenment (and also against orthodoxy's rationalism). Under the formative influence of his pietist upbringing in Moravian schools, of his participation in romanticist circles, and of the Reformation demand for a living faith, for truthfulness as well as truth,[14] Schleiermacher located religion in the center of the heart and dispositions (*im Innern des Gemüts*). Religion is, in his famous phrases in the first edition of the *Speeches*, a "sense and taste for the infinite," an "intuition and feeling of the infinite," of the universe. In the later definition of *The Christian Faith* (§ 3), "Considered purely in itself, the piety that forms the basis of all ecclesiastical communities is neither a knowing nor a doing but a determination of feeling or of immediate self-consciousness." [15] More precisely, then, "the common element in all the quite diverse expressions of piety by which these are at the same time distinguished from all other feelings—thus the self-identical essence of piety—is this: that we are conscious of ourselves as utterly dependent (*schlechthin abhängig*) or, which is to say the same thing, as being in relation to God." [16]

13. Schleiermacher, *On Religion: Speeches to Its Cultured Despisers*, trans. John Oman from the 3d ed. (1821) (New York, 1958), p. 31. Subsequent page references to the English translation are to this edition.

14. See C. Senft, *Wahrhaftigkeit u. Warheit* (Tübingen, 1956). For Schleiermacher's early thought, see W. Seifert, *Die Theologie des jungen Schleiermachers* (Gütersloh, 1960). The classic account of Schleiermacher's early life and development is Wilhelm Dilthey, *Leben Schleiermachers* (1870; 2d ed. Mulert, 1922). A useful summary may be found in the introduction to *Schleiermacher's Soliloquies*, trans. Horace L. Friess (Chicago, 1957). Also of much value for the understanding of Schleiermacher's concept of religion and his theological intentions is the collection of essays from the 1968 Vanderbilt University consultation, ed. Robert Funk, *Schleiermacher as Contemporary*, *Journal for Theology and the Church*, vol. 7 (New York, 1970).

15. This is one of the "propositions borrowed from ethics," which in this context means especially that, since ethics is defined as the science of community, or of the principles of history, faith and the religious life belong to the realm of man as responsible being and as free agent. "The church is a community which originates and can only be continued through free human activity" (*CF*, § 2.2).

16. Ibid., § 4. The translation of *schlechthin* as "absolute," and of *das schlechthinige Abhängigkeitsgefühl* as "feeling of absolute dependence," is to be avoided. I have used "utter" or "simple" dependence. "Unqualified" would also be a possible translation.

What is meant by such expressions, and particularly by Schleier-macher's use of the term "feeling" (*Gefühl*)? We must guard against several sorts of misunderstanding. First of all, Schleiermacher did not say that piety is a special *kind* of feeling, but that "feeling" designates the place in which religion is to be sought. This is to say, in the language of romanticism, that the locus of religion is the innermost realm of human existence. Nor, by distinguishing piety from knowing and doing, did Schleiermacher mean to suggest that religion exists apart from knowing and doing. Theological knowledge and cultic and moral activities are normal and regular signs of religious feeling. The "religious, epistemic, and moral interests" are not to be segregated; "Schleiermacher is not being inconsistent when he recognizes that religious perception carries in itself a cognitive conatus and that a moral, artistic impulse informs religious feeling." [17] It is clear from the *Speeches* and the *Soliloquies* that the religious man cannot really be immoral or aesthetically insensitive. And "to wish to have true science or true practice without religion, or to imagine that it is possessed, is obstinate, arrogant delusion, and culpable error." [18]

Furthermore, *Gefühl* is not a "faculty" parallel to the faculties of thinking and willing. Schleiermacher located the religious at a different level (though not as separate) from knowing and willing. The latter belong fundamentally to the subject-object duality of the middle level of self-consciousness, that is, to the level of "sensuous" self-consciousness. But piety Schleiermacher defined as a "determination" of feeling, and feeling was equated with "immediate self-consciousness" (*CF*, §§ 3 ff.). The feeling of utter dependence belonged to the highest level of human self-consciousness, in which the antithesis between the self and the other which characterizes the sensuous self-consciousness disappears again. This feeling is never present apart from the subject-object relations, but it is presupposed by and manifested in them as something immediate. That is, it is "an immediate existence-relationship." [19] It is that "affective level of existence"

17. Richard R. Niebuhr, "Schleiermacher and the Names of God," in Funk, *Schleiermacher as Contemporary*, p. 182. See *CF*, §§ 3, 4. Partly under Schleiermacher's influence, his onetime Berlin colleague W. M. L. de Wette (1780–1849) emphasized the rational possibility of the discernment or presentiment (*Ahnung*) of the being of God in feeling. See *Ueber Religion und Theologie* (1815) and *Lehrbuch der christlichen Dogmatik* (1813, 1816). De Wette's most important work, however, was his advanced biblical critical study.

18. Schleiermacher, *Speeches*, p. 39.

19. Schleiermacher, *Sendschreiben an Dr. Lücke*, p. 15.

through which the *Eigentümlichkeit*, the irreducible individuality, of the self comes to expression [20] as coextensive with the whole range of human activity. It is thus the deepest (or highest) level of self-existence, not an isolable "religious experience," but an "original relation of intuition and feeling." [21] Religious awareness is irreducibly also self-awareness. And man, at the deepest level of his existence, *is* religious.

The feeling which is piety, however, is never apart from its determination by the "infinite" or the "whole" (*Speeches*) or the "whence" (*Christian Faith*). In the *Speeches,* Schleiermacher freely used a variety of (sometimes confusing) terms to denote that which is the "object" of feeling and intuition: God, the All, the Universe, and so forth. The dominant idea seemed to be the sense of the whole and the unity of the self with it.[22] But neither the fluidity of expression in the *Speeches* nor Schleiermacher's later changes in terminology should obscure the fact that, throughout, he was not speaking of the self in an enclosed or merely "subjective" immediacy, but always of an objective determinant of the self's existence, that is, of its determination by what it is not.

Further, religion is irreducibly particular and historical, not universal and abstract. There is no universal natural or rational religion which alone is true. The "original relation" or "immediate unity" is manifested in great variety. Religion, Schleiermacher said in the *Speeches,* is infinite, to be comprehended only in the sum total of all its forms. Out of the manifold intuitions of the infinite arise, by reflection on feeling, the multiplicity of beliefs and dogmas. So the discussion in the *Speeches* moves between the poles of individual and universe, individuality and multiplicity. This did not of course imply an individualism in religion, for from the *Speeches* onward, Schleiermacher insisted that religion is social because man is by nature a social being (see especially the fourth speech), and in *The Christian Faith* the church was given such an overwhelmingly important role in the redemptive process that Schleiermacher quite con-

---

20. See Richard R. Niebuhr, *Schleiermacher on Christ and Religion* (New York, 1964), 121 ff. This book is a particularly useful treatment of Schleiermacher's idea of religion.

21. *Speeches,* p. 41.

22. "Your feeling is piety, insofar as it expresses, in the manner described, the being and life common to you and to the All. Your feeling is piety insofar as it is the result of the operation of God in you by means of the operation of the world upon you" (*Speeches,* p. 45).

tradicted his own suggestion that one could provisionally distinguish
Protestantism and Catholicism by saying that "the former makes the
individual's relation to the church depend on his relation to Christ,
whereas the latter conversely makes the individual's relation to Christ
depend on his relation to the church" (*CF*, § 24). Indeed, while the
second speech is undeniably the *locus classicus* for Schleiermacher's
new definition of religion, the logic of the *Speeches* moves definitely
forward from that starting point with the individual in relation to
the whole, through the necessarily social expression of religion, to a
culmination (in the fifth speech) in the discussion of the historical
or positive religions, Christianity in particular. Though no one is
required to associate with any of the positive religions in order for
his intuition to be valid, yet positive religions are the "definite forms
in which religion must exhibit itself." Each individual religion selects
"some one of the great relations of mankind . . . to the highest Being, and, in a definite way . . . [makes] it the center and refers to it
all the others." [23] Thus one may even view the discussion of the nature of religion in the second speech as an abstract formula, a description of that which is *presupposed* in the empirical actuality of religion. In a similar way, in *The Christian Faith,* the religious self-
consciousness treated in Part I is an abstraction from the living reality of the Christian religious self-consciousness; "it is always both
presupposed by and contained in every Christian religious affection." [24]

THE STRUCTURE OF THEOLOGY

It is frequently said that the great achievement of Schleiermacher,
his creative breakthrough, was his fresh interpretation of religion in
its own integrity, according to its fundamental intuition and its locus
in feeling or in the immediacy of human existence, whereby the ra-
tionalist-orthodox debate was wholly undercut and a new possibility
for understanding religion was opened. This is correct. Schleiermacher did thus take a step decisive for subsequent theological
endeavors. The *Speeches* was doubtless his most influential work, and
it was a liberating and impelling document for his contemporaries
both because of its penetration to a deeper level of understanding

23. *Speeches,* pp. 217, 223.
24. *CF,* title to Part I.

and because of its fluidity of thought. The *Speeches* did not foreclose but opened new ways; one could move on toward Hegel as well as in Schleiermacher's own later direction.[25]

But equally important for the question of the possibility of theology was the way in which Schleiermacher himself proceeded to develop the justification for doctrinal assertions and to restate the kind of validity and truth those assertions can have. This is why, with respect to the theological question, *The Christian Faith* and the *Brief Outline* are as important as the *Speeches*.[26] The assertion in the *Speeches* that beliefs and doctrines are secondhand, only subsequent expressions of what was originally in the heart and disposition, was not really new; the view was deeply rooted in pietism and romanticism, and Fichte had just made much of the point. But in the *Brief Outline,* and above all in *The Christian Faith,* Schleiermacher set forth the principles by which the movement is made from disposition to doctrine, that is, by which the theological tradition can be both critically evaluated and reinforced. To exhibit the principles for interpretation of the basic assertion that "Christian doctrines are accounts of the Christian religious affections set forth in speech" (*CF,* § 15), we may focus on three critical points: Schleiermacher's conception of the structure of the theological enterprise, his view of the possibilities and limits of speech about God, and the question of theology and history.

According to *The Christian Faith* and the *Brief Outline,* theology as a positive discipline is always the function of a specific mode of faith, in this case Christianity. Theology thus presupposes and is located within the context of more inclusive frameworks of the total intellectual terrain, notably ethics and the philosophy of religion. In ethics, which is the study of the principles of historical existence in the broadest sense, one treats the fundamental nature of piety and of religious association. The philosophy of religion deals with definite religious communions in their historical differentiation according to level and kind.[27]

25. This is not at all to say that Schleiermacher's mature work was inconsistent with his first works. On the contrary. I have here obviously emphasized the continuities rather than attempting a detailed account of the development of Schleiermacher's thought.

26. Thus F. C. Baur, in treating the history of doctrine, could mark the beginning of the most recent period with *The Christian Faith*, not with the *Speeches*.

27. Cf. *KD,* §§ 22 ff.; *CF,* §§ 3–10.

This does not imply that theological assertions are derived from or depend for their validity upon judgments independently arrived at in ethics and the philosophy of religion. To say that would be to destroy the balance and independence of theology and philosophy. The general nature of religion is what is *presupposed by* and expressed in concrete religious existence, and the validation of the statements of ethics and philosophy of religion with respect to Christianity comes only out of the empirical data of Christian piety, just as "philosophical theology presupposes as already known the material of historical theology" (*KD*, § 65).

Theology itself has three main aspects: philosophical, historical, and practical. Philosophical theology, the point of conjunction with philosophy of religion, exhibits the distinctive nature of Christianity by viewing its historical givenness in relation to that of other religious communities. In "apologetics," the essential nature of Christianity (and of Protestantism) is determined by reference particularly to its origin and historical continuity. In "polemics," which looks inward, one seeks to understand the aberrations, diseases, and weaknesses that occur within the religious community. Historical theology provides the proper body of theological study, presenting a knowledge of the whole, in its presently existing condition, by understanding it as a product of the past. It thus includes exegesis or the study of primitive Christianity (and hermeneutics), church history (or historical theology in the narrower sense), and finally the historical knowledge of the present condition of Christianity (that is, the two disciplines of dogmatic theology and church statistics). Practical theology, which develops the rules for the art of leadership in service in the individual congregation and in government of the whole church, is the crown and goal of the entire theological task—thus Schleiermacher's thirty years of preaching in the *Dreifaltigkeitskirche* in Berlin was not incidental to his scholarship, but was an essential expression of it.

In this conspectus of the theological program, the traditional elements were all taken up, but in a radically new and unified way, with new bases, new definitions, and new tasks. It was a program that was to be true to the evangelical faith and to the revelation of God in history, but in a way that would avoid the scholastic artificial mixture of philosophically derived concepts with historically given content and the customary splitting of what should be an organic whole into isolated topics. Several crucial determinants of the program, and its application in *The Christian Faith,* stand out. First of all, theology is carried on in and for the church. Its purpose is finally the care of souls. It is a modest and critical endeavor, seeking to clarify for the believer the nature and implications of his piety. "Dogmatics" is a *Glaubenslehre,* a doctrine of faith. That is, by carefully formulated technical language and systematic arrangement, theology performs a hermeneutic function for the language of piety. It must be responsible both to the theologian's own convictions and to the common beliefs of the community. And theology must be done by one who combines the scientific spirit with deep religious interest.

Second, there is no place at all in the theological structure for argument about the relative truth or falsity of various religions, or for debating the finality or superiority of Christian faith. Apologetics and polemics have an entirely different function from "evidence-theology." And within dogmatics, every effort to prove the truth of Christianity has to be renounced (*CF,* § 11.5). Schleiermacher did assume that every Christian would be convinced of "the exclusive superiority of Christianity" (*CF,* § 7.3), and he allowed to the philosophy of religion the possibility of distinguishing levels of development, in which Christianity appears at the highest level.[28]

But here Schleiermacher was finally unclear. Truth cannot be simply denied to any expression of the religious relation, of the feeling of utter dependence (*CF,* § 7.3). The most that can be affirmed in the philosophy of religion is a higher truth along with similarities. And presumably by Schleiermacher's principles of the independence and interrelatedness of theology and philosophy, and of the empirical and the speculative, the Muslim would also legitimately be convinced of "the exclusive superiority" of Islam. Yet Schleiermacher could say that "this comparison of Christianity with other similar religions is a sufficient warrant for saying that Christianity is in fact the most perfect among the most developed forms of religion" (*CF,* § 8.4). Schleiermacher seemed to alternate between his emphasis on the

28. Just as in the *Speeches* Christianity emerged as the religion of religions, because its original intuition is of "the universal resistance of everything finite to the unity of the whole" and of "the way in which deity treats this resistance, reconciles hostility to itself and sets limits to the ever-increasing alienation by scattering points here and there over the whole that are at once finite and infinite, human and divine." That is, the theme of Christianity is "corruption and redemption, hostility and mediation" (*Speeches,* p. 241).

genuinely individual character of every historical phenomenon and his growing desire to view the Christian religion as the culmination of the process.[29]

Third, dogmatics is radically historically conditioned. It is and should consciously be "contemporary theology": "the science of the coherence of the doctrine that prevails in a Christian community at a given time" (CF, § 19). Every doctrinal form is bound to a particular time and no claim can be made for its permanent validity. It is the task of theology in every present age, by critical reflection, to express anew the implications of the living religious consciousness—by no means, of course, without reference to the whole prior history of the community, but in continuity with it.[30]

Finally, legitimate theological (that is, dogmatic) assertions are shaped by logically ordered reflection "on the *immediate* assertions of the religious self-consciousness"; they always have as their basis "the *immediate* description of the [religious] dispositions themselves." [31] This is the negative side, simply, of the principle that doctrines do rightly and necessarily spring from the religious self-consciousness. But the restriction to direct implications provides an important critical tool for distinguishing the essential from the nonessential and for freeing theology from much troublesome excess baggage. The mode of origination of the world, for example, or the ideas of angels and the devil, can have no proper place in dogmatics; the doctrine of original sin is not a historical assertion about the first human parents; strictly speaking, there can be no *doctrines* of the consummation of the church or the "last things"; and even the doctrine of the Trinity has to come in an appendix, though it expresses all that is essential in the explication of the consciousness of grace.

Further, Schleiermacher insisted that among the three sorts of doctrinal propositions, or, we may say, directions of assertion— "descriptions of the human states of life," "concepts of the divine

29. His view of the several religions in their origin and manifold development side by side provides the basis for a new and genuinely historical interpretation of religion (see CF, § 10, postscript).

30. One must "first exclude from the totality of the dogmatic material everything heretical, and retain only what is ecclesiastical" (CF, § 21). And "all statements that lay claim to being included in the substance of evangelical doctrine must be tested in part by appeal to the evangelical confessional writings, or in default of these, to the New Testament Scriptures, and in part by the exhibition of their homogeneity with other doctrinal statements that are already acknowledged" (CF, § 27).

31. CF, § 16, *postscript;* § 31. Italics mine.

attributes and modes of action," and "assertions about the constitution of the world"—it is the first which constitute the basic form.[32] The latter two sorts of statements are only "permissible in so far as they can be developed out of statements of the first form" (*CF*, § 30.2). They are secondhand assertions, and faith could learn to get along without them. Yet statements about God and the world are not superfluous. They express only what is contained in the first form, they reemphasize individual aspects, and they need to be formulated, Schleiermacher said, to establish continuity with the past (in which the basic form of theological statements has regularly been abandoned for metaphysical assertions), to purify theology from alien elements, and "to maintain clearly and truly the rhetorical and poetic communication" (*CF*, § 30.3).

Schleiermacher's other main principle for determining the shape of dogmatics—and he himself suggested that the greatest value of his systematic theology would be found in its order and structure—was drawn directly from his definition of Christianity as "a monotheistic faith, belonging to the teleological type of religion, and essentially distinguished from other such faiths by the fact that everything in it is related to the redemption accomplished by Jesus of Nazareth" (*CF*, § 11). This meant that theology must be genuinely a christocentric whole,[33] even to the point that one could consider beginning the system with the treatment of redemption and discussing creation only subsequently. Schleiermacher finally rejected that alternative and began in Part I with those elements that were presupposed by and contained in the Christian consciousness; then in Part II he explicated the facts of the specifically Christian self-consciousness, determined by the antithesis of sin and grace.

The resulting scheme for the *Glaubenslehre* was a unique three-by-three framework within which the traditional topics were taken up in a new way. Elements of doctrine arising from the presupposed religious consciousness in general, from the consciousness of sin, and from the consciousness of grace are developed in relation to the self, to the world, and to God (or more precisely, to descriptions of the human states of life, to the divine attributes and modes of action, and to the constitution of the world). The accompanying diagram graphi-

---

32. *CF*, § 30. See also the *Sendschreiben an Dr. Lücke*, pp. 47–48.

33. Or christomorphic (the term is a happy suggestion by Richard R. Niebuhr, in *Schleiermacher on Christ and Religion*, chap. 5, where the unresolved problems of Schleiermacher's order are also admirably discussed). See below, pp. 82–84.

PART I

Elements Presupposed by and Contained in Every Christian Religious Affection

Descriptions of the human states of life	**1** * Description of the religious self-consciousness insofar as the relation between the world and God is expressed in it: CREATION PRESERVATION
Concepts of the divine attributes and modes of action	**2** Divine attributes related to religious self-consciousness, as it expresses the relation between God and the world: ETERNITY OMNIPRESENCE OMNIPOTENCE OMNISCIENCE
Assertions about the constitution of the world	**3** Constitution of the world that is indicated in the religious self-consciousness, as it expresses the general relation between God and the world: ORIGINAL PERFECTION OF THE WORLD ORIGINAL PERFECTION OF MAN

* The arabic numerals indicate the order of the sections within the three major divisions.

Part II

Facts of the Religious Consciousness as Determined by The Antithesis between Sin and Grace

A Development of the Consciousness of Sin	B Development of the Consciousness of Grace
1 Sin as a state of man: ORIGINAL SIN ACTUAL SIN	1 State of the Christian as conscious of the divine grace: CHRIST: PERSON WORK REGENERATION SANCTIFICATION
3 Divine attributes related to the consciousness of sin: HOLINESS JUSTICE (MERCY)	3 Divine attributes related to redemption: LOVE WISDOM
2 Constitution of the world in relation to sin: EVIL	2 Constitution of the world relative to redemption: ORIGIN OF THE CHURCH COEXISTENCE OF THE CHURCH WITH THE WORLD: ESSENTIAL FEATURES MUTABLE ELEMENTS CONSUMMATION OF THE CHURCH

Conclusion: The Trinity

cally shows the new ordering of topics and their distinctive locations in relation to the basis of formulation, with an abbreviated identification of the doctrines taken up in each section. Thus, for example, whatever is valid in the doctrines of creation and preservation is to be understood as a description of human states of life, arising out of elements of religious awareness presupposed by the specifically Christian religious affections. The divine attributes of eternity, omnipresence, omnipotence, and omniscience likewise arise from that presupposed experience, as do the notions of the original perfections of the world and of man.

Within the orbit of specifically Christian experience, then, not only the doctrines of original and actual sin but also the doctrines of both the work and the person of Christ emerge as descriptions of the human states of being. The world becomes a place in which evil is recognized and also, relative to redemption, a place which is reconstituted by the origin of the church, its co-existence with the world, and its consummation. Similarly the divine attributes of holiness and justice and of love and wisdom emerge from the religious consciousness that is determined by the experience of sin and grace.

In general, the final pattern of the *Glaubenslehre* retained the "history of salvation" order, that is, the movement from creation to sin to Christology and eschatology. But a striking feature was the distribution of the doctrine of God throughout the three main parts, or what one could equally well call the development of the whole system as a doctrine of God, for much of Schleiermacher's concern with the structure of the *Glaubenslehre* grew from his attempt to deal with the attributes of God in a properly integrated way. The movement of his thought is toward the culminating statement that "God is love" (*CF*, § 167), at which point the distinction between the attributes and the nature of God vanishes.[34]

THE NAMING OF GOD

An obvious question concerning Schleiermacher's reordering of the systematic theological enterprise and his explication in *The Christian Faith* is this: granted the intelligibility and truth value of "descriptions of the human states of life," what is the scope or "reach"

34. At the same time, that Schleiermacher treated the attributes of eternity, etc., in Part I (and at such length) has undoubtedly tended to give a great emphasis to the speculative elements in his doctrine of God. Schleiermacher's concern with the doctrine of God may also be the reason for his reversal of the order of treatment in Part II (in Part I the order is self-God-world; in Part II, both sections, it is self-world-God).

of assertions about God and the world? Schleiermacher plainly did not want to rest theology in subjectivism or in anthropology alone, for the religious self-consciousness is precisely an awareness of being utterly dependent on something, and that awareness is always given along with the feeling of relative freedom and dependence vis-à-vis the world.

The point of departure for proper language about God, that is, the irreducibly given in Christianity, is the experience or consciousness of sin and grace, or more fully, the self-awareness of redemption in Christ from the deficiency and alienation in our consciousness of God, an experience which presupposes and also gives that consciousness of ourselves as utterly dependent, which is to say "as being in relation to God." From this point of departure, dogmatics proceeds to speak of God as eternal, omnipresent, omnipotent, and omniscient (on the basis of the awareness of utter dependence in general), as holy and just (from the experience of sin), and of the divine love and the divine wisdom (from the consciousness of grace).

Schleiermacher further specified the limits of this language by the statement that "all attributes that we ascribe to God are not to be taken as denoting something special in God, but only something special in the way in which the feeling of utter dependence is related to him" (*CF*, § 50). The reasons for this circumscription seem to be threefold. First, though not necessarily in order of importance, there are the requirements of "speculation" (*CF*, § 50.1–3). If the attributes actually expressed a *cognition* of God—even of distinction in the relation of God to the world—then composition or multiplicity of function would be introduced into God. In rejecting that possibility, Schleiermacher was in line with the tradition of the simplicity of God and the unity of the divine attributes. And according to his own argument in the *Dialektik*, God must be beyond the relativities of finite knowledge and being; the distinctions of the latter cannot be imported into God's being. Thus, with Kant, Schleiermacher held that God cannot appear in a concept or judgment (*Begriff* or *Urteil*). That sort of objectification is epistemologically inappropriate.[35]

Second, religion can have no interest in "God in himself" apart

35. Though Schleiermacher also believed "with Anselm . . . that God informs the mind, as that than which no greater can be thought," and with Spinoza that "a conatus towards God inspires every effort of intellect and will to grasp the part of the whole" Richard R. Niebuhr, "Schleiermacher and the Names of God," in Funk, *Schleiermacher as Contemporary*, p. 180. On Schleiermacher's idea of God, see also Gerhard Ebeling, "Schleiermacher's Doctrine of the Divine Attributes," in the same volume; and Friedrich Beisser, *Schleiermachers Lehre von Gott* (Göttingen, 1970).

from the relation to him. Here Schleiermacher's view was continuous with Luther's constant insistence on the *for us* and Calvin's opening statement in the *Institutes* that the knowledge of God and self are given together. In Schleiermacher's language, theological statements refer to God only as he is apprehended *in* the religious consciousness; theology cannot have any "objective" knowledge but only this relational knowing of God as present, and care must be taken not to assert anything "that extends beyond the immediate content of that self-consciousness" (*CF*, § 35.2).

Third, therefore, the restriction derives directly from the nature of the awareness of utter dependence. The religious interest just as much as the speculative interest is violated by the introduction of diversity into the dogmatic conception of God. "For the feeling of utter dependence, considered in and by itself, could not be always and everywhere the same, if differentiation were posited in God himself" (*CF*, § 50.2). Implicit here is an insistence on the positive reference to God of proper theological language. The feeling of utter dependence is directly and necessarily correlated with, and is the awareness of, an utter causality (*schlechthinige Ursächlichkeit, CF*, § 51). This is not an illusory interrelation or correspondence, but a real one just as the self's relation to the world is real. "The religious consciousness becomes . . . actual only as consciousness of his eternal power," Schleiermacher insisted in his argument that eternity should not be separated from omnipotence (*CF*, § 52.1). Thus while the attributes cannot be said to denote something real (*reeles*) "in" God, that is, in the being of God in itself, "so much at least is certain, that all the divine attributes to be dealt with in the Christian doctrine of faith must go back to the divine causality, since they are meant only to explain the feeling of utter dependence" (*CF*, § 50.3). The attributes of God refer to modifications of divine causality, which must be distinguished because the feeling of absolute dependence is never separable from the diversity and totality of life's elements in the relation to the world.

In short, theology is a very human enterprise. Statements about God can be made with validity and they must be made. Above all, Christian statements characterize the divine causality as love and wisdom (*CF*, §§ 165–69). Such language validly refers to what is given in experience as the Whence, that utter causality which is distinguished from all finite causality, that power which posits self and world together. Yet this is to be said without the presumption of going beyond the limitations imposed by the immediacy of the religious self-consciousness.[36] Properly cognitive statements are restricted to descriptions of the religious self-consciousness itself, and dogmatics, which has a scientific interest, must make clear this methodological limitation. But these are descriptions of the self in its awareness of dependence, and therefore indirectly, or at a second level, proper references to God as present in that relationship. They reflect the self's viewing of God, the actual disclosure of God in the self's experience of itself, but now in the form of dogmatic statements, which both validate and chasten the natural poetic and rhetorical language of piety.

The way in which God is apprehended in the immediacy of the feeling of utter dependence also leads to a conception of the relation of God and the world which does not fit into the common classifications of deism, theism, pantheism—and hence the unsatisfying nature of the debates whether Schleiermacher was a "pantheist" or a Spinozist. He was plainly seeking a view beyond naturalism and supernaturalism. Deism was obviously abhorrent, for it posits an externality of God to the world and the self that is utterly at odds with the feeling of utter dependence, and it makes God only "a being." But ordinary theism or supernaturalism is not much better, particularly insofar as it involves anthropomorphic conceptions of deity (e.g. as personality) or views "miracle" as an entrance of divine activity apart from natural causes. Any "absolute miracle" would destroy the whole system of nature.[37] Even the view that natural causes are intermediate causes seems to represent God as another

36. Similarly, speaking of "revelation" as the basis of a religious community, Schleiermacher says "we might say that the idea of revelation signifies the *originality* of the fact which lies at the foundation of a religious communion, in the sense that this fact, as conditioning the individual content of the religious emotions which are found in the communion, cannot itself in turn be explained by the historical chain which precedes it.

"Now the fact that in this original element there is a divine causality requires no further discussion; nor does the fact that it is an activity which aims at and furthers the salvation of man. But I am unwilling to accept the further definition that it operates upon man as a cognitive being. For that would make the revelation to be originally and essentially *doctrine;* and I do not believe that we can adopt that position, whether we consider the whole field covered by the idea, or seek to define it in advance with special reference to Christianity" (*CF*, § 10, postscript).

37. Miracle, Schleiermacher said in the *Speeches*, "is simply the religious name for event" (p. 88). It refers to a way of viewing, and every event becomes miracle to the truly religious man. Similarly, in *The Christian Faith*, Schleiermacher insisted that nothing is to be excluded as a possible problem for scientific research, yet that in no way prejudices the possibility of an event's stimulating religious feeling (*CF*, § 47.3).

finite being, that is, as a particular finite free cause (see *CF*, § 47.2). That sort of transcendence is to be rejected, as Schleiermacher said from the *Speeches* on.[38] Religiously speaking, that is, with respect to the intimacy of the experience of dependence, pantheism would be better. But God for Schleiermacher is obviously not identical with the world. Any strict immanentism or monism would deny both human freedom and the way in which the world is given along with the self in the experience of dependence. To state it another way, the totality of finite being must also be viewed as utterly dependent. Thus Schleiermacher's suggestion that omnipotence expresses an equating of the compass of the divine causality with the totality of the natural order is balanced by his suggestion that eternity expresses the opposition of the divine causality to the finite and the natural (*CF*, § 51.1).[39] And though he was sympathetic to Spinoza's sense of the intimacy of the God-world relation, or the finite's inherence in the infinite, Schleiermacher wanted to distinguish his view definitely from Spinozism, particularly by insisting on the loving and directed character of the divine willing.

But the root difficulty in these alternative conceptions (including

38. It is significant that the *Speeches* were written in the context of the Fichtean "atheism controversy," which excited the German public from November 1798 on. In his paper of 1798 "On the Basis of Our Belief in a Divine World Government" (*Ueber den Grund unseres Glaubens an eine göttliche Weltregierung*), which led to charges of atheism (and thence to Fichte's giving up his post at Jena), J. G. Fichte had been interpreted, wrongly, as saying that the "living and operative moral order" which is God, the only God conceivable or needed, is merely constructed and supported by human moral will. In his reply to the criticism, Fichte insisted that he meant a supersensible and living moral order, an active ordering (*Ordnen*) rather than an order (*Ordnung*) constructed by the finite ego. But equally important for the ensuing discussions, he made clear that he rejected the ideas of God as personal or as substance because personality was essentially finite and substance meant extension in space and time; from the standpoint of philosophy, God could not be "a being" but rather "pure activity, the life and principle of a supersensible world order." Hence a major consequence of the atheism controversy was the widespread currency of the judgment that the concept of God as personal (or as having any of the attributes of finite beings) is an objectification or an anthropomorphism incompatible with God's infinitude.

39. Whether Schleiermacher was right in saying, in his discussion of omnipotence, that because the feeling of absolute dependence leads us to speak of the divine causality as *wholly* presented in the totality of finite being, therefore everything for which there is a causality in God happens and becomes real (*CF*, § 54), is another matter. The latter assertion certainly does not follow logically from the former. The most that can be said, on the basis of the feeling of dependence, is that for methodological reasons, theology cannot make any statements about a possibility of divine activity that is not actualized.

Spinoza's) is that, for Schleiermacher, God is properly beyond all speculative conceptions. He is beyond the relativities or antitheses of the world of experience. The God-world relation cannot be comprehended in the categories of the self-world relation. God transcends thought in a different way than the world does. As the Whence of the feeling of utter dependence, God cannot be the object of cognition. Thus the divine causality can be spoken of in relation to all finite causality only in a genuinely dialectical fashion.[40]

THEOLOGY AND HISTORY

Within the three directions of theological assertion—toward the self, the world, and God—judgments concerning the past and our relation to it appear in *The Christian Faith* in the form of statements both about the world and about the religious self-consciousness iself.[41] Once again, Schleiermacher's insistence that dogmatic statements keep to the immediate content of that self-consciousness provided the critical tool for reviewing the doctrinal tradition. Two illustrations are particularly illuminating: original sin and the person of Christ, both of which were treated as forms of statements about the human conditions themselves.

Original sin is not, for Schleiermacher (any more than creation), a doctrine about some past event to which men are related. As "the sinfulness that is present in an individual before any act of his own and that is grounded outside his own being" (*CF*, § 70), original sin does indeed refer to the whole of the human race and thus to the first human parents. But the basis for the affirmation is not at all a literary (scriptural) testimony to a first act of sinning, but man's

---

40. Schleiermacher did not put it this way, and it may be that failure to maintain such a perspective—as well as the inconsistencies, especially in Part I of the *Glaubenslehre*, resulting from the introduction of speculative judgments contrary to his methodological principle—accounts for Schleiermacher's difficulties in relating divine and human agency, particularly in respect of the origin of sin. Along the line suggested here, the idea of God in *The Christian Faith* is quite congruent with the presuppositional nature of the transcendental and unconditioned ground of being and knowing in the *Dialektik*. If a single term were to be used to denote Schleiermacher's idea of the relation of God and the world, the most useful would doubtless be "panentheist."

41. Contrary to the opinion of Dilthey and others who have followed him that Schleiermacher was "ein ganz unhistorischer Kopf," Schleiermacher was not only deeply concerned with history but was productively sensitive to the problems of historical understanding. This should be evident both from the *Kurze Darstellung* and the *Hermeneutik* (see Hannah Jursch, *Schleiermacher als Kirchenhistoriker*, [Jena, 1933]).

fundamental awareness of his own incapacity for good, of his need of redemption, which is both a personal act and prior to every individual's act. Thus it is necessary to speak of a common or corporate participation of all men in sin. But nothing can be found in this experience to necessitate, or even to make possible, the judgment that the first human beings were in any different situation, much less the notion that there was some alteration in the nature of those first persons as a consequence of a first sin (see especially *CF*, § 72). Demythologized, the doctrine of original sin refers to "the simple idea of an utterly common guilt that is the same for all" and "a timeless sinfulness always and everywhere adhering to human nature and coexisting with the original perfection that is given along with it." [42]

Sin is apprehended as a universal human condition. Grace, on the other hand, is experienced only as mediated through a specific historical community; thus there is a church history but no sin history. Therefore it seems altogether appropriate that Schleiermacher should treat sin among the propositions that are descriptions of human states of life. So also one might expect regeneration, sanctification, and so on, to appear in this form of assertion. But what does it mean that the *person of Christ,* the historical figure Jesus, is treated under the heading "of the state of the Christian, inasmuch as he is conscious of divine grace" rather than, as one might conceive possible or even expect, among the statements about the world, along with the church and its historical existence? Doubtless this pattern is related to Schleiermacher's Second Adam Christology, which views Christ as the completion of the creation of man and the embodiment of a new possibility for human existence which also can be essentially shared (in dependence on him) by his followers. This is his expression of the archetypal nature or ideality of Christ, his *Urbildlichkeit* (see *CF*, §§ 87 ff.), though that is an inverted way of stating the matter. Schleiermacher's procedure was surely influenced by his insistence on holding together Christ's "person" and his "work."

But more basic for the question of structure was the Christo-centrism of Schleiermacher's thought. Christianity he defined as essentially distinguished from other teleological religions "in that

42. *CF,* § 72.6. Thus for Schleiermacher (along with De Wette, Marheineke, Schweizer and others) the "historical" character of the Genesis accounts had ceased to be an important question.

everything in it is related to the redemption accomplished in Jesus of Nazareth" (*CF*, § 11). This means that the reference to Jesus must be present in every form or direction of dogmatic statement, in statements about God as in statements about the world. Schleiermacher insisted that the whole God-consciousness of Christians is possessed only as something brought into being in them through Christ.[43] God, the world, and the self are all to be understood by reference to Christ. The relation to Christ is among the immediate utterances of the religious self-consciousness. Indeed, what is given in the experience of grace is precisely the regeneration and sanctification of the believer together with its source in the person of the redeemer, in his "distinctive activity" and his "exclusive dignity" (see *CF*, § 92).

Jesus of Nazareth, then, is the indispensable *historical* Whence of the new "divinely effected common life" of the Christian community. That is not to be taken in the negative sense that Christ is only the necessary backward reference of a present experience (Hofmann was later to come close to saying this), but in the positive sense that the living religious self-consciousness is actually bound to, dependent on, an occurrence in the past, that is, an event really *in* man's history. From this sort of historical reference, then, come principles whereby Christian theological statements (e.g. about Christ, about his continuing redemptive activity, and about the authority of Scripture) are both made possible and limited.

Precisely here Schleiermacher made only a half-turn to the new nineteenth-century attempt to construct Christology "from below" (*von unten nach oben*) rather than "from above" (*von oben nach unten*). That is, all doctrines of Christ must start from and be grounded in his humanly historical existence. This was the view that was to be accepted decisively in the nineteenth century. The fundamental form of the christological question became: "given the reality of Jesus' humanity, what does it mean to speak of his divinity?" rather than, as the question had been regularly put by orthodoxy, "given the divinity of Christ, how could he be really man?" Schleiermacher went only halfway in this movement. The controlling ideas in his Christology were the "ideality" (*Urbildlichkeit*) of Christ, the "constant potency" of his God-consciousness, and his "unclouded blessedness." Schleiermacher's thought seems to have moved from these perfections, as apprehended in the pious self-consciousness, to the figure of Jesus in a way that by-passed considerations of historical

43. Cf. *Sendschreiben an Dr. Lücke*, p. 31; *CF*, § 39, § 32.1.

criticism. He relied confidently on the Gospel of John for the portrait of Jesus. And he could interpret the sinlessness of Jesus in a way that denied to him the possibility of temptation or error (*CF*, § 98).

But Schleiermacher did take the half-step. Despite inconsistency in applying his principle and the inadequacy of his idea of humanity, Schleiermacher insisted that the divine act of revelation and redemption in Christ, whose innermost fundamental power was the "being of God" and which could not be explained by prior events, was an event that really took place and was received *in human existence*. And in those terms it must be interpreted. The appearance of the Redeemer in history as divine revelation is "neither something utterly supernatural nor something utterly suprarational" (*CF*, § 13). The virgin birth, the resurrection and ascension, and the prediction of his return in judgment cannot be properly parts of the doctrine of Christ's person (*CF*, §§ 97, 99). And most important, the idea of the presence of God in Christ is itself interpreted by reference to "the power of his God-consciousness" (the relation of his selfhood to God), which was "an authentic being of God in him" (*CF*, § 94).

In a similar way, the continuing redemptive activity and power in the church is radically historicized or naturalized. Not that this ceases, in Schleiermacher's view, to be fully divine activity, but the power of Jesus' God-consciousness is communicated immanently *in* history; the Holy Spirit can even be said to mean "the living unity of the Christian community as a moral person" or the "common spirit" of the church, which is at the same time "the being of God in it" (*CF*, § 116.3). The believer is dependent "horizontally" on Christ through the historical life of the church.[44]

Finally, theology can have no interest in historical "proofs" from miracle or prophecy. Quite apart from the impossibility of such demonstrations, these alleged proofs actually presuppose the faith they are supposed to support.[45] The doctrine of the divinity of Christ is

44. Schleiermacher's depiction of the continued working of redemptive activity in the church represents one of the weakest points in his historical sense. One gets the impression of a steady and unruffled development of growing conformity with Christ, without any of the conflict and interplay of opposites that characterized Hegel's picture of history. Thus subsequent historical studies were far more influenced by Hegel's attempt to find patterns in historical development.

45. See especially *CF*, § 14. The argument is similar to that of Lessing in "On the Proof of the Spirit and of Power" (cf. Henry Chadwick, *Lessing's Theological Writings* [London, 1956], pp. 51–57).

not the premise of faith but the outcome of reflection on faith, whose certainty can only be legitimated directly, in real, living relation to its object. Similarly, the authority of Scripture does not rest on any prior judgment about its "inspiration," nor faith in Christ on the authority of Scripture. Rather, faith in Christ must be presupposed "in order to allow any special standing to holy Scripture" (*CF*, § 128). The possibility and limits of theology have quite another foundation than the inerrancy or uniqueness of Scripture. Thus while Scripture (that is, the New Testament) continues to be "the norm for all subsequent presentations" of Christian faith (*CF*, § 129), it too falls genuinely within history, as the first of a series, and it is thus open to the freest course of historical investigation by "the purest hermeneutical methods" (*CF*, § 131.1).

At least two consequences were to follow from Schleiermacher's program at this point. One was the shaping of a major tradition of hermeneutics as the study of the principles of interpretation (notably of ancient documents), developed especially by Dilthey and, in the twentieth century, by Bultmann and Heidegger. The other was the much more pervasive approval of Schleiermacher's position as freeing theology for the fullest acceptance of historico-critical investigations of Scripture. Here Scheiermacher's statement was to be the archetype for nearly all the later liberal theologies.

4

Religious Truth in Image and Concept:
Hegel and the Speculative Theology

It was Schleiermacher, not Hegel, to whom the later nineteenth century looked as the great regenerator of modern theology. And the reasons for such a judgment are surely substantial. Schleiermacher was, after all, primarily a theologian and preacher who was also deeply and necessarily concerned with philosophy, whereas Hegel was primarily a philosopher who was also deeply and necessarily concerned with theology. That is, Schleiermacher's thinking was done more evidently by one standing within the church, a man as influential through his preaching as through his lecturing. Hegel emerges rather as a speculative worker, carrying to the farthest point the effort to comprehend everything in thought.[1]

1. It may not be unrelated to this difference that Hegel's life story seems less important to an understanding of his thought than that, for example, of Schleiermacher or Coleridge or Maurice or Bushnell. Born in 1770, Georg Wilhelm Friedrich Hegel studied theology in the Tübingen *Stift,* entering in the same year in which Kant's *Critique of Practical Reason* was published (1788); but he was much more interested in the new spirit emerging outside the curriculum—the spirit of Kant, of Spinoza rediscovered, of Herder, of *Sturm und Drang,* as well as of Greek and especially Platonic philosophy. Hölderlin and Schelling were his close friends in the *Stift.* After going on to study at Bern and Frankfurt, where he moved sharply away from the Enlightenment spirit toward that of romanticism, Hegel began in 1801 to lecture in philosophy at Jena, where he was in close association with Schelling. Losing the post at Jena in 1806 as a result of the Napoleonic victories, Hegel went to Bamberg briefly, then to Nuremberg to head the Gymnasium (1808), to Heidelberg to lecture (1816), and finally to Berlin, where he remained from 1818 until his death in 1831.

Most of the major works that Hegel himself published were issued before his coming to Berlin, e.g. *Die Phänomenologie des Geistes,* 1807 (*The Phenomenology of Mind,* trans. J. B. Baillie, 2d ed. [London, 1931]); *Wissenschaft der Logik,* 1812–16 (*Science of Logic,* trans. W. H. Johnston and L. G. Struthers, 2 vols. [London, 1929], familiarly known as the "Greater Logic"); *Enzyklopädie der philosophischen Wissenschaft im Grundriss,* 1817, later editions in 1827 and 1830 (see also the translations from this by W. Wallace, *The Logic of Hegel* [Oxford, 1892]—the "Lesser Logic"—and *Hegel's Philosophy of Mind* [Oxford, 1894]).

The lectures on the philosophy of religion were published from students' notes in 1832 and 1840 (by Marheineke and Bruno Bauer, reprinted in vols. 15 and 16 of the

Yet Hegel clearly looked upon himself as a Christian philosopher, who brought the truth in Protestant faith to fullest philosophical expression. He was a Lutheran. He was proud of redeeming the ancient dogmas, especially of Trinity and Incarnation, for which even Schleiermacher, to say nothing of the Enlightenment, could find no adequate justification. He located Christianity at the highest pinnacle of religious development, and sought to show the *necessity* of Christian truth as genuine truth, not mere feeling, and thus with a claim to universal validity. No less than Schleiermacher, Hegel sought to point a way beyond enlightenment and orthodoxy and to show that religion is a necessary part of human experience. He aimed at a full reconciliation of Christianity and science, theology and philosophy—not just Schleiermacher's covenant of mutual independence. Thus he concluded the lectures on the philosophy of religion by describing their intention "to reconcile reason and religion, to show how we know the latter to be in all its manifold forms necessary, and to rediscover in revealed religion the truth and the Idea." [2] And more than Schleiermacher, Hegel gave impetus and shape to the historical study of the origin and development of Christianity and provided a form for much of nineteenth- and early twentieth-century philosophy of religion. Yet just because Hegel claimed the universal truth of Christianity and incorporated religious truth into the system, this pattern for reestablishing the possibilities of theology was obviously tied more closely to the fortunes of the system as such, and it was thus peculiarly vulnerable to the later nineteenth-century reaction against idealism (when to be called a

---

Sämtliche Werke, anniversary edition ed. H. G. Glockner, 26 vols. [Stuttgart, 1928]). See also the critical edition of Georg Lasson, 1925–29, cited below from the Philosophische Bibliothek reprint (Hamburg, 1966). The translation by E. B. Speirs and J. B. Sanderson, *Lectures on the Philosophy of Religion, Together with a Work on the Proofs of Existence of God*, 3 vols. (London, 1895; reprinted 1962) is based on the 1840 text and is not unusable but needs to be compared with the anniversary edition and the Lasson text. Also of special importance for Hegel's view of religion are *Hegels theologische Jugendschriften*, ed. Herman Nohl (Tübingen, 1907), which has been largely translated by T. M. Knox, with a useful introduction by Richard Kroner, *Early Theological Writings* (Chicago, 1948); and above all, from the literature in English, Emil L. Fackenheim, *The Religious Dimension in Hegel's Thought* (Bloomington, Ind., 1967). One final useful volume is Albert Chapelle, *Hegel et la religion*, 3 vols. (Paris, 1963).

2. *Religionsphilosophie, Sämtliche Werke*, anniversary ed., 16 : 355 (*Lectures on the Philosophy of Religion*, trans. Speirs and Sanderson, 3 : 151). Subsequent references to the *Religionsphilosophie* are to this edition; volume and page numbers in Speirs and Sanderson's translation are set in brackets following the German citation.

Hegelian was a reproach) as well as to the immediate questions posed by the Hegelian "left" (notably Strauss, Bruno Bauer, and Feuerbach) and by Marx and Kierkegaard.

DYNAMICS OF A SYSTEM

Unity was the primary interest and end of Hegel's system—and in this interest as in other ways he represents the fullest flowering of speculative idealism. He was the man of the age.[3] From the beginning Hegel was absorbed by the problem of reconciling the opposites, the paradoxes and polarities of life and thought. Like Schelling in particular, he was imbued with the romanticist longing for a unity that transcended the boundaries which the Enlightenment had sought to make clear and distinct. In appreciation of the *Sturm und Drang* of life, in celebration of the ebb and flow in the manifold expressions of individuality, in protest against form on behalf of freedom, the romanticist was seeking a universality and wholeness different from that sought by the Enlightenment—a unity of life that could not finally be broken into the separate realms of philosophy and poetry, the divine and the human, nature and spirit. But while Hegel shared the romanticist's goal, he could not accept romanticist ways of expressing that unity: through mere deliberate confusion of the boundaries, or through mystical intuition or imagination, or through the absorption of philosophy and religion into poetry. No more could he be satisfied with Schelling's vague "indifference"—this "night in which all cows are black" (see below, p. 91). No mere state of feeling for unity could be adequate. He must have a *rational* unity, expressed by the reason as well as by the imagination and capable of being discovered by logic, though by a new logic able to overcome the problems which rationalism had found insoluble.

The world for Hegel had thus to be an *intelligible* universe. Here he was quite unwilling to give up the Enlightenment's quest. If the Enlightenment had to be spiritualized, romanticism had also to be intellectualized. Hegel carried to the highest pitch the confidence in the reign of reason, but he did this by a system of thought that transcends the merely abstract understanding (*Verstand*) of the Enlightenment. The object of thought, which is and must be the truth in reality itself, is grasped by reason (*Vernunft*). So the rational is the real and the real is the rational. Things thought are completely present in the thinking; and in thinking, thought is completely pres-

3. Kroner, introduction to *Early Theological Writings*, p. 14.

ent in things thought. What stands in no conceptual relationship is in itself simply nothing. The concept (*Begriff*) and the object are fully joined, in that objective truth is the conformity of objects to their concept. Thus philosophy could be defined as "the science of reason, in so far as reason is aware of itself as the whole of being." [4]

But Hegel also meant that knowledge is not a simple result but a process, an undertaking growing out of and resolving the contradiction between the self-certainty of the thinking self and the merely given that confronts it. It is a *movement toward* the identity of concept and object. And therefore the logic which is true rationality and true metaphysics must be of a different sort than that of the changeless definition and the formal deductive system. A logic that can discover the original unity, that can overcome the dualism of the transcendental and the historical and empirical, the chasm between the "eternal truths of reason" and the "accidental truths of history," or the separation of the theoretical and the practical, must be a dynamic logic. It must be a logic of life. This, then, was the decisive new step that must be taken to fulfill the aspirations and redeem the failures of the Enlightenment and romanticism. The logic of true thought is not a rigid universal, a fixed construction, but a recollection of the observed fullness of life, a logic able to penetrate to the mystery of life. Thought, as life, is insistent movement, a passing over into something else.

More specifically, the process of philosophical thinking is dialectical. In contrast to the fixed notions and axioms of the understanding (which remains as a beginning in philosophy, a necessary pattern of initial abstraction), dialectic demands the movement to complementary or antithetical abstractions. It denotes the inner tendency of finite determinations to go out of themselves into their opposites, to negate themselves. From every thesis arises its antithesis. The contradictions are not merely apparent or accidental but necessary. The dialectical is "the moving soul of scientific progress . . . the principle through which alone immanent connection and necessity enters into the content of science." In every philosophical concept there is the dialectical negation, which says what something is not, as well as the abstract form, which says what something is. "*A* is also that which it is not; *A* is non-*A*." [5]

4. *Enzyklopädie*, § 5. "Concept" is now, I believe, a more useful term to translate *Begriff* than is "notion," which has been customary.

5. *Lesser Logic*, § 81 (*Enzyklopädie*, §§ 13 ff.). For a good discussion of the dialectical method, as well as a general introduction to Hegel, see J. N. Findlay, *Hegel: A Re-Examination* (New York, 1962).

But the dialectic is a "moment" in philosophical thinking that is itself overcome in the higher "synthesis" of speculative thought, that is, of reason. The important point here is not the terminology of thesis, antithesis, and synthesis, which Hegel took from Fichte's *Wissenschaftslehre* and which was much more characteristic of the latter than of Hegel. Though a triadic pattern continually recurs in Hegel's system, the triads actually vary greatly; the second term can be much less than a contradiction of the first, and the third term appears in various relations to the first two. More important is the character of concept as event, whereby the concept does not so much exclude its contrary or complement as include it, call it forth, swing over to it, release it, and move to and fro in correlation and interdependence. And the movement proceeds to a reuniting or reconciling, so that reason is characterized by the overcoming of the contrasts in a rich harmony that is at the same time the preservation of the differences. This is a necessary movement, though of course the necessities of the transitions are not to be viewed as deductions; the inevitability of relationship is often more like that of a work of art, or it reflects an appeal to the concrete material of the nature and history that has to be interpreted. All truth is to be found finally in the completion of the circle from unconscious identity to differentiation to conscious unity; from the examination of "being" in the simplest sense, to the self-unfolding of the Absolute. And to stop at any point short of all-inclusiveness is to be in error.

The new shape of logic, then, was a way of thinking appropriate to the world. Hegel insisted that "dialectic is the principle of all the movement and of all the activity we find in reality. . . . Everything that surrounds us can be treated as an instance of dialectic. We know how all that is finite, instead of being stable and ultimate, is rather changeable and transitory: this is no other than the dialectic of the finite whereby it, being implicitly other than itself, is driven beyond what it immediately is, and turns into its opposite." [6] In particular, such thinking was to express and illumine the course of history. It could reflect the whole variety and play of phenomena, but without falling into romanticism's extravagances and disorder, or its unexamined organicism. Rather, diversity could be seen in a pattern of tensions being resolved, of partial and one-sided truth being overcome. Both in the general dominant theme of evolutionary development and in the specific notions of dialectic in history and of the

6. Lesser Logic, § 81.

Idea as working itself out ever more fully through concrete historical expressions, Hegel's vision was of the most profound influence for nineteenth-century historiography.[7] For theology, Hegel was at this point much more decisive than Schleiermacher. Schleiermacher had at times a firm grasp on historical individuality, where Hegel was often weak, but he possessed no real sense of tension and struggle in the movement of history. Thus his view of the history of the Church was that of a gradual and untroubled extension in the Christian community of the perfect embodiment of God-consciousness in Jesus. Hegel's conception of conflict in the center of spiritual reality was both far more stimulating to historical research and far more helpful in illuminating the events. It also produced a more dynamic idea of the relation of the religions.

The new logic was also the necessary means for explicating the grand vision that the Absolute is Spirit. Hegel agreed with Schelling that the Absolute could not be conceived simply as substance (as Spinoza had said) or as ego or subject (as Fichte). But Schelling's mere assertion of a neutral "indifference" was not acceptable either. The opposites must be transcended in a rationally interpretable self-development of Spirit, passing through and taking up the antithesis, so that the whole of reality is disclosed as the self-unfolding of Spirit. The real and the rational are one. The system of reason and the system of the universe are at once an unfolding of the realm of freedom and consciousness. And the whole thrust and task of philosophy is precisely to uncover and to grasp the content of the definition of the Absolute as Spirit.[8]

THE PLACE OF RELIGION

The speculative philosophies of Fichte, Schelling, and Hegel all had a deeply religious stamp and motive. Philosophy and religion were struggling against the same enemies, the rule of eudaemonism, of mere "understanding" (i.e. the rigid or "hard and fast" abstract thought of a formal deductive system, which fixes and defines in such a way as to exclude fluidity and movement, and thus life). They both sought a unitary view of the world and culture, and a movement beyond subjectivity to the objective, to the eternal and the

7. For church history, see especially the work of F. C. Baur and I. A. Dorner (chaps. 7 and 12, below).
8. *Enzyklopädie*, § 302.

universally valid. Philosophy had to be religious, even theocentric. As Hegel put it,

> the object of religion and of philosophy is the eternal truth in its objectivity itself, God and nothing but God and the explication of God. Philosophy is . . . knowledge of that which is eternal, which is God, and which flows from his nature. . . . Philosophy explicates itself only by explicating religion and in explicating itself it explicates religion. . . . Thus religion and philosophy collapse into one. Philosophy is in fact itself worship; it is religion, for in the same way it renounces subjective notions and opinions in occupying itself with God. Philosophy is thus identical with religion, but it is this in a distinctive way, different [in expression] from what one is accustomed to call religion as such.[9]

Hegel's early theological writings make it clear that the possibility of viewing his whole system as a universal philosophy of religion was a natural consequence of a lifelong concern with the meaning of the Christian religion. Indeed, his ideas were shaped as much by reflection on the problems of Christianity as by the doctrines of the philosophers. His Absolute was approached through religion rather than through art (as in Schelling) or ethics (as in Fichte), and for all his sympathy with the romanticists, Hegel had never accepted the idea of the poetic as the deepest insight; that was rather the religious. Two themes in the early essays stand out. One is Hegel's wrestling with the problem of "the positivity of the Christian religion." [10] Here Hegel was still identifying "the aim and essence of all true religion, our religion included, [with] human morality," and he sustained the Enlightenment's suspicion of positivity, that is, of an attachment to particular historical events which yield a revelation that cannot be discovered by reason but must be given from outside. Such positivity was heteronomy, an authoritarian subjugation of human freedom and reason, and Hegel could not attribute it to Jesus but only to the Jewish milieu, to the disciples, and to the development of the church from a moral society into a "state."

The second theme was Hegel's discovery, in religion, of love as the actuality of reconciliation.[11] In Jesus' teaching God is love, living in man. The commandments are annulled as laws but fulfilled in a

9. *Religionsphilosophie*, 15 : 37 [1 : 19–20].

10. See the essay by that title, written in 1795 and following, in *Early Theological Writings* (pp. 67 ff.), and Hegel's earlier "Life of Jesus," in which Jesus appears simply as a teacher of Kant's religion of moral law.

11. See "The Spirit of Christianity and Its Fate" (*Early Theological Writings*, pp. 182 ff.). Hegel's interpretation of Jesus had now shifted strongly away from Kant.

higher mode of reconciliation and love that makes laws superfluous. Love is "a unification of life, it presupposes division, a development of life, a developed many-sidedness of life. The more variegated the manifold in which life is alive, the more the places in which it can be reunified; the more the places in which it can sense itself, the deeper does love become." [12] Love, then, is the actual overcoming of the antinomies in life, the discords of duty and inclination, of law and motive, of objectivity and subjectivity. In the living process which is religion, the pattern of reconciliation, of dynamic unity, is in fact realized.

The clue for Hegel's later idea of the reconciliation of opposites thus came from religion, the region in which all the riddles of the world are solved. What he set out to do was to provide a rational method to express that living reality, to translate life's pattern of disunion and reunion into logical terms. Hence the positivity of religion came to be sharply revalued as part of a new orientation to the historical as such. Reason, in Hegel's mature thought, grasps the truth not by avoiding particularity and positivity, but precisely *in* what really is (which also means that it grasps not just the appearance, but rather the reality which forces itself into existence). The unfolding of Spirit is genuinely *within* history. While the history of Spirit "must be conceived so as to be in harmony with its Idea," the powers that Spirit possesses we learn "from the variety of products and formations which it originates." [13] The universal has to pass into actuality through the particular. Spirit is known "in itself" only because it has appeared "for itself" and "in and for itself" in history.

Religion, in Hegel's system, stands at the highest stage in the unfolding of Spirit, that is, in the final development of subjectivity called "Absolute Spirit." Here Subjective Spirit and Objective Spirit are surpassed and taken up in Spirit's vision or consciousness of itself as the truth of everything.[14] This vision emerges in art, in religion, and in philosophy. In art it is given only immediately and sen-

---

12. Ibid., pp. 278–79.

13. Hegel, *Philosophy of History*, trans. J. Sibree (New York, 1956), pp. 57, 73. See also p. 78: "Spirit is essentially the result of its own activity; its activity is the transcending of immediate, simple, unreflective existence—the negation of that existence, and the returning into itself."

14. This requires the setting of a well-ordered state, which is the highest stage in the development of Objective Spirit, and Spirit's self-consciousness never simply transcends the peculiarities of a national culture, though it is the absolute truth as given in a particular time and way. Thus art, religion, and philosophy are at the same time expressions of a limited culture (to be superseded in later phrases) and eternal.

suously, and as presented to the imagination. In religion, however, the true content is given, a content identical with that of philosophy. In theological language, truth is revealed by God to the spirit in man of which He is the absolute ground. Religion as man's consciousness of God is God's consciousness of himself in man, whereby He is God; and man's knowing of God is also man's knowing of himself in God.[15] In speculative language, religion is the self-consciousness of Absolute Spirit through the mediation of finite spirit.[16]

Like Schleiermacher, Hegel insisted that religion is an essential moment in human experience. Historically and materially, the religious consciousness is the foundation of all higher human consciousness: of rights, duty, truth, beauty. Hegel's emphasis, however, was not on man's dependence but on his freedom and consciousness, on the elevation of the finite consciousness to the infinite, on oneness and the final transcendence over polarity. Further, Hegel was contemptuous of Schleiermacher's identification of religion with feeling.[17] Not that feeling and emotion are not present and important for subjective life; on the contrary, feeling is the *immediate* form in which the consciousness of God is given, it is the *place* where God is in my being, and I am certain of him. But in feeling there is no clear distinction between the subjective and the objective; all is immediate certainty; there is no reflective or analytical clarity; and to stop with feeling is to be able to make no discriminations of truth or value. Feeling is as such not distinctive of man but is shared with the animals—hence Hegel's remark that if religion were the feeling of absolute dependence, the dog would be the most religious being.

Religious expression therefore necessarily leads on to reflective consciousness of the content of feeling, that is, to that which is thought. The content of religion, the objective side, is encountered in the form of representation (*Vorstellung*), which is the characteristic language and level of religion, and in cultus. Hegel's technical term *Vorstellung* includes elements both of sensuous particularity and of universality. A representation is not a mental picture or an

15. "God is God only insofar as he knows himself; his self-knowledge is his self-consciousness in man, is the knowledge man has *of* God, which advances to man's self-knowledge *in* God" (*Enzyklopädie*, § 564). Hegel also recalled the words of Meister Eckhart: "The eye with which God sees me is the eye with which I see him; my eye and his eye are one" (*Religionsphilosophie*, 15 : 288 [1 : 217–18]).

16. *Religionsphilosophie*, 15 : 214 ff. [1 : 240 ff.].

17. Ibid., 15 : 131 ff. [1 : 118 ff.]. See also Lasson's critical ed., 1 : 97 ff.

image simply. It is rather "the picture as it is lifted up into the form
of universality, of thought, so that the one basic characteristic which
constitutes the essence of the object is held fast and is present to the
mind doing the representing." [18] Representation uses sense forms
drawn from direct perception or intuition (*Anschauung*), but for the
purpose of conveying the universal. It signifies truth, *objective* content, which has its validity in itself; and thereby *Vorstellung* stands
against all modes of mere subjectivity, whether of pictorial thinking
or private opinion and wish.

But to say that in representation the essential content is given "in
the form of thought" is not to say that it is posited "as thought."
Vorstellung has not yet freed itself wholly from the sensuous; it is
still concerned with the historically accidental, the narrative in the
phenomenal realm; in seeking to express essential connections, it
still leaves them in the form of contingency. Therefore reflection in
religion must move on to the level of authentic (*eigentlich*) or actual
(*wirklich*) thought (*Gedanke*), from the form of faith to the form of
reason, from representation to concept (*Begriff*), from theology to
theological interpretation to philosophical knowledge in which the
inner necessity of the relations and processes is made plain, thus also
from the subjective and immediate knowing (*Wissen*) of God to
genuine rational cognition (*Erkennen*).

At the center of the religious content is the overcoming of the
"bugbear" of the opposition of the finite and the infinite. Beyond
the level of the antithesis is the recognition, at the level of speculative conception, that man's consciousness of God is God's self-consciousness; that is, that the knowledge of God must finally be understood as a moment in the being of Spirit, of God himself. Religion is
not a "transaction of man" but "essentially the highest determination of the absolute idea itself," a differentiation and affirmation, an
active play and movement within Spirit itself.[19]

From the depiction of religion in general as man's consciousness of
God and the elevation of the finite to the infinite, Hegel moves to
the examination of the definite religions by way of an important dis-

18. Ibid., 15 : 154 [1 : 142]; Lasson ed., 1 : 115 (cf. 110–18, 291 ff.).

19. *Religionsphilosophie*, 15 : 216 [1 : 206]. Religion is not simply knowledge of the
overcoming of the duality of finite and infinite, but as such *is* the overcoming. "Religion is itself . . . this activity of thinking reason and of the man who thinks rationally: the individual's positing of himself as the universal and, annulling himself
as individual, finding his true self as the universal." Philosophy is the same process in
the form of thought rather than representation (ibid., pp. 204–05[194]).

cussion of worship (*Kultus*). Religion must be viewed in every instance from the standpoint of interpenetrating *Vorstellung* and *Kultus*. In contrast to the theoretical expression of the unity in *Vorstellung*, worship constitutes the practical relation, the concrete unification of the self with God and God with the self. Of course, worship is also theoretical and its mode of knowledge is called faith. But worship as the adoration of God in the broadest sense points to the active union of man with God by voluntary surrender of himself to the divine grace as the real power of his own freedom and goodness. Out of the living communion of the self with God springs also moral action, and religion expresses itself in custom and in the state. Worship is thus the presence of the content that constitutes Absolute Spirit in such a way that the history of the divine content is the history of humanity.[20]

The history of specific religions, accordingly, can be set forth by Hegel as the development of the religious consciousness, which is at the same time the evolution of human freedom and spirituality generally. In several series of lectures on the philosophy of religion (1821, 1824, 1827, and 1831), he worked out a rich and remarkably inclusive interpretation of this religious history in its necessary stages of development.[21] The first major distinction was between immediate or natural religion and the religion of spiritual individuality or free subjectivity. The religion of nature is not (to contradict the Enlightenment) the finest but the most imperfect moment in religious development, belonging to the childhood of humanity. It is characterized by an immediate and undisturbed unity of the spiritual with the natural, and God is conceived as natural unity, that is, as less than Spirit. The initial level is the religion of magic, either direct (as in the Eskimos and African peoples, and among the Chinese and the Mongol shamans, where the principle is that of direct power over nature) or indirect (as in the official Chinese religion and in Taoism). The second stage is constituted by the religions of "substantiality," in which the highest power is grasped as a substance, as in the "religion of Being-in-itself" (*Insichsein*)—Lamaism, for exam-

---

20. Ibid., 15 : 220 ff. [1 : 210 ff.].

21. Ibid., 15 : 269–16 : 180 [1 : 261–2 : 323]. Lasson ed., vol. 1, pt. 2, and vol. 2, pt. 1. Hegel did not always follow the same order of development; e.g. in 1827 he reversed the previous sequence and placed the religion of beauty before the religion of sublimity. This should be a warning about the sort of necessity Hegel saw in the movement of the concepts (cf. the note in Lasson, II/1, 250 ff.). Lasson's arrangement of the levels of the development is helpful and I have generally followed it here.

ple—and in the "religion of fantasy," which combines the abstract One of being-in-itself with extravagant imagination, as in the religion of India. The third stage of the religion of nature is that of "abstract subjectivity," which is the moment of transition to a religion of freedom. Here we encounter the strife of good and evil and the resumption into concrete unity of the wild, unrestrained fullness that was expressed, for example, in the Indian movement from the idea of Brahman into the vast Hindu pantheon. The dualism of good and evil is given in Zoroastrianism in a superficial way as a natural manifestation, as in the opposition of light and darkness. This stage also takes the form of a religion of suffering, of estrangement of Spirit from itself, in Syrian religion. And it begins to disclose a "coming of Spirit to itself," not yet as a reconciliation but as a struggle out of strife toward the destiny of free spirituality, in the religion of mystery (notably Egyptian, the cult of Osiris, and the dying and rising god cults generally).

In the religions of spiritual individuality, the spiritual independence of the subject begins. Subjectivity achieves dominance over the natural and finite elements of consciousness, the latter serving as a garment or a manifestation and glorification of spirit. If the religions of nature represent the childhood of man, the religions of spirituality are his adolescence. God here is power, which is wisdom reflected in itself as subject, which acts according to purposes, and the world is viewed in conformity with an end. The variations relate to the determinations of power, of wisdom, and of end.

The first moment is the religion of sublimity (*Erhabenheit*), which is externally represented by the Jewish religion. God is absolute power, wisdom, and holiness, absolutely one and without form. He is infinite activity. The conformity to an end that is a moral end is of an external sort, and the end is limited; the religious family is exclusive. Man is related to the Lord simply as a servant, remaining wholly in human finitude, though he is exalted above all else in creation as being in the image of God, knowing, thinking, perceiving. His worship is thus fear of the Lord, which in self-annihilation is at the same time absolute confidence and faith.

The second moment is the religion of beauty or necessity, exemplified by Greek religion. Here God's "Other" is released as something free and independent. "Freedom is found first of all in the subject" and God is the power that releases the subject and in whose essential nature is found whatever has any value in man. "God is in himself the mediation which is man, man knows himself in God and God and man say of each other: this is spirit of my spirit." [22] The beauty that is worshiped is perceived as immanent in the human. Freedom, the formal element of self-determination, is that moral element from which ethical determinations arise. But the moral determinations have here no inner connectedness; the natural powers and the spiritual are opposed, and essential spirit and finite spirit remain in antithesis. The higher absolute unity, which stands over the gods as their pure and absolute power, is fate (*Schicksal*), simple necessity, and "because particularity is not yet tempered by the Idea and necessity is not the content-filled measure of wisdom, unlimited contingency of content appears in the sphere of the particular gods." [23] The gods are concrete subjective spirituality, but they are finite and they are not holy; they can be arbitrary. They are beautiful because in the imaginative sensuous portrayal they are given an ideal human form—and their defects, which are moral in nature, are due to their being too little rather than too much anthropopathic.

If the ruling principle in the religion of sublimity was unity in the form of abstract subjectivity and utter transcendence, and in the religion of beauty it was empty necessity, the religion of purposefulness (*Zweckmässigkeit*, exemplified by Roman religion) marks a return to a principle of definite limited ends (happiness with a definite content). The gods are practical and prosaic, not joyous and free like the Greek gods, but earnest and serious of purpose. Universality of sovereignty is represented as real and actual, empirical, in *Fortuna publica*, though the power of this god is abstract, not truly spiritual and one. There is a universal family in the Roman people (in contrast to the many families of Greek religion and the one exclusive family in Jewish religion). This is a religion of happiness, that is, of the particular finite self-seeking of the worshipers. God is served for a human end. There is a restless movement in Roman life between the extremes of the universal element, *Fortuna publica*, and independent human ends. As a return to the side of reality, and in the isolation and contradiction of its moments, Roman religion stands as the indispensable middle term in the transition to absolute religion. It is the closing stage of the finite reli-

22. Ibid., 16 : 92, 95 [2 : 220, 224]. On the relation of Jewish and Greek religion to Christianity for Hegel, see Fackenheim, *The Religious Dimension in Hegel's Thought,* pp. 133–38.

23. *Religionsphilosophie*, 16 : 113–14 [2 : 243].

gions, a completion of finitude which is "the absolute misfortune and absolute misery of Spirit," the "highest antithesis of Spirit in itself and this antithesis is unreconciled, this contradiction unresolved." [24]

THE NATURE OF CHRISTIANITY

The history of religions was for Hegel the study of a definite and necessary unfolding, a gradual self-disclosure and self-realization of Spirit which at no point is without truth but which is not yet pure truth. The positive religions were neither to be put down as corruptions of a true natural religion nor viewed simply as inferior kinds of religious expression. They were fragmentary and they could not transcend their fragmentariness, but (at least in the case of Jewish and Greco-Roman religion) they could come to recognize it and thus point beyond themselves. They were necessary stages on the way. Here Hegel's vision of the evolution of the religious spirit was more novel, more dynamic, and more influential than Schleiermacher's typology of religions. And because he sought to give a reason for the development, Hegel's idea could become a most seductive (though also highly problematic) possibility for a new Christian apologetic which would validate Christianity by man's entire spiritual enterprise and which would place Christianity securely at the pinnacle of religion without the rejection of other religions as mere error and idolatry. Christianity was for Hegel the culmination and fulfillment of the religious-historical process. This was its validity. The events of the Gospel were the hinge on which the history of the world turns, because in the Gospel was given the clue to the whole historical process. With the Christian religion has come the absolute epoch in world history, because God has now revealed himself.

Christianity, therefore, Hegel called Absolute Religion, not one among the "definite" religions, but a new and final stage in which all the moments of the preceding stages are taken up. (Thus is posed the question of the "absoluteness of Christianity.") It is the religion of revelation (*offenbare Religion*), that is, positive religion in the sense that it has come to men from outside, with all its historically contingent character, as everything that exists for consciousness must come in an external way. Yet truth must become internal, rational, and essential, so that consciousness of the truth becomes identical with self-consciousness. Thus absolute religion is also the religion of

24. Ibid., 16 : 184 [2 : 320].

truth and freedom,[25] and the appearance of the absolute religion, because it is the religion of freedom, was for Hegel the condition for the actualization of the true state. The Reformation, in its liberation of conscience, was the final breakthrough of the political ideal that emerged with Christianity.

In all its most characteristic doctrines, Christianity expressed in representational forms the essential truth: the "unity of divine and human natures," the "absolute identity" of finite and infinite spirit (which Hegel called the "substance and content" of Christianity), the dialectical movement of redemption and reconciliation. And in contrast to the prevalent disjunctions of philosophy and theology, and the neglect by theologians (especially Schleiermacher) of the ancient dogmas, Hegel set out to recover, to rehabilitate, and to show the necessity of the doctrines of Trinity, of creation, of fall, and of incarnation and reconciliation.

The despised doctrine of the "immanent," that is, inner-divine Trinity (together with the idea of the God-man) was the place where Hegel found above all the center of Christianity and the expression of the true nature of Spirit. The depiction of Father, Son, and Spirit as "persons" and the childishly natural conception of the generation of the Son have finally to be laid aside (demythologized) as only representational in form.[26] But the trinitarian idea remains the ultimate truth and the proof of it is the whole of philosophy. It expresses a *concrete* identity, a rich and living unity rather than the abstract unity or barren identity without difference conceived by rationalism and Judaism. Spirit is the process of differentiation and return: the universal Idea itself, containing the Idea, that is the Idea implicitly; the distinguishing of the Other, the particular, representing the entire Idea in-and-for-itself; and the identity between the two, the One being at home with itself in the Other. Love means a being outside of self and identity with self; knowledge requires the existence of another which yet belongs to it.

> God, who is eternally being-in-and-for-itself, eternally generates himself as his Son, distinguishes himself from himself—this is the ab-

25. Ibid., 16 : 191 ff. [2 : 327 ff.]; Lasson ed., vol. 2, pt. 2, pp. 3 ff.

26. The true nature of personality, further, was for Hegel constituted by the whole trinitarian process, the winning back of self through being absorbed in the other (see *Religionsphilosophie*, 16 : 239 [3 : 25]). Thus Hegel sought to redeem the idea of the personality of God brought into question e.g. by Fichte and Schleiermacher, and opened a way for much later 19th-century interpretation of the Trinity (especially by I. A. Dorner).

solute differentiation [Urteil]. But what he thus distinguishes from himself does not have the form of a being that is other, rather what has been distinguished is nothing more or less than that from which it has been distinguished. . . . God is himself this entire act. God is the beginning . . . but in this he is precisely also the end, the totality; thus it is as totality that God is Spirit. God simply as Father is not yet the True . . . he is rather beginning and end, he is his presupposition, constitutes himself his presupposition (this is simply another form of the differentiation), he is the eternal process. . . . God in his eternal universality is the differentiating of himself, determining himself, positing another to himself and at the same time abolishing and taking up the distinction, thereby being with himself [bei sich], and he is Spirit only by being so brought forth.[27]

From the movement which is God intrinsically, in and for himself in his eternal Idea, we have to go on to the movement in which the Idea passes out of its universality and infinitude into the determination of finitude.[28] Creation, to put it with deliberate ambiguity, is that same going forth which is essential to the nature of Spirit. The eternal being in-and-for-itself is the self-unfolding, the self-determination and differentiation, in manifestation and finitude; but the distinction is just as eternally abolished and taken up (aufgehoben) and what eternally is, is thereby a return to itself. Only in this way does Spirit exist. To ask the question, which Christian orthodoxy at once asked and which gave rise to diverse interpretations among the followers of Hegel, whether Hegel meant to describe an inner-divine process apart from the creation of the world or whether the second moment (the "Son") was itself finally the world, was, for him, to put the matter wrongly. What the Idea is intrinsically cannot be so separated from its manifestation of itself. The Other is the external world, the finite world which is outside the truth; but Hegel insisted that to separate the movement of the Idea in itself and the differentiation in the form of finitude, that is, to regard these as two wholly different realms and acts, is to betray the true content that is given in representational thought. A distinction has

27. Ibid., 16 : 228–29, 237 [3 : 12–13, 22]. Both of Hegel's most immediate theological disciples, Karl Daub of Heidelberg (1765–1836) and Philipp Marheineke of Berlin (1780–1846), but especially the latter, took up the trinitarian idea as central to dogmatics and developed its necessity in speculative fashion (cf. Marheineke, Die Grundlehren der christlichen Dogmatik als Wissenschaft [2d ed., 1827]; Daub, Theologumena [1806], Einleitung in das Studium der Dogmatik [1810], Die dogmatische Theologie jetziger Zeit [1833]).

28. Religionsphilosophie, 16 : 247 ff. [3 : 33 ff.].

to be made, yet the two are said to be intrinsically the same, hence the sameness must be defined exactly so as not to imply the false idea that the eternal Son of the Father is simply identical with the world.[29] Yet it is of course also true that for Hegel God has his self-consciousness in man's consciousness of him, that Spirit thus comes to self-consciousness. God, one may say, is true though not real apart from his manifestation in the world. A similar difficulty appears in the question of the eternity of the world. Hegel could say that God as Spirit is essentially self-revelation. He does not create once-for-all but is the eternal creator and self-revealer ("this is his concept, his definition"). But he also insisted that "questions such as whether the world or matter is eternal or has existed from eternity or whether it has begun in time, belong to the empty metaphysics of the understanding."[30]

The Fall, a doctrine which also particularly interested Hegel and which he defended against Enlightenment attacks, was for him a fall into history. Like Schleiermacher, Hegel insisted that original sin is not properly a doctrine about a first man and an inheritance from him, but a truth about all men and the universality of sin. It is said both that man is by nature good and that he is by nature evil. This means that he is implicitly (an sich) spirit, rationality, created in the image of God. Here we designate both the possibility of his reconciliation and the ambiguity of his existence, for to remain simply what he is implicitly, "by nature," is itself defective. Because he is spirit, man is differentiated from mere natural being; he must emerge into existence as a finite, particular, one-sided consciousness and will—and thus in disunion from the "paradisal innocence" of unreflective harmony with God and nature. History is thus the study of human-alienation (and also, of course, of reconciliation). The biblical story of the loss of innocence through eating of the tree of knowledge is a telling symbol of the fact that man does become evil through the disharmony of self-consciousness, the condition of contrast or isolation that separates the individual from the universal. But only through that separation can being-for-self come into being, though this is of course not to deny the many specific evils of history, nor the content of man's willing as impulse and inclination within the circle of his own desires.[31]

29. Ibid., 16 : 251–52 [3 : 38–39]. Fackenheim finds in this double Trinity, held together in love, the answer to the whole problem for Hegel of uniting philosophy and faith (see *The Religious Dimension in Hegel's Thought*, especially pp. 203 ff.).

30. *Religionsphilosophie*, 16 : 198, 253 [2 : 335; 3 : 40].

31. Ibid., 16 : 257 ff. [3 : 45 ff.]; Lasson ed., vol. 2, pt. 1, pp. 95 ff.

The positing of the distinction between God and man, the consciousness of the opposition of the finite to the infinite, is the precondition of the *explicit* unity of God and man. This is expressed both in the myth of the fall of man, which depicts his becoming a historical creature, and in the course of the development of religion, with its movement from unreflective identity with the infinite to the most intense awareness of the opposition of sinful man to infinite and good God. Thus the way is prepared, the time is fulfilled, for the infinite reconciliation, that is, for the manifestation in self-consciousness of the unity of the divine and the human. This is the appearance of the God-man—the perfect embodiment of the Idea, God's actual coming to self-consciousness in man—which is thus the center of Hegel's whole teaching. Just as the contradiction must be posited before it can be overcome (*aufgehoben*), so the reconciliation can occur only by a process within history. And the truth of the unity of God and man can be received with certainty by man only as it takes the form of a concrete person in whom God and man are one, and indeed Spirit can attain its fulfillment, its reality for itself, only in the consciousness of an individual. The unity of divine and human nature is the Idea of absolute Spirit in-and-for-itself. The movement of reconciliation is further expressed, that is, completed, in death and resurrection. Death is the utter extremity of estrangement and the beginning of the conversion of consciousness. And not only is this death the complete proof of finitude, and a death of shame and dishonor, but God has died, "the negation is itself in God," a moment in his being. Yet "God maintains himself in this process and it is only the death of death. God comes again to life." Resurrection belongs with crucifixion. Thus this death, which is the utmost form of finitude, is "at the same time the abolition and absorption (*das Aufheben*) of natural finitude, of immediate existence and of alienation, the dissolution of the limits." [32] The resurrection and ascension is a "return" from finitude, but now to the concrete universality of the Idea. The identity of finite spirit with infinite Spirit is fully explicit and the reconciliation in Christ can become universalized as the death of death for all men. In the life of the community of those who acknowledge the divine-human unity in Christ, that actuality is recapitulated (through the presence of the Spirit), the representational identification of the divine-human identity with Christ is transcended in the certification of that truth in the life of every man.

32. Ibid., 16 : 300, 302 [3 : 91, 93].

ISSUES AND CONSEQUENCES

In Hegel's legacy to the theology of the nineteenth and twentieth centuries, three kinds of problems were of special import. One, as we noted, was the question of the relation of God and the world. The charge of pantheism was a standard feature of theological orthodoxy's judgment upon him. More important, the God–world distinction was a continuing focus of the debate between the so-called Hegelian right and left wings, with the former seeking to interpret him more nearly in accord with traditional theology. Further, the resultant way of defining the problem—as a balancing of transcendence and immanence or a proper locating of "theism" on a continuum between "deism" and "pantheism"—continued to be a preoccupation of theology down to the radical reformations of the question in the twentieth century by Barth, Tillich, Heim and H. Richard Niebuhr. But it may be asked whether that posing of the problem was not itself a lapse to a more primitive kind of understanding. Quite plainly, Hegel's idea of creation was not the same as the general theological tradition of *creatio ex nihilo* any more than was Schleiermacher's idea. The world was not called into being "out of nothing" by the divine word in "free" decision, nor did it have its being "out there" over against God without any involvement in his being (if indeed this is what orthodoxy taught; such views have often been colored more by the small God-ideas of the English deists than by the grand vision of Aquinas or Calvin, more by Arius than by Athanasius). The world for Hegel was a necessary unfolding of the life of God himself. But his idea was not any simple assertion that the world is God, nor was it even the identity of Spinoza's *natura naturans* and *natura naturata*. Rather, like Scheiermacher, Hegel was attempting to formulate a panentheistic conception of God and the world, to give a new shape to the concepts both of creation and of the personality of God, a new shape demanded by post-Enlightenment thought, especially since Fichte and the atheism controversy.

Second, what was the significance of the figure of Jesus in the process of the self-actualization of Spirit? Hegel's idea of the divine and the human as not two utterly disparate natures conceptually incapable of being joined, but rather as implicitly one, was to be immediately productive of a renewal of incarnation theology (especially in the work of Isaak Dorner). And it would later contribute forcefully to the adoption of evolutionary ideas on the grand scale. But the pointed question was then of the uniqueness of Christ: Was Jesus only a symbol of the pattern of reconciliation which was embodied in the total world-process, as was often charged, or was he a unique and necessary event? Granted that God for Hegel does not transcend historical events in such a way that the appearance of Jesus could be an abrupt or arbitrary intrusion from without, and that Hegel demythologized the biblical accounts generally, still he does seem to insist that the coming of Spirit to full self-consciousness had to occur in one individual, that is, to be known explicitly there if it was to become explicit in all men. But the question of Jesus was to be the special touchstone for nearly all those influenced by Hegel, including Strauss, Baur, Biedermann, Dorner, and Kierkegaard.[33] And it was the followers of Hegel who above all gave shape to the historical question in the succeeding generation.

The most important issue, however, was Hegel's view of the truth of theological statements, their status, their meaning, and their validation—that is, his answer to the question of the possibility of theology. Hegel intended to be the authentic bearer of living Christian truth. But was his a fruitful way beyond orthodoxy and enlightenment, or was his system the embrace that crushed and smothered? The center of the problem is found in his identification of the language of religion as *Vorstellung,* and his distinction of *Vorstellung* from *Gefühl, Anschauung,* and *Begriff.* More specifically still, it was his idea of the relation between the religious form of thinking, *Vorstellung,* and the philosophical form of thinking, *Begriff,* and thus also the distinction between the "form of faith" and the "form of reason" (*Vernunft*). At this point, Hegel was unequivocal about two things: (1) in religion the true content is found and that content is never surpassed as content but only in form; philosophy knows no higher truth than that of theology, its truth is the same; (2) the form of philosophical expression is superior, and the work of philosophy is that of changing the form of religious representation into the form for which it yearns, thereby giving the content a fully adequate form and bringing into view its rational necessity.

33. On Strauss, Baur, and Biedermann, see chap. 8, below; on Dorner, chap. 12; and on Kierkegaard, chap. 13. For an excellent discusssion of Hegel on this point, as well as of his relation to Christian theology generally, see Stephen D. Crites, "The Gospel According to Hegel," *Journal of Religion* 46, no. 2 (April 1966) : 246–63.

But is this finally the justification or the dissolution of Christian faith? Each of these judgments has been asserted, but a fairer estimate seems to be that the distinction of *Vorstellung* and *Begriff*, as Hegel employed it, was a peculiarly double-edged sort of demythologizing, and that just this accounts for the profound influence of the Hegelian formulations on the modern question of the truth of Christianity.

On the one hand, looking to the superiority of the philosophical over the theological *form,* and to the judgment that the witness of Spirit attains its highest form in philosophy, and thus its final self-unfolding (so far), it could be charged that the religious must now be surpassed, that, as Feuerbach put it, speculation only lets religion say what speculation has already said and said much better; it determines religion without being determined by it. Thus the next step is to say that religion has now been superseded—or, less radically, that henceforth the philosophy of religion will wholly provide the basis and the limits, and most of the content, for theology. Religion and theology have no independent basis and character, but become bound to a claim for a universal cultural and philosophical world view.

But in the distinction of form of expression is the other side of the assertion: that Christianity is neither mere feeling nor a kind of truth claim separate from the rest of man's knowing. In both respects Hegel stands in contrast to Schleiermacher. He insisted that knowledge (*Erkennen*) is an essential element in the Christian religion. Christianity is a claim to truth, not a claim independent of other truth claims but necessarily bound up with them, answerable to them and they to it. Therefore the Christian claim is a universal claim. No mere covenant of coexistence or noninterference between theology and the other sciences will suffice. Religion is not *sui generis,* not a discrete and independent mode of human being and awareness—but to deny it that sort of protected and (presumably) unassailable basis is at the same time to assert for it a more inclusive relevance and validity. Just as all history, not only a special "sacred history," is for Hegel the revelation of God, so religious truth is integral to the whole human quest for truth. And at precisely this point, the disjunction between Schleiermacher and Hegel provided the shape of the issue for the nineteenth and twentieth centuries: whether Christianity (and religion in general) was to be defended and interpreted on the basis of its independence and *sui generis* character or on the basis of its unity with the whole of human experience and its embodiment in Western culture.[34]

To put the question in a different form, can theology be sustained as a truly independent enterprise, either on the basis of revelation or of feeling, without becoming simply discrete and isolated from the generality of human culture? Or can theology be sustained as a claim to universal truth without being finally subordinate to the other sciences and thus losing its own integrity?

34. So Crites can suggest that it was Hegel's view that "provided the basis for a major crisis of faith in European thought. . . . That the distinctively modern controversy over the truth of Christianity was not so much that formulated in the Enlightenment as that formulated among the successors of Hegel [Strauss, Baur, Feuerbach, Marx, Kierkegaard]" ("The Gospel According to Hegel," p. 246).

5

Reasoning Faith and Faithful Reason: Coleridge and the Struggle against the Eighteenth Century

The attempt to describe common elements in the theological trends and the problems in Germany, Britain, and the United States is most difficult for the first third of the nineteenth century. This was the period with the least obvious parallels, whereas the last third of the century shows perhaps the greatest sharing of theological tendencies. The climate of philosophical and theological opinion in the early decades of the century in Britain and America was very different from that in Germany. The fertility and liveliness of debate engendered by Kant, Lessing and Herder, by Schleiermacher, Hegel, and Schelling had in fact no counterpart in either England or the United States. And, of course, in the latter nation there was also the special desire to be independent from the influences of the Old World.

Yet the picture is not so simple. In England and America also, though in their own ways and on a different time scale, we see a struggle to bring in the theologically new. If the time of cultural transition which had been so violently signified in Europe by the French Revolution was not widely felt in England until the 1830s, with the passage of the Reform Bill and the coming of Catholic emancipation, England was nevertheless already in a period of rapid (almost revolutionary) social change. And Samuel Taylor Coleridge joined battle with the eighteenth century in a conflict not unlike that in Germany of romanticism and idealism against rationalism (or Hegel and Schleiermacher against supernaturalism). America had had its own revolution and both Germany and the United States were characterized by new and powerful senses of national identity. Pietist and revival influences were potent in all three situations. In Britain and America, the Calvinist-Arminian debate was being carried on, though in both instances this was the death rattle of an old era. That debate in Britain was far overshadowed in significance by a more fundamental conflict of theological world views, and in America it reflected the malaise of New England Calvinism and a turning, under the impact variously of deism, revival, and Unitarianism, to a profound reconstruction of theological foundations, the impact of which would not be fully felt until the middle of the century, notably in the thought of Horace Bushnell.

If we look more closely at the British theological scene at the beginning of the nineteenth century, four principal characteristics stand out. First, the Church of England was marked by an absence of intellectual vitality or excitement. What an earlier historian said about the latter half of the eighteenth century in England applies as well to the beginning of the nineteenth: "Theology was paralyzed. The deists railed no longer; and the orthodox were lapped in drowsy indifference. They boasted of the victory won by their predecessors; but were content on occasion to recapitulate the cut and dried formulas of refutation or to summarize the labours of the earlier inquiries." [1]

Second, rationalism of the more radical sort was present in the materialism of Hartley, for example, or the anarchist reformism of Godwin, but not as a movement of great life and vigor. Third, and much more important religiously, was the evangelical temper and vitality represented by the Methodists, by the beginnings of the great nineteenth-century foreign missionary movement,[2] and by Anglican evangelicals who were deeply concerned with humanitarianism and social reform. But the Methodists produced no important thinker who related their socially profoundly effective revival to the new currents of thought. Nor were the energies of the missionary societies directed to theological reformulation. The great leader of the Anglican evangelicals was William Wilberforce, whose famous "Practical View of the Prevailing Religious Systems in the Higher and Middle Classes in the Country, Contrasted with Real Christian-

1. Sir Leslie Stephen, *History of English Thought in the Eighteenth Century*, 2 vols., 3d ed. (New York, 1902), 1 : 372. Stephen goes on to mark Paley as an exception: "The one divine of brilliant ability was Paley; and Paley's theology escapes, if indeed it escapes, from decay, only because it is frozen. His writing is as clear and as cold as ice."

2. Originating among the Baptists in 1792, this movement had resulted before 1800 in the formation of missionary societies in Scotland, in the Church of England, and in the Netherlands.

ity" (1797) typified the fundamental direction of the evangelicals' interest. Theirs was a practical theology, one of great power and real novelty. But what was new was not any restatement of Christian faith for a new situation, but the understanding of Christian love explicitly as a power of social as well as churchly renewal, with consequences ranging from opposition to the slave trade to the formation of Bible societies.

Fourth, the dominant theological pattern in England was the supernaturalist rationalism of the post-Lockean theology of "evidences"—supremely illustrated in the work of William Paley (1743–1805), his *Natural Theology, or Evidences of the Existence and Attributes of the Deity Collected from the Appearances of Nature* (1802; 20th ed., 1820), for example, and his *Evidences of Christianity* (1794; 15th ed., 1811).[3] This apologetic evidence-theology, which had been spurred to renewal (though hardly reform) by Hume's essay on miracles, still so preoccupied the theological writing of the early nineteenth century that Coleridge's *Aids to Reflection* (1825) at first received little notice in either the popular or the religious press. But in spite of Paley's intellectual gifts—his works are undeniably classics—this was a theology already in a state of *rigor mortis*.

The two really seminal minds, at least in respect of religious thinking, in early nineteenth-century England were to be found outside the ranks of the professional theologians. These were Jeremy Bentham (1748–1832)—legal and social reformer, moral philosopher, founder of utilitarianism—and Samuel Taylor Coleridge—poet, literary critic, famous "talker of Highgate," philosopher, and theologian. John Stuart Mill in his much quoted essays on Bentham and Coleridge (1838 and 1840) wrote that "there is hardly to be found in England an individual of any importance in the world of the mind, who . . . did not first learn to think from one of these two"; and again that "every Englishman of the present day is by implication either a Benthamite or a Coleridgean; holds views of human affairs which can only be proved true on the principles either of Bentham or of Coleridge."[4]

It was Paley, of course, whom Coleridge again and again identified as the theological archenemy. And it was indeed what Paley

---

3. Paley's writings were required reading well through the 19th century in conservative, especially Anglican, circles. The *Natural Theology* has been newly edited by Frederick Ferré (Indianapolis, 1963).

4. *Mill on Bentham and Coleridge*, ed. F. R. Leavis (London, 1950), pp. 39, 102–03.

represented that Coleridge revolted against as both unphilosophical and irreligious.[5] But what Paley exemplified was not far different from the ethical utilitarianism and rationalism of Bentham. Paley also, in his *Principles of Moral and Political Philosophy* (1785) had said that "It is the utility of any moral rule which alone constitutes the obligation of it." [6] His abstract and impersonal, cold and lifeless argumentation, his natural theology, to which Christianity was finally only an appendage, epitomized the same eighteenth-century rationalism that Coleridge had to reject as only "understanding," incapable of perceiving religious truth.

Thus Bentham emerges as the real alternative to Coleridge, the great symbol of what the eighteenth century stood for and therefore of what had to be combated.[7] Although Bentham well deserves to be defended against the oversimplification of which even J. S. Mill was guilty,[8] two themes integral to his philosophy are of decisive importance in contrast to Coleridge. One was the principle of utility itself, the principle (later developed into the idea of the greatest happiness for the greatest number) that every action is to be judged by its tendency to increase or diminish pleasure or happiness. Pleasure and pain are the two sovereign masters that determine what man will do and what he ought to do; they are the only real meaning for good and evil. Utility—in contrast to the so-called principles of asceticism, sympathy and antipathy, and theology—proves to be the only real principle, the actual norm of conduct. The theological or religious sanctions, that is, the sources from which pleasure and pain flow, lose their significance, since we cannot now know the pleasures and pains of a future life, and any present application comes necessarily through the powers of nature. Bentham's philosophy was

5. He wrote in *Aids to Reflection:* "I believe myself bound in conscience to throw the whole force of my intellect in the way of this [Paley's] triumphal car, on which the tutelary genius of modern idolatry is borne, even at the risk of being crushed under the wheels" *(Complete Works,* ed. W. G. T. Shedd, 7 vols. [New York, 1853], 1 : 364. Subsequent references to the *Works* are to this edition).

6. *Works* (Boston, 1811), 3 : 70. For Bentham, see especially the *Introduction to the Principles of Morals and Legislation* (1789).

7. To cite Mill again on the "Germano-Coleridgean" doctrine: "It expresses the revolt of the human mind against the philosophy of the eighteenth century. It is ontological, because that was experimental; conservative, because that was innovative; religious, because that was abstract and metaphysical; poetical, because that was matter-of-fact and prosaic" *(Mill on Bentham and Coleridge,* p. 108). To this summary, one must make two important exceptions for Coleridge: he was metaphysical, and he was theologically innovative.

8. See Mary P. Mack, *Jeremy Bentham, 1748–1792* (New York, 1963), pp. 1–25.

frankly anthropocentric; ontology was for him nearly synonymous with "eudaemonics." His "encyclopedical tree" placed eudaemonics at the apex as the "all-comprehensive name" appropriate to all the human sciences; this was then subdivided into metaphysics and the studies of particular being. Further, pleasure and pain were for Bentham susceptible of being measured in terms of their intensity, duration, certainty or uncertainty, nearness or remoteness, fecundity, purity, and extent.

The idea of measurement in ethics involves the other great theme of Bentham which Coleridge rejected in the eighteenth century's concept of reason. Bentham wanted to create a *science* of morals, which in turn required a new logic, an all-embracing formal analysis with an unambiguous grammar and vocabulary. He never wrote the logic, but his principles of reasoning were clear: his interests were insistently empirical and quantitative; reason proceeded by measurement and analysis, by breaking wholes into parts, and by classification. This quantitative rationalism was also antitraditional. The reform to which Bentham had dedicated himself from his youth (and which sprang in part out of his revulsion from religion) required a fresh beginning, with empirical and "rational" considerations of what is beneficial for man. Insofar as Bentham could look back to the religious tradition for any prior apprehension of truth, he had to go behind both the medieval and the Protestant tradition, back to Jesus within the New Testament. In his book *Not Paul, but Jesus* (1823) it was the Jesus of the Golden Rule, the great utilitarian, the sober seeker for the happiness of men, who was affirmed.

In contrast to the enthusiastically anthropocentric rationalism of Bentham, then, as well as to the "irreligion" of Paley's rationalism, Coleridge may be seen as the real turning point into the theology of the nineteenth century. He was as important for British and American thought as were Schleiermacher and Hegel, notably through his most famous "disciple" F. D. Maurice, along with Julius Hare, Edward Irving, James Martineau, John Sterling, Thomas Carlyle, and P. T. Forsyth in England, and through Horace Bushnell, sometimes called the "liberalizer" of American theology.[9] In his thought he was related to Kant, Schelling, and Jacobi, as well as to romanticism, and he had independent roots among the Cambridge Platonists, but his culminating idea of the fidelity of reason cannot be derived from

9. And see the preliminary essay by James Marsh in the first American edition of the *Aids* (1829).

any of these. In particular, he stands alongside Schleiermacher, both like him and in contrast to him, in offering a fresh answer to the question of the possibility of theology. Mark Pattison, in *Essays and Reviews,* could write that "theology had almost died out when it received a new impulse and a new direction from Coleridge." [10]

Coleridge was remarkably sensitive to the movements of his time, and prior to his decisive meeting with Wordsworth (1795) and the turn to poetry rather than politics, he had gone through an intellectual odyssey that included being a materialist and necessitarian of the school of Hartley, a unitarian of the school of Priestly, and a follower of Godwin with enthusiasm for French Republicanism.[11] His mature religious ideas were set forth in the periodical *The Friend* (1809–10, later revised in book form), in the *Biographia Literaria* (1817), in *On the Constitution of Church and State* (1830), and above all in *Aids to Reflection* (1825) and the posthumously published *Confessions of an Enquiring Spirit* (1840).[12] Out of the mostly fragmentary forms of expression, we may select four chief themes: the problem of faith and reason (i.e. the possibility of theology), the idea of God, the ideas of the Christian Church and the national church, and the authority of the Bible.

THE RATIONAL CHARACTER OF FAITH

Coleridge was above all absorbed by the question of the nature of religious knowing, which was for him a problem of the rational character of faith and of the faithful character of true reason. More than in doctrinal formulations, he was interested in the process of

10. Leipzig ed., 1862, p. 236.

11. "I go farther than Hartley, and believe the corporeality of *thought,* namely, that it is motion" (Coleridge to Southey, 11 December 1794, cited in Basil Willey, *Nineteenth Century Studies* [London, 1949], p. 5). Yet one may argue, with Willey, that "the enthusiasms of this period were largely froth upon his mind's surface; the deeper currents of his nature ran steadily forwards all the while, and were even then not wholly concealed"; and that "the seminal principle, the original impulse, which was in him from childhood, was sense of the Whole as a living unity, a sense of God in all and all in God, a faith in a divine spiritual activity as the ground of all existence." As Coleridge wrote, "My mind feels as if it ached to behold and know something *great,* something *one* and *indivisible*" (Willey, pp. 6, 4).

12. Among the most useful interpretations of Coleridge's theological thought are J. Robert Barth, *Coleridge and Christian Doctrine* (Cambridge, Mass., 1969); James D. Boulger, *Coleridge as Religious Thinker* (New Haven, 1961); John H. Muirhead, *Coleridge as Philosopher* (New York, 1930); and the brilliant chapter in Basil Willey's *Nineteenth Century Studies.* The notebooks are being published under the editorship of Kathleen Coburn (New York, 1957–).

religious thinking, and this was his theme in the *Aids to Reflection*.[13] There were two major options that had to be rejected. One was the religious rationalism that had been revived as the reply to Hume, most disastrously in Paley (and in another way in the Scottish common sense philosophy). For Coleridge, Kant made clear that the metaphysical problems of God and the soul cannot be resolved by the categories of pure or scientific reason. But the opposition to theological rationalism was not based primarily on Kant. Kant made its weaknesses evident, but more important were the demands of genuine *religious* knowing—and in general Coleridge's arguments

13. Coleridge's concept of Reason has often been interpreted as largely derived from German idealism, or as a combination of idealism with a Platonism taken over the Cambridge divines of the 17th century. It is quite true that Coleridge was deeply influenced by Kant, Schelling, and Jacobi—and he had also read Eichorn and Schleiermacher and many other German thinkers. But to account for Coleridge by such influences is a serious distortion. Equally important for Coleridge's religious thought were three quite different bases in his own existence. One was the quality of personal religion, in which prayer and the struggle of sin and redemption were at the center. For Coleridge, in contrast to Hegel, "let us pray" represented a higher level of action than "let us think about God"; the relationship with reality in prayer was too actual to be identified with mere meditation. Similarly, moral experience was a datum more basic than merely phenomenal. Out of his own struggle, especially with opium addiction, Coleridge understood the possibility that conscience can be killed in a man. He knew the reality of remorse, the originality of sin in the self as a conscientious being—and thus the great need and hunger in man that cries out for salvation.

Second, he had a deep sense of social need and a hope for the revitalization of English society and the church—a cause which he wanted to serve (hence, especially, *The Constitution of Church and State*). Third, Coleridge's religious thinking developed from a position within the historical Christian faith. He had little interest in religiousness in general. His thought in *Aids to Reflection* moves from the beginning toward the concluding Aphorisms on Spiritual Religion (which for him meant Christianity). Coleridge's interest is in giving "a reason of his faith" (first Aphorism on Spiritual Religion), not cutting a faith to suit some other reason. It is in the context of this life of Christianity in his own existence that the famous Aphorism 25 (of the Moral and Religious Aphorisms) needs to be understood: "He who begins by loving Christianity better than truth, will proceed by loving his own sect or church better than Christianity, and end in loving himself better than all." This was for Coleridge a freedom grounded in faith rather than in uncertainty or disbelief. (Thus his own aphorism was added to sayings drawn from Leighton, in the preceding aphorism: "He never truly believed, who was not first made sensible and convinced of unbelief. Never be afraid to doubt, if only you have the disposition to believe, and doubt in order that you may end in believing the Truth.") In a similar vein, another of J. S. Mill's comments on the difference between Bentham and Coleridge is relevant. For Bentham, said Mill, the question was always "Is it true?"—and if it did not directly conform to his idea of truth, that was the end of inquiry. For Coleridge the great question was "What is the meaning of it?"—since anything that had been so much believed by thoughtful men and generations had to be accounted for (cf. *Mill on Bentham and Coleridge*, pp. 99–100).

for the "idealism" drawn from the Cambridge Platonists and German philosophy were supports for his conviction of the shallowness and / or actual irreligion of rationalism, orthodoxy, and evangelicalism. "Christianity is not a theory, or a speculation; but a life—not a philosophy of life, but a life and a living process." [14] On the other hand, Coleridge vigorously combated the nonrational idea of faith in both Schleiermacher and the evangelicals. It was not enough to assert "I have felt" and to insist that the immediacy of religious experience refutes all doubters. The internal evidence of the spirit and the will and the sense of need and redemption are the starting point, but emotionalism is no answer to the questions of reason. No more than Pascal (who at more than one point must be recalled in connection with Coleridge) was Coleridge satisfied simply to say "the heart has reasons which the reason does not know." Faith must be a reasoning faith, and reason must be understood more deeply than by either rationalism or the religion of the heart. There are mysteries in Christianity, but these are "reason in its highest form of self-affirmation." [15]

Coleridge's own program may be described in four ascending levels of argument. The first is his distinction between "Reason" and "Understanding." These are different in kind. "Reason is the power of universal and necessary convictions, the source and substance of truths above sense, and having their evidence in themselves. . . . On the other hand, the judgments of the Understanding are binding only in relation to the objects of our senses, which

14. Cf. Aphorism on Spiritual Religion 7 (*Works*, 1 : 233).

15. Preface to *Aids*, *Works*, 1 : 115. A similar opposition to religious rationalism, though without the depth of Coleridge's idea of reasoning faith, was appearing almost concurrently in Thomas Erskine (1788–1870), an influential figure in the 19th-century changes within Scottish Calvinism (see his *Remarks on the Internal Evidence for the Truth of Revealed Religion* [1820], *An Essay on Faith* [1822], *The Unconditional Freeness of the Gospel* [1828], and *The Brazen Serpent* [1831]; the first three of these were translated into French, and the *Remarks* also into German). Erskine's special theme was the "internal aspect," the religion of the heart and the conscience, the direct connection between believing in doctrines and being shaped toward the moral character they commend, the testimony of truth to the conscience (a connection essential to the reasonableness of religion). Through his own shift to the "Christian consciousness," Erskine marked a theological transition not unlike that of Schleiermacher and Coleridge, though apparently independent from both. In his idea that pardon is already actual and universal, and that men do not need forgiveness (since they already have it) but rather the awareness of it (cf. *The Unconditional Freeness* and *The Brazen Serpent*), Erskine was of particular importance both for Macleod Campbell's classic reformulation, *The Nature of the Atonement* (1856), and for F. D. Maurice, though the extent of direct influence on the formation of Maurice's view is unclear.

we reflect under the forms of the understanding. It is, as Leighton rightly defines it, 'the faculty judging according to sense.' " [16] There is, then, spiritual truth to be apprehended—laws and principles that exist outside the mind, and supremely the personal reality of God, in which Truth rests. To them are related Ideas, laws contemplated in the mind, intuitions that are not sensuous. But spiritual reality cannot be known by the understanding. Understanding is directed to the phenomenal world of sense-perception, arranging and generalizing therein. It is "the science of phenomena," it is (when it usurps the role of reason) the "mind of the flesh," it is "discursive," "the faculty of reflection," and it "refers to some other faculty as its ultimate authority." [17] Understanding, simply, is the "scientific" reasoning of Bentham and Paley, the kind of thinking that separates, analyzes, measures, classifies, knows in terms of cause and effect, is concerned with means rather than ends. Within its proper limits this is an indispensable kind of thinking—for science, for much of the routine of life, for all knowledge of the finite.[18] But when only this sort of thinking is recognized, when it pretends to be all, then life, philosophy and religion are denied. And that was the consequence of the eighteenth century: the philosophy of death, "materialism, determinism, atheism, utilitarianism, the 'godless revolution,' 'moral science exploded as mystic jargon,' the 'mysteries of religion cut and squared for the comprehension of the understanding,' 'imagination excluded from poesy.' " [19]

But there is also a knowledge of that with which the self as self is concerned, an intuition of ourselves as related to the whole as a living reality, "something one and indivisible," a knowing that is religious and poetic, a seeing that goes beyond space and time. This is Reason, whose "proper objects . . . do not appertain to the world

16. Aphorism on Spiritual Religion 7. The distinction is obviously related to (and perhaps derived from) Kant's distinction between understanding and reason, but Coleridge differed greatly from Kant in his view of reason's capacity to lay hold, in *knowledge*, of spiritual realities. He was closer to Jacobi (see *Works* 2 : 144), but even more he reached back to the realism of the Cambridge Platonists, though that also was fundamentally qualified in his conceptions.

17. Aphorism on Spiritual Religion 8.

18. Understanding is the "faculty of the finite" which "reduces the confused impressions of sense to their essential forms—quantity, quality, relation, and in these action and reaction, cause and effect, and the like; thus raises the materials furnished by the senses and sensation into objects of reflection, and so makes experience possible. Without it, man's representative powers would be a delirium, a chaos, a scudding cloudage of shapes" (*Literary Remains*, ed. H. N. Coleridge [1836–39], pp. 244–51).

19. Willey, *Nineteenth Century Studies*, p. 29.

of the senses, inward or outward." It is the "organ of the supersensuous," the faculty of the infinite, the knowledge "of the laws of the whole considered as one." This power, which is found only within (and as the self is fully engaged in the search for truth) is alone capable of discernment of "spiritual objects, the universal, the eternal, and the necessary." [20]

Second, reason involves imagination. Though Coleridge drew back from a tendency at one point simply to identify imagination with the higher reason,[21] the imaginative process must be considered an enduring constituent in his idea of reason. The relation of reason to understanding was much like the relation of imagination to fancy in Coleridge's literary theory. Imagination stands above the mind of the flesh. It is a creative act of the self. The "primary imagination" is "the living Power and prime Agent of all human Perception, and as a repetition of the finite mind of the eternal act of creation in the infinite I AM." It denoted the genuine activity of the mind in knowing (in contrast to the mind's supposed passivity, in the Lockean psychology). Equally important, imagination is like (and is perhaps even a dimension of) reason in its special function of seeing the whole in the parts and comprehending the parts as a whole. In the way it makes things real to the self it allows objects to be living (does not kill them by dissection and analysis) and it embraces the interpenetration of the opposites or polarities of existence in man and in nature.[22] Further, imagination has the power to identify with the reality beyond the senses, and thus to bring together the opposites of subject and object. In particular the knowledge of other selves and of God cannot take place through the abstraction and measurement of the understanding, but only through an imaginative act in which there is creative interchange.

Third, reason is intrinsically moral. It includes conscience or the moral sense. It is a will for the good quite as much as it is cognition of being. Here Coleridge drew heavily upon Kant's distinction of

---

20. *The Friend, Works,* 2: 144.

21. See Boulger, *Coleridge as Religious Thinker,* pp. 105 ff. and, for another point of view, I. A. Richards, *Coleridge on Imagination* (New York, 1935).

22. So the stories in the Scriptures "are the living educts of the imagination; of that reconciling and mediatory power, which incorporating the reason in images of the sense, and organizing (as it were) the flux of the senses by the permanent and self-circling energies of the reason, gives birth to a system of symbols, harmonious in themselves, and consubstantial with the truths of which they are conductors" (Lay Sermon, 1816, *Works,* 1 : 436.

the theoretical and the practical reason—though his conclusion was different from the "postulation" of God, freedom and immortality. Reason "contemplated distinctively in reference to formal (or abstract) truth, . . . is the Speculative Reason; but in reference to actual (or moral) truth, as the fountain of ideas and the light of the conscience, we name it the Practical Reason." [23] Conscience or the practical reason can be called in fact the chief witness to spiritual realities. Above all, God gave us conscience. "But what are my metaphysics?—merely the referring of the mind to its own consciousness for truths indispensable to its own happiness." [24] The authority of the conscience is direct and indisputable. Conscience "unconditionally commands us to attribute Reality and actual Existence to those Ideas, and those only without which the conscience itself would be baseless and contradictory, to the ideas of the soul, of free will, of immortality, and of God" [25]—to which ideas one should, for Coleridge, also add original sin and the need for redemption (cf. *Aids to Reflection*). These ideas are not necessary in the sense of being logically necessitated, but to reject them is to narrow and debase reason. They can be denied, but no good man will deny them. Even before he encountered Kant, Coleridge says, he had become persuaded of this point:

> I became convinced, that religion, as both the cornerstone and the keystone of morality, must have a *moral* origin; so far at least, that the evidence of its doctrines could not, like the truths of abstract science, be wholly independent of the will. It were therefore to be expected, that its *fundamental* truth would be such as MIGHT be denied; though only by the fool, and even by the fool from the madness of the heart alone.[26]

The practical reason is, of course, inseparable from the will. Conscience can be described as the point of synthesis of reason and

23. Aphorism on Spiritual Religion 8, *Works*, 1 : 241–42.

24. *The Friend*, *Works*, 2 : 103. In his *Confessio Fidei* (1816) Coleridge began "I believe that I am a free agent, inasmuch as, and so far as, I have a will. . . . Likewise that I possess reason, or a law of right and wrong, which, uniting with my sense of moral responsibility, constitutes the voice of conscience. Hence it becomes my absolute duty to believe, and I do believe, that there is a God" (*Works*, 5 : 15).

25. *The Friend*, Works, 2 : 106.

26. *Biographia Literaria*, in D. A. Stauffer, ed., *Selected Poetry and Prose of S. T. Coleridge* (New York, 1951), p. 212.

will. But this involves the fourth and highest level in Coleridge's
understanding of Reason,[27] a level at which Reason and Faith become one, where Reason is fidelity. Reason itself requires an act of
will, a venturing forth, a throwing of oneself into the act of apprehension of spiritual truth. Just as faith must give a reasoned account
of itself, so a reason that has no fidelity in it is unfaithful to Reason.
Only at this level do the deepest differences of Coleridge's thought
from supernatural rationalism emerge—as do also his differences
from Schleiermacher, Hegel, Kant, and Schelling. "Christianity is
not a theory or a speculation . . . but a life and a living process."
Thus every theology of evidences (or Hegelian proof) is both useless
and a misunderstanding; it is irreligious. The life of faith cannot be
"intellectually more evident" than the law of conscience commands
"without becoming morally less effective; without counteracting its
own end by sacrificing the *life* of faith to the cold mechanism of a
worthless because compulsory assent." [28] The faithful reason—or the
faith that exists in the synthesis of Reason and Will [29]—is characterized by a real venture (Pascal's wager must be recalled, and William
James's "will to believe" is anticipated; just as a contrast must be
drawn with Schleiermacher's feeling of utter dependence, which
notably lacked the biblical note of faith as faithfulness). In the conception of theological foundations, there is a logical movement in
Coleridge's thought from the acknowledged wants or religious needs
of men, through the demands of the moral sense, to the injunction:
"Try it!" The whole program of the *Aids to Reflection,* from "prudential Aphorisms" to "Moral and Religious Aphorisms" to "Aphorisms on Spiritual Religion," is designed to elicit a kind of religious thinking which recognizes that the culminating test is of an
experimental, even pragmatic, sort. As faith is properly the fidelity
of man to God, so to the question "How is Christianity to be
proved?" Coleridge finally offered the answer "Try it!" [30] Courage
is a necessary means of laying hold of the spiritual truth. This did
not of course mean discarding everything else that had to be said

27. Thus in Introductory Aphorism 32 of *Aids to Reflection,* Coleridge distinguished
the "spiritual" faculty from the moral, indicating that the prudential aphorisms
correspond "to the sense and the understanding; the moral to the heart and the
conscience; the spiritual to the will and the reason."

28. *Biographia Literaria,* p. 212.

29. See, e.g. *Works,* 1 : 195–97, 233–35.

30. Aphorism on Spiritual Religion 7, *Works,* 1 : 231, 233.

about religious knowing; rather it was an integral element in the entire way in which one "must give a reason of his faith." [31]

THE IDEA OF GOD

Coleridge's idea of God was never fully worked out, though his published and unpublished works are filled with speculations about the nature of God and the Trinity. Rather, he kept coming back again and again to the question of how God is known, that is, to the nature of religious thinking. Yet two themes constantly interplay in his conception of God, involving both his view of the basis for theology and his relation to post-Kantian idealism. On the one hand, Coleridge shared fully the idealist objection to orthodoxy's anthropomorphism and supernaturalism and especially to deism's mechanical and absentee God. This reinforced the sense of striving that he says was in him from childhood, the sense of the whole and of unity, of "God in all and all in God." "My mind," he said, "feels as if it ached to behold and know something *great,* something *one* and *indivisible.*" Thus Spinoza's "intellectual love of God," and Schelling's "intellectual vision" of God were truer than any deism or Unitarianism. God is the superindividual self, the ground of all the vastness of existence. He is the absolute Will, which is identical with the universal Reason. "The superessential Will is the Root of all the ground, Source and Antecedent of all Reality—Eternal Antecedent and Co-eternal Being, the unnameable." [32]

But on the other hand—and here Coleridge parted from Spinoza and Schelling, and also from Schleiermacher—Absolute Will must not be understood in a way that excludes the personality of God or identifies deity with the totality of nature. Pantheism and atheism come to the same thing. A less than personal God is religiously in-

---

31. Aphorism on Spiritual Religion 1, *Works,* 1 : 199. A further element in the necessity of this experiential verification was, for Coleridge, the incapacity of language to express fully spiritual truth. "Religion necessarily, as to its main and proper doctrines, consists of ideas, that is, spiritual truths that can only be spiritually discerned, and to the expression of which words are necessarily inadequate, and must be used by accommodation. Hence the absolute indispensability of a Christian life, with its conflicts and inward experiences, which alone can make a man to answer to an opponent, who charges one doctrine as contradictory to another, 'Yes! it is a contradiction in terms; but nevertheless so it is, and both are true, nay, parts of the same truth' " (*Literary Remains, Works,* 5 : 307–08).

32. Notebook 37, ff. 34ʳ–34ᵛ. Cf. Boulger, *Coleridge as Religious Thinker,* p. 127 and the whole of chap. 4, where he draws extensively on the Notebooks in showing Coleridge's attempts to describe God.

sufficient.[33] Thus Coleridge spoke of the "personeity" of God, as a way of establishing the "diversity" of the Creator from the whole of his creation.[34] That personal relationship of distinction and nearness is essential to moral experience, to obedience and fidelity and the will in man. God must be conceived as personal (or superpersonal) because the center of religion, or its focus, is prayer, a real "religious intercommunion between man and his Maker." The theological formulation must be accountable, therefore, to the fact that religion is finally "the relation of a Will to a Will, the Will in each instance being *deeper* than Reason, of a Person to a Person." [35]

CHURCH AND NATION

The hunger for unity that was expressed in Coleridge's ideas of faith and of God emerged also in his social thought, where an opposition to sectarianism and "parties" and an antipathy to mere toleration at the expense of principle was joined to a great loyalty both to universal Christianity (for him, Christianity alone rises to the universal) and to the nation (the "people" was not to be swallowed up in a cosmopolitanism of the race).

The immediate point of departure for Coleridge's chief work in this area was the Catholic Emancipation Act of 1829, which led him to develop his ideas of the state, the constitution, and the church in relation to the history of England.[36] Most distinctive in this reflection was Coleridge's concept of the "national church" or the "clerisy," which is the "third estate" of the realm and whose object is "to secure and improve that civilization without which the nation could be neither permanent nor progressive" (*CS*, p. 52). This is something that belongs to the essential elements and proper ordering of any national life. Its "paramount end and purpose . . . is the continued and progressive civilization of the community" (*CS*, p. 97). It is not identical with the ecclesiastical in the common sense of

33. "For a very long time, indeed, I could not reconcile personality with infinity; and my head was with Spinoza, though my whole heart remained with Paul and John" (*Biographia Literaria*, p. 211).

34. He also, most extensively in the Notebooks and the fragmentary *Opus Maximum*, developed formulations of trinitarian doctrine as expressing personeity and providing the only rational alternative to pantheism and atheism.

35. Notebook 26, ff. 52ᵛ–53; cf. Boulger, *Coleridge as Religious Thinker*, p. 168.

36. *On the Constitution of the Church and State According to the Idea of Each* (1830), *Works*, 6 : 29–129. Subsequent references to *Church and State* (*CS*) are cited by page number in the text. For an analysis of Coleridge's political theory, see David P. Calleo, *Coleridge and the Idea of the Modern State* (New Haven, 1966).

that term, but draws rather on the "original and proper sense" of "clergy." "The Clerisy of the nation, . . . in its primary acceptation and original intention, comprehended the learned of all denominations, the sages and professors of the law and jurisprudence, of medicine and physiology, of music, of military and civil architecture, of the physical sciences, . . . in short, all the so-called liberal arts and sciences, the possession and application of which constitute the civilization of a country, as well as the theological." [37] The theological is properly at the head, because "under the name of theology or divinity were contained the interpretation of languages, . . . of ethical science, in relation to the rights and duties of men . . . and lastly, the ground-knowledge, the *prima scientia* . . . the doctrine and discipline of ideas" (*CS*, pp. 53–54).

The national church is in effect a "great national guild of the learned professions," [38] and England is to be thankful for having from the beginning had such a church. This is a treasure to be retained. But the national church is not to be confused with the Christian Church (or with Christianity). To be sure, Christianity supports and gives life to the national church, but that can be called a "blessed accident," in the sense that "Christianity is an aid and instrument, which no State or realm could have produced out of its own elements, which no State had a right to expect. It was, most awfully, a *God-send*" (*CS*, p. 60). There can be a national church without Christianity, and the state for its own good needs to support the clerisy, and thus social unity, even though Christianity does prove at the same time to be the greatest invigoration and nourishment of the national church.

The Christian Church, in contrast, has four essential distinguishing characteristics. (1) It is "no state, kingdom, or realm of this world; nor is it an estate of any such realm . . . but it is the appointed opposite to them all collectively—the sustaining, correcting, befriending opposite of the World." It asks and demands of the state "only protection and to be let alone, i.e. nothing that citizens cannot

37. *CS*, p. 53. The idea of the national church, as of the state or anything else, is not an abstraction or a generalization from particulars, but "is given by the knowledge of its ultimate aim" (*CS*, p. 30). It should be added that there were for Coleridge two "absolute disqualifications" for service in the national church: "allegiance to a foreign power, or an acknowledgment of any other visible head of the Church but our sovereign lord the King; and compulsory celibacy in connection with, and dependence on, a foreign and extra-national head" (*CS*, p. 97).

38. Calleo, *Coleridge and the Modern State*, p. 96.

already demand as citizens" (*CS*, p. 98). (2) The Christian Church is not a "secret community." It is not invisible, not the kingdom of God within, but quite visible, a city on a hill, "an institution consisting of visible and public communities. In one sentence it is the Church visible and militant under Christ" (*CS*, p. 99). (3) The Christian Church is thus not the "counterpole to any particular State," not the church in "church and state." It has "no Nationality entrusted to its charge." Its contrast is the "World." It is to exist in every state and country. Therefore the first and second characteristics require effectuation by the third: "namely, the absence of any visible head or sovereign, and by the nonexistence, nay the utter preclusion, of any local or personal center of unity, of any single source of universal power" (*CS*, p. 100). (4) It follows from the first and third characteristics, that the church is truly universal—"neither Anglican, Gallican, nor Roman, neither Latin nor Greek." Rather, "through the presence of its only Head and Sovereign, entire in each and one in all, the Church Universal is spiritually perfect in every true Church" (*CS*, pp. 104, 105).

Finally, then, Coleridge could thank God for the existence of "a Catholic and Apostolic Church in England." And he could be grateful also "for the constitutional and ancestral Church of England," for that "true Church of England" which "is the National Church or Clerisy" (*CS*, p. 105). The Church of England was certainly to be criticized, but at the same time it was to be more highly praised than any other, for its exemplars of genius and learning, its toleration (in contrast to the sectarianism of Roman Christianity), its apostolic faith, and its liturgical forms. And church establishment was to be recognized as a bulwark of toleration, as well as, in the case of England, a support for the national church. For if the Church of England were to be disestablished, the idea of a national church would wither.

THE AUTHORITY OF SCRIPTURE

By the time of Coleridge's death, the storm of biblical criticism had not yet broken over England. Though rumblings of the developments in Germany had been heard, it was not really until the publication of *Essays and Reviews* in 1860 that extensive and open debate took place.[39] Until the mid-century, there seemed almost to be a

39. In spite of the fact that a translation of the fourth edition of Strauss's *Leben Jesu* was published in 1846 by Marian Evans (who later became more widely known

"conspiracy of silence." When the major changes in biblical studies did come, however, they were deeply under the influence of perspectives that Coleridge had earlier developed. These views were mediated especially by F. D. Maurice; they were operative in the "Cambridge triumvirate," B. F. Westcott, J. B. Lightfoot, and F. J. A. Hort; and they were taken up in the whole program of British and American liberal theology at the end of the nineteenth century.

Coleridge's ideas were most succinctly set forth in the form of seven letters which he had planned should comprise one of several disquisitions to supplement *Aids to Reflection,* and which were published posthumously, in 1840, under the title *Confessions of an Inquiring Spirit* (2d ed. 1849, 3d ed. 1853).

Just as Coleridge attacked the theology of evidences as a fundamental violation of the nature of Christianity and proposed a radically different approach to the question of religious truth, so he rejected with equal vigor what he called bibliolatry (probably taking the term from Lessing); and he offered a new conception of biblical authority and inspiration. Coleridge was well in touch with biblical scholarship on the Continent: he had read Eichorn and Reimarus, Lessing and Schleiermacher—and he seems to have been particularly indebted to Lessing. But he had no interest in pursuing detailed biblical-critical investigations himself, though his notebooks were filled with biblical commentary. His concern was rather with restatement of the principle of biblical truth, which would actually exhibit its authority in the face of both rationalist challenge and orthodox misconstruction. The great enemy, as Coleridge identified it in the *Confessions,* was in fact the "orthodox" doctrine of infallibility. Thus he proposed to answer two questions:

1. Is it necessary, or expedient, to insist on the belief of the divine origin and authority of all, and every part of the Canonical Books as the condition, or first principle, of Christian Faith?
2. Or, may not the due appreciation of the Scriptures collectively be more safely relied on as the result and consequence of the belief in Christ; the gradual increase—in respect of particular passages— of our spiritual discernment of their truth and authority supply-

---

as a novelist under the pseudonym George Eliot). For the most part, as Willey phrased it, the English divines in the first part of the century "recoiled into a more determined insularity. Van Mildert, in his Bampton Lectures (1814), said that acceptance of any biblical 'criticism' indicated moral defectiveness, unsoundness of faith, and disloyalty to the Church" (*Nineteenth Century Studies,* p. 39).

ing a test and measure of our own growth and progress as individual believers, without the servile fear that prevents or overclouds the free honour which cometh from love? [1 John 4 : 18] [40]

Christianity cannot be identified with the contents of the Bible, for though the Bible "contains the religion of Christians," it is not the case that "whatever is contained in the Bible is the Christian religion" (*Conf.*, p. 61). Nor can anything be established by the claim of biblical inerrancy. This is not primarily because of the weakness of the attempts to defend such a view of Scripture—"the forced and fantastic interpretations," "the literal rendering of Scripture in passages, which the number and variety of images employed in different places, to express one and the same verity, plainly mark out for figurative," or the strange and unparalleled "practice of bringing together into logical dependency detached sentences from books composed at the distance of centuries, nay, sometimes a millennium, from each other, under different dispensations, and for different objects" (*Conf.*, pp. 58–59). Much more, the notion of the dictation of the Scriptures by an infallible intelligence violates the living character of revelation and faith. "The doctrine in question petrifies at once the whole body of Holy Writ. . . . This breathing organism, this glorious *panharmonicon*, which I had seen stand on its feet as a man, and with a man's voice given to it, the doctrine in question turns at once into a colossal Memnon's head, a hollow passage for a voice, a voice that mocks the voices of many men, and speaks in their names, and yet is but one voice and the same; and no man uttered it, and never in a human heart was it conceived" (*Conf.*, pp. 51–52).

The authority of the Bible needs no defense or prior establishment just because Scripture is its own sufficient evidence when it is approached in the right way, with a humble spirit that is hungering and thirsting after righteousness. To the one who comes to the Bible with a sense of need and manifold imperfection it will be an organ of living truth; he will find in it copious sources of the bread of life. The Bible is not to be thought true and holy and unquestion-

40. *Confessions of an Inquiring Spirit*, ed. H. StJ. Hart (London, 1956), p. 38. With the first part of the second question, one must compare § 128 of Schleiermacher's *Glaubenslehre*: "The authority of Holy Scripture cannot be the foundation of faith in Christ; rather must the latter be presupposed before a peculiar authority can be granted to Holy Scripture." Whether Coleridge had Schleiermacher's view in mind is not clear. Subsequent references to the *Confessions* (*Conf.*) are cited by page number in the text.

able because we already believe it to be the Word of God; rather "the Bible, considered in reference to its declared ends and purposes, is true and holy, and for all who seek truth with humble spirits an unquestionable guide, and therefore it is the Word of God" (*Conf.*, p. 68).

That is to say, further, that no "evidence" of authority or truth is to be found apart from human need. The proof of the divine authority of the "truth revealed through Christ" is "in its fitness to our nature and needs; the clearness and cogency of this proof being proportionate to the degree of self-knowledge in each individual hearer" (*Conf.*, p. 64). In that assertion, Coleridge did not quite go to the point of identifying the criteria of religious truth simply with man's apprehension of his spiritual wants (and thus of opening the way to thorough subjectivism). Rather, he was echoing one of the fundamental themes of his criticism of the theology of evidences in *Aids to Reflection:*

> Evidences of Christianity! I am weary of the word. Make a man feel the want of it; rouse him, if you can, to the self-knowledge of his need of it; and you may safely trust it to its own Evidence.[41]

This truth is not to be "proved" or even apprehended or understood apart from self-knowledge. The pragmatic, existential character of the "Try it!" is implicit. The right view of the authority of Scripture and the right idea of the nature of faith must here come together. In both respects Coleridge brought to vivid expression the Socratic turn to the self in nineteenth-century theology. What most distinguished his own account of the venture of faith, however, was his effort to explicate the rationality of it, to show that this venture is neither against nor beyond nor apart from reason, but is reason's own highest moment.

41. *Works,* 1 : 363.

6

God's Moral Government or Man's Goodness:

Taylor and Channing

Theological change in America in the first third of the nineteenth century was above all represented by Nathaniel William Taylor (1786–1858), who as professor at Yale shaped the so-called New Haven theology, and William Ellery Channing (1780–1842), who became the symbol of American Unitarianism.[1] The kinds of transition embodied in their work did not at all involve a reordering of the theological enterprise comparable to the work of Schleiermacher or Hegel or Coleridge. That sort of rebuilding was to appear definitely only in the following generation, with Emerson and Bushnell. Through the struggle of Taylor and Channing, the problem of the possibility of theology was defined quite differently than it had been in Europe; there was much more continuity with the eighteenth century in the issues debated and the bases of argument. The move into the nineteenth century was thus begun only hesitantly; yet it was a definite movement away from the old theological order.

Three aspects of the American religious scene at the turn of the new century need particularly to be kept in mind.[2] First, it was the time of national origins. Religious hopes and perspectives had played a major role from the beginning of the settlement of the New World. Now, following the American Revolution, a religious and cultural independence was also being declared; Channing's plea for cultural

1. One might also think of the biblical scholars Moses Stuart, who taught at Andover Seminary from 1810–48, and his student Josiah W. Gibbs, who taught Hebrew and Sacred Literature at Yale (with Taylor), 1824–61—both of whom were informed concerning contemporary German theology. Stuart, for example, translated and wrote a significant and sympathetic introduction to Schleiermacher's long essay on the Trinity. Both men influenced Horace Bushnell. But Stuart was on the whole more a defender of orthodoxy than Taylor, and Gibbs was widely felt to be theologically indecisive.

2. For a general background, see H. S. Smith, R. T. Handy, and L. A. Loetscher, *American Christianity*, vol. 1 (New York, 1960); W. S. Hudson, *American Protestantism* (Chicago, 1961), and H. R. Niebuhr, *The Kingdom of God in America* (New York, 1937).

freedom in his "Remarks on National Literature" (1830) is an example of this trend. American Christianity entered a new stage in the attempt to develop a Christian culture. Two important indigenous shaping forces were the revivals and, with much agonizing, the new relations of church and state following ecclesiastical disestablishment in Connecticut in 1818. It was a time both of construction and of provincialism. The European influences were not those of Kant or the romantics, but of the French rationalists and the "safe" Scottish common sense realism,[3] though American students did begin to go to Germany after 1815.

Second, the old theological order was essentially that of the Calvinist tradition, imbued from the days of the Puritan settlements with the idea of an intensely personal religion, in which sound theology is conjoined with deep emotion and with pragmatic interests in the formation of culture. This theology had been magnificently restated, focused, and transmitted in the second half of the eighteenth century by Jonathan Edwards. In spite of the presence of the Anglicans and Quakers, and more recently the Methodists—thus the small threat of "Arminianism"—and in spite of the "liberal" party out of which emerged Unitarianism, it was Calvinist orthodoxy that in 1800 still dominated American theology. This theology was shared by Congregationalists and Presbyterians (and with less uniformity by Baptists), and it had its center in New England. Following Edwards and the debates over revivals in the Great Awakening, the orthodox tradition was characterized by an intensive (even if finally not very interesting) development involving (a) the "New Divinity," or Consistent Calvinists as they preferred to be thought of, led by Joseph Bellamy and Samuel Hopkins, who undertook to uphold a thoroughly articulated and consistent Edwardsean view of divine sovereignty, of sin and redemption; and (b) the "Old Calvinists" (including N. W. Taylor's father, Nathanael), who were less concerned to refer everything so strictly to divine agency and who were emotionally and theologically more sympathetic to revivals, favoring the use of "means" (e.g. prayer and Scripture reading) by sinners for their conversion. The impact of these debates had lessened with the waning of religious enthusiasm after the Great Awakening and during the Revolution, though the issues recurred with the later revivals.

3. See Sydney E. Ahlstrom, "The Scottish Philosophy and American Theology," *Church History* 24, no. 3 (September 1955).

A third determining element at the beginning of the century was the widespread resurgence of revivals in the Atlantic seaboard states where they emerged especially in the colleges, and on the western frontier. Their spirit was continuous, of course, with the characteristic American emphasis on personal (even individualistic) religious experience and its immediate expression in practical life; and the revivals were also supported by the influence of a popular "romanticist" spirit that stressed feeling. But they were particularly viewed as counterattacks against the postrevolutionary trend toward irreligion and rationalism.[4] This was exactly the purpose of Timothy Dwight, president of Yale College, grandson of Edwards, and mentor of Taylor, who by 1802 had begun a major revival among Yale students. For Dwight, revival meant the defense of "true religion" (along with good morals, sound government, and the established church) against "French atheism" and infidelity, with its logical outcome in Jacobism. From Dwight, the succession in intellectual leadership of the movement passed to his students Taylor and Lyman Beecher, who were very close in theological outlook, and in the 1830s to Charles G. Finney, to whose theology revival was utterly central.[5]

Both the common background in "orthodox Calvinism" and the revivals are signs of the relatively unified (though not uniform) character of American Christianity at the beginning of the century. In spite of theological differences, the churches cooperated freely in the revivals and also in the formation of missionary and bible societies. Denominational or confessional rivalries were much less acute in the early 1800s than they were to become at mid-century.

Against this background, Taylor and Channing emerge as the

4. Actually, the rationalist currents of thought seem to have had less effect in the United States than in Europe. It is probable that in 1790 fewer than 10 percent of the population were church members, but this estimate must also be seen in the light of the traditional requirement of conversion for church membership. Specific Enlightenment influences did not seem to generate such a sharp break in American religious life, nor were the cultural leaders at the end of the 18th century so alienated from Christianity as in Germany or France, for example. The most articulate spokesmen for rationalism and / or deism were Thomas Paine, Ethan Allen and Elihu Palmer. Paine was especially widely read. Benjamin Franklin and Thomas Jefferson were less outspoken in their criticism.

5. Finney (1792–1875) has been called the founder of modern revivalism. See his Lectures on Revivals of Religion (1835), and Lectures on Systematic Theology (1846). After acquiring fame as a revivalist, Finney became a professor and president at Oberlin College. The Oberlin theology, with its emphasis on freedom and perfectionism, was a characteristic expression of popular evangelicalism.

two crucial transitional figures, with overlapping interests and ideas, yet in powerful tension with each other. Taylor was to be the bridge to the critical orthodoxy of Bushnell, Channing to the Transcendentalism of Emerson.

Taylor's theological roots were particularly deep in the revival movement. He has even been viewed as one whose center of interest was not Calvinism at all, but the preaching of conversion, for which the freedom to choose was all important [6]—though to other interpreters he has seemed the last of the Edwardseans, trying to be a Consistent Calvinist while adding the shock absorbers of free will and rational theology.[7] For Taylor, however, the need and possibility of revival meant opposition both to any physical or mechanical necessitation of sin and to the vulgar Pelagianism or romantic humanitarianism that says "do the best you can and God will let you enter his glory." Theology had to be worked out in relation to three sorts of opponents: the secularists, the Unitarians, and the orthodox. The center of Taylor's thought can be marked by his phrases "certainty, with the (dreadful) power to the contrary," and "the moral government of God." [8] "Certainty" here meant the certainty of sin, the "universal depravity" or "entire sinfulness" of mankind, such that men "by nature and in all the appropriate circumstances of their being, will sin." As soon as they are capable of sinning, all men sin. But in that act there is the "power to the contrary." Sin is a moral act, man is not compelled to sin by the nature God has given him. "He sins freely, voluntarily. There is no other way of sinning." Moral depravity, for which man deserves the wrath of God, "is man's own act, consisting in a free choice of some object rather than God, as his chief good—or a free preference of the world and of worldly good, to the will and glory of God" (Concio ad Clerum). Only so understood is sin intelligible.[9] That moral depravity is universal and

6. This is the argument of Sidney Mead, in his Nathaniel William Taylor (Chicago, 1942).

7. One example is F. H. Foster, A Genetic History of the New England Theology (Chicago, 1907), though there are many others.

8. Taylor's theology is most fully stated in the Lectures on the Moral Government of God, posthumously edited by Noah Porter (1859). His central ideas are succinctly sketched in the famous address of 1828, Concio ad Clerum: On Human Nature, Sin, and Freedom, reprinted in Sydney E. Ahlstrom, Theology in America (New York, 1967).

9. A major defect in Edwards's view was, for Taylor, his definition of moral agency and free will. To say that the only liberty is the freedom to do as we please, i.e. to do as we will, is not to go deeply enough into the nature of moral agency; the latter requires the freedom also to choose.

certain—except as prevented by God's supernatural interposition—and that "sin or guilt pertains exclusively to voluntary action" is the testimony of Scripture, of orthodoxy, of common sense, and of the facts of human experience. But the certainty of sin is not a physical certainty; men are sinful "by nature" not in the sense that human nature is the "physical" or "efficient" cause of sinning, but in the sense that men's "nature is the occasion, or reason of their sinning."

In this not altogether unambiguous language, Taylor was seeking to define the rule of God, whose ultimacy and entirety was not to be questioned, as throughout a *moral* government. The model, that is, for interpreting the Calvinistic vision of the sovereignty of God is not the deterministic model of mechanical causality (now rigid in the Newtonian system) but the moral model of human life, in which there is freedom and responsibility. Thus Taylor also continually reiterated the thesis that the universal depravity of mankind is not inconsistent either with the sovereignty or with the moral perfection of God. To suppose that in a moral system, that is, without the destruction of moral agency, God could have prevented all sin is a wholly gratuitous assumption.

A related theme in Taylor's theology was the right and necessity of judgment according to reason and, therefore, of free investigation with clear definitions and correct logic. On the one hand, this meant that Christian truth could and must be rationally stated; God asks of rational beings only a rational faith, including a reasoned view of Scripture. On the other hand, Taylor (like Dwight) believed that the faith truly presented could not fail to be convincing to reasonable men. Revival meant persuasion not only of the heart, but also of the head. By "reason," further, Taylor meant the "principles of common sense"—and more specifically, the principles of the common sense realism developed in Scotland by Hutcheson, Reid, and Stewart in the middle and later eighteenth century as the substitute for Locke and the answer to Hume. Taylor's arguments against "physical" necessitation of sin, for example, leaned heavily on the Scottish philosophers.

The same common sense philosophy, significantly, was reflected in the thought of William Ellery Channing, who gave the most persuasive and influential expression to the principles of "liberal Christianity" or "enlightened religious faith." [10] As pastor of the Federal

10. See his *Works* (Boston, 1900 and numerous other editions), and W. H. Channing, *The Life of William Ellery Channing* (Boston, 1880). The Baltimore sermon and four

Street Church in Boston from 1803 until his death, Channing stood in the long American tradition of pastor-theologians. By the end of his life he was judged by many to be the greatest religious leader of the day and, because it was largely as an essayist that he was known in England and France, a literary star of the first magnitude.

Channing's famous Baltimore sermon of 1819, "Unitarian Christianity," which was at once accepted as the credo of Unitarianism,[11] was divided into two major parts, the first of which was a statement simply of the necessity of the use of reason, specifically in interpreting Scripture but also generally in religion. Channing's arguments were neither extreme nor unusual: all persons and sects use reason, and the question is only one of right use; Scripture is to be interpreted according to the acknowledged principles for interpreting any human writing, and without those the divine authority of the Bible cannot be defended. If reason is unreliable, "Christianity and even natural theology must be abandoned; for the existence and veracity of God, and the divine original of Christianity, are conclusions of reason, and must stand or fall with it." The question of the truth of revelation "is left by God to be decided at the bar of reason." To be sure, God is infinitely wiser than men, but this cannot lead us to expect from him revelations that are contradictory, for infinite wisdom will not allow him to expose us to the possibility of infinite error nor to "sport with the understandings of his creatures."

From those principles, Channing went on to specify five sorts of views "which distinguish us from other Christians." These were, first, the unity of God as one being, person, mind, and perfection, in contrast to the trinitarian doctrine which makes of God a divine society of agents performing different functions—a doctrine both irrational and unscriptural. Second, that Christ is one, not a duality of souls and minds (hence of beings), but one personal being distinct

other brief characteristic works are reprinted in *William Ellery Channing: Unitarian Christianity and Other Essays*, ed. I. H. Bartlett (New York, 1957), which includes "The Moral Argument against Calvinism," "The Evidences of Revealed Religion," "Likeness to God," and "Honor Due to All Men."

11. The Unitarian movement had begun to take shape in the late 18th century. An Episcopal church in Boston, King's Chapel, formally became Unitarian in 1785. In 1805, the Unitarian Henry Ware was appointed to the Hollis Chair of Divinity at Harvard, after two years of struggle between the theological parties, and the "Unitarian controversy" began. The Calvinists organized a rival seminary at Andover in 1808. Ware and his colleague Andrews Norton were important among the Unitarian interpreters, but it was Channing who quickly became the recognized spokesman for the movement.

from the one God as we are distinct. Third, that God is morally perfect: "We consider no part of theology so important as that which treats of God's moral character; and we value our views of Christianity chiefly, as they assert his amiable and venerable attributes." That is, God is infinitely just, good, kind, and benevolent in the "proper" sense of those words; he has the name, the dispositions, and the principles of a father. Hence the doctrines of natural depravity and election have to be resisted unceasingly. Elsewhere, Channing insisted that the chief argument against Calvinism "is the moral argument, or that which is drawn from the inconsistency of the system with the divine perfections." [12] Fourth, that the mediation of Christ means no change in God, but an effecting of moral or spiritual deliverance by instruction, by example, by suffering and death, and by the resurrection of Jesus and his continuing intercession. Finally, that Christian virtue, consisting in love to God, Christ, and man, is founded in the moral nature of man, which is the ground of responsibility, and not in any irresistible grace or infused charity.

In his own development of these themes, Channing was plainly no religious revolutionary, and he could not accept the characteristic Transcendentalist ideas of Emerson and Parker. He wanted to free Christianity from certain immoral and irrational doctrines, but precisely so that the true spirit of Christian piety and the central teaching of the New Testament could flourish. He held to the necessity of scriptural revelation and he defended the miraculous nature of Christianity, arguing against Hume and drawing on both George Campbell and William Paley. He thought it possible to make a rational case for the divine origin of Christianity, notably from the inexplicability of the character of Jesus Christ from the general principles of human nature.[13] Man stood in need of a genuine work of redemption. And Channing's passion for defending the moral character of God was rooted deeply in Samuel Hopkins's idea of disinterested and universal benevolence as the highest good (despite the objectionable use Hopkins made of the notion, finally to justify evil as necessary to the highest good).

Nathaniel W. Taylor with equal vigor insisted on free moral agency, on God's moral perfection, and on the judgment of reason—and he was severely criticized by the orthodox for conceding too

12. "The Moral Argument against Calvinism" (1820), in Bartlett, *William Ellery Channing*, p. 43.
13. See especially "The Evidences of Revealed Religion" (1821).

much to the Unitarians. The question then arises: How shall we interpret the tension between the Unitarian and the Taylorite views? Two focuses of differentiation provide an answer.

The first was Channing's sense, shared by the Unitarian movement generally, of the dignity and the moral perfectibility of man. As Henry Ware put it explicitly in 1820, "The question 'what is the natural character of man,' lies at the very foundation of the controversy between the Unitarians on the one hand and Trinitarians and Calvinists on the other." [14] It is a mistake to interpret Unitarianism as rooted primarily in the idea of the oneness of God. It was, to be sure, a protest against the near tritheism of a vulgar Christianity, which could even introduce moral conflict among the divine Persons (and this even in the sophisticated theological tradition, e.g. by Emmons, of the Hopkinsian school). Unitarianism was even more interested, however, in man and in the defense of his goodness against the doctrines of "depravity." Channing's view was not a blithe humanitarianism or optimism, nor did he go so far as Emerson in the judgment that man is divine. In the sermon "Likeness to God" (1828), Channing could speak of Christianity's "perpetual testimonies to the divinity of human nature"; but that meant essentially the kindred spiritual nature of man which it is his calling to enhance. The dominant note was the perfectibility of man, rather than the immanentism which could lead Emerson to say in 1830 that "God is the substratum of all souls." Channing's was still a Christian humanism. But obviously the grandeur and nobility and capability of man impressed him more than the misery and corruption. Sin he saw as fundamentally frailty in the struggle of growth from a lower love to a higher one. The conflict was not with God or the devil but between the higher and lower principles of human nature. [15] Whereas the seventeenth and eighteenth centuries were astounded by the marvelous works of God in nature, Channing seemed even more

14. Ware, *Letters Addressed to Trinitarians and Calvinists, Occasioned by Dr. Woods' Letters to Unitarians* (Cambridge, 1820), p. 17.

15. Channing, writing in 1799 of his own decision a year earlier to enter the ministry, reported: "There, amidst sore trials, the great question, I trust, was settled within me, whether, I would obey the higher or the lower principles of my nature—whether I would be the victim of passion, the world, or the free child and servant of God" (*Memoir of W. E. Channing*, 3 vols. [Boston, 1851], 1 : 130).

The common saying concerning the differences between the Universalist and the Unitarian points of view was not without a foundation: "the Universalist believes God is too good to damn anyone; the Unitarian believes man is too good to be damned."

than Rousseau (by whom he was impressed, and to whom he has some likeness as a transitional figure) to marvel at the possibilities of human good will. He defined the "one great principle," around which all else turns, as the doctrine that "God proposes . . . to perfect the human soul." God, then, is the good spirit presiding over this world, the morally perfect father educating his children; he is the "life, motive, and sustainer of virtue in the human soul"; he is "a being whom we know through our own souls; . . . who is the perfection of our own spiritual nature; who has sympathies with us as kindred beings." [16] And Jesus is an angelic being, exhibiting the beauty of a human nature willing to suffer for the near and far neighbor, illustrating what man can become and is indeed going to be, a "diviner being."

Taylor and Channing had much in common doctrinally: a profound reliance on moral principles as self-evident intuitions (here both drew on the Scottish philosophy) and a demand for "ethical" formulations in theology; similar opposition to "otherworldly utilitarianism"; insistence upon the freedom of man and the universality of sin. Yet even in those similarities there was the difference between one who suffered over the fact of sin, the brutality and corruption universally expressed in man's nature, and thus saw a desperate need for a supernatural act of deliverance, and one who in the mildness and generosity of his own spirit found evil no great problem. Hence also the difference between the rule of the world by an ultimate moral sovereign and the pedagogy of a kindly and fatherly spirit.

The second focus of conflict was the nature of the appeal to reason. Both Taylor and Channing insisted vigorously on the necessity of rational interpretation. But different contexts and theological stances were involved. For the Unitarian, the demand for consistency was primary. No concept of "total" or "natural" depravity could be squared with the freedom ingredient in a moral act or with God's moral perfection; no doctrine of election with God's justice. Therefore those doctrines must be abandoned. Channing did not doubt the universality of sin, but guilt and responsibility had to be exactly commensurate with free agency and possibility.[17] The same kind of

16. See Channing's sermons on "The Essence of the Christian Religion" (1830–31), "Unitarian Christianity," and "Likeness to God" (1828).

17. Thus Ware, while allowing that Adam's descendants began their lives "under circumstances of increased liability to sin, and greater difficulty of preserving their

reasoning applied to trinitarian and christological doctrine. Taylor also, of course, insisted that the universality of sin is correlated with voluntary action; otherwise sin is unintelligible. But his primary concern seems rather the preservation—and interpretation—of apprehended realities of Christian existence: God's perfection and sovereign rule, man's entire moral depravity, and man's freedom and responsibility. These are known from revelation (for Taylor as for Edwards, God's sovereignty and man's responsibility were revealed facts) and also partly from observation. There is, in short, a structure of things which reason must interpret, not deny. Consistency, that is, freedom from all ambiguity or paradox, is to this extent secondary to adequate representation of all sides of experience.[18] The question to be asked is the *meaning* of freedom, and the true *form* of divine sovereignty.

The distinction between Channing and Taylor, then, is not that one theology was consistent and the other only a half-way compromise mixing old premises and new, but that the one thinker sought primarily to stand within a community of faith and experience whose realities had to be interpreted and newly understood, while the viewpoint of the other was through the claims of a thoroughgoing rationality and, especially, a new vision of human perfectibility. The question of theological foundations was in fact being raised in the debates over God's moral government and man's dignity. Thus Taylor pointed in the direction of the "critical orthodoxy" of Bushnell and the evangelical and christocentric liberalism of the late nineteenth century, whereas Channing was the liberating force for the Transcendentalism of Emerson and could be followed by the thoroughgoing humanism of much of later Unitarianism, as well as by those who sought to hold to his own more christocentric and biblical view. To this extent, the distinction between Taylor and Channing was like that between Coleridge and Bentham.

Yet in at least as important a sense, both Taylor and Channing

---

innocence," insisted that each individual became a sinner for himself, "by a voluntary violation of known duty in obedience to either the appetites or the passions" (*Answer to Dr. Woods' Reply in a Second Series of Letters Addressed to Trinitarians and Calvinists* [Boston, 1822], pp. 51–52).

18. In contrast, Channing said that "Men who, to support a creed, would shake our trust in the calm, deliberate, and distinct decisions of our rational and moral powers endanger religion more than its open foes, and forge the deadliest weapon for the infidel" ("The Moral Argument against Calvinism," in Bartlett, *William Ellery Channing,* p. 47).

stood sharply in contrast to Coleridge and Schleiermacher, and thus they were closer to Bentham and Paley. Their categories for interpreting the relation of God and the world were supernaturalist categories; neither made the turn into the nineteenth century in his understanding of the nature of religious truth. The idea of revelation remained essentially unchanged. They still belonged, that is, to an intellectualist or conceptualist theological tradition. Although there was in Channing the beginning of a romanticist influence and sympathy, notably in his attitude toward nature and sentiment, the ideas of reason in both men were dominantly those of the pre-Kantian Enlightenment. And to this extent they were perpetrators of eighteenth-century patterns of theology as much as harbingers of actually new modes of thought.

PART II

1835–1870

The Possibility of Christology

Introduction: The Shapes of the Problem

In the early 1830s, the generation of those who laid the foundations of modern Protestant theological inquiry came to an end. The publication of David Friedrich Strauss's *Leben Jesu* in 1835 brought a decisive new impulse and complication, leading in the following decades to an intense and widespread concentration on the question of the historical object of faith, Jesus Christ. The way in which Strauss and Ferdinand Christian Baur shaped that question, and the way in which that question focused the problem of the possibility of any theology, must claim early attention. But first it is necessary to sketch in a preliminary way two or three of the other problem areas and tendencies of the period, in order to gain a sense for the whole of a very complex and fruitful theological generation. Here we see again the constant interpenetration of the dominating themes of the nineteenth century.

First of all, there were those thinkers and movements whose outlook can best be understood in relation to the question how, if at all, Christian faith can meet the actual or presumed demands of modern culture. The problem of the possibility of theology was intensified by the internalizing of the critico-historical question, by the progress of the sciences generally, and by the general uneasiness of the passage into the political and social situation of the 1830s and 1840s. The idealist synthesis in Germany broke down amid tendencies to naturalism and materialism. The British Reform Bills, the revolutions of 1848, and the American Civil War all contributed to an intensification of the conflicts between reforming and conservative theological tendencies, and the question of the theological program often merges with the problem of Christianity and culture.

One of the classic formulations of this question was given by Strauss in the *Streitschriften,* in his description of the splitting apart of the Hegelian school into the left- and right-wing groups. For the left wing, in which Strauss included himself, the demands of modern critical science and speculation required that Christianity as traditionally understood be given up. The right wing, on the other hand, chose to return to the old supernaturalism, sacrificing modern thought. To both sides, the conflict between historical Christianity and modern culture seemed finally irresolvable.

This general model for interpretation has been widely adopted in describing the mid-nineteenth century theological scene, especially in Germany. To the "right" and the "left," of course, must be added a number of "mediating theologies," whose principle was that of reconciling the two claims, that is, of holding them together in synthesis or in fruitful tension, in the tradition of the attempts by Schleiermacher and Hegel to unite science and theology. Such was the stated aim, for example, of the journal *Theologische Studien und Kritiken,* founded in 1828 by Karl Ullmann and F. W. K. Umbreit. According to this schematism, one must then distinguish among the many varieties of "mediation." Thus F. C. Baur proposed to differentiate between the "speculative theists" (e.g. I. H. Fichte, C. H. Weisse, and Richard Rothe) and the "right of center" mediating theologians of either the Schleiermacherian type (e.g. Nitzsch, Twesten, Ullmann, Lücke, Umbreit) or the "right-wing Hegelian" type (e.g. Liebner, Lange, Marheineke, Martensen, Dorner). Baur judged both of these latter groups to be moving toward a new supernaturalism.

But this is an interpretative model of strictly limited value. It does point to the perennial question of "Christ and culture," in its opposition of accommodation and resistance or independence, of change and continuity. And it does help to illumine the fundamental theological situation as viewed from the extremes—though that means, for the mid-nineteenth century, mainly those who *rejected* the proposals of Schleiermacher or Hegel or Coleridge (or even Taylor) as unacceptable compromise. But the pattern begins to break down when one looks more closely at the presumed advocates of the "left" and the "right." On the side of the left (the "liberal" side), insofar as that means maximum acknowledgment of the claims of modern thought, is a strange assortment of thinkers including Emerson and Parker as representatives of American Transcendentalism; the Anglican "Broad Church" movement and perhaps also John Stuart Mill and Matthew Arnold; and Strauss, Feuerbach, and Bruno Bauer (following F. C. Baur's classification, though it is noteworthy that he and Strauss differed in their definition of the left wing). Now it is indeed important to consider these movements together and to ask about their common tendencies as well as their differences. The question of Christianity and modernity was real, even desperate for some, and it provides an indispensable tool for inquiring into the theological moods and strategies of the time. But it also becomes apparent at once that radical differences existed, not only as to relative nearness to the tradition (for some, most obviously and immediately Feuerbach and Bruno Bauer, the momentum led out of the Christian faith entirely), but especially concerning the *kinds* of demands that modern critical thought was understood to make. For Strauss, for example, *Wissenschaft* could mean the claims of a consistent Hegelianism; but for Feuerbach it meant the outright rejection of the idealist epistemological principle and the inversion of Hegel's dialectic.

At the other end of the "spectrum," the difficulties of the simple disjunction are no less severe. To be sure, there were many tendencies in the mid-nineteenth century sharply to reject the presumed claims of modern culture and to resist the "liberal" accommodation. Among these must be included the rigid Lutheran confessionalism of the tradition from Löhe to Kliefoth and Hengstenberg in Germany, the Reformed confessionalism of the Princeton theology in America, the Oxford Movement in England, the "biblical realism" of J. T. Beck, and even Søren Kierkegaard. And to this list may be added a parallel in the "fortress mentality" in Roman Catholicism under the leadership of Pius IX after 1848. All these represent in some sense protests against the threatening dissolution of the substance of Christian faith—a danger at least as evident in social and political currents as in scientific and philosophical development. But both the *objects* and the *principles* of protest were sharply divergent. The authority to which Beck appealed was hardly that of the Lutheran (or the Reformed) confessions. And the Christianity on behalf of which Kierkegaard assailed Hegel was quite different from the "historic church" for which John Henry Newman fought, though of course one must also ask whether Kierkegaard can be at all adequately interpreted by such a pattern of analysis.

Over against both the so-called extremes, however, which had in common the sense of deep conflict between authentic Christianity and modern thought, were many thinkers, including some of the most interesting and creative, who might recognize a tension between the claims of Christ and culture, but who decided that the claims were not in conflict and must both be honored. They were not fundamentally anxious about the new claims of the nineteenth century.[1] Thus to call them mediators or synthesizers is usually to be less responsible to *their* view of the situation—or to say only that they stood in the tradition of Thomas Aquinas rather than of Tertullian—as well as to ignore their own unique theological intentions. In respect of the basic decision, these thinkers followed in the line of Hegel, Schleiermacher, and Coleridge, and they generally sought to build on foundations laid down by one or more of those early nineteenth-century fathers, though also in distinctively new directions. The thinkers and tendencies that might be cited here are many, but among the principal figures were I. A. Dorner, Richard Rothe, Julius Müller, F. D. Maurice, Horace Bushnell, the Erlangen theologians, and the Mercersburg school. And of these thinkers Rothe, Maurice, Bushnell, and Dorner have been particularly difficult to locate in "schools." Like Kierkegaard, each could claim his own chapter.

The theology of the mid-nineteenth century was also deeply affected by religious revival in both Germany and America and by a pervasive new interest in the nature of the church. These tendencies were related to each other and, at some points, they both lent support to "conservative" theological movements. The close relation of theology to revival that we observed in N. W. Taylor and Lyman Beecher in early nineteenth-century America continued to be expressed particularly by the great "revival theologian" Charles G. Finney (1792–1875) and in the Oberlin theology, as well as in their opponents. The renewal in Germany of "a vigorous Christian life," as Dorner described it,[2] did not take the dramatic forms that characterized American frontier revivalism, but it represented a neopietism of enormous influence. The most decisive theologian in the German movement was probably August Tholuck (1799–1877) of Halle. The new pietism was important not only for the Halle and Erlangen groups, but also for Müller, Dorner, and Rothe, for example, and later for Ritschl, Herrmann, and Kähler, all three of whom were

---

1. F. D. Maurice wrote about the "Broad Church": "All I can hear from it is a cry to leave the 16th century and believe in the 19th. So long as I believe in God, I do not mean to believe in any century: though I may earnestly believe that He has assigned a work to every century which no other can perform, and which it can only perform when it looks before and behind and ceases to glorify itself" (quoted in C. R. Sanders, *Coleridge and the Broad Church Movement* [Durham, N.C., 1942], p. 14).

2. I. A. Dorner, *History of Protestant Theology* (Edinburgh, 1871), 2 : 396. See also below, chap. 9.

Tholuck's students. Out of the neopietist revival, in addition to a vigorous missionary activity, came more than one theological impulse. One tendency, parallel to the pattern of revival-theology in America, was to concentrate on the specific experience of rebirth as the basis for theological development. This sort of "religious experience" theology could (and did) quickly provide a way back to forms of orthodox theology, especially through the doctrine of sin. Neopietism and revival also tended to support the burgeoning interest in a theology of the church. Emanuel Hirsch has rightly argued that in the nineteenth century the church's nature, task, form, order, and relation to the state and life generally became the object of theological concern as at no previous time, not even in the Reformation; [3] and that this movement has continued into the twentieth century. In the mid-nineteenth century, that interest was expressed especially in the various confessionalist and denominationalist theologies in Germany and America, in the Oxford Movement, in F. D. Maurice and I. A. Dorner, and in the Mercersburg theology, as well as in the Christian Socialist and *Innere Mission* movements and even in the struggle over the slavery in the United States.

Yet it was also widely characteristic of Protestant theology in the middle third of the nineteenth century that the christological problem came to the center of the stage and became a focus for the other concerns, both as the new and burning question of whether (or how) the historical figure of Jesus can be available at all as an object for faith, and as one multisided problem of reformulating the doctrines of incarnation, particularly in relation to the now necessary acknowledgment of the genuine humanity of the historical figure. The question of the possibility of theology in the modern world and the question of the church were decisively reordered by this new consideration of the possibility of Christology. With the exceptions of Feuerbach, J. H. Newman, and Richard Rothe, the most interesting theological endeavors of the period all found their point of departure or their center of gravity in the question of Christ. For Strauss and Baur, the problem was fundamentally one of the knowability of Jesus and of the significance of an individual historical figure for the realization of the ideal. For Kierkegaard it was expressed both in his idea of contemporaneity with Christ and in the absolute paradox of the God-man as the most decisive expression of

3. *Geschichte der neuern evangelischen Theologie*, 3d ed., 5 vols. (Gütersloh, 1964), 5 : 145 ff.

the qualitative distinction between time and eternity (and thus as the center of attack against the confusions of modern Christendom). For F. D. Maurice the central theological question was that of the lordship of Christ, and the nature and principles of his kingdom. Horace Bushnell's first decisive works were about the right understanding of the divinity of Christ. And it was the orthodox view of Christ against which both Unitarianism and the new Transcendentalism continued to define their views of humanity. On the side of reconsideration of the classical doctrines of the God-man, radically different tendencies emerged, in an interplay of efforts to develop Christology both "from above" and "from below." In the remarkable flowering of kenotic Christology in the 1840s in Germany, the possibilities—or impossibilities—of this approach were worked out far more thoroughly than ever before. At the heart of Isaak Dorner's system was a novel conception of a growing incarnation. And in still another direction (though one of less interest), Carl Immanuel Nitzsch (1787–1868), Karl Ullmann (1796–1865), and Alexander Schweizer (1808–88) sought to deal with Strauss's question by using Schleiermacher's idea of the archetypal man as a way back toward the God-man of the ancient church's dogmas.

In the following chapters we shall make use of an overall pattern of organization reflecting the grand theological stances and moods (see chap. 1 above), treating the new disturbing and problematic lines within theology, the conservative reactions, and the chastened or critically orthodox. But in doing so, we shall see the problem of Christ again and again moving to the center in these diverse theological strategies.

7

The Claim of History

DAVID FRIEDRICH STRAUSS (1808–74)

In the preface to the first volume of *Das Leben Jesu,* Strauss asked his readers to suspend judgment until the appearance of the second volume (early in 1836), in which it would become clear how the historico-critical work he was undertaking would leave the essence of Christian faith quite untouched. The supernatural birth of Christ, his miracles, his resurrection, and his ascension would remain eternal truths, whatever doubts might be cast on their reality as historical facts. Even if that unrealistic request had been heeded, it is doubtful whether the storm his book aroused would have been less violent. It was the source of immediate controversy throughout Germany and it quickly became the symbol in Britain and America of negativity in biblical criticism. The book called forth responses—mostly attacks—from nearly every important German theologian of the time, including charges that it was "the Iscariotism of our days"; and it cost him the chance for an academic career.[1] The opposition was so strong and universal that Strauss himself was temporarily shaken in his views, and in the third edition he made important concessions (mainly concerning the Fourth Gospel). In the fourth edition of 1840, however, he returned essentially to his original contentions.[2]

What Strauss set out to do can be put quite simply. As the preliminary to the doctrinal study he planned to write, it was necessary to work out a thorough historico-critical study of the gospel accounts, for the crucial theological question, and also Strauss's point of departure from Hegel, was the relation of the idea of the Christ

1. Strauss was at the time a tutor (*Repetent*) in the *Stift* at Tübingen, where he had also lectured with great success on Hegel. He lost the post even before the second volume appeared. Strauss's responses to the attacks were published in his *Streitschriften zur Verteidigung meiner Schrift über das Leben Jesu und zur Charakteristik des verständ. Supranaturalismus unserer Tage* (Tübingen, 1837 ff.).

2. Strauss's story and the controversy over the *Leben Jesu* are summarized in Albert Schweitzer, *The Quest of the Historical Jesus,* trans. W. Montgomery (New York, 1960), chaps. 7–9. Though the 1st German edition appeared in 1906, this is still a useful account.

to the historical figure. The most recent attempts to deal with the life of Jesus, by Karl A. Hase and especially by Schleiermacher in his not yet published lectures, were altogether inadequate, halfheartedly compromising historical study with supernaturalism. What was needed was a better understanding and a more thorough application of what Strauss called the "mythical" mode of interpretation. In an introductory survey of patterns of biblical interpretation from Greek and Hebrew times, though with main emphasis on criticism since the Enlightenment, he found the beginnings of such a method in Semler, Schelling, Baur, de Wette, Paulus and others; but it was hitherto largely applied only to the Old Testament, or at best to the birth and resurrection reports. No one had taken proper account of the mythical elements throughout the Gospels.[3]

By "myth," Strauss meant the expression of the *Idea* in the form of a historical account. "Evangelical myths" were those narratives relating directly or indirectly to Jesus which might be considered "not as the expression of a fact, but as the product of an idea of his earliest followers." The task of gospel criticism was thus to identify in the Gospels those elements which ought to be judged mythical rather than historical, and to indicate how those stories developed and became attached to Jesus. The criteria for distinguishing the unhistorical or mythical materials were both negative and positive, though Strauss did not think the line between historical and unhistorical an easy one to draw. The negative criteria involved indications that the events could not have taken place in the manner described. Those indications might be discrepancies or contradictions either in the accounts themselves or among the Gospels, or they might be irreconcilability with known universal laws. The basic principle of historical investigation was the essential homogeneity and interconnectedness of all events. This of course excluded miracle in the sense of an interruption or an "arbitrary disturbance" of the chain of events; and for Strauss the vain attempt of modern supernaturalists to introduce direct divine intervention only in exceptional cases simply added another element of confusion to the picture. Among

3. The rationalist opposition to orthodox assertions that the Gospels were wholly reliable eyewitness accounts had generally taken two lines: either the miracle stories were misinterpretations of scientifically explicable occurrences or they were frauds perpetrated by the early Christians. All of these options were rejected by Strauss.

For the following summary of Strauss's definition of myth, see the *Life of Jesus* (*Leben Jesu, kritisch bearbeitet,* 2 vols. [Tübingen, 1835–36; 4th ed., 1840], trans. Marian Evans, 1846), §§ 15–16.

the negative criteria were also psychological laws, describing how individuals act, and "laws of succession," that is, the assumption that occurrences follow certain orders (so that an individual at birth is unlikely to attract the attention he elicits in his maturity). The positive criteria for identifying mythical elements included poetical forms of expression and any striking agreement between the content of a narrative and the ideas prevailing within the circle producing the narrative, that is, a conformity to prior expectations.

Myth was to be found in the Gospels in two forms. "Pure myths" are those having their source (1) in the Messianic ideas and expectations existing in the Jewish mind at the time of Jesus and (2) in the particular impression left by the personal character or actions or fate of Jesus. The story of the transfiguration, for example, is to be understood as coming almost wholly from the first source. The story of the rending of the veil in the temple has a source of the other type, specifically in Jesus's hostile attitude (and that of the early church) toward Jewish temple worship. "Historical myths," in contrast to pure myths, involve some definite individual fact that was seized upon by religious enthusiasm and surrounded and embellished with conceptions culled from the idea of the Christ. In both cases we are to see the operation, not of individual fictionalization or mere error in interpretation or transmission, but of the unconscious myth-building power of the community, expressing its apprehension of the truth through the development of the stories about Jesus.

Using this apparatus, Strauss worked in detail through the Gospels, leaving no possible contradiction or inconsistency unexposed. The resultant picture was of a thoroughly historical and human figure about whom we have very little reliable information. We know, for example, of his home in Galilee, his baptism by John (certainly not including heavenly voices), his mission in Galilee, his claim to be the Messiah, his rejection at Nazareth, the cleansing of the temple (as recorded by Mark), and his trial and crucifixion. Everything else, if not properly called mythical, is at least surrounded by serious historical difficulties.[4]

4. Among the accounts designated mythical by Strauss were: all elements of the birth stories, the visit to the temple at age twelve, the acknowledgment of Jesus by John and the supernatural circumstances surrounding the baptism, the temptation experiences, the general chronology of the ministry, the Samaritan woman story, the miracles, the transfiguration (which story developed to exhibit a repetition of the glorification of Moses and to bring Jesus into contact with his two forerunners), any

Such an individual could not, for Strauss, properly be the object of faith. But this did not mean that the faith of the church was false. As he had promised, Strauss at the conclusion of the second volume of *Das Leben Jesu* sought to show briefly that the result was not loss but gain. Relinquishing the historical reality of the narratives makes it possible to preserve the absolute truth they expressed. Schleiermacher's notion of the actual presence of ideality (*Urbild-lichkeit*) in Jesus was inconsistent with the laws of development, which do not allow us to regard the first member of a series as the greatest. Kant and De Wette, on the other hand, conceived of the ideal simply as a possibility, a moral obligation to which no reality corresponds; but this was to annihilate the essential truth. Hegel had rightly insisted on the *reality* of the unity of God and man, but he had failed precisely at the point of relating the general proposi-tions on the unity of the divine and human natures to the historical individual or to any necessity for historic embodiment. But the diffi-culty can be resolved, and the reality preserved, Strauss proposed, by abandoning the supposition that the unity of God and man is manifested in any single individual. The *Idee* is indeed not wont to realize itself in that way, "to lavish all its fullness on one exemplar and to be niggardly towards all others"; it loves rather to distribute its riches among a multiplicity of instances which mutually complete each other. Thus, in the most famous words of the concluding essay of the *Life of Jesus,*

> This is the key to the whole of Christology, that as the subject of the predicates which the church applies to Christ, we place instead of an individual an idea, but an idea that exists in reality and not a Kant-ian unreal one. Conceived in respect of an individual, a God-man, the attributes and functions that the church's doctrine ascribes to Christ are contradictory; in the idea of the species they concur. Humanity is the union of the two natures, the incarnate God: [i.e.] the infinite spirit divested to finitude and the finite spirit recalling its infinitude. It is the child of the visible mother and the invisible father: of spirit and of nature. It is the miracle worker: insofar as in the course of human history the spirit ever more completely takes control of na-ture, both in man and the outside of him, and nature is reduced

---

specific prediction of Jesus' crucifixion and resurrection (though he may well have had some general intimation of forthcoming death) or of any particular events in connection with the passion, some of the details of the passion story, the miraculous factors attend-ing the death of Jesus, and the resurrection and ascension.

vis-à-vis man to the powerless material of his activity. It is the sinless reality: insofar as the course of its development is a blameless one, impurity always clinging only to the individual but being annulled in the race and its history. It is that which dies, rises, and ascends to heaven: insofar as its ever higher spiritual life emerges from the negative of its naturalness, and its unity with the infinite spirit of heaven emerges from the annulling of its finitude as personal, national, and world spirit. By faith in *this* Christ, particularly in his death and his resurrection, man is justified before God: i.e. the individual also participates in the divine-human life of the race by the enlivening of the idea of humanity in itself, in particular in accordance with the factor that the negation of naturalness and sensuousness (which is itself the negation of spirit), thus the negation of negation, is the only way to true spiritual life for man. [§ 149]

The significance of the *Life of Jesus* was certainly not the perfection of Strauss's historical method, though he made a great advance in the development of the idea of myth as the product of a community. Strauss was immediately and rightly criticized (notably by F. C. Baur) for weakness in genuine *literary* analysis of the Gospels as documents in their historical context, and for relying rather on a basically philosophical employment of the negative myth criteria simply in relation to individual pericopes and stories. In particular, he too easily played the gospel accounts off against each other. Nor was the importance of the work its shattering of the assumption that consistent Hegelianism and traditional Christian doctrine were the same thing, though this the book did, beginning the decline of the "Hegelian school."

Most important was simply the complete and radical application of the critical perspective to the gospel records in their entirety, with the consequent assignment of a vast amount of the material to the categories of the mythical or legendary. Strauss particularly attacked the historical reliability of the Gospel of John, which had been the reliable favorite of the theologians, including Schleiermacher and Hegel. Though by twentieth-century standards, the net result of Strauss's critique is not at all shocking, his conclusions at the time seemed appalling. The question with which theologians had to deal was whether any historical accuracy could be assigned to the gospel accounts, and whether any foundation for faith was to be found in them. And this question cut as deeply with the rationalists as with the orthodox, for the former had taken it for granted that at least some of the record, once the miraculous was stripped away, was unchallengeable. Schleiermacher, too, had eased the tension of theology and biblical criticism by his hermeneutics and also by eliminating the dependence of faith on Scripture or on any presupposition of Scripture's divine authority—and this gain was to endure. But in Strauss the historical problem was forced again and in an unavoidable way into the center of the arena. There were many who felt that confidence could easily be restored in the historical basis of Christianity; [5] but this was an illusion. The foundations were permanently shaken.

The question was really a twofold one. First, by what methods, if at all, is Jesus Christ available? And second, in what way does Christianity depend on or necessitate a historical object for faith? More generally, in what way does history count for theology? F. C. Baur was immediately to take up both of these questions, and through Strauss and Baur together they became permanent aspects (though not everywhere immediately) of the Christian theological problem.

In his *Christian Doctrine, Presented in Its Historical Development and Conflict with Modern Science.*[6] Strauss put the related historical question to the doctrinal development of Christianity. The fundamental task of dogmatics he viewed as the clarification of the relation between modern science and philosophy on the one hand, and the Christian religion and theology on the other. But that meant an essentially historical study, for in history itself we see the truth of the matter. As Strauss described the task, the material out of which a present day dogmatics must be formed is precisely all the forms of the development of Christianity in its relation to philosophy. This required especially that distinctions be drawn, and Strauss was astounded by the ease with which some claimed to accomplish mediation.[7] Whereas in the historical monographs which comprise the *Glaubenslehre* Strauss was generally most restrained in express-

---

5. And innumerable "positive" lives of Jesus appeared in response to Strauss.

6. *Die Christliche Glaubenslehre, in ihrer geschichtlichen Entwicklung und im Kampfe mit der modernen Wissenschaft dargestellt*, 2 vols. (1840–41), hereafter cited as *CG*, with volume and page numbers.

7. "Not everyone possesses the equipment and the endurance with which Schleiermacher so finely pulverized Christianity and Spinozism, in order to mix them, that it takes a sharp eye to distinguish the blended ingredients. In the case of some, the union of the Christian and the modern elements is only the shaking up together of oil and water, which appear to be blended as long as the agitation continues. Still others, and

ing judgments of his own, in an attempt to let his subjects speak for themselves, he had little but scorn for the contemporary *Vermittlungstheologen*.[8] "The true mediation," he maintained, "must be just as much separation and division. It can only be accomplished through a process, by a smelting or fermentation whereby the slag and the dregs are eliminated, or rather eliminate themselves" (*CG*, 1.70–71).

Thus Strauss wrote the *Glaubenslehre* as a series of extensive essays, tracing with great learning and penetration the development of the major individual dogmas from the New Testament to the most recent times. In general the pattern is the same. From vague and even crude beginnings the dogma is slowly erected to a full and even majestic form, usually continuing in this direction until the time of the Reformation. Then, with the emergence of a freer spirit and the renewal of *Wissenschaft* in the humanistic period, the dissolution begins, in which both the inner contradictions and the conflicts with the increasingly powerful philosophy and science are exposed, and the inner kernel of truth is disclosed. From the small cracks in the edifice that appear with the Socinians and the Arminians, the process continues until under rationalism each item of doctrine is increasingly emptied of its Christian content. Then with Kant's destruction of the Wolffian system (and the revival of Spinozism) the final stage of conflict has been reached, and even the powerful efforts of Hegel and Schleiermacher cannot put "Humpty-Dumpty" together again.

The historical outcome, then, in the dissolution of each of the major doctrinal creations, is just the (at present at least) unbridgeable opposition of dogma and science, faith and knowledge, in both form and content.[9] Thus it is that, in Strauss's famous words, *"die wahre*

---

in part not unknown theologians, are like a piece of sausage, in which orthodox church doctrine represents the meat, Schleiermacherian theology the bacon, and Hegelian philosophemes the seasoning (the image is no more ignoble than the reality)" (*CG*, 1.70).

8. For one of the more vivid instances, see the words with which Strauss sums up his devastating critique of Weisse's trinitarian doctrine: "Where is the Athanasian Creed? Give it to me! I will subscribe to it ten times before I will even once call the statements of our philosopher anything but madness" (*CG*, 2 : 501 [cf. 495 ff.]).

9. "Thus let the believer and the knower alike allow the other to go his road peacefully; we let them have their faith, so let them leave us our philosophy; and if the excessively pious should manage to exclude us from their church, we shall consider this a gain: enough false attempts at mediation have now been made; only a separation of the antitheses can lead further (*CG*, 1.356).

Kritik des Dogmas ist seine Geschichte" (the true criticism of dogma is its history).[10]

Although Strauss's *Glaubenslehre* was overshadowed by the publication of Feuerbach's *Essence of Christianity* [*Das Wesen des Christentums*, 1841), its importance should not be underestimated. Nor does the significance of the work lie in Strauss's own view (which went beyond that of *Das Leben Jesu*) of the irresolvable conflict between doctrine and modern thought and his commitment to a thoroughly immanentist and monist view. The concluding words of the book, whose final section treats eschatology, sum up his rejection of transcendence: "With this our work is completed for the present. For the other world is throughout the one thing, and in its shape as future it is the final enemy, which speculative criticism has to fight and where possible to overcome" (*CG*, 2.739). But more important than this, and even more important (for theology, though perhaps not for social history) than that the picture he created was so fondly embraced by a non-Christian culture, was Strauss's setting of the dogmatic question into the sphere of historical study. This was done even more sharply than by Schleiermacher's locating of dogmatics within the context of historical theology, that is, as contemporary theology. Now, with Strauss, theology has a history in a new way. The serious study of the history of theology, and especially of the problem of the development of doctrine, must begin, and dogmatics must justify itself in relation to historico-critical investigation.[11]

10. *CG*, 1.71. "Subjective criticism of the individual is a water pipe that any boy can stop up for a while: criticism as it works itself out objectively in the course of centuries plunges on like a roaring torrent against which all floodgates and dams avail nothing" (*CG*, 1.10).

11. After 1841, Strauss withdrew from theological controversy for twenty years. In the later writings, especially the second life of Jesus, *Leben Jesu, für das deutsche Volk bearbeitet* (1864) and *Der alte und der neue Glaube* (1872, translated into English in 1873), he had given up any hope of reconciliation of Christianity to the modern world. Whether we can have any religion at all depends on "the spirit of the inquiry." "At any rate, that on which we feel ourselves entirely dependent, is by no means merely a rude power to which we bow in mute resignation, but is at the same time both order and law, reason and goodness, to which we surrender ourselves in loving trust. More than this; as we perceive in ourselves the same disposition to the reasonable and the good which we seem to recognize in the Cosmos, and find ourselves to be the beings by whom it is felt and recognized, in whom it is to become personified, we also feel ourselves related in our inmost nature to that on which we are dependent, we discover ourselves at the same time to be free in this dependence; and pride and humility, joy and submission, intermingle in our feeling for the Cosmos" (*The Old Faith and the New*, trans. Mathilde Blind [New York, 1873], 1 : 164).

FERDINAND CHRISTIAN BAUR (1792–1860)

It was Strauss through whom the historico-critical problem decisively and irrevocably entered the stream of Protestant theology. But it was Strauss's teacher, F. C. Baur, the greatest historian of the church and of theology in the nineteenth century (at least until Harnack), who first and most fully developed the idea of a "historical theology," and in whom, it has been said, "the truly historical investigation of primitive Christianity and of the New Testament is first established." [12]

In the theological milieu of the late 1830s and following, Baur saw divergent trends: the threat posed by Strauss's negative results, the disintegration of the Hegelian schools into the right and left wings, the failure of the "mediating theologians" to further with any effectiveness the bold efforts of Schleiermacher and Hegel to hold theology and science together, and the revival of conservatism. The situation called for a positive historico-critical theology: a concern not with the internal conflicts among the theological systems and directions but with the root problem of science and the church, that is, a struggle on a scientific basis for the "positivity" of Christianity. [13]

The necessary starting point and center, for Baur, was Christology. Schleiermacher had been formally correct in insisting that all be centered in Christ. In language reminiscent of Schleiermacher's definition of Christianity, [14] Baur wrote:

12. Ernst Käsemann, in his introduction to vol. 1 of F. C. Baur, *Ausgewählte Werke in Einzelausgaben* (Stuttgart, 1963), p. viii. Strauss studied with Baur both at the lower seminary in Blaubeuren and at Tübingen, to which Baur was called in 1826. Concerning Baur, see Wolfgang Geiger, *Spekulation und Kritik: Die Geschichtstheologie Ferdinand Christian Baurs* (Munich, 1964); Peter C. Hodgson, *The Formation of Historical Theology: A Study of Ferdinand Christian Baur* (New York, 1966); and C. Senft, *Wahrhaftigkeit und Wahrheit* (Tübingen, 1956). For the Library of Protestant Thought, Professor Hodgson has also translated two important items of Baur's work: *The Epochs of Church Historiography* (1852), and the introduction to the *Lectures on the History of Christian Doctrine* (1865). See Peter C. Hodgson, ed., *Ferdinand Christian Baur* (New York, 1968).

13. See *Kirchengeschichte des 19. Jahrhunderts* (Tübingen, 1862), pp. 402 ff.

14. It was Schleiermacher's *Glaubenslehre* that freed Baur from the supernaturalism of the old Tübingen school, and he looked upon this work (more even than the *Speeches*) as inaugurating the new theological era. Though Baur later employed Hegelian categories extensively, it was not until 1835 (in *Die christliche Gnosis*) that the strong influence of Hegel appears in his writing. Baur was by no means simply a disciple of Hegel, and to consider him mainly as a representative of one of the Hegelian schools is misleading, for it quite overlooks the continuing influence of Schleiermacher.

Can one speak at all of the nature and content of Christianity, without making the person of its founder the chief object of consideration, above all else, and without recognizing that the distinctive character of Christianity lies precisely in the fact that it is everything it is solely through the person of its founder, so much so that it would accordingly make no difference at all to construe Christianity, in its nature and content, from the standpoint of its relation to world history, since its entire meaning is so conditioned by the personality of its founder that the historical consideration can proceed only from that personality? [15]

But this statement also suggests Baur's divergence from Schleiermacher. Finally, Baur believed, Schleiermacher fell back into a subjectivism in which faith could have no proper object, because he started only with the present religious consciousness. The historical was thus lost. The only way to get to the historical Jesus is to *start* with him, that is, to start with a critical analysis of the gospel records. This Schleiermacher had failed to do, and consequently, he had also failed at the most critical theological point: the relation of the "ideal Christ" to the historical Jesus. Christ for Schleiermacher's theology necessarily remained the archetype (*Urbild*), the source of present Christian religious consciousness. Though Schleiermacher insisted on the identity of the ideal with the historical Christ, he had no adequate basis for this (and "identity," for Baur, was wrong in any case). Hegel, likewise, was ambiguous as to whether Jesus was necessarily or only accidentally the presupposition of faith. And Strauss proposed to sever the connection.[16]

Baur, however, insisted that Christianity must have a historical foundation which can be known by the historian, and that the relation between the ideal and the historical Christ is a necessary one. This is not a relation of identity: Baur was prepared to go with Strauss to the point of saying that the ideal cannot be entirely realized in a single individual, for that would both eliminate history and return us to the docetism of orthodoxy. The ideal and the historical in Christ are neither identified nor separated. One can in-

15. *Geschichte der christlichen Kirche* (1853 ff., 3d ed., 1863), 1 : 22–23.

16. The main lines of Baur's criticism of Schleiermacher were worked out as early as 1827 (in his inaugural essay at Tübingen). Thus Strauss's view of the problem was influenced by Baur. But Strauss, too, in Baur's judgment, failed methodologically because he did not start with the Gospels as literary documents, i.e. as theological treatises to be set in their historical context; thus Strauss was also weak on the relation of John and the Synoptics, which Baur held to be a crucial matter.

deed argue speculatively or dogmatically that the idea of reconciliation must be historically actualized, that is, it must enter into history
at some particular point. But how this takes place can be answered
only by historical study.[17] Whether the beginning of the church is to
be traced to a single individual or to a group, for example, is a
purely historical question, as is the question whether Jesus possessed
the attributes associated with the idea of the Redeemer. Faith must
therefore be informed and tested by historical study. Faith is not,
however, generated by historical study, and it could conceivably continue even in the face of purely negative results from the study of
Jesus of Nazareth—though in the latter case only by a *sacrificium
intellectus.*

What historical study discloses, Baur concluded, is that there is a
historical basis for the faith of the Church rather than simply myth
and miracle. The figure of Jesus historically (rather than "super-
naturally") comprehended is that of the unique founder of the
Christian community and the man distinguished from all others.
In the Hegelian language of Baur's history of the doctrine of the
Trinity and of the incarnation, Jesus was penetrated by the idea of
God-manhood in the most intense way possible for any individual.[18]
He is thus the one through whom necessarily the idea of the unity of
God and man entered historical reality, and this is what gives Chris-
tianity its character as the absolute religion. But again, this assertion
about Jesus can only be historically based, that is, in the actual lin-
eaments of the figure of Jesus as it is known by scientific study of the
Gospels. Christology must be developed strictly *von unten.* It is in
the humanity of Jesus that his divinity is to be seen.[19]

Baur's view of the christological problem, we observed, was at the
heart of his divergence from Hegel. In general, he drew heavily
upon Hegel's conceptions of the relation between theology and
philosophy, and of the God and the world. Religious faith, for Baur,
was an inherently historical phenomenon, its content inseparable

17. For Baur, the church "includes" Christ as its point of origin, yet its nature is
determined by him.

18. *Die christliche Lehre von der Dreieinigkeit und Menschwerdung Gottes in ihrer
geschichtlichen Entwicklung,* 3 vols. (1841–43), 3 : 996–99.

19. Baur saw this view as basic to Protestant theology, but the assertion obviously
has a quite different force in the 19th century than in the 16th. Similarly, Baur says
we cannot start from the Johannine view, thus assuming the agreement of all four
Gospels, without the disappearance of the human into the divine and the surrender of
the historical conception (*Geschichte der Christlichen Kirche,* 1.24).

from historical forms. Philosophical knowledge was abstract and universal. The content of the two must, finally, be identical: the triune God or Absolute Spirit. And the task of theology was to mediate between faith and knowledge, religion and philosophy. The growing freedom (for philosophy) since the time of the Reformation had made possible a more genuine mediation of philosophy and theology without the subservience of either, a process reaching its fullest development in Hegel, in whom the dualistic limits remaining in Schleiermacher were overcome: "Philosophy and theology have become reconciled to each other and essentially one: philosophy has become theology because it recognizes the content of theology as its own, and only in that content does philosophy have the element of its movement; and theology has become philosophy because the common content of the two in the selfconsciousness of spirit, knowing itself one with the content, no longer has the form of theology but that of philosophy." [20]

Similarly, Hegel's speculative development of the idea of reconciliation as an act within the nature of God—so that man is implicitly, in the idea of the triune God, reconciled with God, on the basis of which there can be a reconciliation for subjective consciousness—was a legitimate development of the church's doctrine, though not the final word.[21] Christianity is the revelation and external realization of the mystery of redemption existing eternally in God.[22] Hegel thus correctly took the step beyond Schleiermacher, transposing the historical process into the nature of God himself. But the ambiguity in Hegel's view, which could even lead to an acosmism, that is, to a denial of the reality of the world by absorption into God, came to sharp focus for Baur in Hegel's Christology, particularly in his inability to provide anything more than an accidental relation between the historical Jesus and the idea of the God-man. Finally,

20. *Lehrbuch der christlichen Dogmengeschichte* (3d ed., 1867), pp. 355–56.

21. Cf. *Die christliche Lehre von der Versöhnung in ihrer geschichtlichen Entwicklung von der ältesten Zeit bis auf die neueste* (Tübingen, 1838), pp. 713, 725; *Die christliche Lehre von der Dreieinigkeit und der Menschwerdung,* 3 : 968.

22. As Baur described Hegel's view succinctly: "In its essential content, Christianity is the self-explicating Idea itself. The absolute Idea is God as absolute Spirit, mediating itself to itself in the process of thought. Christianity is therefore essentially this process itself, the life process of God explicating itself in thought as the nature of Spirit. As the content of Christianity is essentially the doctrine of the triune God, so Trinity, as the nature of God, is the nature of Spirit itself, insofar as Spirit can act in thinking in no other way than in the relation of these three moments to itself" (*Lehrbuch,* p. 355).

the historical was taken up into the abstract dialectic of thought. Thus Strauss's thought was the appropriate and legitimate outcome of Hegel's.

With a proper Christology, however, in which the ideal and the historical are not identified but are necessarily related, and in which the form of that relationship is open to historical investigation, the entire historical process would be saved from being swallowed up. Consequently Baur was more insistent than Hegel that God's self-mediation is historical. This historical process is of course not to be understood in terms of supernatural intervention, of miracle, but panentheistically. Yet history is genuine outward expression and unfolding. God and man remain mutually transcendent; the individual is not absorbed into infinity; the unity of man and God is a concrete unity. Against both supernaturalism, which sees God as intruding into history, and rationalism, which disintegrates history into disconnected moments, history means change within continuity.

Given this conception of history as the self-mediation of the divine life, the task of the historian becomes a work of obvious religious importance. He seeks by all scientific and critical means to comprehend the historically given in its pure objectivity. That does not mean an abstraction from present religious consciousness or from all subjectivity. On the contrary, one must consciously start from the present standpoint of the historical. Objective history is not mere chronicle, but a penetration into the inner movement of things, an exhibition of how the Idea has manifested itself, which is possible as the historian with both receptivity and activity pursues the movement of the subject matter itself and transposes himself wholly into it. Historical method is thus both critical and speculative; only through the latter is there penetration into the objectivity of the course of things.[23] For example, one is able to see the contradictions in primitive Christianity's witness as stages in historical development, and thus really to grasp the objectivity of the history concretely. Here Hegel's dialectic was useful, though Baur's conception of the opposing Judaizing and Paulinizing tendencies in the New Testament, for which he has most commonly been scolded for an *a priori* interpretation that forced a Hegelian pattern on the material, was in fact developed before he was influenced by Hegel. Meaning and pattern are elicited from history, not imposed on it.

23. "Speculation," for Baur, is a way of thinking critically about history, by which the historian reflects on the object in such a way that it appears as what it really is.

Thus in historical study in general one accomplishes the same mediation between subjectivity and objectivity that one seeks with respect to the object of faith.

Theology then, for Baur, is necessarily historical theology. This means, as Schleiermacher had insisted, that dogmatics is contemporary theology and has always to be done anew; it will always be surpassed, and one can never stop with a history of doctrine up to the Protestant confessions—or at any other point. The future is open; the Hegelian synthesis will lead to further antitheses. Historical theology and church history, furthermore, are not to be separated from universal history; there can be no disjunction of secular history and *Heilsgeschichte* (nor any distinction between *Historie* and *Geschichte*). But more than this—and quite independently of any commitment by Baur to a quasi-Hegelian view of the relation of God and the world—Baur's view that *theology has a history* meant that all theological thinking must be historical thinking.[24] Theology must be carried on as a historical discipline, with self-awareness of its own development, and in a relation to its object shaped throughout by the historico-critical method.

ALOIS EMANUEL BIEDERMANN (1819–85)

The primary line of development in the demand for "historical" thinking was to lead at the end of the century to Dilthey, to Troeltsch, and to Schweitzer—to each, of course, in quite different ways. But more immediately it led also to A. E. Biedermann, who continued to try to hold together the claims of radical historical criticism and of speculation. He was at once the most prominent dogmatician to emerge from the so-called young Hegelian group and the academic leader of the Swiss union for a "free" Christianity.[25]

24. Further, the history of theology has a history; thus Baur introduced his histories by tracing the development of the discipline.

25. A pastor in Basel, then professor at Zurich (1850–85), Biedermann was deeply involved in the struggle between "positive" and "freethinking" (*freisinnig*) Christianity in the Swiss church, insisting on the one hand on the necessity of the scholarly freedom that liberal Christianity demanded but on the other hand on the possibility that liberal and conservative could coexist in the church and participate in a common task of proclaiming the gospel.

Biedermann's principal works were: *Die Freie Theologie oder Philosophie und Christentum im Streit und Frieden* (1844); *Unsere junghegelsche Weltanschauung oder der sogenannte neueste Pantheismus* (1849); *Christliche Dogmatik* (1869; 2d ed. in 2 vols., 1884–85); and *Ausgewählte Vorträge und Aufsätze* (ed. J. Kradolpher, with a biographical introduction, 1885). Portions of Biedermann's *Dogmatik* are translated in my *God and Incarnation in Mid-Nineteenth Century German Theology* (New

For Biedermann, as he surveyed the current scene in his early essay "Free Theology, or Philosophy and Christianity in War and Peace," the question raised by Strauss's *Glaubenslehre* and Feuerbach's *Das Wesen des Christentums* was the radical question whether the church had a right to exist at all. It was no longer a matter of special doctrines or forms of the church, but of the truth or falsity of Christianity as a whole. Yet it was much less Feuerbach than Strauss who shaped the problem in Biedermann's mind. Biedermann's early use of the language and the orientation of the "young Hegelians" led to his being attacked as Feuerbachian, but he insisted in his theological recollections that he had never been much impressed by Feuerbach and had from the first been diametrically opposed to Feuerbach's naturalism and sheer sensationalist epistemology.

Strauss, however, had already put the fundamental historical question in the *Life of Jesus,* and it was he who most acutely exposed the theoretical need into which the church had fallen. Strauss, further, was for Biedermann the bridge to Hegel. With respect to Christology, Strauss was and remained correct on the side of the negative critique: the Christian principle cannot be identified with the historical individual Jesus. (Typically, just because of the bitterness and hostility toward Strauss in nearly all ecclesiastical circles, Biedermann was particularly open in expressing gratitude to him.) But in the *Glaubenslehre* Strauss never fulfilled the promise of speculative construction and he never overcame the characteristic tendency of modern speculative philosophy to make Jesus merely accidental to the Christian principle—and Biedermann, like Baur, was quite unwilling to settle either for a mere idea casually related to Christ or for a substitution of the race for the individual.

Behind and beyond Strauss it was Hegel to whom, as Biedermann put it, he owed a great part of the nourishment of his philosophical thinking,[26] and whose language permeates the *Dogmatik.* Hegel was right, Biedermann judged, in seeking a purely conceptual statement of the truth. The task of theology is the purification of the form of religious expression in accord with the demands of rational thought. Here Biedermann joined the "rationalism" that was "in his blood"

York, 1965), pp. 287–382, which also contains a selected bibliography. Subsequent references to the *Dogmatik* (*CD*), unless otherwise noted, are by volume and page numbers in the second edition.

26. *CD,* 1st ed., p. ix.

with the conviction that the practical needs of the church required a strictly scientific dogmatics—that is, a genuine historical science and a philosophical *Wissenschaft* with a definite metaphysics and a definite psychology of religion.[27] But Biedermann was by no means only a belated offspring of Hegel. Hegel was wrong at the fundamental point of identifying religion simply with its characteristic mode of thinking, and wrong also in failing to ground all knowledge in the empirical. Religion, for Biedermann, was not merely a theoretical but a whole personal relationship; he regarded it as the highest reality for man, not to be transcended in philosophy. That very one-sidedness in the conception of religion as theoretical had led to the distortions in Strauss and Feuerbach. Biedermann, therefore, sought to draw nearer to Schleiermacher, "the great regenerator of modern theology," [28] who recognized the specificity of the religious relationship as distinguished from every other spiritual realm, who pointed the way to the interpretation of religion from its empirical (i.e. psychological) reality, and who thereby made possible theology's full rights as a free discipline in its realm.

But for Biedermann Schleiermacher also was guilty of a one-sided identification of religion with feeling, as well as of weakening the mutuality and freedom inherent in the religious relationship through his idea of absolute dependence. And Kant, on the other hand, had identified the religious too simply with the ethical. In epistemology, furthermore, Kant had set the subject of consciousness on its proper basis, that is, in the determinateness of its concrete existence; but he had denied to it the proper object of consciousness. Hegel, conversely, had rightly fixed the object of consciousness but deprived the subject of its real basis. So Biedermann could complain that Kant puts us in the water but won't let us swim, and Hegel wants us to learn to swim in the air (*CD*, 1.103).

Biedermann thus hoped to defend the "spiritual reality of religious truth as the highest reality for man" (*CD*, p. xi) against every attempt to swallow it up in something higher or to reduce it to illusion or to narrow it to merely one of the aspects of the human spirit. That is needed not only in the general analysis of the nature, truth, and independence of religion, but also in the critically historical and speculative task that constitutes the bulk of dogmatics. The latter requires (a) a historical account, with an unfettered and

27. See *Ausgewählte Vorträge*, p. 383; *CD*, 1. xii–xiii.
28. *CD*, 1st ed., p. viii.

unabashed exposé of the antinomies in which the historical coinage of Christian doctrines has fallen, (b) a direct rational critique, and (c) a disciplined scientific formulation of the truth. The truth of the Christian view can be brought to light only through the smelting process in which the true content of representation (*Vorstellung*) is set forth in conceptually valid form.[29] This process of the purification of religious ideas, furthermore, is undertaken first and last in the service of the church—for dogmatics is not a purely theoretical but also a practical discipline, and in whatever form ("liberal" or "positive"), it is part of the common religious task of cultivating the gospel of Christ. For Biedermann specifically this is the service of showing forth the truth of the constitutive principle of Christianity in such a way that philosophy and theology, and faith and knowledge, are reconciled.

The critique of representational thinking, as Biedermann understood and employed it, thus did not lead to the negative conclusion of Strauss's criticism of dogma in its history (though Biedermann drew heavily on Strauss's historical analysis). Nor was it merely a propaedeutic, a means of getting the traditional affirmations out of the way in order to replace them by new assertions. Biedermann, as we noted, agreed with Hegel on the goal: The truth to be sought can only be a truth of genuine *thought;* therefore, in the quest for the nuclear truth of the life of spirit, the spiritual content must be brought to logical, purely conceptual expression. What is given in religious conviction must be brought, for scientific purposes, to a form of expression adequate to that ideal content. But Biedermann sharply disagreed with Hegel (and with Feuerbach, for this was the fundamental error leading to Feuerbach's illusionism) on the identification of religion with the representational. Precisely that which Hegel designated as the definitive element in religion, the representational character, Biedermann rejected as being constitutive, for this would be to reduce religion to a theoretical relation to God.

Biedermann, we may say, tried to take more seriously than Hegel

29. *Vorstellung* Biedermann defined as the second of three essential steps in the process of cognition: the act of perceiving (*Wahrnehmen*) and perception (*Wahrnehmung*); the act of representing (*Vorstellen*) and representation; and the act of thinking (*Denken*) and thought (*Gedanke*). The order of movement here is necessary. One cannot, with Hegel, begin with pure thought, aprioristically. Cognition moves only from perception through representation to the purification of the latter in thought (cf. *CD*, §§ 21–49).

the latter's assertion that in religion the true content is already found. The highest reality for man is indeed given in the religious relationship, and that relation remains what it is whether described in images or representations or concepts, for the center of gravity in religion is the "whole personal relation of the ego to God, which is carried out unitarily in man's thinking, feeling, and willing." [30] The content does not rest in the representational form. It is thus not *religion* that is to be transformed from representation into concepts, for religion is neither of these; religion is the practical relationship. It is man's "personal elevation as finite spirit from the negatively experienced limits of his life to a liberation from those limits by infinite spirit" (*CD*, §§ 69, 737).

Representation, further, is the natural and inevitable language of religion, both in the sense that men all live their lives primarily at this level, and in the sense that the disciplined or scientific statement of religious truth can be wrought only out of what is given first in representational form.[31] So too, the identification of contradiction in representation, between a purely spiritual content and a sensuous form, is itself a positive step toward pure conceptual statement.

Biedermann's theological program is naturally most clearly seen in his Christology, which for him denoted both the heart of the modern theological embarrassment and the center of the theological system. The Christian principle is directly "the new religious prin-

---

30. *Ausgewählte Vorträge und Aufsätze*, p. 413.

31. Thus the portrayal of God as personality, at the level of representation, is both permissible and necessary, even though finitude belongs essentially to the concept of personality. Absolute spirit can only be *thought;* absolute personality can only be *represented.* "The two indeed coincide: absolute spirit as conception [*Gedanke*] and absolute personality as representation. . . . In thinking of God as absolute we know that, and why, we must also represent him to ourselves as personality." (And the psychological nature of our spirit requires that we think first in representations.) Personality is thus "the adequate representational form for the theistic concept of God, i.e. for that which combines all the essential elements of the idea of God in the concept of absolute spirit. But for just that reason 'the personality of God' is in science the shibboleth of merely representational theism, which is not able to rise scientifically above the act of representation to pure thinking. In substance, it is in the right vis-à-vis every pantheistic representation of God; in form it still stands on the same basis with the latter. In the substance of religious content it is one with the pure concept of absolute spirit; but according to form it is still only an unscientific version of the content. . . . Only man as finite spirit is personality; God as absolute spirit is not. Yet the religious intercourse is always a personal one, and indeed not merely in subjective representation but in objective truth, because it goes on between the infinite and the finite spirit within the finite human spiritual life and thus must take place throughout in the form of the latter" (*CD*, §§ 716–17).

ciple that entered human history as the fact of the religious person of Jesus" (*CD*, § 592). Accordingly, theology and anthropology are ordered as postulates of Christology, and soteriology and eschatology as its consequences.

The first task in christological investigation is simply to lay out the historical development from biblical theology to the formulations of the most recent times, including especially those of the *kenosis* doctrine (see below, chap. 9). The result is a judgment much like that of Strauss; the history of christological doctrine is the story of its dissolution, that is, its increasingly obvious involvement in self-contradiction. The church's doctrine has from the beginning tried to hold on to the personal deity of the ego of Christ, to the unity of his person, and to the genuineness of his human life. But this has led from the ancient church's idea of the two natures of the God-man, through the doctrine of the *communicatio idiomatum* (the impartation of properties) to the modern idea of kenosis, in which aspects of deity are actually laid aside in the incarnation—and the natural outcome has been the doctrine of a "transformation of the Logos into a man" as formulated by Gess.[32] This is a complete absurdity, the perfect contradiction in terms. Yet just at this point, and because of the absurdity, the rational nucleus can begin to emerge.

Within its materials the church's doctrine was constantly seeking a consistent expression for its principles of true deity, true humanity, and unity in a personal life. But the materials were representational and, therefore, the more consistent the expressions the sharper the contradictions. The contradictions arose both from the universal (psychologically grounded) problem in every spiritual representation, "that in it consciousness holds a purely ideal reality present in a form taken from sensible reality," and from the specifically historical contradiction "that Christian faith first gave account of its essentially new religious content in forms of consciousness which had sprung directly out of the religious soil which faith broke through and annulled" (*CD*, § 586). A complete working out of the negative task of rational critique of representational forms is thus necessary, in order for the religious content to be grasped in pure conceptual form.

The root of the christological problem emerges as the immediate

---

32. W. F. Gess, *Die Lehre von der Person Christi, entwickelt aus dem Selbstbewusst-sein Christi und aus dem Zeugniss der Apostel* (Basel, 1856). Cf. Biedermann, *CD*, esp. § 407.

identification of the Christian principle with the human person of
Jesus, so that a spiritual principle is described as a person, and a
mythologizing doctrinal form emerges. So far with Strauss. Strauss's
negative conclusions must be maintained: the definitions of Christology cannot be accepted as the definitions of a person. But neither
Strauss's proposal to substitute the race for an individual, nor the
attempt of mediating theology (e.g. Schleiermacher, Schenkel), has
resolved this problem without abandoning or violating what the
church's doctrine actually and rightly sought to express, albeit in
inadequate form. On the other hand, the speculative Christologies
provide proper metaphysical material, but they make the idea of
God-manhood a universal metaphysical truth about the abstract relation of absolute and finite or of divine and human, whereas this
idea is a specifically religious one, that is, a specific determination
of the *religious* reciprocal relation between finite and infinite spirit.

The essential content of Christology is then, for Biedermann, to
be defined as the Christian principle of divine childhood, "which in
the religious person of Jesus . . . entered into humanity as the essentially new religious power of life, and thereby is the intrinsically
unitary actual ground—and thus the principle—of the Christian
religion" (*CD*, § 792). This principle is intrinsically eternally contained in the nature of God and man as their true religious re
lationship, but "it first factually entered as such into human history
in the religious person of Jesus" (*CD*, § 795), and that is what was
essentially new in him and why Christian faith is based on that
personhood. What was expressed in Jesus' self-consciousness of divine childhood, his messianic self-consciousness, his self-consciousness
of the absolute value of the ego vis-à-vis world existence, his drawing
of the absolute ethical command directly out of his self-consciousness
of loving communion with God—all these elements of the concretely
historical form, which it is the business of historical research and
religious psychology to examine, are to be defined purely conceptually as the way in which "God-manhood actualizes itself as the
human spiritual life of divine childhood . . . as finite spirit's self-
consciousness of the absoluteness of spirit" (*CD*, §§ 796, 799). It is
not the historically accidental (mythological and representational)
forms of assertions about Jesus, but the principle of divine childhood revealed in him, that constitutes the self-identical essence of
Christian faith. But Jesus was the first self-actualization of that
principle as a world-historical figure and is thus (to contradict

Strauss) the historical Redeemer, the entrance into human spiritual life of the principle of salvation for natural humanity, the annulling of the discord into which man by nature falls and out of which he cannot by himself emerge.

ESSAYS AND REVIEWS (1860)

It is a vivid indication of a time lag in the nineteenth century between German and British theology—and perhaps of a determined insularity on the part of the latter—that the historical question, and thus the question of biblical authority and inspiration, was not fully confronted in Britain until the publication in 1860 of a group of essays by seven Oxford men, under the title *Essays and Reviews*.[33] To be sure, Strauss's *Life of Jesus* had been translated by Marian Evans in 1846,[34] Coleridge's *Confessions of an Inquiring Spirit* had been published in 1840 (though of course he did not have to be counted as a theologian), B. F. Westcott's *Introduction to the Study of the Gospels* had appeared in 1853, and Dean Stanley's *Epistles of St. Paul to the Corinthians* and Benjamin Jowett's *Epistles to the Thessalonians, Galatians, and Romans* in 1855. Yet *Essays and Reviews* generated a shock not unlike that caused in Germany by Strauss's book, so that "within a year of its publication the orthodox English world was convulsed with indignation and panic"[35] and the controversy over *The Origin of Species* was for a time overshadowed. Two of the authors (the only ones subject to ecclesiastical discipline) were tried for heresy, but they were eventually acquitted.

Complaints came from both sides, initially from the "positivist" Frederic Harrison in the *Westminster Review*, which had been a center for reports on Continental biblical criticism. Harrison greeted the book as the *reductio ad absurdum* of the Broad Church, rejecting the idea that this liberalism could call itself Christianity. The church, in other words, should stay where it was when the positivist left it. The orthodox made the same kind of charge: the threat of the book to them was that it could not be put aside as an attack

---

33. See the excellent interpretation, with an account of the varying responses, by Basil Willey, *More Nineteenth Century Studies* (London, 1956), chap. 4, "Septem contra Christum." (Willey's attempt to relate *Essays and Reviews* to Bultmann is less useful.) See also W. L. Knox and Alec Vidler, *The Development of Modern Catholicism* (London, 1933); and L. E. Elliott-Binns, *Religion in the Victorian Era* (London, 1936).

34. And she had been influenced to give up her evangelical beliefs by the Unitarian Charles Hennell's *Inquiries Concerning the Origin of Christianity* (1838).

35. Willey, *More Nineteenth Century Studies*, p. 137.

from without (or charged to "German rationalism") but was a conspiracy from within.

The content of *Essays and Reviews* does not require extensive analysis. It was essentially a manifesto for freedom and honesty in the discussion of biblical-critical questions, a protest against the "conspiracy of silence" that had dominated the English scene. Rowland Williams reported belligerently on "Bunsen's Biblical Researches." Baden Powell, writing "on the Study of the Evidences of Christianity," followed much in the line of Hume's essay on miracles. C. W. Goodwin discussed the Mosaic cosmogony in relation to the geological sciences, arguing particularly against the biblical harmonizers.[36] Mark Pattison's "Tendencies of Religious Thought in England, 1688–1750" was a first rate and original piece of historical interpretation, clearly the essay of most enduring value. Pattison could deal with the theology of evidences much more effectively than Powell, remarking that "evidences are not edged tools; they stir no feeling; they were the proper theology of an age, whose literature consisted in writing Latin hexameters." [37]

The most immediately relevant and important essay was the last, by Benjamin Jowett, "On the Interpretation of Scripture." It was by no means extreme, either in conclusions or in tone, but was rather strongly affirmative of the "real truths" of Christianity, that is, of the enduring reality of the Christian life. For the sake of that deeper truth, Jowett argued with the weight of his classical scholarship (and out of acquaintance with Lessing, Schleiermacher, Hegel, and Bauer), the results of criticism are not to be ignored or rejected; they are to be welcomed. Christianity cannot be opposed to the love of truth. "Any true doctrine of inspiration must conform to all well-ascertained facts of history or science." And, most horrifying of

36. Goodwin did not deal with Darwin; the only reference in the *Essays* to *The Origin of Species* was by Baden Powell. Goodwin's view of the problem of scriptural interpretation was relatively simplistic, assuming a ready availability of the "plain meaning of the Hebrew record," but his statement of the principles for relating Genesis and science is a useful indication of the temper of the times: "It would have been well if theologians had made up their minds to accept frankly the principle that those things for the discovery of which man has faculties specially provided are not fit objects of a divine revelation. . . . Believing, as we do, that if the value of the Bible as a book of religious instruction is to be maintained, it must be not by striving to prove it scientifically exact, at the expense of every sound principle of interpretation, and in defiance of common sense, but by the frank recognition of the erroneous views of nature which it contains, we have put pen to paper to analyze some of the popular conciliation theories" (*Essays and Reviews* [Leipzig 1862], pp. 189–91).

37. Ibid., p. 235.

all to many of Jowett's contemporaries, Scripture must be "interpreted like any other book, by the same rules of evidence and the same canons of criticism." Yet when this is done, "the Bible will still remain unlike any other book, its beauty will be freshly seen, . . . it will create a new interest and make for itself a new kind of authority by the life which is in it. It will be a spirit and not a letter." [38] Thus discrepancies can be openly recognized, even misinterpretations within the Bible, and yet its eternal import remains invulnerable.

Essays and Reviews certainly worked no universal change in British theology. Six years later, H. P. Liddon was defending the orthodox Christology in his Bampton Lectures, reiterating the Mosaic authorship of Deuteronomy (since Jesus so quotes it, and he after all was omniscient). Yet the book marked a major transition. Perhaps because the impact of biblical criticism came so much later in Britain than in Germany, the *Essays* and Darwin's *Origin of Species* intensified each other's effect. After 1860, according to one interpreter, "a settled state of baffled judgment and a mind empty of beliefs" began to appear in Britain.[39] More positively and specifically put, *Essays and Reviews* made impossible a further concealment of the historical question, it greatly broadened the range of permissible religious opinions, it widened the discussion to include the larger public, and it opened the way for acceptance of the work of the rising generation of biblical critics like B. F. Westcott and J. B. Lightfoot—as well as for the reluctant acceptance of writers like T. H. Huxley as serious positivist challengers to narrow biblical belief.

38. Ibid., pp. 303, 325.
39. Walter E. Houghton, *The Victorian Frame of Mind, 1830–1870* (New Haven, 1957), p. 20.

8

Humanism, Religion, and Culture

Like the theological developments treated in the previous chapter, the several quite different critiques of theology on behalf of man and culture discussed in this chapter may also be called variants of radical theology, deeply concerned about the kind of religious thinking appropriate to the modern world. The standpoint for critique and reordering in these theologies, however, was not the historical question, as in Strauss and Baur, but the problem of the humanity of man and the validity of his culture. Here, in other words, were some of the theological reflections of the crisis in the idea of humanity that emerged toward the middle of the nineteenth century—a multi-dimensioned crisis with which we associate figures as diverse as Feuerbach and Kierkegaard, Marx and Emerson, Comte and Darwin.

THE CELEBRATION OF MAN: LUDWIG FEUERBACH

To this context Ludwig Feuerbach (1804–72) belongs in a peculiar and decisive way. With Strauss he was one of that mixed group of German thinkers called "young Hegelians," and he can be spoken of as representing the "negative development" from Hegel. Much more than Strauss, Feuerbach was part of the stream of "materialistic thought" that swept over Germany and changed Hegel's idealism into materialism. Also, as is widely known, Feuerbach was a prime figure in the transition from Hegel to Marx—even though it was Strauss more than Feuerbach who persuaded Marx and many others that one need not any longer bother with theology.

Feuerbach, nevertheless, belongs within the theological story rather than simply to the rejection and turning away from Christianity. If this is so, it is not because Feuerbach posed for the nineteenth century the great threat of an immanent critique of theology, which was to be the fate of Schleiermacher as well as Hegel. That thesis has been argued by Barth and others, and Feuerbach may indeed have become such for many thinkers in the twentieth century, especially after Freud. But for the mid-nineteenth century it was Strauss who posed the great *internal* theological threat (recall that this was explicitly Alois Biedermann's judgment). Feuerbach was a radical empiricist, for whom existing things were not to be derived from thought; existence is rather known only by sense perception and feeling. He thus built on another basis and represented a turn to a new humanism of a quite different sort from that of idealism and the romantic era.

Yet Feuerbach's "theological" anthropology, his desire to reveal the true nature of religion, his exaltation of man, *real* man, his preoccupation with the problem of theology and of Christian theology in particular, gave him a peculiar place in Germany in the shift away from idealism and Christianity. Because of that, his way of posing the questions for theology has properly come to stand as a parallel to the historical kind of question raised by Strauss; and his "atheism" became a different and more threatening sort of atheism than that of Hume.[1]

For fifteen years Feuerbach was a disciple of Hegel. Thereafter Hegel continued to dominate his thought, but as one whose fundamental premise had to be opposed. The initial break came apparently in the understanding of religion, which for Feuerbach was to be located in the sphere of feeling rather than in that of thought.

1. After a brief period with Daub at Heidelberg, Feuerbach studied under Hegel at Berlin (1824 and following) then went to Erlangen, where he was a *Privatdozent* in philosophy for a time. In part, presumably, because of the unorthodox character of his first published work, *Gedanken über Tod und Unsterblichkeit* (1830), he withdrew from university life and spent the rest of his career as a private scholar. His interpretation of religion is found in *Das Wesen des Christentums* (1841; trans. from the 2d German ed. by Marian Evans, *The Essence of Christianity* [London, 1854]; reissued under the same title with an introductory essay by Karl Barth [New York, 1957]), the work which made him famous as the dominant figure in the philosophical world for a decade; *Das Wesen des Glaubens im Sinne Luthers* (1844; trans. from the 1846 ed. by M. Cherno, *The Essence of Faith According to Luther* [New York, 1967]); *Das Wesen der Religion* (1845); and the Heidelberg Lectures of 1848–49, *Vorlesungen über das Wesen der Religion* (trans. Ralph Manheim, *Lectures on the Essence of Religion* [New York, 1967]). Also important for Feuerbach's overall philosophical view is the *Grundsätze der Philosophie der Zukunft* (1843; trans. Manfred Vogel, *Principles of the Philosophy of the Future* [Indianapolis, 1966]). After the revolutions of 1848, in which Feuerbach was a minor hero because of his philosophical influence on some of the leaders (though he himself played no direct role in political affairs), his star waned. He was left behind by the "scientific socialists" and he was largely ignored by the theologians until the 20th century.

Unless otherwise noted, references to *The Essence of Christianity* (*EC*) are cited by page number in the 1957 ed.; references to *Principles of the Philosophy of the Future* (*PPF*) by page number in the Vogel translation.

More broadly, Feuerbach made the transition from the absolute to
the human as the center for the concept of truth. Hegel's fundamental presupposition, the identity of being and thought, which for
Feuerbach was based on an idea of being rather than on concrete
reality, was to be abandoned in favor of a position based explicitly
and thoroughly on sense perception. Feuerbach wrote in the preface
to the second edition of *The Essence of Christianity:*

> I unconditionally repudiate *absolute* immaterial self-sufficing spec-
> ulation—that speculation which draws its material from within. I
> differ *toto coelo* from those philosophers who pluck out their eyes
> that they may see better; for *my* thought I require the senses, es-
> pecially sight; I found my ideas on materials which can be appro-
> priated only through the activity of the senses. I do not generate
> the object from the thought, but the thought from the object; and
> I hold *that* alone to be an object which has an existence beyond
> one's brain. [*EC,* p. xxxiv]

And in the *Principles of the Philosophy of the Future* he wrote that
the self with which his philosophy begins is not the "abstract and
merely thinking being to whose essence the body does not belong"
but the judgment "I am a real, sensuous being and indeed the body
in its totality is my ego, my essence itself" (*PPF,* p. 54).

Thus Feuerbach could still use Hegel's dialectical logic (though
Marx complained that Feuerbach had really given up dialectic), but
only on fundamentally anti-Hegelian presuppositions. In the themes
that Feuerbach and Hegel had in common, Hegel's scheme was
turned upside down. It remained true for Feuerbach that the divine
is the human and that the human is the divine, but the starting
point and direction of the dialectical movement were precisely reversed: not the Absolute objectifying itself in the human and returning to itself, but the human self objectifying itself, projecting
the infinite as the divine, and returning to itself. Both Hegel and
Feuerbach were profoundly concerned with the theme of self-
alienation, and through them it entered into the fabric of modern
thought. But for Hegel alienation was the result of man's failure
to realize himself as divine, whereas for Feuerbach alienation came
from man's projection of a part of his own being into another imaginary being, the fantasy which is God. Alienation was thus to be
overcome by the removal of the supernatural and the recognition
that the self is entirely in space and time.

What is of decisive importance about Feuerbach's view of religion is not that he rejected a transcendent object of devotion, but the way in which he sought to give an account of the religious reality. As he said concerning the structure of *The Essence of Christianity,* the "negative applications" of Part II, in which he detailed the contradictions in traditional theology, were not to be taken alone, as if religion and Christianity were simply nothing. Of course, religion has been a hindrance to man's material development. There is in fact no metaphysical correlative of faith, no actual experience of God. But the negative consequences rest upon the earlier positive explication of the nature of man and religion. Anthropologically, religion is a very great reality, and an understanding of the illusory character of the objects of religion's assertions is essential for the understanding of man and for his future progress. Thus Feuerbach became the first thinker to develop a full theory of religion as illusion; and this he himself judged to be a turning point in human history.

Feuerbach's theory of religion can be summarized briefly as follows. The possibility of religion lies in the distinction between man and the brute, that is, in consciousness. But consciousness means the possibility of an inner life, the presence of a being to himself as an object of thought, the self-consciousness that is the consciousness a man has of his nature.[2] The basis of religion is to be found in feeling or emotion and in wish. Included in feeling, of course, is human fear, and "the fear of evil that constantly accompanies man is the root of the religious imagination." [3] But feeling is not identical with fear, it is also ecstasy, joy, love, gratitude, a sense of dependence (not Schleiermacher's feeling of utter dependence, but a feeling of dependence that has eyes and ears). The root of religion is also in desire, in man's wish to be and to have what he is not and does not have. Religious fantasy is distinctive in that it has a "practical, egoistic goal." Man believes in gods because he seeks help from them. What he is not himself but wishes to be, he projects into the being of the gods in order that he may get it back from them. Thus the imagination is the most essential organ of religion.

2. In *The Essence of Christianity* Feuerbach argued that no being could be limited to itself; thus self-consciousness is immediately a consciousness of the infinite in its nature, the consciouness of the infinite being precisely the consciousness of the infinity of the consciousness.

3. *Das Wesen der Religion,* p. 234; see also p. 51.

The imagination is to be recognized as an authentic activity of sensuous man; here man may express himself freely and spontaneously. And the products of the imagination are not condemned as false and inadmissible abstractions of speculation so long as it is recognized that the projections of the imagination are different from the objects of sense perception. The error of Neoplatonic thought (whose imagination and fantasy was merely rationalized and transformed by Hegel into concepts) is that, having negated the body, it negates in practice the difference between imagination and perception. In place of the real world there is deposited an "imaginary and intelligible world in which there is everything that is in the real world, but abstracted and imagined" (*PPF*, p. 45. See pp. 44–48).

The proof of this view of religion is to be found precisely in the characteristics of religion itself. In prayer—the simplest act of religion, in which "man addresses God with the word of intimate affection, *thou*," thus declaring "that God is his alter ego"—man confesses to the being nearest to him his most secret thoughts and his deepest wishes, in the certainty that these wishes will be fulfilled. He forgets that a limit exists for his wishes and is happy in that forgetfulness. Here the objective is absolutely identical with the subjective; "prayer is the unconditional confidence of human feeling in the absolute identity of the subjective and the objective, the certainty that the power of the heart is greater than the power of nature, that the heart's need is absolute necessity, the fate of the world." "Prayer is the absolute relation of the human heart to itself, to its own nature." "It is the self-division of man into two beings—a dialogue of man with himself, with his heart" (*EC*, chap. 12). Faith, which is the power of prayer, is "identical with faith in miraculous power." It is that which "unfetters the wishes of subjectivity from the bonds of natural reason; it confers what nature and reason denies; hence it makes man happy, for it satisfies his most personal wishes" (*EC*, chap. 13). Again, the grave is to be recognized as the birthplace of the gods; the negative wish of man not to die becomes the positive wish for life after death. In its last doctrine, religion speaks out unequivocally in its concern for man. Saint Paul said it openly: "If there is no immortality, then there is no God." Similarly, beliefs in creation and providence express openly "the value of man . . . the conviction of man of the infinite value of his existence" (*EC*, p. 105). Providence is always for man's sake.

Religion's way of conceiving God is itself a proof that theology is anthropology. Orthodox theologians readily admit the human projection of the attributes of God but deny the projection of the *subject* of the attributes. Yet no being can exist without attributes, hence this admission is itself a product of unbelief, a subtle disguise for atheism. To deny the objective validity of the attributes as applied to God is precisely to deny what is most important to religion. Unless God has human qualities man can find no contentment in him. It is not the so-called metaphysical attributes but the personal and moral attributes that are essential to religion. These have the material, sensuous, and determinate qualities of objects of the imagination—and when these predicates are acknowledged to be anthropomorphism, doubt has conquered faith, and it is recognized that the *subject* of those predicates, as well as the predicates themselves, is human.

This, then, was the novelty of Feuerbach, in relation to the rejection of God by other empiricists. Religious language cannot be simply rejected; only it cannot be taken at face value. It must instead be interpreted so that we may understand what is really being expressed. Here Christianity is of singular interest. At one level, Christianity is an illustration of the general character of religion. "The difference between the Christian's and the heathen's God rests only on the difference between the Christian's wishes and the wishes of the heathen." [4]

But more than this, Christianity is the "perfect religion" in that it, as distinguished from pagan and Jewish religions, is utterly the religion of the heart and the disposition. Its basic dogmas are the clearest expression of the process of man's alienation from himself and of the fulfillment of the wishes of the heart. In Christianity man most clearly negates himself in order to affirm God. That is to say, whatever is positive in man is elevated to the Divine Being and the remaining concept of man is only negative. Man denies his own goodness and knowledge that he may place them in God, so that the more the divine subject is really human, the greater is the apparent difference between God and man. Of course, the religious man virtually retracts his own nothingness by making himself an object of this rejection of himself. He puts it in God, in other words, in order that he may get it back.

In a peculiar way, then Feuerbach also became highly christo-

4. *Vorlesungen,* 1851 ed., p. 298.

centric in his thinking about religion. He had, of course, no interest in the question of the historical element in the story of Christ, though he also had no interest in denying the reality of the human figure as something for the imagination to work on. But the "real Christ," which is central, is the embodiment of all the qualities admired by man and the clearest exhibition of the human nature of God. It is a "complete misunderstanding of religion to trace religious facts back to historical facts." [5] The incarnation is "nothing else than the practical, material manifestation of the human nature of God." The love of God for man is embodied in Christ because man is contemplating himself as an object; "the descent of God to man is necessarily preceded by the exaltation of man to God. Man was already in God, was already God himself, before God became man, i.e., showed himself as man" (*EC,* p. 50). The identity of God and man is thus entirely intelligible, not as a doctrine of speculative philosophy deducing the incarnation from metaphysical grounds, but as an expression of the deepest truth of the religious process.

As a protester *against* theology Feuerbach was not finally as important as Karl Marx. The distinctiveness and power of Feuerbach lay rather in his explanation of the origins and functions of religious conceptions in the life of sensuous man. His sort of atheism was to be an internal threat to theology because it demythologized God from within religion, which was itself shown to be a true affair of the heart. It said that theistic language is not at all meaningless: it is full of meaning, but it is finally disclosed to be talk about man himself. In this way Feuerbach could come to pose a more serious threat to theology than either Hume or Strauss.

The great positive point of Feuerbach's exposé of religion was to call on man for inward change, for a reorientation of consciousness made possible only by removal of the false notions of God. This was to be the true overcoming of man's alienation. The real question was no longer one of the existence or nonexistence of God, but of the existence or nonexistence of men, and Feuerbach wanted to call

5. *Das Wesen der Religion,* p. 293. Feuerbach welcomed Luther's insistence that Christ is decisive for the Christian knowledge of God. See appendixes 21 and 22 of *The Essence of Christianity.* In the second edition of *The Essence of Christianity* and in *The Essence of Faith According to Luther,* Feuerbach elaborates the judgment that Luther's view of Christianity is a particularly apt illustration of his theory. Feuerbach could even refer to himself as a second Luther. What he did was simply to make explicit the implications of Luther's exclusive stress on the "for us" in assertions about God and Christ.

men to be men, real flesh-and-blood men, for whom sensuousness (*Sinnlichkeit*) is the principle of reality and truth.[6] The old philosophy could say "I am an abstract and merely a thinking being to whose essence the body does not belong"; but the new philosophy begins by saying "I am a real sensuous being and indeed the body in its totality is my ego, my essence itself" (*PPF*, p. 54).

Feuerbach's effort, therefore, is not properly described as a deification of man, as Barth and others have tried to say. To affirm that there is no measure other than man is not to say that man is unlimited and not measured. It is to say rather that man is to be recognized and celebrated precisely in his actual humanness. As Feuerbach insisted "it is not I but religion that worships man although religion, or rather theology, denies it" (*EC*, p. xxxvi).

Theology had long ago become anthropology, particularly since Luther. Feuerbach wanted to take the next great step—to let man be man. As he put it in the concluding words of his Heidelberg lectures, his principal aim was to change "the friends of God into friends of man, believers into thinkers, worshipers into workers, candidates for the other world into students of this world, Christians, who according to their own confession and understanding are half animal and half angel, into *men, whole men*."

THE DIVINITY OF MAN:
EMERSON AND THE TRANSCENDENTALISTS

If Feuerbach's critique of theology was a protest on behalf of man's freedom and authenticity, so also was that of Ralph Waldo Emerson.[7] But it would be hard to imagine two thinkers whose

6. In the earlier works, including *The Essence of Christianity* and *The Principles of the Philosophy of the Future*, Feuerbach stopped somewhat short of the assertion that the real human being is individual man. He held on at times to the idea of generic man, of the species, and this was attacked as a contradiction of his argument in *The Essence of Christianity*, where the idea of generic man became the basis for interpreting the attributes of infinity, immortality, omniscience, and omnipotence. But beginning with the Luther book, Feuerbach shifted his emphasis to the individual, concrete man—and in still later writings he moved all the way to a materialistic position.

7. The descendant of a long line of New England clergymen, Emerson (1803–82) studied at Harvard College and Harvard Divinity School and was for a short time pastor of the Second Church in Boston. Resigning in 1832 because he could no longer conscientiously administer the sacrament of the Lord's Supper (he did not believe that Christ intended to establish such a continuing observance), he settled down in Concord, Massachusetts, to spend the rest of his career as an essayist, poet, and lecturer on a wide range of topics, most of them nontheological but suffused with a religious feeling. Emerson's works have been issued in numerous editions: *Complete*

ideas of man were more opposed. The man Emerson celebrated seems to have hardly anything in common with Feuerbach's "real man," the man of whom Feuerbach could come to say in all seriousness "Der Mensch ist was er isst." Emerson too could utter the shibboleth "The divine is the human and the human is the divine"— but on his lips the words have an accent closer to Hegel's than to Feuerbach's, and yet quite different from either. Feuerbach rejected the transcendent in order to affirm the humanity of man. Emerson affirmed the transcendent in order to show the divinity of man.

Emerson's was a man in harmony with a benign and supportive nature. He shared the romantics' delight in nature; for him the fields and woods minister "the suggestion of an occult relation between man and the vegetable." This nature "never wears a mean appearance." She is the symbol of spirit, the inviolable order of consistency and law, which promises us something more than the attributes of brute nature, which leads beyond the senses to unity, morality and spirit. To spirit, nature is "a remoter and inferior incarnation of God" ("Nature," pp. 7, 5, 36).

Emerson's was also self-consciously an American man. In the Phi Beta Kappa address, "The American Scholar" (1837), which was enthusiastically received, Emerson brought to sharp focus the American desire for intellectual independence from Europe. "We have listened too long to the courtly muses of Europe." "Perhaps the time is already come . . . when the sluggard intellect of this Continent will look from under its iron lids and fill the postponed expectation of the world with something better than the exertions of mechanical skill. Our day of dependence, our long apprenticeship to the learning of other lands, draws to a close" (pp. 62, 45).

This American scholar is free from enslavement by the inherited learning of the past. Rightly used, books are "the best of things"; but their one right use is "for nothing but to inspire." "Man Thinking" must be superior to his instruments. Hence books are "for the scholar's idle times" (pp. 49, 50). History and the sciences serve us

---

Works, 12 vols. (Boston, 1903–04); *Journals,* 10 vols. (Boston, 1909–14); and *Letters,* ed. R. L. Rusk, 6 vols. (New York, 1939). His views on man and religion are well represented in the small volume *Nature,* the addresses on "The American Scholar," "An Address" (to the Harvard Divinity School graduating class of 1838), "The Transcendentalists," "The Lord's Supper," and the essays on "History," "Self-Reliance," "Spiritual Laws," "The Over-Soul," and "Nature." Page references in the text below are to the excellent collection, *The Selected Writings of Ralph Waldo Emerson,* ed. Brooks Atkinson (New York, 1950).

most only when they support the creativity in the self. Man Thinking is educated by nature, by books, and also by action, for in the
American world the scholar is not a recluse but one for whom life
is the dictionary—though he finally finds his help and truth in himself alone. The true man, "inspired by the Divine Soul which also
inspires all men" (p. 63), is man in the act of creation. Not the
record, not the thought, not the mere thinker or parrot of others'
thoughts, but man thinking in complete self-trust.

Third, Emerson's man was an individual and largely unhistorical
man, one to be freed from both society and history. Society, with its
love for names and customs rather than realities and creators, is
"everywhere in conspiracy against the manhood of every one of its
members" and "history is an impertinence and an injury if it be
anything more than a cheerful apologue or parable of my being and
becoming" ("Self-Reliance," pp. 148, 157). As each individual man
is an incarnation of universal mind, the world exists "for the education of each man," all history becoming subjective, verified in
private experience, so that "there is properly no history, only biography" ("History," pp. 126, 127).

Finally, Emerson's man was a divine reality. In more radical
fashion than the other so-called Transcendentalists Emerson took
up Unitarianism's concern for man's goodness, gave it warmth and
inner power, and carried it to the farthest extreme. If Channing
(and Parker) thought man perfectible, Emerson thought him divine.
There is no division of natural and supernatural such that the
latter intrudes by miracle. The one universal spirit is immanent in
the soul and is the ground of man's self-confidence. Revelation is
the disclosure of the soul. The one thing of value in the world is
the active, creating soul, which sees and utters absolute truth. Even
though in most men obstructed or unborn, this divinity is contained
in every man. "Ineffable is the union of man and God in every act
of the soul. The simplest person who in his integrity worships God,
becomes God; yet forever and ever the influx of this better and universal self is new and unsearchable" ("The Over-Soul," p. 275).

Emerson was not one to agonize over evil or error. There is
struggle, of course, as man, the bearer of spirit, seeks to conquer the
world (this plainly spoke to an America become conscious of her
strength). But evil is "merely privative," "so much death or nonen-
tity." Only "benevolence is absolute and real" (Divinity School Address, p. 69). At such points Emerson found support in the religions

of Asia, which he greatly helped to introduce to America, though his own understanding of Eastern religions was poor. He was much impressed by the Hindu (or more properly the Vedanta) concept of *maya,* commonly interpreted to mean that the world is illusory; and he took up the theme of the unreality of the phenomenal. He also found continuity with his own doctrine of the "Over-Soul" in the Indian concept of Brahman (see his poem "Brahma").

Emerson's man is virtually infallible in his intuitions. Of course the generality of men have not actualized this potentiality, but man is nevertheless able to intuit directly and individually the absolute right and the true, that is, the transcendent spiritual reality. No criteria were offered for identification of the transcendent reality, but there was no doubt of the individual's ability to intuit directly and without dependence on others.[8]

Emerson's Divinity School Address, which so shocked the Unitarian clergy that it was nearly thirty years before he was again invited to speak at Harvard, was the most important statement of the relation of his ideas to the theology and ecclesiastical life of the day. His starting point is the mystery of nature and "the sentiment of virtue," which is the essence of all religion. Man learns that though he now lies in evil he is born to the good, to the perfect. He is not to be virtuous but virtue. "The intuition of the moral sentiment is an insight of the perfection of the laws of the soul," which are such

---

8. It was this idea which gave what cohesion there was to the so-called Transcendentalists. Others in the group, besides Emerson and Theodore Parker (1810–60), were William H. Furness (1802–96), George Ripley (1803–80), Orestes A. Brownson (1803–76), Frederic H. Hedge (1805–90), James Freeman Clarke (1810–88), and William Henry Channing (1810–84). All of these except Brownson were Harvard College and Divinity School men. The others were theologically more conservative than Emerson. More basic than their belief in an order of truth transcending the sphere of sensory experience, which according to George Ripley in 1840 was why they were called Transcendentalists, was the abounding faith in human intuition of that moral and spiritual truth. This vague though vigorously asserted idea had for them a quite ill-understood ancestry. It was anti-Lockean (and that was part of their conflict with the old-line Unitarians), and it drew variously on Platonism, German idealism, romanticism, Coleridge, and especially Victor Cousin. The degree of their confusion on the historical roots is illustrated in Emerson's idea that Kant's use of "transcendental deduction" and "intuition" involved the direct cognition of transcendent realities. Even Parker, who was widely read in German thought, could confuse Kant's postulates of the practical reason with cognitive intuitions of faith. James F. Clarke did better in relating the intuitionist theme to Coleridge's Reason (Coleridge's distinction between Reason and Understanding was very popular among the Transcendentalists) and to Schelling's *Anschaaungsvermögen.* A good collection of Transcendentalist writings is Perry Miller, *The Transcendentalists: An Anthology* (Cambridge, Mass., 1950).

that "he who does a good deed is instantly ennobled. . . . If a man is at heart just, then insofar is he God" (p. 68). It is the perfection of these laws that has always suggested that the world is the product of one mind, and that good is positive and evil merely privative. And thus is awakened the religious sentiment

> which makes our highest happiness. Wonderful is its power to charm and to command. It is a mountain air. It is the embalmer of the world. It is myrrh and storax and chlorine and rosemary. It makes the sky and the hills sublime, and the silent song of the stars is it. By it is the universe made safe and habitable, not by science or power. Thought may work cold and intransitive in things and find no end or unity; but the dawn of the sentiment of virtue on the heart, gives and is the assurance that Law is sovereign over all natures; and the worlds, time, space, eternity, do seem to break out in joy. This sentiment is divine and deifying. It is the beatitude of man. It makes him illimitable. Through it the soul first knows itself. [P. 70]

The intuition of this absolute truth cannot be received second-hand. Emerson called Jesus as a witness to this point. Jesus was a member of the true race of prophets, expressing what has dwelt deepest in the minds of men in the East as well as in Palestine. It was only Jesus, however, who "estimated the greatness of man. One man was true to what is in you and me. He saw that God incarnates Himself in man, and evermore goes forth anew to take possession of His world. He said, in this jubilee of sublime emotion, 'I am Divine. Through me God acts; through me speaks. Would you see God, see me; or see thee, when thou also thinkest as I now think' " (p. 72).

Historical Christianity, however, has corrupted this truth. First of all, "it has dwelt, it dwells, with noxious exaggeration about the person of Jesus." The soul properly knows no persons, but historical Christianity has distorted the truth of Jesus into an exaltation of one man and a subjection of others. It has profaned the soul by aiming to convert men by miracles rather than by the reception of beautiful sentiments. Secondly, the Moral Nature has not been explored "as the fountain of the established teaching in society" (pp. 73, 75).

Now, however, we are come to a time of freedom from this oppression and distortion. There is famine in the churches. The creed of the past is passing away and the hold of that worship is waning for persons of religion and character. But worship ought not to be lost. And the remedy is to be found in the contrast of the Church with the Soul: "in the Soul then let the redemption be sought. . . . The stationariness of religion; the assumption that the age of inspiration is past, that the Bible is closed; the fear of degrading the character of Jesus by representing him as a man; indicate with sufficient clearness the falseness of our theology. It is the office of a true teacher to show us that God is, not was; that he speaketh, not spake" (p. 80). True Christianity is a faith like Christ's in the infinitude of men.

Thus Emerson called the graduating ministers to be newborn bards of the Holy Spirit, breathing new life through the still useful forms, the "two inestimable advantages Christianity has given us," the Sabbath and the institution of preaching.

It can hardly be supposed that Emerson's influence was due to the power and rigor of his thought. He was rather a visionary and an inspirer, bringing especially to Americans a new sense of religion (though he was also widely read in Britain). There was in him a breath of religious freedom, not only from the old orthodoxies but from and within a Unitarianism that had already become established and conservative. Pronouncements of human freedom and unlimited human competence were also both natural and satisfying to a nation savoring its independence, sensing its growing power, and expanding apparently without limit.

The theme of freedom from old forms was also given classic expression in Theodore Parker's sermon, "The Transient and Permanent in Christianity" (1841), a statement often ranked in importance with Channing's Baltimore sermon on Unitarianism and Emerson's Divinity School Address.[9]

For Parker the difficulty in historical Christianity, as in other areas of life, is that more attention has been paid to particular phenomena than to the permanent underlying truth. It is especially the theologies that are transitory, notably the doctrines concerning the origin and authority of Old and New Testaments and the doctrines relating to Christ. The permanent in Christianity is in the

---

9. Unlike Emerson, Parker stayed in the ministry, even though for much of his career he was excluded from the pulpits of most of his fellow clergymen. On Parker see especially John Weiss, *Life and Correspondence of Theodore Parker*, 2 vols. (New York, 1864); Henry S. Commager, *Theodore Parker*, 2d ed. (Boston, 1947), an interesting biography; J. Edward Dirks, *The Critical Theology of Theodore Parker* (New York, 1948); H. Shelton Smith, "Was Theodore Parker a Transcendentalist?" *New England Quarterly* 23 (1950): 351–64; and Perry Miller, "Theodore Parker: Apostasy within Liberalism," *Harvard Theological Review* 54 (1961): 274–95. The standard edition of Parker is the *Collected Works*, 15 vols. (Boston, 1907–10).

utterly simple words of Jesus of Nazareth: "Absolute, pure morality; absolute, pure religion; the love of man; the love of God acting
without let or hindrance"; the truth of God's being and the call for
perfect obedience to his law (i.e. "doing the best thing in the best
way, from the highest motives"). Christ and the Father abide within
men, and thus real Christianity gives men new life. This is the truth
that is of God, the pure ideal religion that Jesus taught, the absolute
value that never changes.

In comparison with Emerson, Parker was not only less effusive in
his repudiation of traditional theological concepts, he was also much
more the scholar and the historian. The Transcendentalist faith and
freedom and its sentimental romanticism were qualified by the
more critical spirit of the Enlightenment. Widely read in the German thought of the preceding half-century, Parker was deeply interested in the historical question as raised by Strauss, and he devoted
several years to a translation and elaboration of W. M. L. De Wette's
critical introduction to the Old Testament.[10]

Parker was also more active than Emerson in the Transcendentalist crusade for social reform, though Emerson gave strong support
to its ideals. Parker was a particularly active participant in the antislavery movement. This side of Transcendentalism's religion, however, was most vigorously expressed by William Henry Channing,
the son of William Ellery Channing, and by Orestes A. Brownson,
who passed through Universalism and Transcendentalism on his
way from Calvinism to Catholicism. In general the Transcendentalists' was a religiously based radical social ethic that included opposition to war, to capitalism, and to intemperance, and that led to
several social experiments, including some inspired by the Christian
socialism of Charles Fourier. A view of the Kingdom of God as the
ideal social order to be realized on earth led not only to concern for
the plight of the industrial laborer but on occasion also to opposition to hereditary property.[11]

RELIGION, CULTURE, AND MAN: COMTE, MILL, CARLYLE, AND THE ARNOLDS

The most explicitly humanistic religion in Britain in the mid-
nineteenth century was doubtless that of the disciples of Auguste
Comte, introduced to Britain by John Stuart Mill's *System of Logic*

10. Parker, *A Critical and Historical Introduction to the Canonical Scriptures of
the Old Testament*, 2 vols. (Boston, 1843).
11. See, for example, Brownson's 1840 essay "The Labouring Classes."

(1843) and J. H. Lewes's *History of Philosophy* (1845–46). The promise of the deliverance of man from evil through the new science of sociology was widely popularized in the decades following Mill's *Logic,* and many shared the new hope for the reconstruction of society on a scientific basis.

For Comte, the great discovery of the law of the three necessary stages in the evolution of man's thought—the theological, the metaphysical, and the positive—was not only to illuminate the past but to direct change in the present. Sociology, brought now into the series of positive sciences, could at last enable men to overcome intellectual and moral anarchy and could provide a sure base for a new order. In the *Système de Politique Positive* (1852), Comte proposed his "Religion of Humanity," which was to supersede revealed religion at all points. It was not only to serve in a general way the traditional functions of harmonizing feeling, reason, and activity, thus fulfilling all that was true in the "partial religions" but without their superstitions; it was also in Comte's grand scheme to offer surrogates for a broad range of traditional worship patterns, both private and public. Among these were included, for example, the nine social sacraments and the new positivist calendar to replace the church calendar of saints (hence the description of Comte's religion as "Catholicism minus Christianity"). In this religion, humanity was explicitly and definitively to occupy the place of God, a new and true object of worship, one that was fitting and dynamic.

But Comte's thought could hardly be taken as characteristic of mid-nineteenth century Britain. Not only was he eclipsed at the point of proposals for social change by Karl Marx, who offered a real program as the basis for action, but Comte's unwavering confidence in the truth of his view and in the possibility of worshiping humanity also went counter to one of the deepest elements in the Victorian experience. Despite the appeal of the vision of utopia, the Victorian mind was profoundly characterized by uncertainty and doubt.[12] The idea of evolutionary progress was revived under the tutelage of Carlyle and Mill, and although characteristically Victorian doubt never reached the point of ultimate skepticism about the possibility of knowing truth or value, there was still a pervasive suspicion about belief. This doubt was not generally a religious scepti-

12. This is admirably shown by Walter E. Houghton, *The Victorian Frame of Mind, 1830–1870* (New Haven, 1957). The idea that the Victorian period was a time of untroubled religious certitude is simply a delusion.

cism as such, for the framework of thought continued to be basically Christian. But as Houghton puts it in discussing the question of hypocrisy, the Victorians'

> vision was blurred or blinded by a powerful current of emotion: the fear of finding there an ominous or horrible doubt, or, to put it in positive form, of finding a ghastly suspicion that atheism and materialism were true, and human life, therefore, a meaningless existence in a meaningless universe. In that state of mind self-deception was almost impossible to avoid, and the refuge of 'believing' what one needed so desperately to believe almost inescapable.[13]

John Stuart Mill provides a helpful testimonial to this experience:

> Scarcely anyone, in the more educated classes, seems to have any opinions, or to place any real faith in those which he professes to have. . . . The multitude of thought only breeds increase of uncertainty. Those who should be the guides of the rest, see too many sides to every question. They hear so much said, or find that so much can be said, about everything, that they feel no assurance of the truth of anything.[14]

Also, though Mill's education by his father was such as systematically to exclude any religious belief (see his *Autobiography*—yet he was also warned against being publicly imprudent in antireligious statements), Mill embodied another theme characteristic of the Victorian humanization of religion, namely, the utility of religion. In his own modification of utilitarianism, which called for seeking the happiness of others, Mill recognized that altruism had to be taught as a religion—though, of course, a religion of humanity rather than Christianity. In the *Three Essays on Religion,* Mill maintained his rejection of orthodoxy because of its lack of intellectual verification and its immorality as a defender of social privilege, but he allowed for the previous value of Christianity as the upholder of moral ideals through the precepts of Jesus.[15] That role for religion was not to be abandoned but continued in an earthly form, better than the former religion because freed of intellectual difficulty and moral imperfection:

13. Ibid., p. 404.
14. Diary of J. S. Mill, 13 January 1854, in *Letters,* ed. H. S. R. Elliott, 2 vols. (London, 1910), 2 : 359.
15. The *Essays* were published posthumously in 1874. The first two essays, *Nature* and *Utility of Religion,* were written between 1850 and 1858, and the third, *Theism,* between 1868 and 1870.

The essence of religion is the strong and earnest direction of the emotions and desires towards an ideal object, recognized as one of the highest excellence and as rightfully paramount over all selfish objects of desire. This condition is fulfilled by the Religion of Humanity in as eminent a degree, and in as high a sense, as by the supernatural religions even in their best manifestations, and far more so than in any of their others.[16]

The flavor of the characteristic Victorian concern for man and his culture, in relation to religion, is better expressed, however, by the Arnolds, father and son, and by Thomas Carlyle. In them, too, a strong national religious consciousness comes strongly to the fore.

Thomas Arnold (1795–1842), though he wrote relatively little in theology, being rather a classics scholar and an educator, the famous headmaster of Rugby, must be recognized along with Coleridge as a prime source of free theology in England and one of the chief "Broad Churchmen" of the century.[17] The themes articulated in Arnold's *Principles of Church Reform* (1833) and other writings were hardly such as to please the Tractarians. Arnold's was the party of inquiry, Newman's the party of authority, with quite different grounds for reform in the church. Arnold stood for acceptance of the spirit of the age, in the belief that it could be Christianized. And one of his chief concerns was the reconciliation of all the Christian sects in one body, the state church, which was to be open to all Englishmen who wished to be called Christians (except for the Unitarians), free with respect to form in doctrine and in ritual and requiring only acceptance of the essentials of Christian faith. Most important for our present purposes is Arnold's identification of "the putting down of moral evil" and "the moral improvement of mankind" as the essential aim of both church and state. Together

16. *Three Essays*, p. 109. In the essay on theism, Mill even moved to the point of allowing that perhaps the evidence points to a Being of complete goodness, though of limited power, and that perhaps Christ has not been wrongly chosen as the "ideal representative and guide of humanity."

17. Others commonly counted among the Broad Churchmen are Thomas Arnold's (and Newman's) teacher, Archbishop Richard Whateley, J. C. Hare, A. P. Stanley (who, according to Alec Vidler, was the most typical of the Broad Church), Charles Kingsley, F. D. Maurice (but see below, chap. 10), Benjamin Jowett and others among the contributors to *Essays and Reviews*, and Alfred Lord Tennyson, who was the poet of the movement. The term *Broad Church* seems to have appeared sometime before 1850. Jowett said it was first proposed by Arthur Hugh Clough. Its general use dates from an article by W. J. Conybeare ("Church Parties," *Edinburgh Review* 98 [October 1853]: 330 ff.), in which Conybeare describes the movement as being called "Moderate, Catholic, or Broad Church by its friends; Latitudinarian or Indifferent by its enemies."

church and state have the object of promoting the improvement of man and his culture. Right action is the common ground of Christians, thus the religion of the gospel is necessary to the state for its moral ends.

Thomas Carlyle (1795–1881), the archetype of the Victorian non-churchly theist, cannot quite be described as a "celebrator" of man; but no one felt more deeply than he the crisis of man threatened by dehumanization and by a world of uncertainty and doubt.[18] Enraged by the animalism and shoddiness that he saw engulfing England, the depersonalization of mere economic man, industry's use of persons as things, the placing of commercial value on everything, the dominance of competition as a guiding policy, and the pursuit of merely secular happiness, he wanted desperately to overcome the spiritual paralysis of the age. There was no hope in the church, no possibility of a reformed church, whether of Oxford or of Coleridge, Hare or Maurice. Creed and sacrament were "Hebrew old clothes," fit only for discarding. One could not quite wish to kick the fat priests into the canals, "for what would follow were they gone? Atheistic Benthamism, French Editorial 'Rights of Man,' and 'Grande Nation.' That is a far worse thing, a far untruer thing." Yet the church belongs to the past. It is now incredible. And "when the brains of the thing have been out for three centuries and odd, one does wish that it would be kind enough to die." [19]

But that was not the end of religion. Carlyle was nothing if not a man of religious temperament. No disciple of Coleridge, whom he found personally distasteful and could describe as unprofitable and tedious, "a man of great and useless genius: a strange, not at all a great man," and even "a mass of richest spices putrefied into a dunghill," Carlyle nevertheless shared Coleridge's diagnosis of the evil of the world as resulting from eighteenth-century rationalism and the death of the spiritual in materialism and utilitarianism.[20] Carlyle profoundly distrusted Coleridge's belief that the church could be revivified, but he was a passionate partisan of reverent wonder and faith, even of "the Old Eternal Powers" that "live forever." His God has been described as "a sort of amalgam of Jehovah, Odin, Calvin's predestinating God, and the Soul of the World; his

18. See *Sartor Resartus* (1834), *The Life of John Sterling* (1851), and James A. Froude's biography *Thomas Carlyle, A History of His Life in London, 1834–81*, 2 vols. (London, 1884).

19. *Life in London*, 1 : 264–65.

20. For his views on Coleridge see especially Carlyle's *Life of John Sterling* (1851).

faith a blend of Old Testament monotheism, pantheism, and philosophic necessitarianism." [21] The name of God is obsolete, but not the reality of the "eternities," the "abysses," the "silences," which were over against that threat from which Carlyle himself had been delivered: "the Universe . . . void of Life, of Purpose, of Volition; even of Hostility: it was one huge, dead, immeasurable steam engine rolling on in its dead indifference, to grind me limb from limb." [22] From that threat there is release into passionate assertion of self and "the immensities and eternities," the infinite reality that executes judgment on the nations just as surely as did the God of the Old Testament. The language and superstition is dead, but wonder in the temple of the universe lives. Salvation is not in the church, but man may recover himself under the tutelage of spiritual heroes as they appear.

The language was not at all the same, but elements in Carlyle's thought lead on to Matthew Arnold (1822–88).[23] Unsympathetic to Carlyle's anger and stridency, and much more a conservative reformer in the tradition of Coleridge, Arnold too was deeply sensitive that the acids of modernity had eaten the foundations of traditional religion. "Two things about the Christian religion must surely be clear to anybody with eyes in his head. One is, that men cannot do without it, the other, that they cannot do with it as it is" (preface to God and the Bible). "Culture" was Arnold's great word for the inner perfection of humanity proper, in opposition to the prevailing anarchy of the spirit. There is no doubt of Arnold's sincerity in his conviction of the permanent value of religion. But it is equally certain that for him religion is a function of that "culture" which includes religion and poetry, education and criticism. At the highest levels poetry passes into religion, and religion into poetry. If Arnold wanted deeply to provide a new ground for religion, to restore a possibility of belief to men whose simple faith had already been lost, to place religion on an unshakable foundation of experience, there was also in him a subtle appeal to religion as useful for, indeed essential to, the development of moral culture.

Arnold was tenderhearted toward those for whom popular reli-

21. Basil Willey, Nineteenth Century Studies (London, 1949), p. 113.

22. Sartor Resartus, bk. 2, chap. 7, an account that Carlyle identified as reflecting his own experience.

23. See Arnold's Culture and Anarchy (1869), St. Paul and Protestantism (1870), Literature and Dogma (1873), God and the Bible (1875), and Last Essays on Church and Religion (1877).

gion was still possible; better Christianity with *Aberglaube* than no Christianity at all. But better still religion seen as centering in conduct, not speculation: "Conduct is three-fourths of life"; the essential element for faith is "the eternal not ourselves that makes for righteousness." There is a moral power behind the universe and man has a moral tendency. Religion provides the emotion necessary for transformation, it is "ethics heightened and kindled, lit up by feeling, . . . morality touched by emotion" (*Literature and Dogma,* p. 21). The church is a national society for the promotion of goodness. Doctrine is supported by righteousness rather than righteousness by doctrine.

The Bible, Christianity, and the church were not, for Matthew Arnold, to be abandoned or replaced. They remain for us as the supreme inspirers. But the old and cherished images are to be cherished precisely in their poetry and mythology, for it is as poetry that they have the power to communicate the emotion that makes morality into religion. Arnold had no theory of religious language like that of Bushnell (see chap. 11 below). But he had the same sense for the power of image and symbol, and a far more intuitive appreciation of the poetic. Through the poetry of religion, the most exalted mood of culture, could agnosticism be overcome, goodness be promoted, and a Christian humanism be maintained.

9

Strategies for Restoration and Conservation

The mood of restoration and recovery, of diastasis and defense, was strong in mid-nineteenth-century Christianity. In Roman Catholicism, the uprisings of 1848, following upon the shocks of the French Revolution, sparked the shift to the "fortress mentality" of the later pontificate of Pius IX. German Protestant theology in the 1850s and 1860s, as Martin Kähler recalled it forty years later, was dominated by the "positivistic" dogmatics of biblicists and confessionalists.[1] Doubtless this reflected the more general reaction to "liberalism" and the consequent suppression of revolutionary tendencies. In the United States, the mid-century was a period of renewed denominational rivalry and even hostility (accompanied by anti-Catholic nativism). The ecumenical spirit that had marked the early nineteenth-century revivals in America was replaced by the party spirit, by preoccupation with the distinctiveness of the particular denomination—its theology, its polity, its rights (and likewise its own missionary and Bible societies). In part, this theological mood and strategy was concentrated on the reassertion, or preservation, of biblical authority and classic theological forms. In part, it represented a kind of concern about the church—its nature, status, and role—that was quite new in Protestantism.

Among the broader impulses supporting such tendencies was doubtless the reaction of an ever-present conservative piety to the threat of dissolution of the Christian substance in modern culture generally and in the new theological liberalisms of the century in particular.[2] During the Victorian period in England, the basic sense

1. *Geschichte der protestantischen Dogmatik im 19. Jahrhundert* (Munich, 1962), pp. 147 ff.

2. One of the reasons why Frederick William III had pressed for the union of Lutheran and Reformed in Prussia (1817) was to overcome rationalism. And more than one major theological appointment in the 1820s and 1830s in Germany was arranged by ecclesiastical authorities specifically to counter rationalist dominance; indeed, one could almost speak of a purge of the universities. In the United States, Princeton Seminary (in 1812) and later Andover (in 1834) were established to preserve Calvinist orthodoxy against dilution and betrayal.

was that of living in an age of transition. The new shape of thought, which the previous generation of Coleridge and Bentham had struggled to construct, had not yet emerged. Though the traditional forms of thought were breaking down, nothing had emerged in the intellectual world to match the coming of bourgeois industrial society. Everywhere, the revival of traditional Christianity was related to a new sort of awareness of the tenuous situation of Christianity in the modern world. Especially since the French Revolution there was evidence in Europe of the dechristianization of public life, accompanied by the increasing development of education, of intellectual and cultural life generally, and of commerce and science, independent of any concern for the church. The idealist synthesis was collapsing, and the pietist-orthodox lines drew sharply apart from those of the historico-critical development. There was a frequent call, among evangelicals and conservatives, for the renewal of piety, for a "believing theology" and "believing pastors."

Whether the moods of conservatism and revival in the midnineteenth century were confident movements to restate the classical truth in the face of merely new forms of the age-old attack of the world upon Christianity, or whether they were themselves functions of doubt and thus a new kind of quest for "certainty" as a deliberate recoil to authority, is a question that naturally arises. Houghton's judgment about the Victorian mind, that "most of the time . . . [it] contained beliefs and not doubts—but the beliefs were shaky," has much validity for the Continental and American minds as well.[3]

Traditional theologies generally received vigorous reinforcement from religious revival, particularly in Germany and America, but also in the Reformed churches of Switzerland, France, Scotland, and the Netherlands. Revival in Scotland had been led by the great preacher and organizer Thomas Chalmers (pastor in Glasgow, 1815 and following), who founded a system of parish poor relief and strongly supported missions; and by the mid-1830s the Evangelicals

3. Walter E. Houghton, *The Victorian Frame of Mind, 1830–1870* (New Haven, 1957), p. 21. Houghton adds: "This was particularly true of religious beliefs; and in calling the period one of doubt, I do not mean to imply that it was one of religious skepticism. On the contrary, Christian faith was characteristic of the frame of mind. If most Victorians had reservations about one or more theological doctrines, they instinctively looked for the hand of God in the events of life; interpreted success as the reward for virtue, or suffering as the punishment for sin. They thought of death quite literally as a reunion with the loved ones who had gone on ahead. The churches were crowded; Bibles (on chains!) were placed in railroad stations; sermons outsold novels. But here, too, as in other areas, belief was shaky."

became dominant over the "Moderates" in Scottish church life. Partly through impetus from Scotland, revival occurred in Switzerland and France, and in turn in Holland. By the fourth decade of the century in the Reformed churches in all these countries the Evangelicals were pressing strongly for reassertion of the distinctive Protestant theology (as opposed to rationalism) or even of the Reformed confessions, and for the greater independence of the church from the state bureaucracy.[4]

During the 1820s and 1830s in the United States, the revival movement reached new heights, spurred on in dramatic fashion by Charles G. Finney (1792–1875), with his controversial "new measures" for breaking down resistance to renewal and inducing conviction of sin—measures well calculated to intensify emotional reaction. Initial opposition to Finney by the religious establishment gave way to wide acceptance, and the "revivalist system" and interpretation of the faith was deeply impressed on American church life.[5]

In Germany, a chief center of revival (along with the Berlin circle of von Kottwitz) was the Franconian church, in Nuremberg and Erlangen, notably under the leadership of the Reformed pastor and professor Johann Krafft (1784–1845), in the third and fourth decades of the century. Thence renewal spread to Saxony, Leipzig, and to the first confessionalists. Neopietist revival thus reinforced the lay conservatism that had never been overcome by "rationalism" and that joined in the movement "hard back" to the Bible and the confessions of the church, that is, to the "objective" aspects of Christianity. In Germany particularly the demands of "practical" Christian action also gave support at least to moderate conservative views. Out of revival had come enormous concern and energy for philanthropic and social as well as Christian missionary societies, a great many of which were taken up by 1848 in J. H. Wichern's "Inner Mission" (which for him meant witness in the total everyday life, though not political or social reconstruction).[6] Both "missions" and

4. Hence the separatist movement in the Netherlands in the 1830s and the Scottish "Disruption" of 1843, which was influential in Switzerland, in France, and even in Sweden.

5. In addition to the revival of 1830, which has been hailed as the greatest in modern times, that of 1857–58 was particularly widespread and popular.

6. A chief result of the great Kirchentag of 1848 was the "Central Committee for the Inner Mission." The Inner Mission as such was supported by the Erlangen Lutherans but rejected by most strict confessionalist Lutherans, who began to support

"*innere Mission*" seemed to require as their basis a Bible and a Christianity whose validity was not seriously in doubt. And there was always the sideward glance at the Roman church, with its apparent stability and inner strength, its security in truth for faith and practice.

In quite specific ways, attention to the conception of the church itself was called forth by developments in the relations of the various churches to the political community. In Europe, Britain, and the United States alike, the question of church and state was newly expressed in the first half of the nineteenth century. In Britain, the occasion was the Reform Bill of 1832, which prompted the Tractarian movement's attempt to restore the church's integrity and her true authority and function. In America, the problem was shaped by the unique religious pluralism of the nation's multiplicity of imported denominations, by the separating of church from state even in those states (especially in New England) where establishment had been the rule, by the peculiar character of the American frontier, and by the growing and finally all-consuming struggle over slavery. In Germany the situation of the evangelical churches was altered after the Napoleonic wars. The Peace of Westphalia (1648) had made the Confession the basis of the legal existence of the Protestant churches. With the general coincidence of political and confessional boundaries, this had been a relatively unproblematic arrangement. But with the political rearrangements arising out of the Napoleonic era, a confessionally mixed state became for the first time a normal political form. And one consequence of this new pluralism was to be an intensified emphasis on the Confession.

At least three major sorts of theological movement in the mid-nineteenth century may intelligibly be viewed in relation to the pervasive mood of restoration (or preservation and defense) and of churchly self-consciousness. One is the frankly and vigorously restorationist (even repristinating) and "objectivist" programs whose best expressions can be seen in Lutheran confessionalism, in the "biblical realism" of Johann Tobias Beck, in the Princeton theology's effort to maintain an orthodox Calvinism against the "New Theology," and in H. P. Liddon's defense of the divinity of Christ. A common

---

voluntary Christian "social action" later, though largely as mere organized charities.

The general consequence of the revolution of 1848 for German Protestantism was the increased identification of the church with political and economic conservatism, and thus its estrangement from labor and political liberalism.

characteristic of these programs was their refusal to accept the historical question. Another sort found expression in the creative new struggles for a better doctrine of the church, especially of its basis and the authority of its tradition for the present. These movements emerged most notably in the Oxford Movement in England, in the Erlangen theology in Germany, and in the Mercersburg theology in America. A third was the astonishing development of kenotic christological theory, mainly among German Lutheran thinkers, which may be seen as a last great attempt to save the classical christological dogmas and to accommodate them to a genuinely human historical figure of Jesus.

CONFESSIONALISM, REPRISTINATION, AND BIBLICISM

The Idea of the Confessional Church in German Lutheranism

The paradigm of Protestant churchly resistance to the new historical critique, to "subjectivism," and to accommodation was without doubt the "confessional" Lutheranism that appeared in Germany.[7] This movement to return to the Lutheran confessions was given early impetus by the Kiel pastor Claus Harm's new "Ninety-five Theses," delivered in the summer of 1817, attacking Enlightenment religion and the Prussian church union. As a full-scale effort, it was shaped especially by Friedrich Julius Stahl (1802–61), professor of law in Berlin, and by Wilhelm Löhe (1808–72), the spiritual father of Bavarian confessionalism with a vision of a great North American Lutheranism; and it was most extensively developed theologically by August Vilmar (1800–68) in Hessen, K. F. August Kahnis (1814–88) in Breslau and Leipzig, Theodor Kliefoth (1810–95) and F. A. Philippi (1809–92) in Mecklenburg, and Ernst W. Hengstenberg (1802–69) in Berlin.[8]

7. A parallel tendency in the German Reformed tradition, though of less extensive impact, appeared notably in F. H. Kohlbrügge (1803–75), who influenced a small school in Reformed circles in Germany, the Netherlands (Kohlbrügge had taught privately in Utrecht for ten years), Switzerland, and America. Kohlbrügge's themes included an uncompromising reassertion of the Calvinist "dogmas" and a strict biblicism with even a "mechanical" doctrine of inspiration. Cf. Karl Barth's lively and critically sympathetic chapter in *Die Protestantische Theologie im 19. Jahrhundert, ihre Vorgeschichte und ihre Geschichte* (Zurich, 1946), pp. 579 ff.

8. See Stahl, *Die Kirchenfassung nach Lehre und Recht der Protestanten* (1840), a profoundly influential work; Löhe, *Drei Bücher von der Kirche* (1845), *Kirche und Amt* (1851); Kliefoth, *Acht Bücher von der Kirche* (only vol. 1 appeared, 1854); Vilmar,

The theological program represented by these men was openly and vigorously restorative. Its spirit was that of a self-conscious minority seeking to defend the church against the dominance of rationalist and idealist views, to hold to the objectivities of Christian truth against subjective vagaries, and so to reprise the distinctive doctrine and order of the early Lutheran church (hence the label *Repristinationstheologie,* though in no case was the result a simple and unaltered repetition of sixteenth- or seventeenth-century Lutheran orthodoxy).[9] In determined opposition to all modernization—since a liberal or "free Protestantism" was the most dangerous form of anti-Christianity—and to any mixing with non-Lutheran views, they mounted both a theological and a political program. Through the *Evangelische Kirchenzeitung* (1827 and following), which became a primary focus for the conservative party, Hengstenberg campaigned against both social and religious liberals, and he attained a great influence over ecclesiastical appointments. The movement came closest to the ideal of a pure Lutheran repristination under Kliefoth and Philippi, at the same time giving Mecklenburg a reputation as the most intolerant church in Germany.

The fight for uncompromised biblical authority and inerrancy was led most vigorously and single-mindedly by Hengstenberg. He was indeed perhaps the only one in the group who maintained the old inspiration theory without any qualification. Even Philippi wanted to distinguish between an externally dictated "inspiration of words" (*Wörterinspiration*), which was to be rejected, and a "verbal" inspiration (*Verbalinspiration*) in which the divine and human spirits were so closely united as to prevent any error from the human component or distortion of the pure Word of God. For Hengstenberg, the inspiration of Scriptures was the foundation of all theology. To believe that Moses wrote the Pentateuch and that the messianic prophecies actually described the person and life of Jesus was a matter of religious duty (particularly against Schleiermacher, Hengstenberg zealously emphasized the validity of the Old Testament). Opposition to historical criticism was an obligation of faith.

Die Theologie der Tatsachen wider die Theologie der Rhetorik (1856), *Geschichte des Konfessionsstandes der evangelischen Kirche in Hessen* (1860).

The 1830 celebration of the Augsburg Confession anniversary and the beginning of the publication of Luther's letters and of the Erlangen edition of his works were also important for the movement.

9. Kahnis was sharply attacked from Mecklenburg and Hanover as heterodox on several points.

Against conservative or liberal views stressing the "organic" character of biblical truth, Hengstenberg distinctively insisted that God
acted in history quite without regard to "law" or historical condition, and this arbitrary action was itself a particularly clear and even
necessary sign of revelation. The "isolation" of a biblical word (e.g.
of prophecy) was a proof that "God speaks here." "Who will pre-
scribe for God the rules he is to follow in his revelations? Who will
say that what he never does, as a rule, he may never do?" [10] In
Hengstenberg, further, both the defense of Scripture and the recovery of ecclesiastical orthodoxy were powered by an intense pietist
experience of renewal, derived in his case mostly from his own reading of the Bible, of Luther, and of Melanchthon (though Neander
and Tholuck also influenced him). Hengstenberg thought it possible
to show precise agreement between what he had experienced from
the biblical word and what was taught in the Augsburg Confession
and Melanchthon's Apology.

But the view of the church held by the confessionalists was by no
means simply a return to the Lutheran symbols and fathers, zealous
as they were to protect those symbols against attack or alteration.[11]
Their characteristic idea of the "confessional church" (*Bekenntnis-
kirche*) was newly minted, pressed to the extreme, and invested with
a hitherto unknown evangelical fervor. Further, the demand for a
"churchly" theology, and the condemnation of opposing views as
"unchurchly," was new (and this helps to explain the passion of
the later attack on Ritschl's claim to be a church theologian). Even
the rationalists of the eighteenth century had beeen admitted to be
men of the church. Now the church was to be understood as strictly
constituted by its confession, which was "the essence of the evangelical church." There was no middle ground between fidelity to the
confession and the abandonment of Christianity. No church could
be older than its confession, for it is the confession that holds every
church together. The confession was both the rule of faith and life
and the unifying center for fellowship; without agreement here
there could be no true Christian fellowship. Not only the doctrine
but the very life of the church rested on its confession. Further, as
Vilmar contended, the confession could have its sustaining and life-

10. Hengstenberg, *Christologie des Alten Testaments*, 3 vols. (1829–35; 2d ed., 1849–
57), vol. 1, pt. 2, p. 193.

11. See Emanuel Hirsch's detailed treatment of "The conflict over the idea of the
Church," *Geschichte der neuern evangelischen Theologie*, 5 vols. (Gütersloh, 1964),
5 : 145–231.

giving power in the community only in its completeness, without alteration or exception. Theological problems might permit a certain balancing and tentativeness, but not the church's confession.[12]

The confessional principle was itself symptomatic of a broader thrust toward the objective forms of the church's life, notably pastoral office, sacrament, and worship, as well as Bible and confession. The church was "a continuing incarnation of God." [13] The invisible and the visible church were one and inseparable. The true community of faith was a divinely established *institution* (*Institut*), an establishment (*Anstalt*), a system and order (*Ordnung*). Thus it could even be declared that the doctrine most distinctive of Lutheranism was not justification but the sacrament, and the sacraments could be described as working *ex opere operato* and having an indelible effect.[14] Further, especially in Löhe, Kliefoth, and Vilmar, the objectivity and validity of Word and Sacrament depended on the apostolically established ministerial office (*Amt*). This office, which stands over against the congregation, was in itself defined as a means of grace. The Word was bound to the preaching, the sacraments to their administration. Thus a doctrine of sacramental objectivity and effectiveness in ordination was developed (especially by Kliefoth), and Vilmar could insist that the faith and life of the church were bound to the presence of the ministerial office, and that it was in the person of the ordained clergyman that Christ is present to the community in saving act, in power and judgment.[15]

The principle of authority in the church was developed particularly by Stahl, and in a way fraught with consequences for Lutheranism in Germany. With Hengstenberg he led the majority of the conservatives to the banner of "throne and altar." For him, the valid principle in the church, as in the civil community, was the *Legitimitätsprinzip*. The priesthood of all believers was not a *constitutional* principle. It represented the true equality in faith of minister and layman before God, but in the legally constituted church there must be a super- and a sub-ordination, that is, a genuine power of government, to which every Christian is in conscience bound to be obedient. The chief task of that church government (or

---

12. See Vilmar, *Die Theologie der Tatsachen wider die Theologie der Rhetorik.*

13. Kliefoth, *Einleitung in die Dogmengeschichte* (1839), p. 14.

14. See Franz Delitzsch, *Vier Bücher von der Kirche* (1847), pp. 30 ff.

15. The parallel, in this emphasis on sacrament and ministry, to the contemporary Oxford Movement is evident. The Lutheran confessionalists also liked to speak of true Lutheranism as the proper center between the Roman and the Reformed conceptions.

Kirchengewalt) was to maintain the purity of the church, its community in faith on the basis of confessional agreement. Stahl also vividly represented the political and social conservatism and authoritarianism toward which the confessionalists tended. His concept of the "Christian authoritarian state" (*christlicher Obrigkeitsstaat*), whose principle was "authority, not majority" and whose perfected form was legitimate monarchy, was an important formulation of that tendency.

"Biblical Realism": Johann Tobias Beck

Johann Tobias Beck (1804–78), who served as professor first at Basel and then from 1843, at F. C. Baur's urging, at Tübingen, could hardly be called a confessionalist. He was almost as sharp a critic of the church as Kierkegaard—and like Kierkegaard and Rothe he belonged to no school.[16] His polemic was not only directed against the ecclesiasticism of confessionalism—he insisted that one has responsibility to confessions only as they are subject to Scripture, and a right and duty to improve confessions on the basis of Scripture—but also against the sort of activism represented by Wichern's *Innere Mission,* that is, against any "Christian action and effort, by which they mean to force success by outward busyness and industry, thereby more and more losing sight of the inner preparation of hearts, theirs and others, for the Kingdom of God." [17] Beck stood against both right and left in contemporary Christianity, against activism and quietism, against modern culture and especially against its theological science. That is, he sought a fundamental disengagement from all the current tendencies. But this distinctive independence and individuality was grounded in a rigorous objectivism with

16. At the same time it should be emphasized that Beck did belong to and represent a strong "biblicist" tradition. In this respect he had an important predecessor in the Bremen pastor Gottfried Menken (1768–1831), who was of considerable influence through popular writings and exegetical sermons. Menken had little concern for ecclesiastical orthodoxy, opposing e.g. the Heidelberg Catechism's doctrines of the wrath of God and fearing tendencies to repristination, and he developed a detailed demonology (*Beiträge zur Dämonologie,* 1793). In opposition particularly to Enlightenment thought, he was a vigorous biblicist, defending the unconditional and exclusive authority of Scripture, which he viewed as the witness to a saving history whose center is Christ and which actualizes the Kingdom of God (apocalyptically understood). Both in his biblicism and in his eschatologism, Menken made contact with the older pietism (notably via Collenbusch and J. A. Bengel); and he was also a father of neopietism.

Beck, in turn, was an important influence for Wolfgang Gess and later for H. Cremer, Martin Kähler, Adolf Schlatter, and Fritz Barth.

17. Beck, *Christliche Reden,* 6th *Sammlung* (1870), p. 487.

respect to Christian doctrine, to Scripture, and to the divine reality that works in Christian existence.

Christian doctrinal science, for Beck, meant real knowledge— gnosis, not speculative but "believing" gnosis. It is the (rational) reproduction of something given which is exclusively the biblical revealed truth. The Bible is the true image of the "organic" truth of revelation. All "truly Christian knowledge" is determined by its having as its exclusive object the "perfect and perfecting knowledge deposited in holy Scripture." This is the only field for religious knowledge for Christianity; it is the all-sufficient content of "all Christian knowledge and science." [18] Anything not so biblically given can have no *objective* truth or significance for Christian religious knowledge. If not contrary to biblical truth, it may have subjective value for subjective religion, but not the value of objective and universal Christian truth. The Christian revelation, that is, is an utterly objective reality, a "creative realization of the eternal and historical revelational fullness of God," which is given in Scripture and is to be reproduced in a scientific theological articulation.[19]

Two themes were particularly distinctive in Beck's thought. One was his conception (wholly antithetical to Hengstenberg's idea) of the organic wholeness of the biblical truth. The revelation contained in Scripture is itself an ordered "organism of truth," developing in a coherent way and perfecting itself.[20] Scripture offers in its different books just such an organized whole of truth—which is not to be known by general hermeneutical methods, but by a "spiritual" *(pneumatische)* exegesis, that is, one in which the spirit of the believer, who alone can interpret Scripture, acknowledges that *pneuma* which is the spirit of the Scripture itself. Scripture has an inner unity, and the task of theology is not at all to provide a system for biblical doctrine but rather to express the organic reality as a conceptual organism. The scientific theological system should thus reproduce the real life-system of the biblical doctrine, for which the coherent activity of God is central.

The second theme was directly correlative. It was the conception of the kingdom of God as a supernatural realm, a heavenly reality already in being, which grows and works in humanity. Christianity is the revelation in actuality of a "new, previously transcendent life-

18. Beck, *Vorlesungen über christliche Glaubenslehre*, ed. J. Lindenmeyer (1886), p. 533.
19. Beck, *Einleitung in das System der christlichen Lehre* (1837; 2d ed., 1870), p. 151.
20. Ibid., p. 246.

system of the world"; it is "the organization of the divine spiritual life through the mediation of the divine Logos in human personality for the formation of a new world." The fundamental reality from the foundation of the world is thus "an independently existing kingdom," an "organized life-system," which in Jesus Christ enters into organic union with human nature. Justification is no mere forensic act, but an act of divine creative power. This new life-system works as the gradual "beginning of a new man, a new history and finally a new world." The new "life-type" is produced in the head of mankind, Christ, then gradually reproduced first in individual men through spiritual rebirth, then in history through the community, and finally at the end of the whole development even in physical natural life.[21]

The Princeton Theology

The confessional resurgence of the mid-nineteenth century was strongly reflected in America in both the Lutheran and the Reformed traditions.[22] Among the Lutherans, it was particularly focused on the efforts, led by Samuel S. Schmucker (1799–1873), to create an "American Lutheranism" which would blend Lutheran pietism with elements of the broadly based "New School" nonsectarian revivalist outlook (in the tradition of Taylor and Beecher) in a Protestant united front or confederation of denominations. This led even to the proposal to revise the Augsburg Confession, eliminating for example the doctrines of baptismal regeneration and of the "Real Presence" in the Lord's Supper, and indeed most of the characteristically Lutheran themes.[23] Against such tendencies, a vigorous confessional reaction developed. Its principal theological representatives, all of whom favored strict adherence to the unaltered Augsburg Confession, were Charles Philip Krauth (1792–1867), his son Charles Porterfield Krauth (1823–83), and C. F. W. Walther (1811–87).[24]

But Lutheran confessionalism in the United States was largely de-

21. *Vorlesungen über christliche Glaubenslehre*, pp. 383 ff.

22. And in the Episcopal church as well, not only through the influence of the Oxford Movement but also in its continuation of a long-standing high church tradition (led in the early 19th century by Bishop John Henry Hobart, 1775–1830).

23. See Schmucker's "Fraternal Appeal to the American Churches, with a Plan for Catholic Union on Apostolic Principles" (1838) and the "Definite Synodical Platform" (proposed in 1855).

24. See especially Charles Porterfield Krauth, *The Conservative Reformation and Its Theology* (1871).

rivative from the contemporary movement in Germany, especially through the new waves of immigrants, some of whom had left Germany in opposition to the attempts there to unite the Lutheran and Reformed churches. The chief indigenous "confessional" movement in the United States—and certainly the most important in view of its endurance as a bastion of Presbyterian orthodoxy, and later as a haven sought (properly or not) by all sorts of conservative revivalists and Fundamentalists in the face of the threats of biology and biblical criticism—was the Princeton theology. Its principal architect was Charles Hodge (1797–1878), who taught at Princeton Seminary from 1822 and who could express pleasure that during his career of over fifty years no theological novelty had lodged in the school.[25]

Strictly speaking, of course, Hodge was no confessionalist. Though zealous to defend the tradition of the Westminster Confession, one of his fundamental principles was the completeness and the perspicuity of Scripture. "The people of God are bound by nothing but the Word of God." And the Scriptures are sufficiently plain that, while an individual Christian would not dissent from the faith of the universal Church (i.e. the body of true believers), there are no officials in the church to whom the individual need submit as final authority in biblical interpretation. Hodge was even able to speak of the "right of private judgment" as a central Protestant principle and "the great safeguard of civil and religious liberty" (*ST*, 1.86). But this did not at all mean sympathy for nonsectarian revivalism or nondenominational missionary activity. For Hodge, Christianity existed only in particular forms with particular tenets: "No such thing exists on the face of the earth as Christianity in the abstract. . . . Every man you see is either an Episcopalian or a Methodist, a Presbyterian or an Independent, an Arminian or a Calvinist; no one is a Christian in the general." [26] Hodge's view was typical of the denominational self-consciousness that flourished after 1830 among Congregationalists, Baptists, and Methodists as well (especially in

25. The first professor of the seminary and "founder" of the Princeton theology was Archibald Alexander. Its tradition was continued by Charles Hodge's son, Archibald Alexander Hodge (1823–86), and later by Benjamin Warfield (1851–1921) and J. Gresham Machen (1881–1937). References to Charles Hodge's major work, *Systematic Theology*, 3 vols. (New York, 1875), are indicated in the text by *ST*, with volume and page numbers.

26. See Hodge, "The General Assembly of 1836," in *Biblical Repertory and Theological Review* 8 (1836) : 430–31.

tightening organizational lines), though his was a more rigorous concern for theological purity.

The most immediate opponent of the Princeton theology was Taylorism and the "New School" tendency, not only because of its "ecumenical" interest in revival, in missions, in temperance and antislavery causes, but because of its "Arminianism" and its liberalism. Calvinist orthodoxy was being lost in New England, and Princeton set out to preserve it, something that Andover and Hartford proved unable to do. To the defense, Hodge brought a massive and erudite restatement of the seventeenth-century Reformed theology, especially as formulated by the elder Turretin.

Hodge was no mere repristinator. Philosophically, he owed much to the Scottish realists, notably in his understanding of "first truths" or "laws of belief" that God had implanted in man's nature (these included moral truths). And he was not fearful of the appeal to Christian experience: "the true method in theology requires that the facts of religious experience should be accepted as facts, and when duly authenticated by Scripture, be allowed to interpret the doctrinal statements of the Word of God" (*ST*, 1.16). In this vein, Hodge himself showed certain New School tendencies.

Further, Hodge was quite prepared to make concessions to astronomy and geology, seeking to reconcile their theories with Scripture. His basic principle was that the Bible cannot possibly contradict the facts (as distinguished from the theories) of science. Interpretations of the Scriptures may of course have to change, as they have in the past. (Facts and the Bible are from God; interpretations and theories are of men.) Science has often "taught the church how to understand the Scriptures." The Bible can now be explained "without doing the least violence to the language, according to the Copernican system"; and "if geologists finally prove that [the earth] has existed for myriads of ages, it will be found that the first chapter of Genesis is in full accord with the facts, and that the last results of science are embodied on the first page of the Bible" (*ST*, 1.171).

But Hodge envisaged no such possibility for reconciliation with Darwinism. Darwin's theory (whatever his personal views about God may have been) was inherently atheistic. It denied teleology and any living relation of God to the being of the world, and it was directly counter to the biblical teaching of man's creation in the image of God. Even a theistic version of the Darwinian hypothesis was unacceptable because it threatened the total Christian view of man's origin and destiny.[27]

The most characteristic and influential feature of the Princeton theology, articulated with great thoroughness by Hodge, was the conception of the inspiration of Scripture, and its objective authority and infallibility. Here was to be found the fundamental basis for Christian faith, and no concession could be made to "higher criticism." The Scriptures are infallible because they were given by the inspiration of the Holy Spirit, that is, by a supernatural influence that, without being mechanical or destroying the individualities of the biblical authors, preserved them from any error whatsoever *in teaching*. The writers might have been in error in what they themselves thought and said, concerning the relation of the earth and the sun, for example, but they did not teach any such errors.[28] The question is not whether there are inaccuracies in the Bible, but only whether there are erroneous teachings—and there are none. The Bible's own clear testimony is to its full and objective authority. Its inspiration is "plenary," not partial. Though plenary inspiration was to be distinguished from a mechanical "verbal" inspiration, the former did mean that "all the books of Scripture are equally inspired. All alike are infallible in what they teach." And that includes "all the contents of these several books." No distinction need or should be made between "moral and religious truths" and "statements of facts, whether scientific, historical, or geographical." The question again is only one of teaching. And inspiration extends to the words of the Bible, and not only to the ideas.

The implications for theological method are clear. It is the proper business of theology above all to "set forth what the Bible teaches." But this must be done in a genuinely scientific way, quite parallel to the activities of the natural sciences. In this theme also, Hodge revealed his concern with the contemporary threat of the sciences: "The Bible contains the truths which the theologian has to collect,

27. See Hodge, *What is Darwinism?* (New York, 1874).

28. The biblical men, "as to all matters of science, philosophy, and history, . . . stood on the same level with their contemporaries. They were infallible only as teachers, and when acting as the spokesmen of God. Their inspiration no more made them astronomers than it made them agriculturists. Isaiah was infallible in his predictions, although he shared with his countrymen the views then prevalent as to the mechanism of the universe. Paul could not err in anything he taught, although he could not recollect how many persons he had bapitized in Corinth" (*ST*, 1.165).

authenticate, arrange, and exhibit in their internal relation to each other." The Bible is the theologian's "storehouse of facts," just as nature is to the man of science. It contains *all* the facts concerning God and our relation to him. Even though some of these might be taught elsewhere, in our nature or in religious experience, for example, they are "recognized and authenticated" in Scripture. The method of theology is therefore not "speculative" or "mystical," but strictly inductive—a true scientific method, beginning with the collection of facts according to the same rules that govern the man of science, and proceeding to the deduction of the principles from the facts. Thus "God's system" rather than the theologian's can be ascertained and exhibited. "As natural science was a chaos until the principle of induction was admitted and faithfully carried out, so theology is a jumble of human speculations, not worth a straw, when men refuse to apply the same principle to the study of the Word of God" (*ST*, 1.14–15).[29]

The "Absolute Divinity" of Jesus Christ: H. P. Liddon

The most striking illustration of the reassertion of creedal authority in mid-Victorian England is offered by Henry Parry Liddon (1829–90) in his Bampton Lectures of 1866.[30] A major second generation leader of the Oxford Movement until the publication of *Lux Mundi* in 1889, which was to give a new Oxford impetus to theology and which appalled him as a betrayal of the achievements of the movement, Liddon well expressed the temper of that conservatism for which no modification is finally possible in the presentation of any article of Christian faith. Especially considering the fact that

29. Along with Hodge, for contrast and as a corrective to oversimplified views of mid-19th-century theological responses to science, one should note the work of such "judicious conservatives" as James McCosh, president of Princeton University, and Albert Barnes of Philadelphia. In his *Method of Divine Government: Physical and Moral* (1850), McCosh argued against the "god of the gaps" and in favor of a single universal providence working by natural law. McCosh very easily adopted evolution as a means of God's providential action. Barnes argued that science and religion cannot be in conflict. Science is a help in purifying religion of false and nonessential myths. Not everything in the Bible is revelation; but nothing significant in the Bible will ever be denied by science (see his *Ely Lectures on the Evidences of Christianity in the Nineteenth Century*, 1867).

30. *The Divinity of Our Lord and Savior Jesus Christ* (1867). Liddon was also widely accounted one of the best English preachers of the latter half of the century. A quite different sort of defense of orthodoxy, combining epistemological skepticism with biblical positivism, may be found in the work of H. L. Mansel (see the discussion below, chap. 10, in connection with F. D. Maurice).

because of the illness of the appointed lecturer, Liddon was asked to give the lectures on short notice, the work is an impressive statement, erudite and thorough even if not creative. It shows an unusually wide acquaintance with foreign theological scholarship of many varieties. Liddon cites not only Kant, Fichte, Schelling and Hegel, Schleiermacher, Strauss, Baur, Dorner, Schenkel, Ewald, and Hengstenberg but also Renan, Channing, and Bushnell. Strangely, however, there are no references to contemporary German kenotic Christology. The sense of the mood of the era is particularly interesting. Liddon was consciously writing in a time of "widespread unsettlement of religious belief," which people thought of as "a transitional period"; and he acknowledged the great extent to which the claims of "Divine Revelation" (and thus any approach at all to the classical Christology) were rejected outright. Indeed, he could judge the influence of Mill and Spencer to be so great in Oxford as to make serious theology impossible. But in the Bampton Lectures, Liddon chose not to write for those who could not take the step of accepting the trustworthiness of the scriptural record, but primarily for that large group who "shrink with sincere dread from anything like an explicit rejection of Christianity," who have a concern for moral truth, and yet who are suspicious of dogma.[31] Against this antidogmatic sentiment, with its idea of the separation of religion from theology, he set out to show that the cause of morality is the cause of dogma, that an argument for the perfect moral character of Jesus is compatible only with the Nicene Creed's assertion of his "absolute divinity." Here, as elsewhere, no modification is possible in the presentation of the truth of Christian faith.

Liddon had no interest in further development or reinterpretation of the ancient christological doctrine, but rather reasserted and defended it by appeal to the biblical foundation. Without denying or overshadowing the complementary assertion of Christ's perfect manhood, the church has insisted that Christ was God, not as a poetic assertion but as a strict and proper statement, the word God being used in "its natural, its absolute, its incommunicable sense," not the God pantheistically united to the world but God as "essentially distinct," utterly independent of creation. The attributes of deity were actually present in Jesus. The life of Christ is one "which is supernatural throughout, which positively bristles with the super-

31. See ibid., especially the preface to the 2d ed. (1868) and the appended Note H (1881).

natural, which begins with a supernatural birth, and ends in a supernatural ascent to heaven, which is prolific of physical miracle, and
of which the moral wonders are more startling than the physical." [32]
The alternative answers to the question of what men think of Christ
are finally two: either the ancient Ebionite or modern Socinian answer that Jesus was finally only a good man, or the answer of orthodoxy that he was God incarnate. The Arian attempt to define him
as a highest created being quickly reduces to the former view.

In defense of the traditional view, Liddon adduces in a preliminary way the arguments from prophecy, that is, from the anticipa-
tions of incarnation in the Old Testament, and from the growth of
Christianity in the world. The "success" and "progress" of Christ's
supernatural design to establish the Kingdom of God can only be
accounted for on the basis of his divinity. But such arguments cannot stand alone. They are quite subsidiary to the evidence from
Christ's testimony to himself, together with the perfection of his
character. According to the New Testament account, when it is not
mutilated by critical violence, the Christ of dogma is the Christ of
history. He worked miracles and the mystery of his humanity is en-
compassed by miracles of his conception and birth, resurrection, and
ascension. He never confessed to sin, he taught with authority, he
claimed to judge all men, he said he was the Messiah, the Son of
God. Evidence of that "persistent self-assertion" of Jesus is spread
throughout the Gospels. Such a contention, of course, demands the
assumption of the reliability of the biblical record, and Liddon was
prepared to argue *in extenso* for the organic unity of Scripture and
especially for the authenticity of the Fourth Gospel's account of
Jesus' teaching (mainly on the grounds that this Gospel was fully
accepted as an authority in the second century). But given that presumption, the impossibility of holding on to the moral perfection of
Christ without the dogmatic claim of his divinity becomes apparent.
Christ was either God or he was no good man but a blasphemer.
If he was God incarnate, then he can be hailed as the perfection of

32. Ibid., pp. 26, 12; cf. pp. 30 ff. It is striking how phrases appear here that were to
become touchstones, or shibboleths, of later British and American fundamentalism.
I do not mean, of course, to charge Liddon with the naïveté and simplicism of popular Fundamentalism. He was deeply concerned with the problem of intelligibility,
and he refers to the doctrine of *anhypostasia* as the answer to the question how
divine and human can be joined without denial of the human. But the answers to
these questions were given in the ancient church and neither new philosophy nor
new history makes them unsatisfactory.

sincerity, unselfishness, and humility, but if he was not God, he was certainly not any of those things, just because of his claims to pre-existence and authority.[33]

Thus at least for Liddon there was a clean choice. The attempt to appropriate Jesus as a moral ideal must be joined with the doctrine of his divinity, or it collapses. One may have Christ as orthodoxy has described him, but not otherwise. One may accept the Christian claim in its fullness, or one may reject Christ and the whole basis of revealed truth.

CONFESSION AND CATHOLICITY: THE STRUGGLE FOR
CREATIVE THEOLOGIES OF THE CHURCH

Newman and the Oxford Movement

The Oxford Movement must be considered as more nearly akin to the Lutheran confessionalism of Löhe and Stahl than to the "religious experience"-oriented theology of the Erlangen school or the ecumenical efforts of the Mercersburg theology.[34] Certainly the spirit of the "Tractarians" was one of sharpest protest against the spirit of the age on behalf of the church's ancient traditions and her divinely established authority. Certainly also, their appeal to Scripture and to the early Fathers was often uncritical.[35] It could hardly be said that

---

33. See ibid., pp. xii, 194 ff. The stress on the consciousness of Jesus was characteristic of 19th-century Christology, and particularly in Britain it led to a preoccupation with the issue of his infallibility. Liddon took great pains to show that Jesus' disclaimer of knowledge of the time of the coming of the Kingdom (Mark 13 : 32) was not really inconsistent with the infusion of omniscience into his human soul (pp. 466 ff.), and that Jesus' ascription of the Pentateuch to Moses must stand as a sufficient refutation of modern theories of a later origin (pp. 475 ff.).

34. Some useful contributions to the study of the Oxford Movement include E. R. Fairweather, ed., *The Oxford Movement* (New York, 1964), an excellent selection of documents from the movement, with valuable introductions and bibliography; Y. Brilioth, *The Anglican Revival: Studies in the Oxford Movement* (London, 1925), and *Three Lectures on Evangelicalism and the Oxford Movement* (London, 1934); Owen Chadwick, *The Mind of the Oxford Movement* (London, 1960); W. G. Peck, *The Social Implications of the Oxford Movement* (New York, 1933); C. Dawson, *The Spirit of the Oxford Movement* (London, 1933); S. L. Ollard, *A Short History of the Oxford Movement*, 3d ed. (London, 1963); L. Bouyer, *Newman: His Life and Spirituality* (London, 1958).

35. John Tulloch wrote sharply, in his account of the movement: "There was endless building up out of old stones. This was confessedly Newman's idea of what the church needed. But what the stones themselves were really worth was never asked" (*Religious Thought in Britain during the 19th Century* [1885], p. 113). This was a caricature of the reality, but it was not altogether false in representing an attitude toward an-

they were sympathetic to the new historical or theological science in Germany (i.e. to what they knew of it; only Pusey and Wilberforce were well-informed). One of the lesser factors in the background of the Oxford Movement was indeed a report by a High Churchman from Cambridge, Hugh James Rose (1795–1838), on "The State of Protestant Religion in Germany," offered after a brief visit to the Continent. Rose described a horrible state of affairs, the dissolution of religion in a search for novelty and in theological caprice. For Newman, in 1837, no argument was required to assert that "Germany had become rationalistic, and Geneva Socinian"; and he could speak of "the connexion of foreign Protestantism with infidelity" as "so evident" that it need not claim our sympathy.[36] And the emphasis on dogma as the center of religion was one of the primary themes.

Yet there were decisive differences from the Continental confessionalism. The primary enemy for the Tractarians was not a new biblical science or a speculative or mediating theology, or even an articulate rationalism, but an age blighted by worldliness, a church about to be swallowed up in spiritual decay and death, even in "national apostasy," and incapable of being rescued by contemporary Protestantism. Because of this, the first generation Oxford Movement had as deeply the spirit of reform as of repristination, as much concern for holiness as for ecclesiastical structures. It did not become wedded to political conservatism. Further, the movement was not a call to loyalty to a particular confession, but to the broad tradition of the "undivided ancient Church" (often not clearly delimited, to be sure). It could embrace certain ecumenical tendencies (e.g. in Robert Wilberforce). And the theology of the Oxford renewal was not a systematic whole but a quest which could lead some of its thinkers (notably Newman and Wilberforce) into the Roman church and which could also support significant renewal in the Church of England.

On the whole, the influence of the movement was much more the result of its pastoral and devotional power—through which both the

---

tiquity that was present. There was also a strong romanticist strain in the Oxford men's vision of history (as well as in the way their religious passion was expressed in their poetry).

36. *Lectures on the Prophetical Office of the Church*, introduction. (See Fairweather, *The Oxford Movement*, p. 110.)

forms and the inner spirit of Anglican religious life were deeply affected—than of its intellectual power. The characteristic ideas of church authority, of dogma, and of inspiration and revelation were intellectually vulnerable primarily because the Tractarians were unwilling to accept the historical question. Hence some of their most cherished positions were overrun almost simultaneously by post-Darwinian science and by biblical criticism (after the storm broke with the publication of *Essays and Reviews,* 1860). Yet in Newman in particular (though Pusey and Wilberforce have also to be counted important thinkers) there was both a spiritual power and a genius of mind that has "enriched the common religious experience of Christendom." And for Newman, all the objectivity of authority in the church was inseparable from an inner principle of certitude—a certainty at once of self-existence and of the being of God—out of which Newman contributed to the general nineteenth-century search for a better understanding of the nature of religious assent.

The Oxford Movement began as a struggle for inner renewal, for reform, and for the freedom of the church by men who were already bound in close association at Oxford by their "High Church" or "Anglo-Catholic" views—notably John Keble (1792–1866), Edward Bouverie Pusey (1800–82, Regius Professor of Hebrew and the principal leader of the movement after 1845, so that it was also frequently called Puseyism), John Henry Newman (1801–90, the leader until his entrance into the Roman church in 1845), and Richard Hurrell Froude (1803–36), who along with Robert Isaac Wilberforce (1802–57) was a pupil of Keble at Oriel College.

The immediate occasion for a public call to action was the Church Temporalities Bill of 1833, introduced by the new Whig administration. Its specific provisions were innocuous enough, involving a badly needed reorganization of the Irish church, for example, suppression of ten sees and the redistribution of revenues. But in the immediate background were the acts of 1828–29, relieving both Protestant Dissenters and Roman Catholics of many civil disabilities and thus constituting a first step in limiting the remarkable privileges that the Church of England had possessed. Further, the new Reform Bill emerged in the context of the Benthamite liberals' general overhauling of the political and social structure of the nation (which would include of course the church, as the religious aspect of the nation). There was talk of far-reaching proposals: that the Church of England should include every form of Christian creed and practice followed by Englishmen (except the Roman Catholic), that drastic liturgical reforms be made and that the church be disestablished.

The "calamity," as Keble called it, of the 1833 act was the principle that underlay both it and the other unrealized proposals—that a secularized government should act as if the church were one of the several departments of state. "National Apostasy" is not too hard a term, Keble said in the sermon of that title (which Newman accounted the true beginning of the movement),[37] to describe the present scene of "the growing indifference, in which men indulge themselves, to other men's religious sentiments," of "scornful impatience . . . when Christian motives are suggested and checks from Christian principles attempted to be enforced on their public conduct," and of "infringement on apostolic rights." That the church, even in matters of its own organization, should be at the mercy of a legislature whose members might be non-Christian! Against this the church must declare her rights and independence—and many of the early tracts were but manifestos and assertions of a long familiar claim that now required new acknowledgment and obedience. Later on, for example in Pusey's tracts on Baptism (Tracts 67–69), in Newman's *Lectures on the Prophetical Office of the Church* (1837) and *Lectures on Justification* (1838), and Wilberforce's *Doctrine of the Incarnation* (1848), the theological substance was more seriously developed. The need, said Newman, was for a "second Reformation"; the first Reformation, Froude said, "was a limb badly set—it must be broken again in order to be righted." [38]

The proper question, then, was: Who is to reform the church and on what principles? Newman clearly identified the opponents in this struggle. On the one side was "liberalism," which was trying to reform society and the church on the "antidogmatic principle." But one cannot live without dogma. Newman had from the age of fifteen, he tells us, the sense of the necessity of a definite creed, along with the luminous certainty of the self and the Creator, the mistrust of the reality of material phenomena, and the sureness of the supersensual world. From that time on, he wrote in 1864, "dogma has been the fundamental principle of my religion; religion as a mere sentiment, is to me a dream and a mockery. . . . Such was the principle

37. Preached 14 July 1833. On 9 September Newman published (unsigned) the first three of the ninety tracts that were to appear.

38. Newman, *Apologia Pro Vita Sua* (1864; New York, 1956), p. 149; Froude, *Remains*, 4 vols. (London-Derby, 1838–39), 1 : 433.

of the movement in 1833." Private conscience cannot be the ultimate authority, and the proof of this is found in the sheer latitudinarianism and indifference to which the exaltation of private judgment has led.[39]

Nor could the importance of dogma be compromised by defining the essence of Christianity in a way that did not include doctrine. Even so orthodox a divine as Renn Dickson Hampden offended through his argument for the admission of Dissenters to Oxford and his desire to distinguish between religion and theological opinions. In *Observations on Religious Dissent* Hampden said that "The real causes of separation are to be found in that confusion of theological and moral truth with Religion, which is evidenced in the profession of different sects. Opinions on religious matters are regarded as identical with the objects of faith; and the zeal which belongs to dissentients in the latter, is transferred to the guiltless differences of fallible judgments." [40] The principle there enunciated seemed to the Tractarians nothing less than a fundamental rationalist undermining of the historic dogmas, and they put Hampden in the same camp with Schleiermacher and the Scotsman Thomas Erskine. Thus Hampden's appointment as Regius Professor of Divinity seemed another step in the liberal antidogmatic attack on the church.

Liberalism also meant, more broadly, the utilitarian spirit and program, with its questioning of the utility of all ancient institutions and its exaltation of this-worldly happiness as the great good—and therefore its particular conceptions of social reform. For the "religious liberal," while the transcendent world was of course to be affirmed, the main question was how to make man's life here and now as perfect as possible. God's aim was also the happiness of man, and religion was justified by its contribution to the well-being of society. For the Tractarians, however, holiness was more important than adjustment and peace. This world was strictly ancillary to the other, the transcendent world.

On the other side, the enemy was evangelicalism, which was also ostensibly against dead religion. But evangelicalism was utterly powerless to reform the church because it had no real internal principle.

39. *Apologia*, pp. 127, 163. With respect to this, Newman could say, "I do not shrink from uttering my firm conviction that it would be a gain to the country were it vastly more superstitious, more bigoted, more gloomy, more fierce in its religion than at present it shows itself to be" (*Parochial and Plain Sermons*, 8 vols. [London, 1908–18], 1 : 320).

40. 2d ed. (London, 1834), pp. 7–8; cf. Fairweather, *Oxford Movement*, pp. 61 ff.

Protestantism had rejected papal and minimized priestly authority, thus opening the way for the subjection of church to state. It had exalted private judgment, encouraging sect and schism. It had weakened the doctrines of sacramental grace, abandoned much of ritual and symbol, scorned asceticism, and impoverished the devotional life, constricting piety to "personal experience" of "blood-atonement." Protestantism was worldly and unspiritual, no protection at all against the forces of unbelief. Like all other intermediates (including, as Newman the Roman Catholic judged, his own earlier idea of the *via media*), it was a mere halfway house to atheism. The only real principles were Catholic truth and rationalist atheism, and when they meet, "then, indeed, will be the stern encounter, when two real and living principles, simple, entire, and consistent, one in the Church, the other out of it, at length rush upon each other, contending not for names and words, or half-views, but for elementary notions and distinctive moral characters." [41] Protestantism also—as Newman knew it in the forms of English evangelicalism—was plagued by its subjectivism, its concentration on the interior state of the soul, on the consciousness of sin rather than on sin itself. It was a hypochondriac religion, even idolatrous in worshiping religion rather than God, in preaching justification by faith rather than justification by God. Thus the objectivity of God's work and gift in Jesus Christ was utterly compromised. The only cure for the Church of England was to de-Protestantize it.

The Tractarians' positive theme, then, was the recovery of the supernatural reality of the Christian life, an "objective supernaturalism" centering in an incarnational theology of the church and the sacraments. Though it came to full systematic statement only in Wilberforce's *Doctrine of the Incarnation of our Lord Jesus Christ in Its Relation to Mankind and to the Church* (1848), the incarnational theology was crucial for the outlook of the movement as a whole and was an element of its enduring influence.[42] The Ox-

41. *Apologia*, p. 207, cf. p. 290.
42. "The Tractarians saw the Incarnation, the Church, and the sacraments as contiguous and inseparable elements in God's redemptive economy. For the Tractarians, as for all orthodox Christians, the heart of Christianity was the story of God's own saving and self-revealing action, which culminated in the hypostatic union of humanity with deity in the person of the Mediator. But they did not stop here. To their minds it was no less clearly a part of the Christian message that the saving person and work of the Mediator were effectually 're-presented' in the Church by means of certain sacramental 'extensions of the Incarnation.' It was, they insisted, supremely fitting that the life-giving flesh and blood of God's Eternal Son who was made man should be communicated through fleshly signs wrought by human hands.

ford men thus insisted on the dogmatic and supernatural element in the Church of England, on its nature as no mere human organization but a living branch or member of the Catholic church, independent of and transcending the state. The apostolic succession of the bishops could be called "the real ground on which our authority is built," as Newman said in Tract 1. It was the presupposition of the communication of grace in the sacraments, the only guarantee for the maintenance of true doctrine, and the basis for the integrity and independence of the church vis-à-vis political authority. Thus also it was the proper point of appeal to recall the clergy to the sacramental nature, the dignity and the authority of their office.

Not less important was the "apostolic tradition of dogma." This meant, as Keble put it in a sermon of 1836, the principle of a doctrinal "charge, trust, deposit," left in the hands of the apostles, a "treasure of apostolic doctrines and church rules" (including the sacraments). It meant an apostolic tradition "divinely appointed in the church as the touchstone of canonical scripture itself," whence Scripture in turn became "a test for everything claiming to be of apostolical tradition." It meant, further, the subsequent necessity of constant appeal to tradition, for the "system and arrangement of fundamental articles" (including the creeds), for the interpretation of Scripture, and for the "discipline, formularies, and rites of the church of Christ." The rule for the unwritten system of primitive tradition is the Vincentian canon—antiquity, universality, catholicity. Thus Keble sums up, in shaping our course in these times "we are to look before all things to the integrity of the good deposit, the orthodox faith, the creed of the apostolical Church, guaranteed to us by Holy Scripture, and by consent of pure antiquity." And we are to beware of novelty, that is, a "novelty relative to the primitive and original standard, [which] is the thing above all to be deprecated in the whole of theology." [43]

The appeal to apostolic tradition, to the theology and life of the "early and undivided church," was at the heart of the idea of the *via media*, which was to be abandoned by Newman (and which be-

---

Indeed, they were prepared to argue that the failure to recognize the 'extensions of the Incarnation' stemmed from a feeble apprehension of the twofold truth of the Incarnation itself—on the one hand, that man's salvation comes from God alone; on the other, that God's saving action really penetrates and transforms man's world and man's life. If we do not understand this thoroughgoing incarnationalism, we shall miss the deepest motive of the Tractarian concern for the integrity of the Church" (Fairweather, *Oxford Movement*, p. 11).

43. Sermon on "Primitive Tradition" (Fairweather, *Oxford Movement*, pp. 63–89). Cf. *Sermons, Academical and Occasional* (2d ed., Oxford, 1848).

came more difficult for any to maintain in view of the growing ultramontanism of some Anglo-Catholics like William Ward, the episcopal repudiation of Tract 90, and the extreme anti-Catholicism of the Evangelicals). Both Keble and Newman in their earlier writings were as eager to dissociate themselves from Rome's errors (e.g. what Keble called "metaphysical or grammatical subtleties" such as transubstantiation) as from Protestantism.

Newman's *Lectures on Justification* [44] are generally accounted the most important of his efforts to give theological substance to the *via media,* though his own conclusions are strongly anti-Lutheran and obviously do not represent any "middle" way between balancing errors. "Justification by faith only" (and especially justification as being only "counted" righteous) Newman called an "erroneous" doctrine; justification by obedience was a "defective" doctrine. The Lutheran view was an "utter perversion of the truth," because it denied that justification directly produced renewal; and eventually Newman could dismiss the "Protestant" doctrine as a "system of words without ideas, and of distinctions without arguments" (Lectures 7, 8). Yet the proper doctrine was distinct also from the Roman view that made justification consequent upon obedience. Rather, justification and sanctification were "substantially" the same thing, parts of one gift of a justifying sacred presence that creates renewal.

In respect of "tradition," the contrasting errors were Roman misuse and addition, and Protestant abandonment of both the principle and the substance of the tradition. Instead of the principle that the Church was prior to Scripture and that Scripture comes by tradition, Protestantism had tried to rest on the sole authority of Scripture, without note or comment, interpreted simply by private judgment. But this was a self-destructive principle and it made truth but a matter of opinion.[45] Newman challenged the Romanist view confidently "on the ground of antiquity." The Romanist accepted the appeal to antiquity as the great teacher, but he was wrong in believing that his peculiar doctrines were to be found in antiquity. Thus, the controversy with the Romanist was mainly about "facts"; with the Protestant it was about "first principles." Rome held to the foundation, but overlaid the truth with corruptions and subordinated the witness of antiquity to the contemporary church.[46]

44. London, 1838. Lectures 6–8 are reprinted in Fairweather, *Oxford Movement.*
45. See *Lectures on the Prophetical Office,* 1837.
46. Thus Newman's attempt in Tract 90 (1841) to interpret the Thirty-nine Articles in the most Catholic sense possible, while it aroused a sufficient outcry and official

In this vein, Newman could say in the *Apologia* that the ecclesiology of the *via media* had been founded on three points: "the principle of dogma, the sacramental system, and anti-Romanism" (*Apologia*, pp. 221–22). And for him the third point was shaken when in 1839 Nicholas Wiseman charged in an article in the *Dublin Review* that the Anglican claim to continuity with pure antiquity was essentially like that of the Donatists, and when in his own study of the Monophysites Newman then began to view the principle of the Anglican appeal to antiquity as similar to the arguments of dissident and heretical groups in all ages. The *via media* for Newman foundered with the collapse of the appeal to pure antiquity, and he was led eventually to his *Essay on the Development of Christian Doctrine* (1878), according to which antiquity could be no court of final appeal, because the Church is not static and incapable of growth, but has the power of manifesting, publishing, and interpreting the unchanging faith to an everchanging world—and is thus capable of inexhaustible expansion.

John Henry Newman's own most impressive influential theological contribution—with the possible exception of the essay on the development of doctrine, which was much more freeing to those who later read it than the actual argument warranted—was his interpretation of the nature of religious assent.[47] Here Newman both articulated the characteristic Tractarian theme that the deepest and truest

---

condemnation to shake his own confidence in the possibilities of the Church of England, was not a peculiarity of Newman's movement toward Rome. Rather, "the idea behind Tract 90 was integral to the theology of the Movement" (Chadwick, *Mind of the Oxford Movement*, p. 53). If Anglicanism was truly a continuation of the early and undivided church, "the doctrine of the Old Church must live and speak in the Anglican formularies" (Newman, *Apologia*, p. 231). Thus the principle could be laid down in Tract 90: "Never mind what the Reformers intended. The point is what they say. Wherever their words can, by any manner of means, bear a Catholic sense, they shall be made to bear it; where they are ambiguous, a Catholic interpretation shall be put upon them." In spite of what may have been their intentions, the Reformers did not destroy the Catholic element in the Anglican church. It is thus "a duty which we owe both to the Catholic Church and to our own, to take our reformed confessions in the most Catholic sense they will admit; we have no duties toward their framers." The duty is to show that not only the *Book of Common Prayer* but the Articles are by God's grace at least not uncatholic, i.e. that a conscientious Anglican can truly aim at being Catholic in heart and doctrine.

47. Cf. both the University Sermons (especially those published in 1843 under the title *Sermons Chiefly on the Theory of Religious Belief*) and *The Grammar of Assent* (1870). Though the latter, more systematic statement incorporates some new emphases, especially a concern for "certitude," and new terms, Newman's conception of faith and its relation to reason remained essentially continuous, and the *Grammar* should be read in conjunction with the Sermons.

safeguard of faith is "a right state of heart" and came close to parallel-ing Coleridge's understanding of the relation of faith and reason.[48]

Faith Newman described as an "intellectual act," "an act of rea-son," "an instrument of knowledge and action." Yet as such it is distinct from "what is commonly called Reason." For while faith has no right to accept as true doctrines that cannot be "approved" by reason—and in this sense is "justified" and judged by reason—none-theless reasoning, with its power of analysis and criticism and its demands for evidence, cannot be the origin and ground of faith. Faith is more "a principle of action" than of intellectual assent, and "action does not allow time for minute and finished investigations." Faith is an engagement of the whole man. It is a process of reason that includes and springs from the conscience, from hope and desire. Religious certainty must be hungered and thirsted after. Thus more arguments from "evidences of revelation" do not *produce* faith and may be irreligious (though not useless, being a possible encourage-ment for believers). "A mutilated and defective evidence suffices for persuasion where the heart is alive; but dead evidences, however perfect, can but create a dead faith." [49]

Hence Newman's persistent theme that "faith is created in the mind, not so much by facts, as by probabilities" (*University Sermons*, p. 182). That is not to say that facts and arguments are irrelevant to faith, but that in faith action and judgment are demanded *now*, and that such action and judgment always involve "antecedent considera-tions"—the moral temperament, "previous notices, prepossessions, and (in a good sense of the word) prejudices." Because faith is an act "done in a certain moral disposition" (*University Sermons*, p. 232), its safeguard is in the heart, in holiness and obedience. Because it is not an act of demonstration or an inference and because the heart is reached more through the imagination than through reasoning, faith's affirmation must and may be given where there are no more than strong probabilities:

48. Newman evidently arrived at his view independently. He said of his first read-ing of parts of Coleridge in 1835, "I am surprised how much I thought mine, is to be found there" (See H. F. David, "Was Newman a Disciple of Coleridge?" *Dublin Re-view*, October, 1945). The "reason" of whose "usurpations" in the realm of morals and religion Newman spoke in a sermon of 1831, and whose activities he described as "either external, or at least only ministrative, to religious inquiry and knowledge," was what Coleridge had called "understanding," or the merely analytical and dis-cursive reason.

49. *University Sermons* (1844 ed.), pp. 173–80, 192. Newman's polemic against evi-dences was less sharp, however, than Coleridge's.

We are not justified in the case of concrete reasoning and especially of religious inquiry, in waiting till such logical demonstration is ours, but on the contrary are bound in conscience to seek truth and to look for certainty by modes of proof which, when reduced to the shape of formal propositions, fail to satisfy the severe requisitions of science.[50]

"Life is not long enough for a religion of inferences; we shall never have done beginning, if we determine to begin with proof." Faith is what can be died for, and "no man will be a martyr for a conclusion." [51]

Thus faith is also inescapably a venture. Here especially is the choice between creeping along the ground, being sure of every step, and soaring to attain great ends and to know great subjects. "Faith ventures and hazards; right faith ventures and hazards deliberately, seriously, soberly, piously, and humbly, counting the cost and delighting in the sacrifice" (University Sermons, p. 232).

In the Grammar of Assent, Newman's idea of the nature of genuine religious knowing was elucidated especially through the distinction between "notional" and "real" assent. Notional assent is an intellectual assent to a truth or an idea, the mind's contemplation of its own creations, a "theological" as distinct from a "religious" act; or it is the mere acquiescence in a notion or an abstract truth or a cliché (or in a catchword like liberalism, or progress, or "justification by faith"). It is the kind of assent that largely characterizes contemporary religion in England. "Real" assent, however, is "felt in the heart, and felt along the blood"; it affects the imagination and moves the will. The materials for a "real apprehension of a Divine Sovereign and Judge" and the objectivity of revealed truth come from the conscience, which is both a moral sense and a sense of duty, "a judgment of the reason and a magisterial dictate." Along this line of real assents, our "illative sense," which judges degrees of truth and by which we proceed through statements to a "therefore," can lead us from the convergence of probabilities to a genuine religious certitude (distinct from logical or scientific certainty), to a laying hold of the truths of revealed religion in an act that always involves a leap or a willing and trusting, and finally to an acknowledgment of the authority of the church.

50. Grammar of Assent (1870; New York, 1955), p. 320.
51. Ibid., pp. 90, 89.

The Erlangen Theology

The distinctive Lutheran theological program and perspective associated with the faculty at Erlangen was founded by Adolf von Harless (1806–79), brought to classical expression by Johannes C. K. Hofmann (1810–77) and Gottfried Thomasius (1802–75) and in the later nineteenth century carried on especially by Franz Herman Reinhold von Frank (1827–94).[52] In the immediate background of the movement was not only religious revival in Franconia, but also the neopietism mediated by Friedrich August G. Tholuck (1799–1877). Professor from 1826 at Halle, where he had been brought in an attempt to break the grip of the "rationalism" that had dominated the theological faculty since the later eighteenth century, Tholuck was of significant influence on a remarkable variety of nineteenth-century thinkers including Julius Müller, Richard Rothe, J. T. Beck, August Vilmar, Charles P. Krauth, and later Albrecht Ritschl, Wilhelm Herrmann, and Martin Kähler, as well as Harless and Thomasius, who studied under Tholuck at Halle, and Hofmann.[53]

The distinguishing mark of the preaching and theology of Tholuck was his locating of the center of gravity for Christian thinking in the specific experience of sin and regeneration. The idealist philosophy, in its pantheist tendency, had to be rejected because it contradicted that consciousness, particularly the consciousness of sin. From the experience of sin and redemption, both the content and the truth of the Christian view were to be determined, and thus under neopietist influence the evangelical preaching and the revival theology of the mid-nineteenth century were alike strongly directed to the ideas of the fall and original sin. For Tholuck, regeneration formed the pre-

52. For a general history of the school, see F. W. Kantzenbach, *Die Erlanger Theologie, Grundlinien ihrer Entwicklung im Rahmen der Geschichte der theologischen Fakultät, 1743–1877* (Munich, 1960).
Among the later Erlangen theologians should also be mentioned Heinrich Schmid, Franz Delitzsch, Theodosius Harnack, and Gerhard von Zezschwitz.

53. Tholuck's first work, *Die Lehre von der Sünde und dem Versöhner oder die wahre Weihe des Zweiflers* (1823; 9th ed., 1871), was his most influential. Tholuck had not long before experienced a "rebirth" under the influence of the Herrnhut pietism of Baron von Kottwitz. In his other chief work, *Die Geschichte des Rationalismus* (4 vols., 1853–65), Tholuck was led back to deal with the whole of late Protestant orthodoxy (through the 17th century); in the process he was changed from a conventicle pietist into a church theologian—which helps to account for the fact that many of those influenced by him became confessionalists.
Among Tholuck's immediate predecessors in the German theology influenced by pietist revival should be mentioned Gottfried Menken (1768–1831) and the great church historian and associate of Schleiermacher, August Neander (1789–1850).

condition of all theological knowledge. In the Erlangen theology, then, this emphasis on the particular experience of sin and rebirth both complemented and shaped the influence of Schleiermacher, so that the latter could become a bridge back to classical Lutheran positions.

Thus the confessionalism of Erlangen was of a quite different shape and principle than that of Stahl or Philippi or Vilmar. Thomasius rightly rebutted the charge that he was a repristinator: "it is true that we have been faithful to the Confession of our church and have sincerely pleaded its cause in the many directions from which it was challenged; it is not true, however, that the Confession has ever been for us a merely external law or bond, but rather one emerging from within; because we had in it the expression of our own persuasion and because we were persuaded of its conformity to Scripture we have declared for it: I believe, therefore I speak." [54] And Hofmann, for example, was vigorously attacked by Hengstenberg and others. The Erlangen view both of the confessions and of Scripture was different. Especially because of the appeal to the immediacies of experience, theirs was a distinctive sort of attempt to reaffirm the Lutheran heritage—as Hofmann proclaimed in his "defenses of a new way of teaching old truth." [55] At the same time, it should be noted that the Erlangen thinkers always stressed their agreements with orthodoxy, hence only in controversy did it become fully clear that they were not mainly confessionalists; whereas, for example, the "mediator" Julius Müller was relatively orthodox but always pointed out exactly where he differed from traditional doctrine and thus gained the reputation of being heterodox.

The characteristic Erlangen interweaving of the three factors—experience, Scripture, confession—came to clear expression in Adolf von Harless, who had studied and habilitated at Halle, where through the influence of Tholuck and a deep conversion experience he moved away from the dominance of Spinoza, Schelling, and Hegel. He was brought to Erlangen in 1833 at the request of the church authorities and against the plans of the faculty, who wanted the "rationalist" exegete Rückert.[56] Harless's own awakening, which he described in terms reminiscent of the seventeenth-century pietism of Francke,

---

54. *Das Wiedererwachen des evangelischen Lebens in der lutherischen Kirche Bayerns* (1867), pp. 285 ff.

55. *Schutzchriften für eine neue Weise, alte Wahrheit zu Lehren*, 4 vols. (1856–59).

56. See Kantzenbach, *Die Erlangen Theologie*, p. 121. In 1845, Harless went to the Konsistorialrat in Bayreuth, and taught at Leipzig, then in 1852 he became president of the Oberkonsistorium in Munich.

was particularly centered in the words of John 5:44 and 7:16–17. Thus the experience was precisely one of "soul-saving truth" received from Scripture. This was prior to any sense for the special value of the Lutheran confessions. He reported: "Only after I had experienced and known at the hands of scripture what *saving* truth is, did I turn to the confessional writings of my church. I cannot describe the surprise and emotion with which I found that their content conformed to that of which I had become certain from the Scriptures and from the experience of faith." [57] Thomasius put the matter similarly in his history of the Bavarian Lutheran revival: "In our new evangelical life and our practical interest we were Lutherans even before we knew it; we were such in actuality without reflecting on the confessional feature of our church and on the confessional differences which separate it from others. . . . So we had become Lutherans freely from within." [58]

For Harless (more than for Hofmann) personal religious experience and scriptural authority were given indissolubly together. Scripture was the "objective foundation," the "objective correlate" of what is appropriated in personal experience. From these together, then, he moved to reappropriation of the whole complex of Lutheran confessional doctrine, which thus also stood theologically in necessary connection with the foundation. True Christian theology cannot be the product merely of individual opinion and insight, but must be based on and lead back to the common faith of an ecclesiastical community. Thus the confession becomes the necessary organizing principle of Christian theology. Harless distinguished—and this marked a fundamental difference from the confessionalists—between two aspects of the visible church: church (*Kirche*) and "churchdom" (*Kirchentum*). Church is the essential and unchangeable saving order; churchdom is the historically conditioned *legal* order. Only the first is divinely established. Christianity is necessarily communal and churchly, but the tie to the church is not fundamentally one of law. Hence while Harless's conception of the proper form of church government was not greatly different from that of Stahl, the status was different. So too the confessions have an indirect authority, as expressions of the believing community, which in *Kirchentum* is brought to legally binding form. They have an ecclesiastically established authority within the institutions of churchdom and they are the basis

57. Theodor Heckel, *Adolf von Harless* (Munich, 1933), pp. 27–28.
58. *Das Wiedererwachen*, pp. 244–45.

for institutional structures; but they are subordinate to the ultimate substance. Similarly, it was characteristic of Erlangen generally to view the relation of the Lutheran church to God's true Church on earth as one of identity in substance but not in form.

When Harless left Erlangen to minister to a church (1845), he was succeeded by J. C. K. von Hofmann, in whose potent blending of revival theology, Schleiermacherian elements, and a mild biblicism and confessionalism Erlangen found its most important theologian since the establishment of the university.[59]

In the introduction to Hofmann's *Schriftbeweis,* the characteristic elements emerge as distinctions in that independent being of Christianity with which the theologian has to deal and by which his work is tested: a threefold being "in the immediately certain fact [*Tatbestand*] of the rebirth of the Christian, in the history and existence of the church, and in holy scripture." [60] Hofmann was less interested, however, in emphasizing historical development, for example in the confessions, as a distinct element. On the one hand, the theological requirement was to give a systematic account of the given in present experience, a "scientific self-knowledge and self-declaration of the Christian." On the other hand, with respect both to Scripture and church history, there was theology's historical task: an investigation "of the historical development of the church and of the total meaning of holy scripture." [61] Each of these endeavors was in principle to be pursued independently of the other and their conclusions compared. Their concurrence in result constituted the proof of theology, a proper "biblical proof." These two foci, and the relation between them, give us Hofmann's fundamental theological interests, and in each area he had something distinctive to say.

The catchword for the exegetical task was "salvation history" (*Heilsgeschichte*). Hofmann viewed his own efforts in relation to two opposite errors in biblical interpretation. Traditional theology had

59. Hofmann had studied both at Erlangen and at Berlin and had already taught at Erlangen until 1842, when he received a call to Rostock. At Berlin, he was much more excited by the historian Leopold von Ranke than by Schleiermacher, Hegel, or Marheineke—and it is not unimportant that throughout his career he had little interest in philosophy as compared with history and literature. See his *Weissagung und Erfüllung,* 2 vols. (1841–44); *Der Schriftbeweis,* 2 vols. (1852–56; 2d ed., 1857–60), one of the most widely cited of mid-19th-century German works; *Schutzschriften für eine neue Weise, alte Warheit zu Lehren* (1856–59); *Enzyklopädie der Theologie* (posthumous, 1879). See also C. Senft, *Wahrhaftigkeit und Wahrheit* (Tübingen, 1956).

60. *Schriftbeweis,* 2d ed., 1 : 23.

61. *Enzyklopädie,* p. 29.

erred in not acknowledging the historicity of Scripture. Rationalism, on the other hand, failed because it did not address Scripture with an appropriate stance, a living relation to saving truth. Against orthodoxy, then, it had to be affirmed that the Bible has a history, that it is to be investigated as any other document. It is not to be protected as necessarily infallible: "Holy Scripture is something better than a book without errors." This is not to suggest that Hofmann was a biblical critic in the line of a Baur. He regularly drew the conservative conclusions about the biblical historical record, and he was given to harmonizing (e.g. of the resurrection accounts). What he did insist on, however, was that God's activity and thus the Bible should be considered as a whole and not piecemeal, neither removed from history nor swallowed up in general history but recognized in its own character as salvation history. To say that the Bible was historical meant that it is not a collection of isolated events or revelations, not a "textbook of so-called truths" but "the monument of a history." The Word of Christ is not primarily doctrine but history. In the Bible we have no real doctrinal writing but "history and its application." [62]

The implications for exegesis are plain. Individual texts can be interpreted only from the whole *Heilsgeschichte*. Thus Hofmann was particularly sharp in criticism of Hengstenberg's contention that God can and does act without any regard for historical connection: individual incidents and predictions can have significance for us "only when we have found their relation to the one event in which the decree of God concerning Israel and the human race has been essentially carried out. In this remark I have already pronounced against those who prize prophecies more highly the more isolated they are" and who think that they can thus more easily prove the divinity of the revelation they believe in.[63] Prophecy, and this means the whole relation of the Old Testament to the New, is not a mere prediction, but itself bears "the germ of the future."

But to recognize the Bible as the record of salvation history, thus as an organic whole, requires a living relation to that with which the Bible is concerned, a knowledge by experience (an *Erfahrungs-mässigkeit*). The true "historical" understanding is not finally separate from the pole of personal experience, but calls in fact for the believer's relation to Christ. Hence the other, systematic side of the

---

62. Hofmann, *Biblische Hermeneutik*, p. 8; *Schriftbeweis*, 1 : 25; *Weissagung und Erfüllung*, 1 : 47.
63. *Weissagung und Erfüllung*, p. 3.

theological task. This systematic activity, Hofmann insisted, is not a "description of the Christian religious dispositions." [64] Nor is it a reproduction of scriptural or ecclesiastical doctrine, nor a derivation of knowledge out of some first principle. Rather, it is just the "unfolding of the simple fact which makes the Christian a Christian and distinguishes him from the non-Christian, in an exposition of the manifold riches of its content." Theology is really a free science only when that which makes the Christian to be a Christian also constitutes the theologian as a theologian in scientific self-knowledge—in Hofmann's famous dictum, "when I the Christian am for myself the theologian the most proper material of my science." [65]

Hofmann's word for this dimension of the theological task was *Tatbestand,* the "matter of fact" of rebirth in Christ, the actual state of affairs that makes a man a Christian in distinction from the non-Christian. This was, for Hofmann, the simply indisputable and self-sufficient datum, the "relation to God mediated in Christ." That did not mean merely a consciousness or disposition in the self, but the fact that the Christian knows himself, in the experience of rebirth, to be in fellowship with God, and he lives in that fellowship not as an isolated individual but in relation to humanity. This fact is given for systematic theological reflection in the same way that natural or historical facts are given for natural scientists or historians. Christianity is the life that has begun in me an "independent being," "which is not dependent on the church, nor on the Scripture, but to which the church appeals." Of this "fact" I am as certain as I am of my existence. Hofmann thus never doubted the availability of this *Tatbestand* as an object of knowledge and predication. The "basis" of Christianity is not actually the "history of Christ and his apostles"; Christianity rests first of all on "the present Christ," who points back to the historical Christ as the presupposition of his presence. [66] Hence one can speak of having theological knowledge with "certainty"—and Hofmann was a pioneer in the nineteenth-century preoccupation with the question of certainty. [67] Neither in the Bible nor in dogma

64. *"Beschreibung der christlich-religiösen Gemütszustände"*—Hofmann here plainly meant to go beyond Schleiermacher, who had spoken of *"Beschreibungen menschlicher Lebenszustände"* as the primary form of theological assertion (*Chr. Gl.,* § 30), and of all doctrines as *"Auffassungen der christlich frommen Gemützustände in der Rede dargestellt"* (*Chr. Gl.,* § 15).

65. *Schriftbeweis,* 1 : 11, 10.

66. *Enzyklopädie,* p. 28.

67. This was also to be a special theme of F. H. R. Frank of Erlangen. See his *System der christlichen Gewissheit,* 2 vols. (1870 ff.).

is certainty available, since both have to be historically investigated, but only in immediate experience.

Out of the fact of rebirth in Christ, then, Hofmann proposed to develop directly the whole doctrinal system, from the Trinity and Creation to the Last Things. And here he gave classic expression to the movement, under the influence of the revival theology, from Schleiermacher back to the theological tradition, from "experience" to orthodoxy. The fact of Christ, of which we are sure, requires a preceding history, reaching back into the eternal idea of redemption and God's movement out of his self-identity into the otherness of the historical. That present fellowship requires a fulfillment—hence a full eschatology. In principle, the whole shape of Christian truth can be discovered, unfolded, and established without reference to historical investigation; the purpose of the latter is only "confirmation" that the systematic unfolding corresponds to the shape of the salvation history and the church's doctrine. "The question is only whether the result of historical investigation stands in accord with what has been achieved systematically" (i.e. whether exegesis can find support for the system in Scripture).[68] Yet Hofmann's own efforts and interests were manifestly directed to the historical questions. In his *Schriftbeweis* the "independent" systematic statement of the eight sections of the doctrinal whole occupies only twenty pages, which are followed by sixteen hundred pages of biblical analysis. It must therefore be asked whether in fact, for Hofmann's own theological procedures, the unfolding of the experience of rebirth was (or could be) accomplished so independently, or whether the experiential and the historical did not mutually serve to interpret and establish each other. That is, just as the perception of the salvation-historical character of Scripture as a whole required a living relation to the subject matter, so the actual unfolding of the *Tatbestand* had to be carried out and justified by the historical argument. The two tasks finally come together, in a genuine (though not necessarily vicious) circularity of "proof."

Flexibility with respect to confessional authority was implicit in Hofmann's understanding of the theological task. He saw in the church and its confessions and doctrines the medium or reflex or expression of the *Tatbestand* of Christianity in relation to Christ. "We discern this Christianity again in that of the Lutheran Confession." [69] The major doctrinal point at which Hofmann himself di-

68. *Enzyklopädie*, p. 26.
69. *Schriftbeweis*, 1 : 8.

verged from traditional Lutheran views, and for which he was vigorously attacked (even by other Erlangen theologians), was in atonement doctrine, where his salvation-history scheme of theology necessitated an abandonment of the accepted substitutionary satisfaction theory, with its concentration on the death of Christ and the overcoming of the divine wrath. Rather, for Hofmann, Christ appeared as man on earth as the historical actualization of the eternal inner-divine will of love to restore the fellowship with God broken by sin. He did this not so much by an act of dying as by a human form of being and willing and doing that throughout (thus also unto death) was characterized by obedience to the divine call. Thus the love and fidelity of Jesus to the Father, reflecting the inner-divine love of Son to Father, mediates a new relation of God and man, and those who receive this divine act in faith become participants in the new humanity of which Christ is the head. Christ is not a substitute in the sense of doing something for man that man is not therefore obliged to do. Rather he restores a relationship which is, in him as the new Adam, restored in man.[70]

The significance of this departure in atonement theory was twofold. First, though Hofmann's idea was uniformly rejected by the Lutheran confessionalists of all varieties, it was—both in its merging of the significance of the death of Christ with the whole life-career and in the "second-Adam" theme—a point of departure for a great deal of later atonement theory among the so-called mediating theologians. Second, Hofmann's defense of his orthodoxy by appealing to Luther against the "orthodox" in this important area was the real beginning of modern Luther research. That had been prepared for by De Wette's edition of Luther's letters (1825 and following) and the Erlangen edition of the works (1826 and following), but to drive a wedge between Luther and Lutheranism at such a crucial point was to necessitate a thorough reconsideration of Luther's Lutheranism, and thus to open the way to Albrecht Ritschl.

The Erlangen principle of confessional authority, and the balancing of Scripture and experience, was probably best expressed by Gottfried Thomasius. In his book on the Lutheran church's confession

70. "I do not call his accomplishment a 'substitutionary' satisfaction because it seems to me that the expression 'substitution' [*Stellvertretung*] improperly designates Christ's relation to humanity. . . . As the man Jesus, he is not another beside and outside humanity, but the Son of Man, in whom humanity has its other Adam" (*Schutzschriften*, 1 : 19, where Hofmann was replying to Philippi and Stahl, in defense of the idea of reconciliation he had set forth in the *Schriftbeweis*).

"in consequence of its principle," [71] Thomasius sought formally to show how the teachings of that church's confessions in general, and the Formula of Concord in particular, grew from Luther's doctrine of justification by faith, as an "organic life-principle" of the church. His own dogmatics [72] was shaped in such a way that each doctrinal section was divided into three parts: first an extensive theological analysis (articulating the logic of Christian experience), then a section of scriptural proof, and finally a section headed "Ecclesiastical Consensus," usually with extensive citation, to show that Thomasius's doctrine (especially the kenotic Christology—see below) could claim either the explicit approval or the inner "tendency" of the theological tradition. And in the foreword to the first volume of the dogmatics, he described his own theological purpose in revealing and yet characteristic fashion:

> The term dogma I intend here in its proper sense, according to which it means the conceptual expression for the common faith of the church. I am concerned precisely, not with the individual and the specific, but with that which has verified itself to the church as conforming to Scripture and which is sanctioned by its consensus. Consequently my work looks much more backward than forward; it is not intended to offer anything new; rather, even the new or individual elements that it possibly contains should be looked at only as development of the old and the common. I have intentionally limited myself to this. For I fancy nothing is more needed for the edification of the church in our days than that we first arrive again at an understanding of the great foundations and basic ideas of its confession, and as God wills at a unanimous conviction; then we can always go on to the extension of the details and of what lies further off. That I have in mind, however, no mere repetition of old official definitions and forms, the book itself will show. The task of dogmatics, as I think of it, is rather to reproduce the dogma constantly anew and afresh out of its deep inner grounds and life-roots, and thus to give it a form in which it may appear as the expression of the one biblical and ecclesiastical faith, which is by nature at once always old and young.

71. *Das Bekenntnis der evangelisch-lutherischen Kirche in der Konsequenz seines Prinzips* (1848). Thomasius was called to Erlangen in 1842. See my *God and Incarnation in Mid-Nineteenth-Century German Theology: Thomasius, Dorner, Biedermann* (New York, 1965).

72. *Christi Person und Werk. Darstellung der evangelisch-lutherischen Dogmatik vom Mittelpunkte der Christologie aus* (1853–61; 2d ed., 1856–63; 3d ed., rev. F. Winter, 1886–88).

The designation "Lutheran" I surely could also have omitted; for it is not at all our view in the use of this name that in the "Lutheran" there is found something beside or outside the universally Christian and evangelical. We are rather persuaded of possessing, in the genuinely Lutheran, precisely that which forms the truly universal, which is in particular the correct, scriptural center between the confessional antitheses. But just because of this we need not be ashamed of the name of our Luther.[73]

The Mercersburg Theology

Compared with the Oxford Movement or the Erlangen theology, the Mercersburg theology was of far less enduring impact on the nineteenth century.[74] It emerged in the little theological seminary of the German Reformed church, in a village in Pennsylvania. It was the work really of only two men, John Williamson Nevin (1803–86) and Philip Schaff (1819–93). As a vigorous movement it lasted no more than a decade, from 1844, when young Schaff came to join Nevin at Mercersburg, until 1853, when the college and seminary

73. Ibid., 1 : 4–5. Both Thomasius's method in his *Domatics* (see also below, p. 235–39) and his understanding of the confessions were related to the principles of what he himself considered his most original work as well as his chief lifelong interest: his history of doctrine (*Die christliche Dogmengeschichte*, 2 vols. [1874–76, vol. 2, ed. D. G. Plitt; 2d ed., 1886–89], pp. 7–8). Here Thomasius was an important bridge between the work of Baur and Neander and that of Harnack. His new method was to seek the most vital question or questions for each period of the church's history, and then to organize and interpret the dogmatic development around those questions, rather than taking up in order all the traditional loci in each epoch. Thus the period of the Greek fathers was dominated by the doctrines of the person of Christ and of the Trinity; for the Latin Fathers it was the questions of sin and grace, etc. (Kähler considered this an epoch-making development in the writing of the history of dogma; cf. his *Geschichte der protestantischen Dogmatik im 19. Jahrhundert* [Munich, 1962], pp. 182–83).

74. See the excellent selections, introductions, and selected bibliography in James H. Nichols, ed., *The Mercersburg Theology* (New York, 1966). I would dissent, however, from Nichols's associating the Mercersburg theology so closely with the Lutheran confessionalism of Löhe et al. Nevin and Schaff were much closer in spirit and in teaching to the Erlangen theology and to the "mediating theologians" than to the strict Lutheran confessionalists. Yet Nevin and Schaff were, like the Tractarians, deeply concerned for the location of institutional authority and were more "defensively" oriented vis-à-vis the relation of the church to the world than were e.g. Maurice or Rothe. See also James H. Nichols, *Romanticism in American Theology: Nevin and Schaff at Mercersburg* (Chicago, 1961). Nevin's most important works were: *The History and Genesis of the Heidelberg Catechism* (1840–42), *The Anxious Bench* (1843), and *The Mystical Presence* (1846), the latter a historical and systematic work on the Eucharist. Schaff's major works during the Mercersburg period were: *The Principle of Protestantism* (1845), *What is Church History?* (1846), and *History of the Apostolic Church* (1853).

moved to Lancaster. Nevin retired to private life and Schaff subsequently went on to a second, better known and more independent career as the great church historian at Union Theological Seminary in New York. Thereafter the ecumenical momentum was lost, the interests of the American churches were almost entirely captured by the debate over slavery and the Civil War, and the distinctive Mercersburg elements were finally largely sacrificed to denominational interests.

Yet the Mercersburg theology was an episode of intrinsic interest and striking vitality—in fertility matched in the United States only by Horace Bushnell and by Emerson. Further, in its breadth of theological horizon and its degree of interrelationship, the work of Nevin and Schaff was unparalleled in America and hardly matched in England and Germany. The most immediate object of their concern was the highly individualistic and subjectivist tradition of American evangelicalism (in whose atmosphere Nevin had grown up). They debated vigorously with Charles Hodge, whose pupil and temporary replacement Nevin had been. Nevin was deeply influenced by Coleridge, both philosophically and in his view of Scripture. Both men were naturally at home in contemporary German theology and they were of great importance in introducing German thought into the American scene.[75] Nevin and Schaff were particularly involved in exchange with Dorner, who represented a comparable breadth of horizon in Germany. Among the Roman Catholics, they were principally interested in Johann Adam Möhler and Orestes Brownson. They followed closely the development of the Anglo-Catholic movement—with a special affinity for R. I. Wilberforce—and in contemporary American discussions the Mercersburg theology was often associated with "Puseyism." They had much in common with F. D. Maurice, and they engaged in some debate with Horace Bushnell.

Even before the "second conversion," which led him into the German Reformed church and to Mercersburg in 1839, Nevin had been reacting against the growing "party spirit" in American evangelicalism and biblicism, as well as against the divisiveness of the slavery

75. Nevin was familiar at least with Schleiermacher and Hegel, with Olshausen, Ullmann, Neander, Liebner, Tholuck, Rothe, Nitzsch, Müller, and Dorner—and his early colleague at Mercersburg was Frederick Rauch (1806–41), who had studied at Heidelberg and was a disciple of Daub. Schaff came to Mercersburg (as Rauch's replacement) fresh from his studies at Tübingen (with Baur and Dorner), at Halle (where he was secretary to Tholuck), and at Berlin (with Schelling and especially with Neander; he was also close to Gerlach).

issue. Schaff had been stimulated by Gerlach's "Evangelische Katholizität," with its early enthusiasm for the Reformed–Lutheran union in the Prussian Evangelical church. The meeting of the two men at Mercersburg meant the confluence of profoundly similar interests and views, and immediately after Schaff's arrival they published Schaff's *Principle of Protestantism* (1845), with Nevin's sermon on "Catholic Unity" as an appendix. This was in effect the manifesto of the movement, and it was followed by an extensive literature of books and articles (especially in *The Mercersburg Review, The Weekly Messenger,* and *Der deutsche Kirchenfreund*).

The central theme of the Mercersburg "manifesto" was the evil of sectarianism, and the imperative of unity within the church. In the *Principle,* Schaff described the two great maladies of the time as rationalism and sectarianism, the former as a "one-sided theoretic religious subjectivism" most fully exhibited in German Lutheranism, the latter as a "one-sided practical religious subjectivism [that] has found its classic ground within the territory of the Reformed Church, in the predominantly practical countries, England and America." [76] The "sect system," Nevin called "an immense evil," "an abomination in the temple of God"; its spirit is Antichrist. "The whole Christian world" must be brought "not only to acknowledge and feel, but also to show itself evidently one." And it is thus the duty of the church to take every possible occasion "to advance in a visible way the interest of catholic unity." In language strikingly like that of F. D. Maurice, Nevin insisted that this cannot be accomplished by a "no-sect party in the Church," which "must ever be found itself one of the worst forms of separatism, aggravating the mischief it proposes to heal." [77]

But concern for unity in the church presupposes a genuine theology of the church, which was just what Nevin and Schaff found lacking in the typical American antitraditionalist, individualist outlook, now powerfully reinforced by revivalism, especially in the form of Finney's "new measures," with their gimmickry, disorder, and even greater subjectivism.[78] The typical foci for American theologies were either biblical inspiration and "evidences" or conversion and re-

76. Theses 54 and 55 of the 112 in which Schaff summarized the *Principle.*

77. See Nevin, "Catholic Unity," "The Church," "The Sect System," and "Antichrist, or the Spirit of Sect and Schism" (in Nichols, *Mercersburg Theology,* pp. 33–76, 93–119).

78. Nevin had warned against this tendency in *The Anxious Bench,* where he was concerned about the Pelagianism of the revival theology as well as its divisiveness.

generation (hence also justification and atonement). Thus Schaff began his 112 Theses in the *Principle of Protestantism:*

1. Every period of the Church and theology has its particular problem to solve; and every doctrine, in a measure every book also of the Bible, has its classic age in which it first comes to be fully understood and appropriated by the consciousness of the Christian world.
2. The main question of *our* time is concerning the nature of the Church itself in its relation to the world and to single Christians.

For the Mercersburg theology, however, and most explicitly for Nevin, a theology of the church must be thoroughly christological. The theology of the new Mercersburg liturgy (1857, rev. 1866), he defended because "In the first place it is christological, or more properly perhaps, christocentric; in the second place, it moves in the bosom of the Apostles' Creed; in the third place, it is objective and historical, involving thus the idea of the Church as a perennial article of faith." [79] (In the debate with Dorner over the principle of Protestantism, the divergence was finally one of christological views, as Dorner also saw it.) The central christological point, for Nevin, was to see that "the mediation of Christ" is itself simply "the constitution of his person." In agreement with R. I. Wilberforce, whose book on the incarnation elicited a review essay from Nevin, the latter held that the incarnation is not a mere device instrumental to the work of redemption; "it is itself the Mediatorial Fact." Such a doctrine of genuine incarnation leads to recognition of the Church as "the historical continuation" of the life of Jesus Christ in the world. The idea of a sect or of an unchurchly spirit is essentially docetic and unhistorical. This is the Antichrist that "turns all religion into a mere idea," that knows nothing of "a real revelation of Christ in the flesh."

One of the significant features of the consequent doctrine for Nevin and Schaff was their judgment that the whole history of the church must be taken up in a true evangelical catholicity, within the orbit of the Apostles' Creed, but without restricting the truth to any period, apostolic or medieval or Reformation, or absolutizing either confession or bishop. The truth and reality of the church in any given age depends necessarily on a living connection with all previous ages. In their idea of the development of the church and its doctrines, Nevin and Schaff drew on the distinction between doctrine and religion (in the tradition of Schleiermacher and Neander—and here they differed sharply from Newman and from the Lutheran confes-

79. See Nichols, *Mercersburg Theology*, pp. 14, 260–81.

sionalists). They also showed the influence of the romanticist love for tradition and enthusiasm for conceptions of organic unity and development.

Further, in language similar to that of Baur and Dorner, they could use idealist categories to describe the manifestation in history of the total reality of the church and the interplay of doctrinal tendencies. Thus Nevin spoke in his sermon "The Church" of the "Idea" of the church, "in the true sense" of the term idea, "by which it expresses the very inmost substance of that which exists, as distinguished from its simply phenomenal character in time and space." As such, the church "is a living system, organically bound together in all its parts, springing from a common ground, and pervaded throughout with the force of a common nature." The "actual church" is the manifestation, the visible externalization of the "Ideal" church in a process of historical evolution necessarily spread over a long span of time. And the pattern of development (i.e. "rational and necessary" as distinct from the irrational and tyrannical sect distinctions) can even be depicted in the form of historical dialectic: for example, the division between Protestantism and Catholicism, and the further split into the two great confessions, Lutheran and Reformed, have this rationality. Thus, as Nevin said in "The Sect System" (1849), "They have their ground in the Idea of Christianity itself; they form necessary *momenta*, or moving forces, in the process by which this Idea is carried forward to its final completion; they can be studied accordingly, and understood in the way, for instance, of comparative symbolism."

In this context one can understand the "evangelically catholic" character of the Mercersburg view of the church. The church was "the historical continuation of the life of Jesus Christ in the world" not merely a witness to a truth apart from herself, but "in the fullest sense the depository of the life of Christ himself," therefore a "visible, catholic, historical, and life-bearing church." The church was theanthropic, the supernatural made permanent and historical. The Eucharist, as the "real spiritual presence" of Christ, naturally became the principal focus of theological attention. "The Eucharist forms the very heart of the whole Christian worship," Nevin insisted in his major work,[80] for its soul is the "actual communication with the humanity of Christ." But the principle of a sacramental theology was

---

80. *The Mystical Presence: A Vindication of the Reformed or Calvinistic Doctrine of the Holy Eucharist* (1846). Extracts are printed in Nichols, *Mercersburg Theology*, pp. 197–244.

not merely a patristic and catholic principle. For the Reformation had meant a reformed catholicism, a real "advance of the religious life and consciousness of the Church, by means of a deeper apprehension of God's word," but not a "revolutionary separation from the Catholic Church," or a leaping back to the apostolic Age.[81] Nevin's *Mystical Presence* was precisely an attempt to show—contrary to "modern Puritanism" and Princeton—that the Reformed doctrine of the sacraments, in particular the Eucharist, was a development out of, and not against, the patristic doctrine. The Reformed and the Lutheran churches both needed to be recalled to their true heritage. "The old Reformed doctrine included always the idea of an *objective force* in the sacraments." The sacrament exhibits, represents, and seals the grace that is really *there,* "not the name of the thing only, and not its sign or shadow, but the actual substance itself." And Calvin always insisted on a real (i.e. true) spiritual presence of Christ in the Lord's Supper. On the basis, then, of the "old Reformed view" of the Lord's Supper, Nevin proposed to give the doctrine a "proper scientific form," in the light of a better modern psychology.

Nevin's and Schaff's understanding of the relation of Catholic and Protestant truth—in which Protestantism represented a necessary reformation in the church, but not by any means the totality or final summation of Christian truth—and their insistence on the "whole" historical view, points to a final element in their ecumenical outlook: the hope and expectation of future evolution in Christianity, through which the evangelical catholicity and the catholic unity of the church could be more adequately actualized. The actual church is a process, not yet complete or perfected, but always looking and pressing for its completion; it falls short, in every age, of the perfection for which it is destined—this is involved in the very idea that the historical church is both the true Church and yet never simply free from error and sin. Thus there is hope for an evolution from the present divided churches into something better, if the sect spirit can be overcome. The "remedy" is not a "violent overthrow" of present church structures and "outward denominational distinctions" by a "return" to primitive beginnings; this is to create a new *"no-sect"* sect, as had the experiment of Alexander Campbell. Nor is the way a "liberality" that dissolves the substance of Christianity into something indistinguishable from life as mere nature. Nor can the goal be achieved by federation, "free construction of catholic unity by counsel and

81. See Schaff, Theses nos. 30, 31.

compact among the different sects themselves." Rather, redemption from the plague of sectarianism can begin only "with a revival of true and hearty faith in the ancient article of the one holy catholic Church." [82] The form of a new development can never be specified in advance; but on the grand scale of history, without denying the value and truth either of Catholicism or of Protestantism, and without overlooking their defects, the church may now as at all past times be seen as transitional in form and "interimistic." The church is destined to go forward through its present difficulties toward a final form that will also be a realization of the beginning—a Johannine type that once more will fulfill the Petrine and the Pauline.

THE NEW VENTURE IN KENOTIC CHRISTOLOGY

One is tempted to speak of a stampede, especially among the moderate Lutherans in mid-nineteenth-century German theology, toward versions of kenotic Christology. Both there and in the later and more hesitant movement among British thinkers (e.g. in Gore, Fairbairn, and Mackintosh, at the end of the nineteenth century), the new lure of the idea of a self-emptying of the divine in the incarnation (Philippians 2) seems to have come from a convergence of several of the most powerful forces in the theological scene. The Christologies of kenosis were partly a response, though largely negative, to the biblical-historical question as shaped by Strauss and Baur. Equally important was the new critique of classical christological formulas and the new ideas about the development of doctrine. At the same time, however, and above all, the idea of kenosis seemed a way to conserve the fundamental interests of the classical "two-natures" Christology and yet to recognize (in a way the traditional formulas had not) a genuinely human figure in Jesus of Nazareth, a person with actual human limitations of knowledge and power, with a "gradually dawning infant consciousness" and a real growth—a person for whom sleep and death were real. The characteristic focus of this concern for the humanity of Jesus was again typical of the nineteenth century: it was peculiarly the self-consciousness and the knowledge of Jesus that provided the test questions—and this was in turn related to the problem of the personality of God. Finally, the emergence of kenosis doctrines often involved specific confessional interests, as in Thomasius.

The first definite nineteenth-century move in the kenotic direc-

82. Nevin, "Antichrist, or the Spirit of Sect and Schism," see Nichols, pp. 113–19.

tion seems to have been taken by Ernst Wilhelm Christian Sartorius (1797–1859), in the *Beiträge zu den theologischen Wissenschaften*.[83] Though Sartorius himself later drew back somewhat from his earlier suggestions, especially as they involved the mutability of God, kenosis theories spread so rapidly in the 1840s and 1850s that Isaak Dorner could write in 1856 of kenoticism as the then "almost predominant" theory.[84] Among those variously caught up in the movement were König, Hofmann, Thomasius, Gess, Gaupp, Liebner, Ebrard, Hahn, Godet, Edmond de Pressensé, Delitzsch, Schmieder, Steinmeyer, Besser, and Kahnis—and Dorner also was powerfully attracted to it for a time.

The most extreme form of the doctrine was that given by Gess, for whom the incarnation meant not merely that the Logos laid aside, or emptied itself of certain aspects of divinity, but that the eternal Son actually changed himself into a man.[85] The "ego of the pre-earthly Son" he held to be the same as "the ego of the Jesus living on earth. But the pre-earthly Son is God, the earthly Son is man." In becoming man, the Son allowed his eternal self-consciousness actually to be extinguished, regaining it as a man with a thoroughly human development, acquiring righteousness just as every other man. Thus the self-emptying, or laying aside of divinity, in the incarnation was complete: the Logos ceased to be God and became man, though in some way maintaining an identity of ego.[86] And with this sort of statement may be associated the dramatic imagery of Frédéric Godet: Will it not be with a cry similar to "Father, into thy hands I

---

83. See also his *Dorpater Beiträge* (1832), 1 : 348 ff., and *Die Lehre von der heiligen Liebe*, vol. 2 (1844). Roots of the new 19th-century element are to be found at least in Zinzendorf and in Samuel Collenbusch (1724–1803).

84. Dorner, *Briefwechsel Zwischen H. L. Martensen und I. A. Dorner, 1839–1881*, 2 vols. (Berlin, 1888), 1 : 282. Dorner surveyed this development extensively in the first of his essays on the proper understanding of the immutability of God, in the *Jahrbücher für deutsche Theologie*, vol. 1, pt. 2 (1856), pp. 361 ff., reprinted in his *Gesammelte Schriften* (1883), pp. 188 ff., and more briefly in his *System of Christian Doctrine* (see the translation in my *God and Incarnation*, pp. 191 ff.). See also Ernst Günther, *Die Entwicklung der Lehre von der Person Christi im 19. Jahrhundert* (Tübingen, 1911), pp. 165–200.

85. Wolfgang Friedrich Gess, *Die Lehre von der Person Christi, entwickelt aus dem Selbstbewusstsein Christi und aus dem Zeugniss der Apostel* (Basel, 1856), pp. 304 ff.

86. Both Dorner and A. E. Biedermann considered Gess's view the only consistent outcome of the kenotic movement, and thus its final disproof (cf. Dorner in the *Gesammelte Schriften*, pp. 232–33, and Biedermann in my *God and Incarnation*, pp. 304 ff.).

commit my spirit," that "the Word plunges into the voluntary annihilation which was the condition of his incarnation"? [87]

It was Gottfried Thomasius, however, through whom the new kenoticism became a major center of debate and in whose hands the theory was given its most impressive form. His first major essay on Christology, the two-part *Beiträge zur kirchlichen Christologie* (1845),[88] was a response to the recent attacks on the church's doctrine by Strauss and Baur, whose criticisms were to some extent shared by Dorner (though from a more positive point of view). The charges of inconsistency and of denial of the true humanity of Christ were not really new, Thomasius judged, apart from their Hegelian flavor and presuppositions. And they had often been replied to. But they were not without validity. The intention and direction of the church's doctrine (its *Tendenz*) was unassailable. The objections did not apply to the basic content of the dogma, the affirmation of the one Christ who is true God and true man. Yet the form of the ancient creedal definitions, and the ideas of hypostatic union—in particular the valid and necessary doctrine that the humanity of the Redeemer was anhypostatic, that is, without finite *hypostasis* or "person"—did not show how these primary affirmations could be combined with the idea of a full human personality in the modern sense of the word, or how one could be serious about a genuine human development in the Redeemer's life without postulating some sort of double ego.

Just at this point, Thomasius believed, Lutheran Christology had taken a great step forward by seeking to work out more fully the doctrine of the impartation of properties (*communicatio idiomatum*). That is, the divine and human natures were not only joined in the unity of one hypostasis or persona; they were also actually imparted to each other, in as complete a penetration as could take place without destroying the integrity of each. The purpose of this step was the highly practical one, springing directly from the experience of reconciliation, of showing that Christ suffered not only as man but as God, and that he is received in the Lord's Supper not only as God but also as man. This was the intention and direction of the Lutheran christological development. But

87. "The Earthly Life of the Son of God and His Glorification," *Revue chrétienne*, no. 3 (1858) : 160.

88. Published first in the *Zeitschrift für Protestantismus und Kirche*. Thomasius was concerned specifically with Strauss's *Glaubenslehre* (1840–41), Baur's history of the doctrines of Trinity and Incarnation (1841–43), and Dorner's history of Christology (1st ed., 1839).

the consequences were not always fully or consistently drawn. The problem of how the divine attributes could be imparted to the humanity, without annulling the latter, was not fully resolved. The charge of inconsistency, in that the *communicatio* was interpreted only as a one-way impartation from divine to human rather than as a mutual exchange, was not without foundation. And on all sides, in the discussion of the human possession or use of the divine glory and power during the state of humiliation, difficulties remained for conceiving a really human historical life of Jesus.

Thus Thomasius saw two possibilities. Either we gave up the *communicatio* in favor of a mere juxtaposition of divine and human —but this the Lutheran church had rightly rejected as a retreat; or we go forward, in accord with the inner tendency of the Lutheran Christology, to a deeper and more perceptive grasp of the concept of kenosis, and accept the idea of a self-limitation *of the divine* in the incarnation. The latter was the step for which Thomasius argued, and it was the novel element in relation to seventeenth-century Lutheran Christology. That is, the earlier theologians had allowed at most a surrender (according to the humanity) of the *use* of the divine attributes (some permitted only a concealment); further, they had insisted that the subject of the act of self-emptying was the *incarnate* Word, who thus *as man* surrendered the use of the divine powers but *as divine* continued to rule heaven and earth omnipotently, omnisciently, and omnipresently.[89] Thomasius, however, suggested that the Logos himself, in the act of incarnation, underwent a self-limitation, divesting himself of those aspects of divinity that were incompatible with a genuinely human existence: "The eternal Son of God, the second person of the deity, gave himself over into the form of human limitation, and thereby to the limits of a spatio-temporal existence, under the conditions of a human development, in the bounds of an historical concrete being, in order to live in and through our nature the life of our race in the fullest sense of the word, without on that account ceasing to be God." Only in this way could there be an actual entering into human existence, a real becoming man. Of course, the Logos did not surrender that essential deity which made him to be God, but rather gave up the divine "mode of being" in favor of a "humanly creaturely form of exis-

89. For details see my translation of Thomasius in *God and Incarnation*, pp. 25–101, where the principal portions of Thomasius's Christology in his dogmatics are set forth, along with references to the *Beiträge* and other writings.

tence," thus renouncing "the divine glory which he had from the beginning with the Father and exercised vis-à-vis the world, governing and ruling it throughout." [90]

That is to say, in the language of Thomasius's initial proposal in the *Beiträge,* the incarnation was "intrinsically" *(an sich)* a self-limitation of the Son of God. In free renunciation he gave up the "divine form of existence"; he "withdrew into himself" the attributes in which the divine glory is manifested; he determined "to have his divine essence only in unity with the human, to give his divine being over into the form of human existence." "He possessed the divine glory only *potentia* and no longer *actu.*" In particular, this kenosis involved the divine consciousness, for if God was to be truly man he had to have a human consciousness, and he had to develop in a fully human way his consciousness of his divine essence and glory. Thus "the Logos retained neither a distinct being of his own nor a distinct knowledge of himself outside his humanity. He became a man in the literal sense." [91]

Yet the Logos did not cease to be God (as, for example, Gess would have it). The Christian experience of redemption requires both that the Son of God have become genuinely man, sharing to the fullest extent in human experience, and that he have retained what was essential to divinity.

How, then, can the self-limitation be described as sufficiently thoroughgoing to make plausible a unitary, actually historical life, and at the same time a continuity of existence of the Logos? Thomasius's answer to the question involved several themes of his later argument.[92] One was the insistence that if kenosis is *voluntary* self-limitation, it is an expression of the divine rather than any denial of it. For the essence of God is wholly life and will, *actus,* and the self-limitation in the incarnation was an utterly free act and an expression of the divine love. God, therefore, did not cease to be God by setting a limit to himself but expressed his complete mastery of him-

---

90. *Christi Person und Werk,* § 40.

91. *Beiträge,* pp. 93 ff.

92. Notably in *Christi Person und Werk,* where Thomasius sought to develop a theological structure in which the whole pattern of doctrinal assertion would explicitly spring out of Christology. The doctrines of God, creation, man, and sin were subsumed under the heading of "presuppositions of Christology," both eternal and historical. The doctrines of the Holy Spirit, the Church, sacraments, and the Christian life were developed as consequences of Christology, under the rubric "the work of Christ."

self. The surrender of the divine "glory" or the "form of God" Thomasius also sought to interpret as a withdrawal to "potence" (*Potenz*). That did not at all mean reduction to impotency or mere possibility, but "power concentrated in itself, enclosed in itself: *potentia.*" It was thus a "withdrawal" by "an act of self-limitation (self-determination) from the periphery of self-revelation and activity to his innermost center . . . to the root of his concrete being, which is essential absolute will." [93]

A correlative element in Thomasius's theory, and the idea for which he became best known, was the distinction between the "immanent" and the "relative" attributes of God. The immanent attributes—those which were essential to the being of God as God, expressing inner determinations of the absolute personality and inner trinitarian relations—were especially absolute power, truth, holiness, and love. The relative attributes—those that expressed relation to a world, and thus depended on the existence of a world—were above all omnipotence, omniscience, and omnipresence. Absolute power thus was distinct from omnipotence (its activation in relation to the world), and absolute truth was distinct from omniscience. The relative attributes could actually be given up in a withdrawal to potence or to the immanent attributes. Kenosis meant the complete laying aside or "self-divesting" (not self-emptying; Thomasius used the term *Entäusserung,* but rejected *Entleerung*) of the attributes of omnipotence, omniscience, and omnipresence for the period of Jesus' earthly life. He was no omnipotent man, though as man, in a humanly developing way, he possessed "absolute power as the freedom of self-determination, as the mighty will completely his own," and he possessed "absolute truth . . . as the knowledge of the incarnate one concerning his own essence and the will of the Father."

Finally, this conception of incarnation was supported by Thomasius' insistence on the susceptibility of human nature to penetration by the divine (*natura humana capax divinae*). Human nature, because created in the image of God, could be "wholly taken up into the divine and completely penetrated by it," without any human consciousness or will distinct from that of the Logos, yet without ceasing to be human. And the Logos could exist wholly "in the flesh." Thus in the earthly life of Jesus, the *communicatio idiomatum* was genuine and mutual, the divine actually accepting the

93. Ibid., appendix "Against Dorner."

limitations of manhood and the human actually receiving the properties of the divine. And in the state of exaltation, after the resurrection, the transfigured human nature could fully share in the Son of God's reassumption of the relative attributes of omnipotence, omniscience, and omnipresence. None of these properties is incompatible with the essence of resurrected humanity, even corporeality. So the incarnation, the actual being-man, has become "the permanent form of existence for God the Son." [94]

It is plain that Thomasius's effort to resolve the christological problem—especially as a problem of the *unity* of the God-man and of his real humanity—remained within the orbit of the traditional concerns with the "person" and the "natures" of Christ. This was his intention. And while his view was profoundly shaped by the interest in exhibiting a genuinely human existence for Jesus, it was little affected by the new historical discussion. In these respects, Thomasius was typical of the kenotic movement. His own theory was roundly attacked as incompatible with the Formula of Concord. It raised peculiar problems for trinitarian doctrine (how could the inner-trinitarian life avoid disruption when the Son of God gave up his omnipotent rule of the world? [95] And Thomasius candidly allowed that his interpretation finally depended upon the acceptability of his distinction between the relative and immanent attributes.

Yet the collapse of the kenotic christological movement was not due simply to such internal difficulties. Nor was it only that in this movement the idea of kenosis was carried to the limit of its possibilities within those presuppositions that were necessary for a theory of kenosis to be proposed at all, that is, within presuppositions that demanded pursuit of the metaphysical and even psychological questions. More important was the question, which the kenotic movement did not originate but helped dramatically to illustrate, whether the classical ways of posing the question of Christ were any longer viable at all. The new mood of the later nineteenth century, which was symbolized in Germany by Albrecht Ritschl, was one that would sweep aside both the kenoticists and their critics. [96] It was a program for cutting loose from the spirit of "speculation" altogether, and from the "metaphysical" in theology, and a turning to the historical

94. Ibid., §§ 37, 45, 46.
95. Thomasius sought to deal with this criticism in § 46 of his dogmatics (see *God and Incarnation*, pp. 81 ff.
96. Including both the "orthodox" critics and men like Dorner and Biedermann.

and the "practical" as the new foundations and forms in theology. The christological question, as a problem of the constitution of Christ's person, of the two natures, was to be given up in favor of other ways of posing the question, restricted to "historical" or "value" or "existential" judgments. And to that transition the venture into kenotic Christology contributed much, even though in a negative way.

10

Toward a Critical Orthodoxy:

Frederick Denison Maurice

I have in this book attacked no wrong tendency to which I do not know myself to be liable. I hope I am conscious to a certain degree, though very insufficiently, of the danger I am in of substituting the denunciation of it for the practical correction of it in the only sphere over which I have any control. I am not ignorant, also, that the hints which I have offered in opposition to systems may, themselves, be turned by myself or others into a system. . . . But since a school, which should be formed to oppose all schools, must be of necessity more mischievous than any of them; and since a school, which pretended to amalgamate the doctrines of all other schools, would be, as I think, more mischievous than that, I do pray earnestly that, if any such schools should arise, they may come to nought; and that, if what I have written in this book should tend even in the slightest degree to favour the establishment of them, it may come to nought.

F. D. Maurice, The Kingdom of Christ

Both his contemporaries and later thinkers in the century applied to F. D. Maurice the most widely varying judgments. For example, from the liberal side alone, the leading British Unitarian thinker of the mid-nineteenth century, James Martineau, wrote in 1856 that "for consistency and completeness of thought, and precision in the use of language it would be difficult to find his superior among living theologians"; yet the most characteristic thinker of the Broad Church, Benjamin Jowett, complained in 1872 that Maurice "was misty and confused, and none of his writings appear to me worth reading." [1] Martineau's judgment is not easy to sustain, for Maurice was not a systematic thinker and he did not develop his most profound ideas, even his idea of the Lordship of Christ, with theological clarity and intellectual toughness. He never reconciled the tension between his relativism and his realism.

1. Cited in the excellent study of Maurice by Alec Vidler, *The Theology of F. D. Maurice* (London, 1948). Vidler has collected a remarkable group of divergent opinions, pp. 9 ff.

Yet Maurice has come increasingly to be recognized as the most seminal theological mind (with the possible exception of John Henry Newman) in mid-nineteenth-century Britain. He was also the bridge between Coleridge and the famous Cambridge triumvirate of historians and biblical scholars—Westcott, Lightfoot, and Hort —through whom critical biblical study took solid root in the English church; and he powerfully shaped the later Liberal Catholicism and Evangelical Liberalism. He has often been associated with the Broad Church, but he was with them only in the most independent way. He was peculiarly a man of no "school." Like his American contemporary Horace Bushnell,[2] Maurice cannot easily be called a mediating theologian, for he did not seek (or occupy) a middle ground, nor did he have the intention of synthesizing Christian faith with culture or some prevalent system of thought. Insofar as Maurice and Bushnell sought theological reconciliation—and they were both regularly in the midst of controversy with the theological parties of their time, Maurice in England, Bushnell in New England— it was by a critical reappropriation of the gospel and the theological tradition. This theological aim may appropriately be named "critical orthodoxy" (though one might also speak of it as "critical comprehensiveness" or even "critical relativism"). It was highly orthodox in its Christocentrism, but critical in respect of authority and Scripture.[3]

Again like Bushnell, even though he did hold a chair in "divinity" for a time, Maurice was not a professional theologian in the usual sense, by comparison for example, with the scientific theology of the German tradition following Schleiermacher. One is tempted to look on both these men, especially Bushnell, as "folk theologians." Yet it would be better to speak of them as representing a different

2. See chap. 11, below.

3. The term has a grounding in what Maurice himself called "criticism" as distinguished from "compromise": "we can do the world most good by setting forth our beliefs in our different modes, and by expressing or manifesting our conviction that they are reconciled in a Truth of which we have a strong and vital, though an imperfect perception. This is my idea of criticism and of what you and Paul name compromise. Criticism . . . will be always negative, cruel . . . unless it becomes an interchange of thoughts between men who care much for each other and more for Truth. Compromise must always tend to the impairing of moral vigor, and to the perplexing of the conscience, if it is anything else than a confession of the completeness of Truth, and of the incompleteness of our apprehension of it" (Maurice to J. M. Ludlow, 1861, in *The Life of F. D. Maurice, Chiefly Told in His Own Letters*, ed. Frederick Maurice, 2 vols., 3d ed. (1884), 2 : 319–20.

style of theologizing, whose driving force was not completeness or rigorous systematization, nor philosophical interconnections, but a more immediate relation to the life of a church congregation (Bushnell) or social needs and the national community (Maurice), as well as to the conflicts within the Christian community.[4]

THE METHOD

What Maurice called his "system phobia" was one symptom of a complex, many-faceted theological stance and method which was at the same time a unitary direction of thinking pervading a large and unsystematic literature. Like Coleridge, to whom he was close in deepest principles, Maurice had a hunger for wholeness, unity, and reconciliation. In an autobiographical sketch he wrote that "The desire for *Unity* has haunted me all my life through; I have never been able to substitute any desire for that, or to accept any of the different schemes for satisfying it which men have devised" (*Life*, 1 : 41). This hunger was doubtless intensified, if not initiated, by the tensions over religious differences in Maurice's family. One by one his three older sisters had broken with the Unitarianism of their minister father (which was of the "old-fashioned" nondogmatic sort), and finally their mother also, in 1821, took the step (so painful that she could only do it in writing) of telling her husband that she could no longer worship with him. Later on, Maurice saw those early years and all the struggles and crises of his experience as part of a divine pedagogy leading him to seek the unity of a truth transcending all humanly devised schemes. We see in this one expression of the concreteness of Maurice's thinking: theology is not speculation, but reflection on the immediate relation of himself, his family, and his society to God. This involves directly a search for wholeness, a search that Maurice conducted by setting himself alongside his

---

4. Maurice (1805–72) began to read law at Cambridge and completed the course but did not take the degree because he was not at that time willing to make the required subscription to the Thirty-Nine Articles. He later gradually decided for the Anglican priesthood, took a degree at Oxford, and was ordained in 1834. He was a chaplain to medical students (1836), then professor at King's College (1840)—first of English literature and modern history, later of divinity (1846) in the newly established theological department. He was dismissed in 1853, when he also resigned the principalship of Queen's College, which he had helped to found. Continuing his chaplaincy to lawyers at Lincoln's Inn (1846 ff.), he founded a Workingmen's College in 1854. Finally, he was elected Knightsbridge Professor of Moral Philosophy at Cambridge (1866). Maurice's *Life*, edited by his son Frederick Maurice, is an indispensable source for the interpretation of his thought.

hearers as those who were in fact related to the same reality to which he was related, to apprehend with them God acting and speaking. In this understanding of the immediacy of theological thinking, Maurice again found himself close to Coleridge. Of all Coleridge's works, it was to the *Aids to Reflection* that Maurice felt a "deep and solemn obligation," just because "I do not know any book which ever brought to me more clear tokens and evidences" of the author's being "himself engaged in the conflict with an evil nature and a reluctant will, and that he had received the truths of which he would make me a partaker, not at second hand, but as the needful supports of his own being." [5]

The method of Maurice drew in a related way on Plato, who was more congenial to Maurice than was Aristotle because "it was a Being to satisfy the wants of men that Plato sighed for; it was a first Cause of Things to which Aristotle did homage." And it was from Plato, as well as the Bible, that Maurice said he learned an alternative to system-building. "Not to frame a comprehensive system which shall include nature and society, man and God, as its different elements, or in its different compartments, and which therefore necessarily leads the system-builder to consider himself above them all, but to demonstrate the utter impossibility of such a system, to cut up the notion and dream of it by the roots, this is the work and the glory of Plato." [6] The Platonic method was one of "always seeking for principles," and through this Plato, at least indirectly through the classes of Julius Hare at Cambridge, showed Maurice that "there is a way out of party opinions which is not a compromise between them, but which is implied in both, and of which each is bearing witness." [7]

What then is the sort of unity that Maurice sought, which was neither system, nor compromise, nor mediation? The answer can finally appear only in the substance of Maurice's theology, but at least one preliminary distinction is in order. Maurice saw the partiality of every theological view, including his own. As one closely acquainted with all the main "parties" of his time, he insisted that every party or sect had hold of some truth, but that it is a partial or

---

5. F. D. Maurice, *The Kingdom of Christ*, ed. Alec Vidler, 2 vols. (London, 1958), 2 : 355 (from the dedication to the 2d ed., 1842).

6. *Moral and Metaphysical Philosophy*, 2 vols. (1882), 1 : 218, 150–151.

7. *Life*, 1 : 56. Archdeacon Hare was also a thinker familiar with German scholarship and theology.

one-sided truth, and to believe it the whole truth and to deny truth to others is to move at one toward the mischief of sectarianism and eventually to self-defeat. For example, the truth of the Quaker doctrine of an inner light is not to be affirmed to the exclusion of the truth of the sacramental. One is to attend always to the "positive" in another's faith rather than to the "negative" judgment on the ill-understood ideas of others. No one should confuse his view with the whole truth. Yet Maurice was not merely echoing J. S. Mill's dictum that most men are generally right in what they affirm and wrong in what they deny. Nor did he believe that the "whole" truth is something to be found by adding any number of parts or striking median positions between competing claims. The "partiality" of which he spoke was rather the limitation and "corruption" of every perspective on a truth to which the beliefs of men and parties may witness but which they do not contain. It is the greatness of the truth that defines the partiality of every man's view of it. The struggle for a whole truth is therefore always a fight against self-centeredness or preoccupation with one's own view; it is a struggle against one's self on behalf of the reality one views. Conversely, to form a party is to separate oneself from another rather than to stand beside him looking at a truth objective to both.

Maurice's conviction (and thus his method) is well illustrated in the complexity of his relations to the Broad Church and to the Tractarians. He was initially attracted to the latter group,[8] for he saw in the Tractarian movement a recovery of the principle of a social faith and a movement away from formalism on the grounds that "if forms exist at all they must have a meaning in them, otherwise they are shams and delusions." [9] But he drew back from what seemed a tendency that he later decried in a comment on Newman's *Essay on Development*, namely, the substitution of a catholic system for a catholic church. The notion of a catholic "system" is self-contradictory, for every system leads to exclusion, thus to new parties and

8. Some leaders of the Oxford Movement welcomed *Subscription No Bondage* (1835), in which Maurice stated his reasons for signing the Articles of Religion on entrance at Oxford (1829), whereas he had declined to subscribe at Cambridge in 1826 in order to take a degree (see *Life* 1 : 173 ff., 2 : 503 ff.). Maurice argued in *Subscription No Bondage* that the requirement at Oxford was not actually a test of one's own religious convictions, but a statement of the basis on which instruction in the university was to be given.

9. *On Right and Wrong Methods of Supporting Protestantism* (1843), p. 10 (cited in Vidler, *Theology of F. D. Maurice*, p. 105).

divisions. Maurice's love for the "ancient" creeds (*Life*, 1 : 525) did not entail the elevation of doctrine or correct opinion to a place of first importance. Thus Newman's "dogmatic principle," which did seem to imply this, had to be rejected along with the antiquarianism and external ceremonialism of the later Tractarians.

But on the other hand, Maurice could no more readily agree with those for whom opinions in religion were matters of indifference, nor with a "liberalism" that would simply "include all kinds of opinion" (*Life*, 1 : 184). The "breadth" of the Broad Churchmen he judged also to be narrowness. That Maurice has affinities with the Broad Church, especially at those points where Coleridge was its mentor, is undeniable; but to explain him as a Broad Churchman, even as the best of them, is to misunderstand. The Broad Church movement seemed to him both eclectic and a "party," another system, even though one paradoxically too concerned with theological ideas (e.g. in contrast to worship) and too ready to tolerate all opinions, thus being anti-theological.

The principle of Maurice's opposition to both Tractarians and Broad Churchmen, as also to Evangelicals and even to Quakers, was that the ground and unity of truth cannot be ideas or opinions, but only the "realities" to which they witness. To any proposal, for example, to "forget our differences and meet on the ground of our common Christianity," he replied, "I will do no such thing; I consider that your whole scheme is a flat contradiction and a lie. . . . You come forward with the avowal that you fraternize on some ground other than that of our union with Christ, and then you ask me to fraternize with you on that ground." But that is the sectarian principle, which is "an outrage on the Christian principle, as a denial of it." The "common Christianity you speak of [is] the mere *caput mortuum* of all systems! You do not really mean us to unite in Christ, as being members of his body; you mean us to unite in holding certain notions about Christ" (*Life*, 1 : 259).

No theme was more insistently sounded by Maurice than this. Both Puseyite religion *about* God and Carlyle's religion of man amounted to the same thing: "religion against God . . . the heresy of our age . . . leading to the last, most terrific form of infidelity." [10]

10. *Life*, 1 : 518. Thus when Maurice said he "felt as a theologian, thought as a theologian; that all other subjects in my mind are connected with theology, and subordinate to it," he meant the word specifically "in its old sense. I mean by theology that which concerns the Being and Nature of God. I mean the revelation of God to man, not any pious or religious sentiments which men may have respecting God" (*Moral and Metaphysical Philosophy*, 2 : ix).

To seek principles rather than systems and realities rather than opinions—these seemed to Maurice to be correlative if not identical movements of thought. By such a movement the theologian stood in continuity with the Bible and the creeds (and the Book of Common Prayer), which "deliver us from partial ideas of God, and from dependence on particular systems of doctrine, whether religious or philosophical," [11] by directing attention to the reality of God and not to their own religious ideas.

As such a theologian, moreover, Maurice had no need or place for apologetics, defensiveness, or imperialism. The theologian seeks to speak the truth that *is,* to witness to God acting and speaking; and therefore he can expound the truth as he sees it in the confidence that "God can take care of His own cause." The Christian is therefore also free to devote himself to the concrete service of man—and in this connection Maurice could write of his "unspeakable obligation" to Auguste Comte: "he has cleared the ground of much rubbish . . . he has compelled us to abandon all apologies for our faith, and simply ask ourselves what we suppose it can do for mankind." [12]

THE KINGSHIP OF CHRIST

The principal truth that Maurice wanted to declare, the conviction that ran through all his writing and gave it consistency, was that Christ is "the actual Head of man"—not only the potential or future head of mankind, or the head only of those who believe in him, but now in fact the real Head and Lord of all mankind. His first book he called *The Kingdom of Christ.* In 1853 he could say that the Lordship of Christ was the truth he "was sent into the world to proclaim." Twenty years earlier he had written to his mother:

What, then, do I assert? Is there no difference between the believer and the unbeliever? Yes, the greatest difference. But the difference is not about the fact but precisely in the belief of the *fact.* God tells us . . . "Christ is the Head of *every* man." Some men believe this; some men disbelieve it. Those men who disbelieve it walk "after the flesh." They do not believe they are joined to an Almighty Lord of life. . . . But though tens of hundreds of thousands of men live after the flesh, yea, though every man in the world were so living, we are forbidden by Christian truth and the Catholic Church to call this the real *state* of any man. On the contrary, the phrases which Christ

11. *What is Revelation?* (1859), pp. 374–75.
12. *Social Morality* (1869), p. 416.

and His Apostles used to describe such a condition are such as these: "They believe a *lie*. They make a *lie*. They will not believe the *truth*." The truth is that every man is in Christ; the condemnation of every man is, that he will not own the truth; he will not *act* as if this were *true*, he will not believe that which is the truth, that except he were joined to Christ, he could not think, believe, live a single hour." [*Life*, 1 : 155; cf. 2 : 161.]

The critical question was that of an adequate (and true) basis for man's convictions. What is the real point of beginning for self-understanding, as found in Scriptures and creeds? Is it to be the truth or is it to be a lie? The answer is obvious: Sin is a corruption and a lie, therefore the beginning and basis for reflection cannot be man in his sin but God in his grace and power and thus man as created and redeemed in Christ. Otherwise we by implication make the devil the king of the universe. This was the point at which Maurice discovered his deepest difference with the "Evangelicals." [13] They seemed to begin and thus to rest their theology on sin, depravity, and punishment. But that for Christian thinking is self-contradictory. In other words, the only possible place to begin is with how God looks upon man rather than with how man looks upon God—and for God, according to Scripture, "mankind stands not in Adam but in Christ" (*Life*, 2 : 358). The only possible security and deliverance is found in Christ's being the Lord even when man rejects him. God looks upon men in Christ; they are and have always been His adopted sons; their "proper constitution" is in Him. The historical event of Jesus Christ is the manifestation of what has been true from the beginning and will always be true.[14]

This assertion of the kingship of Christ was unquestionably Mau-

13. "He [a German reviewer of *The Kingdom of Christ*] has taught me to see more clearly than I ever did what the ground of my difference with the Evangelicals, both of England and Germany, is. The latter, though so much wiser and more cultivated, still seem to make sin the ground of all theology, whereas it seems to me that the living and holy God is the ground of it, and sin the departure from the state of union with Him, into which He has brought us. I cannot believe the devil is in any sense king of this universe. I believe Christ is its king in all senses, and that the devil is tempting us every day and hour to deny Him, and think of himself as the king. It is with me a question of life and death which of these doctrines is true; I would that I might live and die to maintain that which has been revealed to me" (*Life*, 1 : 450).

14. Maurice's idea has some resemblance to the views of his famous Scottish contemporary, Macleod Campbell, whose thought culminated in *The Nature of the Atonement* (1856). Both Campbell and Maurice were influenced at this point by Thomas Erskine of Linlathen (see his *Unconditional Freeness of the Gospel*, 1828, and *The Brazen Serpent*, 1831).

rice's most original and influential concept. He did not seek to develop from it any formal theories of incarnation or atonement (in contrast with contemporaries like Dorner, Thomasius, and Bushnell), though it is important to note that Maurice stood firmly in the Johannine tradition of Christology, and his emphasis on Christ as the true root of mankind has interesting relations to the second-Adam Christologies developing in Germany. Nor did he show much concern for the historical problem of Christ, as posed either by Strauss or by Kierkegaard. His own interests and method were expressed not in the systematic development of such issues but rather in the continual recurrence, in different contexts and different ways, of themes rising out of his central conviction.

One of those themes was the grounding of man's unity and reconciliation in the unity of the Trinity. Maurice could say "I not only believe in the Trinity in unity, but I find in it the center of all my beliefs" (*Life*, 1 : 41). The Trinity for Maurice was primarily a doctrine of unity, and he said that he owed the depth of his belief in the Trinity in great measure to his training in his Unitarian home. But here again, he insisted, the point was not a *doctrine* of unity but the designation of a *reality* of unity, a living being in whom there is an eternal communion, a full and perfect love between Father and Son, out of which come both creation and reconciliation. The social nature of man is rooted in the social nature of God, and the reconciliation of man into the Kingdom of God is grounded in the perfect reconciliation, eternally real, within the Trinity-in-Unity. In these senses, the Trinity is the "ground on which the Church stands and humanity stands." [15]

Second, grace is prior to sin, both in reality and for our knowledge. To be sure, grace and sin are always seen in a polarity, but for Maurice it was not at all an evenly balanced one. As Christ rather than Adam is the real Head of mankind, so we understand sin only as we look at the grace of Christ and see ourselves as God sees us in Christ. Sin is a lie. Yet that is not to make light of the oppressive plight into which man thrusts himself, of the real struggle that is going on between the divine and the demonic. A lie is not a mistake. Sin is not equated with "error." Sin is a tragic refusal, a turning away.[16] Sin is selfishness and separation, the assertion of indepen-

---

15. F. D. Maurice, *Theological Essays* (1853; London, 1957), p. 302; cf. pp. 281 ff.

16. As H. R. Niebuhr put it, "Maurice is so deeply aware of the sin of self-love and of the tragedy of human divisiveness, the exploitation of man by man, the self-

dence. It is the self-centeredness which represents man's trying to be god to himself, to assert that he is not a part but the whole, or that his view is the whole view, thus to make himself the center of the universe. Sin is also the attempt to be apart from the race, the social reality in which man is constituted, whether by commercial exploitation or by hoping for a separate forgiveness, or by claiming a unique righteousness and truth, or claiming in any other way to be "special." Thus, "it is better, safer, truer language to speak of individual depravity than of universal depravity." [17] To call sin a lie, to define Adam's sin as disbelieving the law by which mankind is constituted —the principle that man was made in the image of God—is therefore to say that sin is the desperate self-contradiction in which man attempts to live, the refusal to acknowledge his real relation to God in Christ. Thus again the emphasis must come back to the truth and grace which expose sin as sin. The second Adam is prior to the first Adam; the fallen Adam before and in us represents man asserting that which he cannot be—independent—and the second Adam is the one who was head of man from the beginning and in whom we are to see ourselves truly.[18]

Third, it is already evident that for Maurice man is essentially a social being, and redemption and morality are intrinsically social. The constitution of man, the structure of creation as grounded in the triune being of God, is a set of relations in which man is a relative, by nature a son, a member of the family. This is the "spiritual constitution" of mankind, in which all the natural human orders of family, nation, and church—which are human by being more than human—are to be seen.[19] This theological understanding of man's social nature was the foundation for the "Christian Socialist" movement, which was the response of Maurice and his associates, including the novelist and pastor Charles Kingsley and the lawyer J. M. Ludlow, to the Chartist and socialist movements and the revolutions of 1848. A Christian view of man is necessarily social and a truly social view of man demands a spiritual grounding. Thus, Maurice wrote to Ludlow in 1850, " 'Tracts on Christian Socialism' is, it seems to me, the only title which will define our object, and will

---

glorification of nations and churches, that he needs to say little in an explicit way about fall and corruption; it is a deep undercurrent of all his thinking" (*Christ and Culture* [New York, 1956], p. 222).

17. *Lincoln's Inn Sermons*, 6 vols. (1891), 5 : 267.

18. Cf. *Life*, 2 : 358; *Gospel of St. John* (1885), p. 500.

19. See *Kingdom of Christ*, 1 : 227–57.

commit us at once to the conflict we must engage in sooner or later with the unsocial Christians and the un-Christian socialists." [20] Society requires a reconstituting in accord with the principles of its constitution, which means on patterns of cooperation and copartnership rather than the structure-violating principles of competition. In this sense "socialism" is a proper expression of existence in love.

One cannot say that Maurice's doctrine of Christian Socialism proved to be relevant to the actual patterns of social change. He partook too much of a sentimental utopianism, and he could not conceive the possibility that the church was not at the center of the complex of culturally important institutions. But in the latter points, as in the demand that Christianity be concerned for the reconstituting of society, Maurice was an earnest of the future.

The call for a social morality was one side of Maurice's understanding of the proper relation of church and culture, one expression of a "living politics." The other side was his idea of the national church, which supported his hope for the Church of England. Church and state are interdependent and mutually supportive:

> The Church wishes to make men feel that they are subjects, but its own influence is one which especially aims at setting them free; the state wishes to have a free intelligent people, but it has itself only the power of keeping men servants. If any great work is to be done for man, if God's gracious purposes to him are to be fulfilled, one would think that these two powers must be meant continually to act and react upon each other, and to learn better, by each new error they commit, their distinct functions, their perfect harmony.[21]

The church deals with the inward and spiritual origin of men's conduct, the state with the outward form and visible conduct. The "national church" becomes the appropriate ecclesiastical form. The function of a national church is to educate the nation, "to purify and elevate the mind of a nation . . . to tell the rulers of the nation, and all members of the nation, that all false ways are ruinous ways, that truth is the only stability of our time or of any time. It should exist to make men tremble at the voice of God speaking to them in their consciences," [22] and in this way to uphold the national life and testify that the national life has a divine ground. The nation, clearly, is called to be obedient not to the church but to God.

Finally, then, if Christ is in truth the Head of all mankind, what

20. *Life*, 2 : 35. See also *Social Morality* (1869).
21. *The Kingdom of Christ*, 2 : 203–04.
22. *Lincoln's Inn Sermons*, 2 : 93.

is the special significance of the church? It is the permanent witness to
the true constitution of humanity in Christ and therefore a place of
restoration and reconciliation to God and an anticipation of the Kingdom. The "world," on the contrary, Maurice defined as the state of
mankind founded on a lie. It is "a miserable, accursed rebellious
order," denying its true foundation and seeking to create "a foundation of self-will, choice, taste, opinion"; therefore "in the world
there can be no communion," whereas "in the Church there can be
universal communion," because "the Church is the witness for the
true constitution of man as man, a child of God, an heir of heaven"
(Life, 1 : 166). "The world contains the elements of which the
Church is composed. In the Church, these elements are penetrated
by a uniting, reconciling power. The Church is, therefore, human
society in its normal state; the World, that same society irregular
and abnormal. The world is the Church without God; the Church is
the world restored to its relation with God, taken back by Him, into
the state for which He created it." [23]

It follows that the sacraments are first of all signs of reality, not
creators of reality. Pusey's tract on baptism (1835), which seemed to
teach the doctrine that by baptismal regeneration a separate individual becomes something he actually was not before, a child of God,
opened the breach between Maurice and the Tractarians. Against
this view, as similarly against the Evangelicals' notion of conversion,
by which a man "became" a member of Christ, Maurice insisted on
baptism as a sign of man's true state and law, a "sacrament of constant union," witnessing that the truth, and man's growth in it,
does not depend finally on him but on God. "Baptism tells me that
I am God's child and may live as if I were," and it at the same time
speaks of the lawlessness within that is to be conquered (Life,
2 : 242). It is the assurance that what is true for mankind is true for
the person baptized, thus it is an initiation into a new covenant and
a permission and possibility for obedience to the true law of one's
being. Similarly, the Eucharist is a sign of the setting up of Christ's
Kingdom on earth, testifying that by a completed sacrifice the race,
constituted and redeemed in Christ, has once for all been brought
into a state of acceptance and union with God.[24]

Once again, it is plain that the principle of the church must be
one of inclusion rather than exclusion (the sectarian principle). "The

23. *Theological Essays*, pp. 276–77.
24. *Kingdom of Christ*, 2 : 71; cf. 2 : 58–91.

Church must either fulfill its witness of a redemption for mankind, or be cut off" (*Life*, 2 : 357). Further, the church's witness entails the *universal* possibility of conversion from self-centeredness to Christ-centeredness, and of the participation of all the societies in the true spiritual society. The notions of a predestination to damnation and of an everlasting punishment are the errors of negative Christianity which has given up the conviction "that God is always righteous, always maintaining a fight with evil, always seeking to bring his creatures out of it." In spite of the seemingly almost infinite "possibilities of resistance in a human will to the loving will of God," Maurice found himself "obliged to believe in an abyss of love which is deeper than the abyss of death. I dare not lose faith in that love." [25] "I cannot believe that he will fail with any at last. . . . His will must surely be done, however long it may be resisted" (*Life*, 2 : 575–76). Maurice also repudiated theories of universal redemption; his case rested instead on the view that "eternal" in the gospel is neither the simple prolongation nor the negation of time. It is "something real, substantial, before all time," the character and dimension of God's working and world. Eternal life is "the righteousness, and truth, and love of God which are manifested in Christ Jesus." [26] Eternal death is not at all a future or temporal reality, but is simply "to be without God," that is, to be in that state of sin and being lost which is an abyss of death—yet even below that, according to the gospel, is an abyss of love.

THE KNOWLEDGE OF GOD

Maurice's "critical" method and his theology of the rule of Christ were inseparably interwoven with a third motif of his thought: the knowledge of God, in particular through the revelation in Scripture. His idea of revelation was brought to focus especially in the debate with H. L. Mansel (1820–71), which Maurice judged to be the most important controversy of his life.[27]

25. *Theological Essays*, p. 323. This was the essay that led to Maurice's discharge from King's College in 1853.

26. *Theological Essays*, pp. 316, 306.

27. For Maurice's writings against Mansel, see *What is Revelation?* (1859) and *Sequel to the Inquiry, What is Revelation?* (1860). These works, especially the former (a violent response), are not generally regarded as Maurice's best, and he plainly did not have the technical intellectual tools or the developed doctrine of revelation and religious knowledge that might have enabled him to defeat Mansel in argument. Yet the positions he defended in these works Maurice believed to be absolutely essential to Christian faith. On the Maurice–Mansel controversy, see Don Cuppitt, "Mansel's

In the Bampton Lectures for 1858, entitled "The Limits of Religious Thought Examined," Mansel had coupled a defense of "orthodoxy" with the denial that the nature of God can be known. One of the few Kantians in England at the time, Mansel was also indebted to the "philosophy of the unconscious" of the Scottish thinker William Hamilton (1788–1856). With wit as well as keen dialectical skill, he moved through all the ways of claiming knowledge of God to the conclusion that "the knowledge of the Absolute and Infinite is made impossible by the very constitution of our minds," and that indeed we cannot make logically coherent statements about the Absolute. The transcendent is by definition incognizable and inconceivable. Metaphysical or speculative knowledge of God is excluded—though that does not exclude deep religious consciousness and moral conviction, nor the possibility of external "evidences" for truths once revealed.

Not only in religion, but everywhere, there is an ultimate inexplicability, a restriction to the phenomenal; the highest principles of thought and action that we can attain "do not tell us what things are in themselves, but how we must conduct ourselves in relation to them." In analogy with the general constitution of mental faculties, then (here the form of Mansel's argument has much in common with Joseph Butler's *Analogy*), we may believe that in religion God "has given us truths which are designed to be regulative, rather than speculative; intended, not to satisfy our reason, but to guide our practice; not to tell us what God is in His Absolute Nature, but how He wills that we should think of Him in our present finite state." [28]

From his denial of any "knowledge" of God's nature, Mansel might have moved (as many, including Maurice and Martineau, thought he should) to Herbert Spencer's Unknowable or a complete agnosticism as the final word about God. Or he might have turned to an articulation of the symbolic character of religious assertions. Instead he sought to use the skeptical conclusions about natural knowledge of God as an apologetic device for holding to the necessity of a "revelation" of God in Scripture which is beyond critical judg-

Theory of Regulative Truth," *Journal of Theological Studies*, 1967, pp. 104–26, and the brief summary of the debate in H. G. Wood, *Frederick Denison Maurice* (Cambridge, 1950), pp. 113–29. Mansel was Waynflete professor of moral and metaphysical philosophy at Magdalen College, Oxford, from 1855 and dean of St. Paul's after 1868.

28. *The Limits of Religious Thought Examined* (1859), pp. 290–96.

ment. No attempt could be made to rationalize Christian dogma. "In this impotence of reason, we are compelled to take refuge in Faith and to believe that an Infinite Being exists, though we do not know how." We learn from Scripture, whose authority is supported by "external" testimonies, notably miracles, what God wants us to think of Him—that is, what we ought to believe as a guide for life, even though the ideas themselves are unintelligible. (This does not mean, of course, that we should think of that revelation as a deception, only that it must be accepted without the possibility of criticism.) What is so revealed is the "traditional" Christian doctrine— though Mansel was wary about specifying the precise contents of scriptural revelation, thus he did not lose the support of divergent orthodoxies.

To Maurice, Mansel's argument was simply a capitulation to atheism, a destruction of the possibility of faith. Revelation can only mean God's making himself known, the bringing of light and truth in the place of uncertainty and confusion. We do—and we must— know God. The Bible declares to us what He is.

The issue between Maurice and Mansel was not over the possibility of natural theology, nor Maurice's "fanatical mysticism," as he thought Mansel must view it (*Life*, 2 : 312). Maurice did not insist on the adequacy of theological ideas, but rather on the partiality of every theological position. The root conflict was over the nature of revelation and religious truth. For Maurice, religious truth was neither speculative nor regulative, for both conceptions leave us in the realm of opinion. He insisted that the root of the matter is "facts" and "reality," not doctrines. The knowledge of God is "personal" (one may well say, existential); it is a relationship in which God's own Being is met and apprehended, inseparably from man's response and obligation. To Maurice (as to Coleridge), the only real knowledge of God is related to human needs and desires; "the witness of the heart, the Conscience, the Reason," is that "the spirit of man within us demands the knowledge of God, demands the perception of Eternal Truth and Goodness." [29]

Maurice's characteristic assertion about Scripture, therefore, was that the Bible is a book of facts—the facts of creation, redemption, the history of God's establishment of His Kingdom. It is not a collection of opinions, even men's opinions about God—to view the Bible that way is to turn the bread of life into stones for casting at

29. *What is Revelation?* p. 262.

one's enemies and to substitute religion for God. The Bible is the record of God's acting and speaking with his people on earth, thus an unveiling of the very heart and character of God. It is the means by which the Spirit of Truth addresses mankind, educating us as to what we are (not what we should be, but what we actually are) and to our position in God's Kingdom, setting forth thus the eternal principles of the divine kingdom, the constitution of mankind in Christ, and God's manner of dealing with his people.

The historical question did not impress itself on Maurice as a fundamental one. Scripture he judged to be revelatory as it relates men to God, not to itself or to the details of historical events—hence Maurice's lack of anxiety over the work of biblical criticism and his refusal to join the hue and cry about *Essays and Reviews,* as well as his lack of interest in pursuing the details of criticism.[30] He could rely freely on the Johannine report of the words of Christ, and could take the opening chapters of Genesis as actual history, but he had no interest in denying the results of criticism or in defending, for example, the chronology of the Gospels, the age of the patriarchs, or the authorship of Hebrews. He distrusted the "negativity" of the criticism in *Essays and Reviews,* but no more than the traditional defense of the authority of Scripture. His view was that both made the Bible a book of dogmatic opinions or theological propositions, or a collection of allegories, or a mere account rather than a real vehicle of communication. Actually, "the more firmly we believe the Bible to be from God" the less serious will be the sacrifice of a "mere sentimental feeling which attaches a particular passage to a particular man." [31] It was important for Maurice that the Bible be considered as a whole, that is, as a record of the gradual manifestation of the Kingdom. Yet even in his insistence upon this point, the Bible remained a sign of the Kingdom, a *means* to the apprehension of permanent principles and to the knowledge of the living God. Revelation is a living word, to be received only by understanding and trusting it to be the guide for life, thus as "the unveiling of the Righteous Being to the hearts and conscience of the only creature that is capable of being righteous." [32]

In Maurice's idea of Scripture we confront once more the central

30. Likewise, and for the same reason, the discoveries of Darwin posed no threat for Maurice.

31. Maurice, *The Prophets and Kings of the Old Testament* (1853), p. 274.

32. *Lincoln's Inn Sermons,* 5 : 250.

problem of his thinking: the seminal insights were reiterated again and again but not worked out. His relativism, which held that everyone's thought about truth, including his own, is only partial, was important and new among theologians. But he did not at all develop this idea with a theory comparable, say, to Bushnell's essay on language. Similarly, drawing on Coleridge's view of the authority of Scripture, Maurice attained genuine freedom from biblical literalism; but he never squared this with his quite uncritical realism about "biblical facts." He left thus as many problems as he resolved.

11

Toward a Critical Orthodoxy:

Horace Bushnell

The subject of which I speak, is language; a very different instrument, certainly, from what most men think it to be, and one, which if they understood more exactly, they would use it more wisely. In the misuse of abuse of this instrument, a great part of our religious difficulties have their spring. We have misconceived, as it seems to me, both its nature and its capacities, and our moral reasonings are, to just the same extent, infected with error. Indeed, it is such an instrument, that I see not how anyone, who rightly conceives its nature, can hope any longer to produce in it a real and proper system of dogmatic truth. He will doubt the capacity of language to serve any such purpose. He will also suspect that our logical or deductive processes under it, are more likely, in general, to be false than true. And yet, in the matter of Christian doctrine, or Christian theology, we are found committing ourselves most unsuspectingly to language and a logic, as if the instrument were sufficient, and the method infallible.

> Horace Bushnell, "Preliminary Dissertation on the Nature
> of Language, as Related to Thought and Spirit"

THEOLOGICAL LANGUAGE AND A RIGHT SENSIBILITY

The method that F. D. Maurice called "criticism," as distinguished from compromise, has striking parallels in what Horace Bushnell (1802–76) named "Christian comprehensiveness." [1] Neither the term nor the argument of the essay by that title is adequate to Bushnell's method and theological contribution, yet at least one of his central theological intentions was made visible: the desire to recognize and

---

1. In an essay by that title, published in the *New Englander* 6 [1848] : 81 ff.; abridged in H. Shelton Smith, *Horace Bushnell* (New York, 1965), 108 ff. (This volume provides an excellent selection from Bushnell's major writings, with valuable introductions and bibliography. Among Bushnell's works, see especially *God in Christ* [1849], *Christ in Theology* [1851], *Nature and the Supernatural* [1858], *Christian Nurture* [1847, 1861], and *Vicarious Sacrifice* [1866; vol. 2 later replaced by *Forgiveness and Law*, 1874]. For Bushnell's life, Mary Cheney, *Life and Letters of Horace Bushnell* [New York, 1880] is indispensable. See also Barbara M. Cross, *Horace Bushnell, Minister to a Changing America* [New York, 1958].)

reconcile at a higher level the truths present in the varieties and antitheses of sects and dogmas. This did not mean mere inclusiveness or
"synthesis." Bushnell argued, for example,[2] that we have to reckon
not only with three schools, the two extremes and their reconciliation, but with five "stages or modes" in the struggle for truth. There
are also the neutralists, who are peacemakers and moderate men but
who are a "wooden-headed school" because they do not seek "the
truth as a positive form and law" but simply "divide distances, and
settle themselves down as nearly midway between the poles as possible." This attempt at a median position, while it may have wide
appeal to those tired of controversy, is essentially negative, properly
called neuter because its thrust is to say simply "neither" to both
extremes. Then there are the "liberals." The liberal is an open and
generous thinker, and "where the liberal spirit is connected with a
rigid and earnest devotion to truth, it is a condition of health to itself and a mark of respect to others." This sort of liberalism Bushnell
could welcome, and in such a sense he would not have objected to
the frequent description of him as the liberalizer of American theology. But "liberalism" seemed all too often to rest on indifference
to truth and thus (like neutrality) to be simply negative, insipid, and
impotent.[3] True catholicity or comprehension involves the most
furious struggle for truth, and it does not either compromise or mediate between extremes but seeks to uncover the truth in each view.

The decisive elements in Bushnell's methods are hinted at when
he speaks of the way the truth is uncovered—by "dissolving" the
form of a dogma and viewing its content "historically," by taking
down the "drapery of language," and thus by separating out the "real
truth of feeling." Further clues are given in Bushnell's insistence on
the plurality of causes "for repugnant or opposing" religious theories.[4]
The causes include the infinity of the object of thought. Equally
important are the differences of personal temperament, of impulses
and of wants, that give rise to differences of opinion. Finally, there
is a source of incompleteness and distortion in the nature of language
itself.

In the last two points Bushnell approached a conception of religious truth different from that of any of his opponents. This was
more fully spelled out in a remarkable "Preliminary Dissertation on

2. Against the Hegelian-oriented views of the French philosopher Victor Cousin.
3. See Smith, *Horace Bushnell*, pp. 113 ff.
4. Ibid., p. 118.

the Nature of Language as Related to Thought and Spirit." [5] All language, Bushnell asserted, has two departments: the "literal," in which words or sounds are "names for physical objects and appearances"; and the figurative or analogical department, which includes all terms for thought and spirit. The latter department is called figurative because all its terms have originally a physical root or base. Communication concerning thought and spirit is possible only through the physical images in the terms, which provide "forms" that are suitable "by reason of some hidden analogy" to represent interior ideas and sentiments. The critical point, for Bushnell, was that *all* words expressing intellectual or moral ideas are figurative. The theologian—and here Orthodox and Unitarian alike erred—cannot assume that in religion only some terms are figurative and some literal. Except for references to physical fact and history, all religious words are figurative. They are "signs of thoughts to be expressed . . . only hints or images, held up before the mind of another, to put him on generating or reproducing the same thought" (*GC*, p. 46). Religious language is figurative, not because it refers to the supernatural or the infinite, but because it always expresses feeling and subjectivity, the personal experience of the user. Religious terms therefore never become wholly unambiguous; words like sin, hope, fear, and love are always understood in relation to the entire personal history of each individual. Further, words of spirit always affirm something false, "contrary to the truth intended."

It follows then that "the same essential truth" may be expressed not only in varying ways, in forms strange or monstrous and repugnant (e.g. the ransom concept of atonement), but even in contradictory forms. The figurative or analogical character of religious language naturally leads to multiplicity in representation, and Bushnell could say that "we never come so near to a truly well-rounded view of any truth, as when it is offered paradoxically" (*GC*, p. 55).

From all this, the consequences for theological method are evident. The so-called logical method of "proving" religious truth by strict

---

5. Published as a preface to the three addresses in *God in Christ* (Hartford, 1849), the essay caused little excitement compared to the outcry over the addresses themselves. Yet it stands among Bushnell's most important works and is indispensable for understanding his method. The main outlines of the linguistic theory (pp. 12–38) were mediated to Bushnell by his Yale teacher Josiah Willard Gibbs. Bushnell, however, put the theory to distinctive use, namely in the demonstration of the limits of theological language. Page references in the text are to the 1849 edition of *God in Christ* (*GC*).

definition and by deduction from prior proposition or previous insight is utterly inappropriate; it is the source of indefinite multiplication of "opinion" and falsity. In relation, for example, to such symbols as Trinity, Atonement, and "the bondage and freedom of sin," the infidel is wrong to reject everything as a mass of contradiction, the orthodox believer is wrong to force everything into a system with one image made dominant, and the Unitarian is wrong to extract certain manageable and measurable assertions and reject the others. Bushnell wished to reject the rationalist or conceptualist view present in all those approaches. Any reader of the Bible should know that "religion has a natural and profound alliance with poetry." [6] Scripture does not set forth or encourage systems of scientific theology but living symbols. Thus dogmatism is a contradiction of the nature of religious assertion.[7] Orthodoxy's insistence on the letter of creedal or other formulas is wrong, since "the letter is never true." Yet the Unitarian protests against creeds is no better, for it makes the same error about language. Rather than being oppressed by creeds, we do well to accept several at once, "letting them qualify, assist and mitigate each other," and recognizing that the best creed is that which stays closest to the concrete, as, for example, the Apostles' Creed (GC, p. 83). The rationalist Orthodox doctrine may be subjected to rationalist Unitarian critique, but both rationalisms are wrong.

The "very cautious and salutary skepticism" (GC, p. 95) that Bushnell maintained about theological language, if it was not to be merely the liberal suspicion of theology that he deplored, had to be complemented by a conception of how spiritual truth is apprehended. Bushnell was certainly not disposed to give up either the task of theology or the claim to religious knowledge. By exposing the truth behind conflicting forms, he wanted in fact to give appropriate expression to "the real moment of all our Orthodox

6. GC, p. 74; see also pp. 74–77. Poets are identified as the "true metaphysicians," p. 73.
Not only the orthodox Calvinists like Nathanael Emmons and Bennet Tyler and the Unitarians like W. E. Channing and Henry Ware but also Nathaniel W. Taylor represented the kind of rationalism that Bushnell wanted to leave behind. This distinguished him from American mediating theologians (or "judicious conservatives") like James C. McCosh and Albert Barnes, who in respect of the relation of science and theology were not far from the outlook of Bushnell's Nature and the Supernatural.
7. "Definitions . . . are only changes of symbol, if we take them to be more, will infallibly lead us into error" (GC, p. 72; cf. the discourse "Dogma and Spirit," pp. 277–356.

formulas unabriged" (*GC*, p. 11). Bushnell's response to this problem was his insistence on the "experimental" (experiential) nature of theology. This meant, first, insisting on the interiority of religious truth, on the priority of life over opinion and of spirit over dogma, and on the distinction between faith "of the heart" and intellectual assent. This view of the "subjectivity" of religious truth was mediated to Bushnell especially by the Puritan tradition as reshaped in the evangelical revivals and by Coleridge, to whose *Aids to Reflection* Bushnell said he was more indebted than to any other extra-scriptural authority. Moreover, theological assertions he believed fully intelligible only in relation to the experience of the one who makes them. It is not simply that—as pietists, Wesleyans, revivalists, and many others had also affirmed—Christian existence requires an inner experiencing or confirming of the truth expressed in doctrine, but that theological articulation can arise only out of personal experience. The meaning of religious terms is relative to the experience of the user, so even "scientific theology" cannot be dissociated from personal history. "Until the internal relation between [a man's] spiritual history and his opinions is known, he is very nearly certain to be a suspicious character" (*GC*, p. 10).

A further aspect of Bushnell's experiential theology was his view of the "immediate" knowledge of God (which had roots in Coleridge's concept of Reason, Victor Cousin's idea of "spontaneous reason," and Jonathan Edwards's "sense of the heart"). Bushnell thought it possible to know God Himself by a wholly "immediate" illumination, an "inward discovery of His infinite spirit and person" like the immediacy of self-knowledge or self-feeling, that is, direct and intuitive in contrast to the other self-knowledge we have through language and reflection. This true knowledge of the heart, which Bushnell spoke of as received by a "congenial" or "right" sensibility, is as truly perceptive as "reason" or "mere intellect." Such knowing, for Bushnell, is not reducible to a natural possibility of human experience. It is rather the work of the Spirit of God, restoring the immediacy that sin has broken. A proper theology will then reflect the immediacy of a spiritual knowing of God; and it will "more resemble an experience than the dry judgments and barren generalizations hitherto called theology." It will therefore deal, like Scripture, in "bold and living figures, often contradictory or antagonistic in their forms." [8]

8. See "Dogma and Spirit," p. 308.

Finally, experiential theology draws heavily on the aesthetic and moral sensibilities rather than on the cognitive and the discursively rational. It is the aesthetic discernment that is appropriate to the inadequacies of language and the richness of expression in image and symbol. Our moral experience, furthermore, can be confidently used as a control for statements about God and his relation to man. Thus in his final discussion of the Atonement, Bushnell said he intended to interpret everything by reference "to the moral pronouncements of human nature and society; assuming that nothing can be true of God, or Christ, which is not true in some sense *more humano*, and is not made intelligible by human analogies. We cannot interpret God, as anyone may see, except by what we find in our own personal instincts and ideas." And again he spoke of "the grand analogy, or almost identity that subsists between our moral nature and that of God; so that our moral pathologies and those of God make faithful answer to each other, and He is brought so close to us that almost any thing that occurs in the working or exigencies of our moral instincts may even be expected in His." [9]

ORGANIC SOLIDARITY IN SIN AND REDEMPTION

One striking illustration of Bushnell's attempt to transform the terms of the Orthodox-Unitarian debate, and a point of material divergence from both sides, is found in his first published work, *Discourses on Christian Nurture* (1847).[10]

The debates over "free moral agency," or natural versus moral ability or inability, Bushnell held, had been carried on under false premises that failed to take account of the actuality of social existence (*CN*, p. 71). An isolation of the individual agent was presupposed on both sides, whether natural goodness or depravity was

9. *Forgiveness and Law,* pp. 12–13, 35. Clearly we have here one of the legitimate bases for identifying Bushnell as the father of American liberal theology, his influence being powerfully reinforced by the later Ritschlian theology.

10. The discourses were later expanded and published under the title *Christian Nurture* (1861), to become the best known of Bushnell's works and the book of greatest influence on subsequent American theories of religious education. Citations here are to the 1914 edition of *Christian Nurture* (*CN*).

The debates in the background of Bushnell's argument had been focused particularly in Henry Ware's idea of the essential goodness of man and Bennet Tyler's insistence on "total depravity," with N. W. Taylor's view falling somewhere between the two (see above, chap. 6). For a good survey of the whole controversy, see H. Shelton Smith, *Changing Conceptions of Original Sin: A Study in American Theology since 1750* (New York, 1955).

affirmed. Both also presupposed a mechanical view of human growth involving discontinuity rather than continuity. In relation to these disputes, Bushnell insisted that every child is truly born into a world of sin and in bondage to sin. The Orthodox claim is correct, and in the sense of the Old School. But the truth of this claim had not been rightly understood and the Unitarian protest against the "immorality" of the notion of natural depravity was therefore justified. Being "born" means much more than the physical act of generation; it is a social as much as a biological process. It means being formed in the organic unity of a family. We have to speak not just of "influence," that is, of "persuasive or governing power exerted deliberately toward some end," but of "organic courses," of bonds so intimate and internal that they are unintended and unconscious. The parents' feelings, character, principles, and spirit "must propagate themselves whether they will it or not." [11] Further, within this organic social matrix the self comes to be itself only in a continuous process of gradual becoming (this is not of course to exclude moments of decisive turning or development). There is no single moment at which a person becomes a moral agent, passing from "moral nullity" to independent moral agency. Only gradually does a child pass out from dependence in the sphere of his parents' moral agency to a proper responsibility of his own. Neither virtue nor sin, therefore, can be interpreted adequately as the product of separate and independent choice. The self is a social self, and virtue is a state rather than an act or a series of acts.

Only in such terms, and that means in social, psychological, and historical terms rather than metaphysical terms, could the realities of sin and redemption be adequately denoted. In a way that bypassed both the Orthodox assertion and the Unitarian denial, Bushnell insisted on an organic unity of man in sin. There is not and cannot be a "transfer" of sin and guilt from one to another, for one may rightly be said to be responsible only for what is his own; yet the race is socially and historically as well as biologically one, and there are moral connections by which persons are corrupters of others. We cannot build, therefore, on any notion of the radical goodness of human nature (as did the Transcendentalists and Uni-

11. A child will never have a wholly distinct character from his family: "the odor of the house will always be in his garments, and the internal difficulties with which he has to struggle, will spring of the family seeds planted in his nature" (pp. 93–94).

tarians). The development of Christian virtue involves a real struggle with evil.

Similarly, there is organic unity in redemption. The same laws of man's existence can be wielded with regenerative purpose. Christ initiated an order of relations or organic causes, operating redemptively in history. True Christian education, then, means nurturing a child within the laws and processes of the Christian family, which are no less divine for being organic, so that, in the words of Bushnell's dramatic thesis, he "is to grow up a Christian and never know himself otherwise." This is the exact opposite of the revivalist idea that a child is to be brought up for future conversion, that is, brought up first to see himself simply as a sinner, and then at some isolated point to be transformed.[12]

SYMBOLS OF INCARNATION AND ATONEMENT

A review even of the titles of Bushnell's work discloses how much he shared the mid-nineteenth-century preoccupation with christological problems. Those problems, to be sure, were not shaped for him by the historical questions of Strauss or Baur. They were formed rather by the Unitarian–Orthodox–Transcendentalist debates. Yet the contrast is far from complete, for in nearly all the ways of putting the question of Christ we see the tendency to ask how an actual man can be spoken of as God rather than how the eternal Logos can be truly human. Here Bushnell's reflections on the Incarnation and the Trinity can profitably be read in parallel with those of Dorner or Thomasius. Bushnell does indeed say in his first "Discourse on the Divinity of Christ" that Christ "is in such a sense God, or God manifested, that the unknown term of his nature is the human," and that "we want Jesus as Divine, not as human." [13] But the context of such statements is the contrast between "divinity" and "mere humanity," in opposition to tendencies to divide what the Scriptures plainly present as a "simple historic unity" by the theory of two distinct subsistences, for example, or of Divine Person–human soul–human body. The "metaphysical or speculative difficulties" are to be dismissed not only because of the inherent difficulties of representing the infinite by finite, hence relative, symbols and significances

12. On the same principle, Bushnell rejected the Baptist insistence on believers' baptism (pp. 116–17).

13. GC, pp. 123, 126–127; this is asserted against the Unitarians.

but also in order to affirm that the divine is truly and fully expressed and seen *in* the "humanities [sic] of Christ" (*GC*, p. 156). Thus while Bushnell's argument was throughout directed to asserting the genuineness of God's presence in Christ, that presence is definitely given in the human personality, the growing, obeying, suffering state of Jesus. Much of the outcry over Bushnell's book and the question of his "orthodoxy" (though his views were no more pleasing to the liberals) stemmed precisely from his movement away from a Christology *von oben nach unten* toward a Christology *von unten nach oben,* and in the latter framework nevertheless to assert the encounter in Christ with nothing less than God himself. Bushnell's own solution to the problem was twofold: (1) to reject as unworkable and unfounded the traditional attempts to investigate the mystery of Christ's person in the categories of divine and human subsistences, persons, souls, and natures; and (2) to speak of full *manifestation* or expression (i.e. genuine self-expression) of God in Christ, such that just in the suffering and obedience of Jesus the Absolute Being, in His feeling and love, His real union with man —His life—is communicated to mankind and the world is redeemed.[14]

The center of Bushnell's interest in Christology was not, however, the restatement of Incarnation or Trinitarian doctrine, but the idea of Atonement, in which again he sought a way out of the apparent Orthodox-Unitarian impasse. His first statement, one of the discourses to which the dissertation on language was a preface, is in some ways the most interesting. There one sees again the effort of this "critical" theology to be orthodox, yet with a character quite altered by the view of theological language. The Orthodox view that Christ, the innocent one, suffers evil or punishment in substitution for those who are guilty, and that thereby God is able to justify or pardon, is simply offensive to our most sacred moral sentiments. So far, the argument has much in common with that of Channing. But Bushnell was not willing simply to abandon those Orthodox views, for that would be to leave unexplained how such doctrines could have sustained the "spirits of so many believers and martyrs . . . through so many centuries." He hoped rather to "reclaim and

14. Bushnell's idea of an "instrumental Trinity" (cf. *God in Christ* and *Christ in Theology*) was heavily dependent on Moses Stuart's translation, with extended commentary, of Schleiermacher's essay "On the Discrepancy between the Sabellian and Athanasian Methods of Representing the Doctrine of the Trinity," *Biblical Repository and Quarterly Observer* 6 (July 1835) : 1–116.

restore," in a shape open to none of the moral objections, "all that is real and essential to the power of this Orthodox doctrine of Atone- ment." One must speak, therefore, of both subjective and objective views, or of a subjective-objective view (see *GC*, pp. 192–203).

The necessary, because Biblical, point of beginning, is the so- called subjective side, the assertion that it is men who need to be reconciled rather than God. As perfect and eternal life, Christ enters a world ruled by sin even as a "corporate authority," an "organic force of social evil," bringing a new life that "becomes a historic power and presence" and forms a new organic "society of Life" (*GC*, pp. 208–09). Christ "lives confidence into the world" (*GC*, p. 214). In such a view, we do not at all overlook God's law and justice, his abhorrence of sin, which is at the heart of theories of Atonement, and thus we cannot go the way of the Unitarians, with a notion of simple forgiveness. On the contrary, in order to make men penitent, the law and its sanctity were brought even closer to men and recon- secrated by Jesus' teaching about it, by His own obedience to the humanly desecrated law, by the "expense and painstaking" in sor- row and suffering of what Christ undergoes for love of man, and by His final acceptance of violent death, which is "not a sacrifice in any literal sense" but which has an expressive power in correspon- dence to blood in the sacrifice (*GC*, pp. 216–38). Yet because this life and death of Christ is not a mere proclamation of law but the mystery of God Himself in the form of a servant, it has subduing and transforming power over the human will.

But this "subjective view," while true, is not adequate by itself to interpret all the symbols of Scripture and the faith of the ages— such terms, for example, as Atonement, sacrifice, wrath, bearing the sins of many, propitiation, and expiation. The spiritual life of the church cannot be wholly mistaken in being sustained by such images. Thus Bushnell proposed also, as a necessary complement to the subjective, an "objective ritual view," which recognizes that here as elsewhere "it is the constant effort of our nature to work itself, report its thoughts and play its sentiments, under forms of repre- sentation that are objective" (*GC*, p. 247). All religions have such objective or ritual aspects, through which "sentiments, states, and moral effects" are conveyed and effected in the worshipers.

The objective theories of Atonement are "altar forms" for Chris- tian worship. They are the outward performance of what is really done within us, but they convey in artistic and ritual form the true impressions. The objective representation of vicarious Atonement thus becomes the operative vehicle for Christ's power in the world.

This, then, is the deeper truth of "orthodoxy," of an orthodoxy critically appreciated and reclaimed in accord with new understandings of the nature and possibilities of theology. Later stages in Bushnell's thinking on Atonement (and similarly on Christology and Trinitarian doctrine) reflected even more strongly his intention to stand within the classical theological traditions, and he was able to make more positive use of the "orthodox" formulations. But this movement was itself, as he made clear, an outcome of a deepening understanding of *human* experience, evidenced, for example, in a new sense of the vicarious quality in all love, which caused him to write *Forgiveness and Law* in 1874. Thus it was a further exemplification of his view of the experiential nature of all sound theology.

12

Mediation, Speculation, and Criticism

THE PROGRAM OF MEDIATION

The epithet "mediating theology" has its proper origin in the program announced for the theological journal *Theologische Studien und Kritiken*,[1] namely, to serve the "true mediation" (*wahre Vermittlung*) between the idea of Christianity and the modern scientific consciousness—that is, to effect the valid reconciliation of historical Christianity and contemporary culture. Those who more or less shared this goal formed no definite school or party, either in method or in teaching. Some were primarily in the Hegelian sphere of influence—both Marheineke and Daub belonged among the mediators in the broad sense—and the term *Vermittlung* inevitably recalled the role this word had played in Hegel's thought. The majority were more indebted to Schleiermacher. Yet with respect to the deepest level of theological need, the holding together of the demands of faith and culture, these thinkers did not judge Hegel and Schleiermacher to be greatly at odds, and they drew freely from both the great synthesizers. Their common mind, or better the commitment that they acknowledged and that often led to a sense of sharing in a common theological direction, set them off sharply from both the "free theology" and the confessionalists. Some of those labeled mediators were largely popularizers of the gospel of reconciliation and synthesis. Others found it all too easy to use (i.e. to misuse) Schleiermacher as a springboard back to traditional formulations. More important, however, were those thinkers who sought not simply mediation between rationalism and supernaturalism, or

1. Founded in 1828 by Karl Ullmann and F. W. K. Umbreit of Heidelberg, in association also with Schleiermacher's close friend Friedrich Lücke, C. I. Nitzsch, and others. For a half-century this journal continued to be a special forum for those interested in reconciling Christianity and culture, and Rothe and Müller were later among the editors. The *Vierteljahrschrift für Theologie und Kirche* (1845 ff.) and the *Jahrbücher für deutsche Theologie* (1856 ff.) shared a similar concern. A useful study is Ragnar Holte, *Die Vermittlungstheologie, ihre theologischen Grundbegriffe kritisch untersucht* (Uppsala, 1965).

between Hegel and Schleiermacher, but whose efforts were directed to a genuinely critical renewal of Christian theology.

The first generation of an explicit mediation theology was represented by Carl Immanuel Nitzsch (1787–1868, professor at Bonn and Berlin) and Karl Ullmann (1796–1865, of Heidelberg and Halle, later director of the Bavarian Church Council). In them a strong biblical orientation was fused with revival impulses and with the influence of Schleiermacher, in whose work they found a basis for recovery of classical theological positions. In these respects, they were to have much in common with the Lutheran revival of the Erlangen type, but they were typical of mediation theology in being suspicious of confessionalism. Nitzsch, for example, was deeply involved in church political life as one of the primary supporters of the Old Prussian Union of Reformed and Lutheran. He was the author of a source book on common doctrine and of an ordination formula which was promptly dubbed the "Nitzschänum," in analogy to the Nicaean formula. Support for the Union—and for the *Kirchentag* and the *Innere Mission*—was characteristic of the mediating theologians, as was interest in the idea of the "Protestant principle," which had been stimulated especially by the Catholic Johann Adam Möhler's *Symbolik* (1832). Nitzsch wrote one of the responses to the *Symbolik* (*Eine protestantische Beantwortung der Symbolik Dr. Möhlers*, 1835). The favorite idea of the two coordinate principles of Protestantism, the formal principle of Scripture and the material principle of justification by faith, which was developed notably by Dorner, apparently goes back to De Wette's *Lehrbuch* (1816).

Nitzsch's *System of Christian Doctrine* and Ullmann's *Sinlessness of Jesus* and *The Essence of Christianity* were among the most widely read works of their day and embodied the characteristic themes of mediation theology.[2] Schleiermacher was right in seeking the principle of religion in feeling, but this had also to be understood as a genuine source of objective religious knowledge and of ethical norms (Nitzsch's *System* was noteworthy for its inclusion of ethics, as well as for the strongly biblical cast of the formulations). Christianity is not a doctrine, but a principle of life whose center is the person of Christ. Thus Christology is basic for all theology. Chris-

2. Nitzsch, *System der christlichen Lehre* (1829; 6th ed., 1851; trans. 1849). Ullmann, *Die Sündlosigkeit Jesus* (1828); the first essay was offered in *Studien und Kritiken* and later published separately as a book (7th ed., 1863). *Das Wesen des Christentums* (1845; 5th ed., 1865) is especially useful as a statement of typical themes.

tianity is divine and supernatural in essence and origin, but human
and natural in its actualization. Scripture is a combination of divine
and human, infallible and fallible. Without falling into the mis-
takes of the old inspiration doctrines, theology could yet find in
Scripture a basis for objectively valid doctrine. Schleiermacher's idea
of Christ as the archetypal and ideal man was taken up and developed in the direction of the two-natures Christology. But his conception of the God–world relation was suspect because of its seeming pantheistic tendency—hence the movement was toward a more
supernaturalist scheme.

Similar notes were sounded by Schleiermacher's successor in
Berlin, August D. C. Twesten (1789–1876), and by the Zurich theologian Alexander Schweizer (1808–88). Along with Nitzsch, Schweizer particularly continued Schleiermacher's deep commitment to
practical theology, and his essay "On the Dignity of the Founder of
a Religion" is a classic illustration of the effort to exploit the concept of Jesus as the greatest human religious genius in order to
make contact with a widely accepted cultural idea and at the same
time to lead on to the doctrine of Christ as the mediator, the re-
vealer and son of God.[3] Through all the areas of theology, for
Schweizer, the covenant of Christianity and culture that Schleiermacher had sought is sealed, the tensions of philosophy and revelation, of reason and history, are resolved, nature and grace are balanced, all "miracle" is absorbed in the one miracle of the primal
divine causality and the dependence of the world, Protestantism
emerges as the realization of the true essence of Christianity, as
Christianity is the expression of the pure essence of all religion—
and the theological "right" and "left" are alike rebutted.

In Julius Müller (1801–78, professor at Halle and close friend of
Tholuck) the openness of the mediating theology to neopietist revival was most pronounced. Typically, his starting point was the
givenness of present personal Christian experience, awakened by
God's word and spirit in the heart, which could be a source of scientific statements of doctrine that trace the experience back to the

3. Schweizer, "Ueber die Dignität des Religionsstifter," *Theologische Studien und
Kritiken*, 1837. See also *Die christliche Glaubenslehre nach protestantischen Grundsätzen*
(1863–69); and *Begriff und Einteilung der praktischen Theologie* (1836). For Twesten,
see *Vorlesungen über die Dogmatik der evangelisch-lutherischen Kirche* (1826 ff.). Twesten's judgment of the relation of this work to Schleiermacher's *Glaubenslehre* reveals
the spirit of the mediating theologians: whereas Schleiermacher assumed a standpoint
"above" the Christian consciousness, Twesten meant to stand "in" it.

effective divine causality—and without Schleiermacher's limitation
of cognitive statements to the immediacy of experience. Thus a way
was opened for speculation and for reconciliation of theology and
philosophy in a theistic philosophy. Müller's distinctive contribution was worked out in his one great book, on the doctrine of sin,[4]
in which the revival concentration on the experience of sin was
given its fullest theological expression. Sin was held to be the point
at which the syntheses of Hegel and Schleiermacher broke down,
for sin is essentially guilt, violation of the law, disobedience to God,
a responsible and culpable act of the self. *Contra* Hegel, the experience of sin makes clear that good and evil are not subject to dialectical mediation, but stand in unconditional antithesis (for this
judgment, Kierkegaard valued Müller's work highly). Against
Schleiermacher, for whom the basic correlation of dependence and
causality had led to denial of an actual confrontation of God and
man and to the identification of sin with the consciousness of sin,
thus with mere negativity or hindrance to the finite self-consciousness, the experience of guilt required the presupposition of a primal
freedom of choice expressed in rebellion against God. The critique
of Schleiermacher and Hegel was worked out in great detail in
Müller's first volume, along with objections to the other current
explanations of sin as a consequence of the metaphysical imperfection of man, for example, or as a result of his corporeality, or on
dualistic hypotheses. Müller's own proposal involved an elaborate
analysis and defense of freedom as the possibility of sin,[5] and a concept of a pretemporal fall, a decision arising in "an extratemporal
mode of existence of created personality" (i.e. in a "realm of the
intelligible," which is as it were "the bosom in which the embryos
of all personal beings are contained"), which enables us to account
for the experienced universality of sin and the ruin of human nature. Of course, it is only the possibility of evil that is conceptually
explicable; in its actuality, evil is strictly inconceivable.[6]

Among the other well-known theologians committed to the task
of "true mediation" were K. H. Sack (1789–1875), professor in Bonn
and then church official in Magdeburg, who was another of Schleiermacher's students and who sought to fulfill his call for a philo-

4. *Die christliche Lehre von der Sünde*, 2 vols. (1838–44; 6th ed., 1877).

5. His assertion that freedom in the formal sense means *"das Auchanderskönnen"*
(*Die christliche Lehre von der Sünde*, 2 : 33) is interestingly parallel to N. W. Taylor's
insistence on "the power to the contrary" (see above, chap. 6).

6. Ibid., 2 : 204–05, 486 ff., 224 ff.

sophical theology; Daniel Schenkel (1813–85), of Heidelberg; the French Swiss thinker Alexander Vinet (1797–1847), of Basel and Lausanne; Dorner's associate in the founding of the *Jahrbücher für deutsche Theologie,* Karl T. A. Liebner (1806–71), of Göttingen, Kiel and Leipzig; the Dane H. L. Martensen (1808–84), professor in Copenhagen and later bishop of Seeland, who was the object of Kierkegaard's attack and a lifelong associate of Dorner and whose brief and simple dogmatics made all theological problems seem easy to solve, and in the Netherlands, the theological faculty at Groningen, under the leadership of Petrus Hofstede de Groot (1802–86).

THE INCARNATION AS PROGRESSIVE:
ISAAK AUGUST DORNER

The most important figure among the mediators proper was Isaak Dorner (1809–84), who as a student at Tübingen was a pupil of Baur and a contemporary of Strauss, and who taught at Tübingen, Kiel, Königsberg, Bonn, and Göttingen before being finally called to Berlin in 1862 as both professor and member of the superior church council. His *System,* though written at the end of the theological era and amid signs that its day was already passing, was the most impressive of those produced by the mediators.[7] Even before Strauss's *Life of Jesus,* Dorner had been drawn to the christological problem as central for theology and was at work on the first portion of what was to be his masterpiece, the *History of the Development of the Doctrine of the Person of Christ.*[8] He embodied the dual

7. In letters to Martensen, Dorner wrote concerning the publication of his own system that his work would not be acclaimed by the rising theological generation. It was not so much the strict Lutheran confessionalists or the biblicists—whom he thought were sure to be dissatisfied with what he had done, in spite of his own sense of nearness to the Lutheran spirit and his intention to be truly biblical—who would oppose him. It was quite another sort of theological mood, which he recognized, that stood against his effort (as also against all those of a mediating or speculative or even gently confessional sort). Albrecht Ritschl was already the new representative man, the one who tried to accomplish what the new theology most deeply wanted accomplished: a cutting loose from the spirit of speculation, and even from the metaphysical in theology, and a turning to the "practical" as a new foundation and form for theology.

8. *Entwicklungsgeschichte der Lehre von der Person Christi* (Stuttgart, 1839 ff.; 2d ed., 4 vols., 1846–56; trans. from 2d ed., 5 vols., Edinburgh, 1861–63). This work remains an important source. Dorner's other major writings included the *Geschichte der protestantischen Theologie* (Munich, 1867), trans. *The History of Protestant Theology,*

commitment to *Wissenschaft* and to the church, and with Müller he was the strongest supporter of the Union. He not only worked out all his thought in relation to the history of theology, but he also had an unusually wide acquaintance with contemporary thought outside Germany.

Hegel and Schleiermacher were most prominently and explicitly in Dorner's background. Hegel's influence was evident in the concern for objectivity and cognition, but more especially in the dialectical pattern for both historical and systematic interpretation. The christological development, for example, Dorner traced with a keen view to the contentions both of Strauss and of F. C. Baur's history of the Trinity and the Incarnation, seeking to validate the intent of classical Christology against any finally negative judgment such as that of Strauss. At the same time, however, he did this in a "critical" way that accepted many of the objections of Strauss and Baur. This history he saw not as the working out of a unilinear tendency, but as a dialectic of factors in imbalance and disproportion, out of which the adequate formulation was yet to be wrought. Similarly, Dorner interpreted the development of the conception of God from Greek and Hebrew religion as continuing dialectic between genuine personal life and unchangeable self-identity. In the *System* also the dialectical argument was prominent. The true understanding of faith emerges as the transcendence (and synthesis) of antithetically inadequate notions of the merely "historical" faith and of the purely "ideal." Here as elsewhere the final solution must arise out of the moments that have emerged in history; the inner course of history determines the sense of further progress.

More decisive for Dorner than Hegel, however, was Schleiermacher. The latter's ideal of the "prince of the church," the Christian who combines the highest and most universal attainment in scholarship with the fullest responsible leadership in the church,

2 vols. (Edinburgh, 1871) and the essays in *Gesammelte Schriften aus dem Gebiet der systematischen Theologie, Exegese und Geschichte* (Berlin, 1883).

Dorner's interest in theology outside Germany (he visited both Britain and America) was reciprocated by extensive translation of his works into English (including his *System of Christian Ethics*, 1887), but unfortunately the quality of the translations cannot be said to have done a service to Dorner's thought or to communication in general.

Two important sections from Dorner's work have been translated in my own *God and Incarnation in Mid-Nineteenth Century German Theology* (New York, 1965), the "dogmatic discussion" from his essay on the immutability of God, and the central portion of his idea of the incarnation from the *System*.

was plainly also Dorner's. The "religious" and the *wissenschaftlich* interests he continually identified as the twin authorities of legitimate theological development. Those interests are finally convergent, and Dorner judged that they have certain immediate aims in common, for example, the purification of theology from "sensuous" elements; but they are not to be confused. *Wissenschaftlich* denotes not merely science in the narrow sense, nor only systematic thinking, which might conceivably operate within the bounds of a subjectively private (or communal) view; it designates that which is coercive and universally valid for thought, and which is thus genuine cognition. Yet knowledge and practice must also go together, and any description of Dorner as a "speculative" thinker must be balanced by a recognition of his own paralleling of scholarship with intense involvement in "practical" church affairs and by his testing of theological conclusions against the immediacies of religious life. His reconsideration of the idea of the immutability of God, for example, concludes with the discussion of implications for the sacraments, for ministerial office, and for worship.

Like Schleiermacher, Dorner wrote a *Glaubenslehre,* a system of doctrines of faith. It was Schleiermacher's great service, Dorner contended, to have given faith the place it deserves in Protestant theology, to have decisively overcome the supernaturalist and rationalist error of supposing that one moves through knowledge to faith, to have understood that doctrine is the articulation of the religious consciousness of the community. But faith must be seen as a real starting point and not a termination. Faith properly understood moves on to knowledge, and therefore Schleiermacher's restriction of knowledge to assertions about the religious consciousness itself must be replaced by actual cognition of the objects of religious awareness.[9] Dorner called the first section of his system a "pisteology," that is, "the doctrine of faith as the precondition of the knowledge of Christianity as the truth." His constructive effort was throughout directed toward attaining an objective knowledge of religious and ethical truth as real (not merely ideal or ideational) truth. Faith, he wrote in an essay on the task of present-day theology with which he began the publication of the *Jahrbücher für deutsche Theologie,* this "self-disclosing faith, this divinely certain fundamen-

9. At this point, Dorner drew not only on Hegel, but on Jakob Böhme and the Böhme-influenced ethical and rational mysticism of F. C. Oetinger (1702–82), as well as on Schelling.

tal Christian knowledge, must in analyzing itself be recognized as a mere point of mediation through which the knowing and loving in which God reveals himself becomes to man just as much knowledge of God and his love as he has knowledge of his own redemption." [10] And he called generally for renewed attention to the "objective" doctrines of Christianity—God, Trinity, Christ's person and work —thus overcoming the one-sided development of the Reformation principles of faith. In contrast, for example, to Schleiermacher's willingness to allow at best a Sabellian kind of distinction in the divine activity, Dorner held that the doctrine of God as triune in himself was to be developed as a central article in the Christian concept of God and the decisive argument against the errors of pantheism and deism. And the doctrine of the person of Christ was Dorner's special theme from his earliest to his last writings.

The goal of systematic theology Dorner declared to be "to bring the immediate factual certainty that faith has in respect of its content to scientific cognition, or to the consciousness of the inner coherence and the objective foundation of this content" (*System*, § 1; cf. §§ 6–12). The first stage in the development of faith's certainty is that of "mere historic faith," which may be either acceptance of tradition and the common faith of the church within which one's life has been shaped, or faith in the Scriptures (a higher form of historic faith). But neither of these forms is adequate. Mere historic faith does not correspond to the true nature of Christianity, which seeks contact with God, nor with doctrines or past history, nor can it provide scientific certainty. Efforts to demonstrate the divine authority of Scripture, in biblical supranaturalism, have failed and must fail. And freedom must be allowed to biblical criticism. Thus doubt is inescapably cast on the standpoint of simple *fides historica;* it cannot be restored again in the old form.

The second stage is then a recoil from the historical to the ideal, to the eternal truths of the spirit, to a level of ethico-religious truths that are nonhistoric and uniform. But this does not correspond to the ideal of Christianity, which claims to be a real principle, that is, to realize itself in history, indeed to have attained absolute realization in the person of Christ and to be at the same time eternally living.

10. "Die deutsche Theologie und ihre dogmatischen und ethischen Aufgaben in der Gegenwart," *Gesammelte Schriften*, pp. 30 ff. (reprinted from the *Jahrbücher*, vol. 1, pt. 1, 1856). The return to "objectivity" from the "subjectivity" of both pietism and rationalism was a favorite theme of the mediating thinkers.

Religious certainty emerges only at the third stage. And it does this only because the religious impulse is associated with the conscience. Its road is one of "ethico-religious self-knowledge founded on experience." Hence it is not lost in theoretic doubt but moves through an even deeper level as doubt necessarily becomes practical. A moral disposition powers the religious impulse in its quest for an existential certainty; it turns every merely theoretical question back upon the subject in his own existence (see especially § 10); and the ethical is a decisive principle for every doctrine. Religious doubt is the awareness of sin, and it passes to religious certainty through "the repentance not to be repented of," that is, to a certainty in which God and self are given together, a unity of subjective and objective in which self-knowledge is knowledge of being loved by God in Christ.

Religious certainty in turn is the presupposition for the attainment of scientific certainty, for the self-verification of Christianity which is the task of the whole of dogmatics. This movement to objective knowledge is not a "retrogressive" inference from the religious certainty of faith, but an explication and verification of the knowing that is present within the faith itself. Further, as the disclosure of objective truth, faith cannot of course be without connection with rational knowledge generally. Faith presupposes universally valid rational knowledge, just as the Christian life is built as a second creation on the first; and it includes the germ of a new knowledge within itself. Thus Dorner could not consider the arguments for the existence of God as superfluous, but sought to rehabilitate them in the new form of scientific grounding of Christian knowledge (*System,* §§ 16 ff.).

From faith, then, in its initial religious certainty, one goes on to cognition of the truth that is apprehended as true in itself. Here philosophy and theology have a common cause—and common enemies: abstract idealism and mere historical empiricism. The positive philosophy that Dorner believed could assist in the development of the Reformation faith was by no means simply that of Hegel, and it especially did not involve the "pantheistic tendency" evident in those Dorner considered to be Hegel's most consistent disciples. The "ethical principle" immanent in the evangelical principle of faith must be set at the center. The highest concept of God becomes not mere being but absolute, primal good, because of which God needs existence, aseity, livingness, and intelligence. And the ethical is not a mere subjective ideal but complete reality in God—and therefore the guarantee of the value of the world and the bridge to history.

Dorner's own most interesting proposals for doctrinal reformulation appeared in his ideas of the immutability of God and of a "progressive" incarnation. The review of the former notion was itself necessitated by the growing popularity of kenotic Christologies.[11] Some of the interests that had led to kenoticism were shared by Dorner, and he was himself drawn to the idea for a time. But he finally rejected it as introducing an intolerable kind of change into the being of God, as well as failing to solve the christological problem. Yet the question could still be asked whether mutability is in every respect to be excluded from the concept of God, whether the highest interests of Christianity have not been done a disservice by insistence on a "bare, absolute immutability" of God. The idea of immutability cannot be dissolved in the attempt to express the religious concern for God as living, but the scholastic identification of immutability with a rigid simplicity of God's nature, which has dominated the church's theology even since the Reformation, must be rejected.

The world, Dorner insisted, really makes a difference to God. Even though God may will and know eternally what emerges only gradually in time, his efficacious, productive willing of the emergents is in no way as eternal as his idea of the world. God's effective action produces novelty in the world, and this means "a change in God's living self-activation." At the highest level, God has created really free beings (not as a self-limitation, but as an exercise of his omnipotence). By living in men, and men in him, God "leads a historical life in the world," he "enters into contact with time." The relation between God and man, an ethical relation of love, is genuinely reciprocal. God's knowledge of the world is affected by the decisions of free beings; though he knows by self-awareness all the possibilities for the activation of freedom, the knowledge of the actuality for which freedom decides can come to him only from the world. The knowledge of an event as actual is different from the knowledge of it as possible. Though God's knowledge is not, like human empirical

11. The first of Dorner's three essays "On the proper version of the dogmatic concept of the immutability of God, with special reference to the interrelation between God's transhistorical and historical life" was an extended analysis of current kenotic theories. Cf. *Jahrbücher für deutsche Theologie* (1856), 361 ff.; (1857), 440 ff.; (1858), 479 ff. (*Gesammelte Schriften*, 188–377). For the third essay, see my *God and Incarnation*, pp. 115 ff.; page references in the text are to this translation.

knowledge, primitively passive, there is nonetheless an element that accrues to his knowledge from the world; "temporal history is reflected into the divine knowledge itself." God's knowledge is thus "conditioned by contemporary history, interwoven and advancing with it" (p. 134), and his decision involves that interplay. The idea of all as eternally and identically present for God is inadequate. Further, there is variety and alteration in God's presence to the world.

With respect then to omnipotence, omniscience, and omnipresence, as well as to the simplicity of God, the older dogmatic notions must be altered. "God is not immutable in his relation to space and time, nor immutable in his knowing and willing of the world and in his decree. . . . In all these respects there takes place also on his side change, alteration, a permitting of himself to be determined" (p. 150). God's true immutability, however, must be maintained in the interest of both piety and science, against pantheistic dissolution of the Being of God into the process of the world, or acosmism, or polytheistic conceptions of God as *a* being rather than the universal principle of being and life. That true eminence and unchangeability Dorner found in God's "ethical" essence and self-identity, that is, in God's being conceived as "ethical in himself." As necessarily ethical being and at the same time ethically free, he "actualizes himself eternally as self-conscious, holy, and free love" (p. 155). For the sake of that eternal self-identity, then, exists everything that may be called a divine attribute—not only simplicity, omnipotence, and beauty, but also consciousness and knowledge, exist for the sake of love.

On one side, this line of thought led back to Dorner's emphasis on the trinitarian idea, which he regarded as expressing the unity of the ethically necessary and free. As a particularly significant participant in the struggle, which began with Schleiermacher, to relate the classical terms *persona* and *hypostasis* (both in the christological and trinitarian usages) to modern conceptions of personhood centering in self-consciousness, Dorner resisted the tendency (especially among the kenoticists) to identify the members of the Trinity with centers of consciousness and agency. That could lead only to tritheism, and to a doubling of the personality of Christ. Rather, "personality" should be ascribed unequivocally to the unity of God and the divine "distinctions" described as "modes of existence" or "modes of being" (*System*, § 32).

On the other side, Dorner's idea of the God–world relation involved a special emphasis on the receptivity and susceptibility of man to God, which was a central theme in his new conception of the incarnation.[12] The interest in a genuinely human historical life of Jesus, which the New Testament presents to us, must be fully protected. Christ's earthly life is not accidental; it is the only way to a right knowledge of his glory. The kenotic doctrine shared the concern for the earthly life but was incompatible with the idea of God, and it did not (e.g. in Thomasius) actually overcome the defects of the classical doctrine, which led either to a doubling of the personality of Christ, or to a truncation of it in the doctrine of the *anhypostasia,* where the idea of the joining of human nature to the *hypostasis* (or *persona*) of the Logos seemed explicitly to involve the impersonality of Christ. Personality, for Dorner, is not to be understood as having the identity of a substance or a point, but as having the organic unity of a process of consciousness and will. Human personality, as finite, is something that intrinsically comes into being; it is essentially historical. As created by and dependent on God—and specifically God as the Logos, as the eternal principle of freedom, of progress, and of history—human personality is furthermore intrinsically receptive to the divine activity and presence. And it knows its need for fulfillment.

The answer to the christological problem, then, is to be found in the idea of a developing (*werdende*) incarnation. From the beginning, God's creative love has prepared in the sphere of human nature a "universal or central receptivity" for itself, a historical preparation for incarnation. And development is "the essential form of the actualization of the God-man" (*System,* § 104). The incarnation, the uniting of God and man, begins with the first moment of Jesus' existence. But neither at the beginning nor in the course of the historical life does it involve an arbitrary or magical kind of miraculous interruption of creaturely being.[13] The incarnation "is not to be

12. This was also central to Dorner's careful development of the idea of miracle, in which he sought to avoid any element of the magical or the arbitrary, without at the same time reducing the idea to a simply subjective viewing of natural occurrences (cf. *System,* §§ 54ff.).

13. "On the one hand, it [the incarnation] is a miracle, i.e. an original and immediate act of God; but on the other hand it is mediated and serves, not the dismembering of the world order, but its strengthening and final fulfillment. This is so because the divine principle that fulfills revelation in incarnation is the same one that was already active in the pre-Christian world, particularly in the history of religion and indeed even in creation, viz. the Logos" (*System,* § 100).

conceived as finished at one moment, but as continuing, even as growing, since God as Logos constantly grasps and appropriates each of the new facets that are formed out of the true human unfolding, just as, conversely, the growing actual receptivity of the humanity joins consciously and willingly with ever new facets of the Logos." [14]

Dorner's christological reflections were of immense influence in mid-nineteenth-century theology. His distinctive idea of a developing incarnation was vigorously debated (especially by the Lutherans as tending to the Calvinist "error" of failing to "unite" the divine and human), and by the time of the publication of his *Glaubenslehre* his approach was already being overtaken by the Ritschlian turn away from "metaphysics" in theology; yet his Christology was the most significant effort of its time to reshape the classical doctrine in a way that ascribed to Jesus a genuinely human historical existence. It also incorporated two other themes that were favorites among the mediating theologians. The first grew out of Schleiermacher's stress on Christ as the second Adam, the head of humanity, which was widely accepted and was devleoped in Dorner's well-known idea of the "central individual." This meant that Christ, as a particular human individual, was at the same time the universal human center, holding the central position in humanity through the uniqueness of his union with the Logos, and being the focus for all the moral and spiritual excellences of man.[15] The second theme was the necessity of the incarnation, not only because of sin but because the idea of God-manhood belongs necessarily to the divine idea of humanity and the world. The God-man is a new creation, a higher reality, but one toward which all God's activity moves; thus it is the factual resolution of all problems of the relation of God and world. The incarnation can be shown to be necessary from the ethi-

---

14. *System,* § 104. Further, "in spite of this development within the *unio,* the Logos is from the beginning united with Jesus in the deepest ground of being, and Jesus' life was always a divine-human one since an existent receptivity for deity never remained without its fulfillment. Human development and the immutability of deity are congruous in that God as Logos can enter history without loss of self, for the purpose of a progressive self-revelation in humanity, and humanity is capable of being set increasingly in immutability, again without alteration of its essence" (ibid.).

15. This did not mean that in Jesus' career all those individual human qualities were "productively exhibited," but that because of the perfect and full receptivity in him, the "universal spiritual endowment is to be ascribed to him" (cf. *System,* § 103). One sees here also the mediating theologians' tendencies to find in Jesus the fulfillment of the Goethean ideal of humanity.

cal being of God. Thus "the Christ of history, the Christ of faith, and the Christ of the Idea are one." [16]

SPECULATION, CRITICISM, AND SECULARITY: RICHARD ROTHE

Of all the mid-nineteenth-century German theologians, Richard Rothe (1799–1867) of Heidelberg is the thinker who has most often claimed a chapter of his own, both because of his genius and because he fits so poorly into any system of classification.[17] He has been labeled the "personification of mediation theology" and "the most brilliant example of speculative theology" (Kähler) and even the "paradigm for the theological intentions of the whole century" (Barth).[18] Yet he was unquestionably a most original theologian. Obviously indebted to Schleiermacher and Hegel and influenced by the revival, he belonged to no school and he founded none. Like F. D. Maurice, he was opposed to theological parties. In 1828 he wrote "everywhere I see parties, and where something has become a party, there is certainly not the genuine, i.e. the whole, truth." [19] His influence on subsequent theology was diverse (e.g. on Albrecht Ritschl and Ernst Troeltsch). He was a man of the deepest piety and devotion to the cause of genuine Christianity; he had the fullest confidence in the possibilities of rigorous speculative thinking; and he was among the most radical in his theological conclusions. Rothe was quite conscious of himself as being in conflict with both the theological liberals and the orthodox, with the former because of his "supernaturalism and belief in revelation" and with the latter because of his attitude toward Scripture (z. Dog., pp. v–vi). On the one

16. Emanuel Hirsch, Geschichte, 5 : 386.

17. Rothe studied at Heidelberg with Daub, later at Berlin with both Hegel and Schleiermacher. In Berlin he was also involved in the pietist circle gathered around Baron von Kottwitz (though he later became critical of pietism). After a period as director of the seminary in Wittenberg (1828 ff.) he was called to Heidelberg in 1837, went to Bonn (1849–54), then returned to Heidelberg. Rothe's great work was the Theologische Ethik, 3 vols. (1845–48; 2d ed., rev. and enl., 5 vols., 1867–71), hereafter cited as TE[1], and TE[2]. Also of particular importance are the three essays "The Concept of Evangelical Dogmatics," "Revelation," and "Holy Scripture," published in Theologische Studien und Kritiken and later expanded in Zur Dogmatik (1863), hereafter cited as z. Dog.; and the Stille Stunden (1872), a collection of aphorisms published from Rothe's literary remains.

18. Martin Kähler, Geschichte der protestantischen Dogmatik (Munich, 1962), pp. 103 ff., and Karl Barth, Die protestantische Theologie im 19. Jahrhundert (Zurich, 1946), pp. 544–45.

19. Quoted in Stephan Schmidt, Geschichte der deutschen evangelischen Theologie (Berlin, 1960), p. 137. Rothe's stress of individuality was also reinforced by his unusual modesty about his work.

hand, he was persuaded that Christianity can live for the thinking man of the present only when the ideas of the supernatural and of miracle were grasped anew in the heart. He could even speak of his own views as naïve. But he was equally persuaded that the traditional treatments of those ideas were impossible. Though insistent on the "essential identity" of the content of doctrinal formulations with Scripture, he set himself against "Bibliologie." Most sharp was Rothe's critique of the authority of dogma. In contrast particularly to the confessionalist trend, but also to many of the mediating thinkers for whom the task of theology was the recovery of the classical formulations, Rothe held that the trinitarian and christological doctrines, for example, must be thoroughly rethought. The scientific goal of dogmatics must be to free us from faith in dogma as such. For the piety of the present, dogma is not an end or a protection, but only offers the "constant danger of a false step" and hinders piety (z. Dog., pp. 32 ff., 53 ff.).

A chief clue to Rothe's thought is that among all the successors of Schleiermacher, he most fully shared the latter's desire to speak to the nonchurchly world. Against the growing confessionalism and ecclesiasticism of the sixth and seventh decades of the century, he could even say that a principal task for faith was to free Christianity from the church, and his theology pointed to the goal of the secularization of Christianity. This interest was expressed, for example, in the establishment of the German Protestant Union, the most liberal of the Protestant associations of the time, of which Rothe was a principal founder.[20] Formed "to strive for the renewal of the Protestant church in the spirit of evangelical freedom and in accord with the total cultural development of our time," the Protestantenverein, as Rothe described it, was especially concerned to overcome the estrangement of the educated classes from Christianity, to prevent it from becoming simply a "peasant's religion." The Union was to enable the church to affirm the values of modern cultural life and to assist in its construction so that it could be purified and sanctified, thus to recognize in modern culture not something anti-Christian but a turning in history that could fulfill Christianity in a transition from a churchly to a secular-ethical form. In the revolutions of 1848 Rothe saw not simply a need for renewed evangelism and social concern, as did most of the pietist and mediating thinkers, nor certainly any occasion for retreat into insularity, as did the confessional-

20. Der allgemeine deutsche Protestantenverein, founded in Frankfurt, 1863.

ists, but rather the travail of birth into a new life. All this necessitated, of course, complete freedom for scholarship and an increased concern for truthfulness in believing rather than for conformity in theology.

A dominant purpose of speculation, indeed, Rothe understood to be the criticism of dogma. Speculative theology is quite distinct from dogmatics. The latter is, as Schleiermacher proposed, always a form of contemporary theology, a positive and historically critical discipline.[21] And Protestant theology has a "sacred duty" to subject church doctrine to a "candid, impartial, uncorrupted, strict judgment." The critique and improvement of dogma cannot be carried out by dogmatics itself, however, but only by "an utterly closed organic system," in which the particular emerges as absolutely conditioned by the whole, hence only by a speculative theology (z. Dog., pp. 49–50). In its procedures, theological ethics has "absolutely nothing to do with the church's tenets, but must proceed purely speculatively." And speculative theology does not arise when piety is wholly satisfied with the regnant dogmatic system. Only in Protestantism was there a soil on which speculative theology could genuinely grow, and this only late in Protestantism. The appearance of such a theology is indeed itself a symptom that the church in question is already in a process of dissolution leading to a metamorphosis. Speculative theology must therefore be heterodox in the good sense.[22]

Rothe's principal work, therefore, he offered as a "theological ethics," a form of speculative theology. It was properly an *Ethik,* both formally as carrying out in full Schleiermacher's proposal for an inclusive theological development in the categories of the good, of virtue, and of duty; and substantively in that the task was the de-

21. Also, in a pattern obviously related to Schleiermacher's, though of less originality or interest, Rothe proposed a twofold structure of dogmatics: the doctrines developed from the consciousness of sin—God, man, and sin; and the doctrines derived from the consciousness of grace—on the objective side, the doctrine of redemption (i.e. of Christ), and on the subjective side, the doctrine of salvation (cf. z. Dog., pp. 16 ff.).

22. Cf. TE[1], pp. 25–26 (TE[2], pp. 48–49), and p. 39. On the last point, Rothe recalls Schleiermacher's assertion in the *Kurze Darstellung* (§§ 203–08) that orthodoxy, whose function is to hold on to what is generally acknowledged, and heterodoxy, which keeps doctrine mobile and open to new formulations, are equally important to theology. Also, of course, Scripture does serve as an authority for speculative theology, since the results of the latter cannot finally be in disharmony with the essential content of Scripture, allowing for the difference between scriptural imagery and speculative conceptuality (cf. TE [2], § 50, and z. Dog.).

velopment of the concept of the ethical in the broadest sense (including both the morally good and the morally evil). The result was the delineation of a universal moral process culminating in inclusive moral community.

The work was to be strictly theological, not philosophical, by virtue of its starting point. "I declare expressly," Rothe said disarmingly in the preface to the first edition of the *Theologische Ethik*, "that this work contains nothing of philosophy, but solely theology, or more exactly theosophy, although I should certainly wish for it consideration from the philosophical side, and that I make absolutely no claim to understand anything of philosophy." [23] The fundamental distinction was that philosophical speculation begins simply with the self, with the *cogito ergo sum* as the primary datum, that immediately certain reality from which thinking proceeds. Theological speculation, however, begins with the religiously determined self-consciousness, that is, with the consciousness of God, for the religious self-consciousness is simultaneously and immediately conscious of God. The awareness of God is as certain as is the awareness of self. Theology presupposes piety and makes no claims to demonstration on any other basis.[24] It begins its thinking with God. Rothe could thus describe theological speculation as "theosophy": philosophy conceives God out of the world; theosophy conceives the world out of God.

Speculation, then, is that thinking which proceeds from first principles by the necessities of thought. It is utterly organic and unified thought, which alone is able to develop genuine, wholly finished concepts. In contrast to reflective, *raisonnierendes* thinking, speculative thought is *a priori* and constructive, self-productive by inner logic. The task of speculation is to generate the whole from the point of beginning. Yet this does not at all mean, for Rothe, that speculation is indifferent to empirical reality. On the contrary, it is as much concerned "as is the most convinced empiricist." When the

23. *TE¹*, p. viii. Rothe also noted that Müller was the only theologian with whom he carried on extended debate because, while on one side he had the deepest sympathy with it, Müller's book represented the theological tendency of the present from which Rothe had to distinguish himself most clearly. Specifically, sin for Rothe was a necessary transitional stage in the process of God's formation of self-determining men in fellowship with himself.

24. This limitation entails no weakness, Rothe judged, because piety is itself a constitutive, essential determination of man, so that only the fully religious man corresponds to the concept of true man (cf. *TE²*, p. 41).

system is completed, speculative thought must turn its attention with all sharpness and strenuousness to the empirical world—and if the speculative construction does not accord with empirical actuality, this is clear evidence that thought has not proceeded rightly and the system must be reconstructed.[25] After all, the interest out of which speculation emerges is precisely to come to know this actuality better than it can be known by empirical, reflective thinking. And theological speculation springs in the first instance not from the "scientific" interest, but out of the directly religious interest that piety has in knowing clearly everything it possesses. So speculative theology stands alongside historical theology and practical theology. It is important for the former (e.g. for dogmatics) especially as a critical tool; it is important for the latter as relating the church to the other realms of life.

For the immediate awareness of God in religious consciousness, speculation seeks the most all-embracing rational expression. This is the concept of the absolute (in the most abstract, neutral sense), which in turn leads to the notions of the utterly unconditioned, the singular, and the eternal, thence to the good and indeed the absolute good. But if absolute being is really to be thought, then it must be by means of those categories essential to thinking, that is, by means of ground and consequence. Hence the absolute must be conceived as cause and effect, as self-caused—and so on to the concepts of pure being, pure potency, absolute self-generating process and life, spirit as the absolute unity of thought and existence, unity, personality, and the attributes or modalities of glory, sovereign will, blessedness, and livingness.[26]

From the concept of God as absolute person, thought leads on to the necessary creation of an eternal world (for this, of course, Rothe was roundly attacked). By a logical necessity (from self-affirmation), God must conceive that which he is not. This does not itself mean that he must create, but to do so is more appropriate to his utter perfection, thus creation is a *moral* necessity (and a free act). As absolute spiritual person, God from an inner necessity of self-determination is never without a world. That world of individual, finite

25. Even God is to be considered empirical, inasmuch as he reveals himself (*TE²*, p. 19*n*).

26. Rothe's pattern of argument is throughout closer to that of Schelling than to that of Hegel. In the 2d ed. of *TE* (though not in the 1st) he cites Schelling frequently, along with another "speculative" theologian, C. H. Weisse (1801–66). See Weisse's *Philosophische Dogmatik oder Philosophie des Christentums*, 3 vols. (1855–65).

beings is, as the counterpart of God, above all a world of spirit and moral process, and whatever in the world is not spirit does not belong to the world-goal itself but is only an instrument for the perfecting of spirit.

On this basis, then, Rothe was able to articulate an inclusive world scheme, from the level of mere material existence to the highest level of spirit, from creation through the moments of sin and redemption (even more than for Schleiermacher, the emphasis is here on creation; the plan of redemption is already contained in the plan of creation, Christ is the second Adam) and from all the spheres of human moral community to the ultimate goal of a transearthly kingdom of spirits.

In Rothe's theological program as a whole, three further points are particularly noteworthy. The first is his evolutionary conception of the world process and man's emergence in it, by which, before Darwin, Rothe set the stage and prepared the lines for the liberal view of Darwinism and generally altered the terms of the question of Christianity and natural science. Creation is a continuing process, directed to the production of personal spirits, who are coworkers toward the moral purpose of the world. God can begin only with the nonspiritual, the material, working out the higher levels from the lower. The soul, including both animal and human soul, emerges as a more highly organized level of development of material nature. Human life (i.e. the "human animal") is the level of the emergence of personality or ego, the unity of rational consciousness and activity of will, out of animal life (i.e. the "mere animal" soul, in which there is already a distinction between consciousness and activity, though not yet cognition and will). Yet as not itself material, personality is a surprising appearance, a new order of creaturely being, with the moral task of self-determination.[27] And in this emergence, the sensuousness and egotism wholly normal to animal being become impulses to be overcome for the sake of man's ethico-religious development. Sin thus has its ground in the necessary materiality of man's origin; it is the resistance, the contradiction, the abnormality, which is at the same time teleologically ordered to the creative-

27. See TE^2, § 83: "In its origin, creaturely personality . . . is the product of the material, humanly animal natural organism or ensouled body in its livingness, and simply the result of its organic (somatic-physical) life-functions. . . . Genetically considered, and consequently originally, it is thus of not merely natural but material extraction. Considered in itself, nevertheless, personality is certainly not material" (cf. §§ 71–84).

redemptive process. (Plainly, Rothe had no place for a traditional notion of original sin or a fall from righteousness, and he was quite ready to leave to natural and historical science the question whether the emergence of man came with a single human pair or via a multiple origin.)

Second, Rothe gives a classic statement of a view of revelation as personal encounter, a conception that was to dominate the theology of subsequent generations.[28] To be sure, revelation is a supernatural, miraculous occurrence—though this is always to be understood within the scheme of God's total activity in the world process as Rothe viewed it, thus as a teleologically ordered supernaturalism in which God could introduce new elements into the natural order that became truly parts of that order (this was a conception of miracle widely taken up in the nineteenth century). Revelation thus is also natural, since it is a form of history; data which the world cannot produce out of itself are planted in the human circle of history—and a new idea of God emerges. But a decisive point, for Rothe, is the distinction between revelation and Scripture. The old view had identified them, conceiving revelation as the supernatural communication of doctrine through the divine inspiration of Scripture. Against this idea modern theology took up its work, and one of the most important of its enduring results was the distinction between revelation and the Bible.[29] Neither the Old nor the New Testament is infallible; nor did the authors so intend their writings. Contradictions, obscurities, and historical errors are present. The old inspiration doctrine is simply destroyed. More particularly, however, it must be emphasized that "in revealing himself, God reveals *himself; God* and *exclusively* God is the object that divine revelation reveals, God and nothing else." [30] Revelation is thus in no sense a "magical infusion" but an utterly moral, personal event that takes place through human functioning. "Through an unequivocally supernatural, peculiarly divine history, God himself as acting person

28. See "Offenbarung," z. *Dog.,* pp. 55–120.

29. Related to this, for Rothe, was the abandonment of the old concerns with general and special revelation, i.e. of different sorts of revealed truths, and the distinctions of "above reason," "against reason," etc., which embodied a false view of reason as a thing. Reason, rather, means just thinking—the process—and a man has reason to the extent that he can actually think (z. *Dog.,* p. 57).

30. z. *Dog.* p. 61. Indirectly, of course, revelation sheds light on all else, so that God leads us into all truth. But revelation does *not* mean the communication of astronomy, etc., to men.

enters into natural history and places himself in such nearness to man that he can be evident even to man whose eyes are darkened by sin" (z. Dog., p. 68). This manifestation, the "objective" side, plainly requires a matching inspiration, an inner working whereby it is received and recognized. As stemming from men inspired in this sense, the Bible is not revelation, but a document or deed of revelation, a collection of testimonies to the divine manifestations and inspirations, through which God can speak to religious sensitivity. Only in Christ, however, do manifestation and inspiration utterly coincide—thus again revelation is the personal presence of God. This coincidence in Christ, furthermore, in no way requires a restriction of God's saving activity to the realm of biblical religion. God's revealing activity is only a special form of his saving work; he has throughout human history been leading men to salvation, though one would not call that activity "revelation" where it was not fruitful in God-consciousness.[31]

Rothe's attack on *Bibliologie* can also be seen in his conception of the development of religious knowledge. The most primitive level, in feeling, is the intimation or presentiment of God (*die Gottes-ahnung*), which objectifies itself in an individually determined image (*Bild*) or symbol. At this level, objective religion is on its theoretical side a "mythology." That is not a negative term, for "it belongs essentially to the perfection of religion, even the Christian religion, to have a mythology, a religious fantasy-world." By an inner necessity, then, there is a movement to a universal form, to a perception by the understanding, a thinking perception, first in the form of mere *Vorstellung*, which is a real knowing and meaning but not yet free from the subjectively individual, a thought (*Gedanke*), but lacking the pure form of thought, thence to proper knowledge in a fully universal form that has been thought through. This last is what is objectified in doctrines, but these need still to be worked into the organic unity of a system of thought or doctrine, and similarly the religious community's intentions into dogmas and these into dogmatics. All of these must always be subject to criticism by reference to the content of Scripture, to the source in religious feeling, and to the scientific standpoint, that is, by internal consistency, by

31. Christology did not occupy the central place in Rothe's theology that it did in that of most of his contemporaries. He intended to be a more inclusively theocentric thinker. The current Christocentrism seemed to him linked to the ecclesiasticism that had to be fought.

relation to contemporary concepts, and by the results of nontheological sciences (see z. Dog., pp. 4 ff., 38 ff.; and TE², §§ 409 ff.).

Finally, and most distinctive in his outlook, Rothe contended that the church is a merely transitory form in the process of developing moral community (cf. TE², §§ 405 ff.). Primitive Christianity itself was much more than a mere religion. It was the emergence of a perfect and "whole new human life and existence," a new history and period in creation. Christ was properly no cleric but a high-priestly king, the founder not of a church but of the Kingdom of God, an ethico-religious community of redemption. The church did come into being by an inner necessity, as the "religious" means to the redemptive world-historical work, to the moral effects leading to an inclusively human religious and ethical common life. But the church was at the same time a break with the authentic nature of Christianity, because the church is specifically a religious community, not an ethical. It is the community purely of piety. It does embrace all the four main spheres of human community—artistic and scientific life, social and civil life—but only as "religious"; it does in this way transcend the national differences that cause separation in a moral community, and it is thus "immediately" universal. But the fulfillment of the goal of a genuinely religio-ethical community requires reaching into the "material" nature (i.e. the totality of the secular), which contradicts the idea of the purely religious. Thus by definition the church can be only a transitory phenomenon. The goal of the moral process, that is, the renewed whole of human natural life, filled with spiritual-ethical content, for which Christianity in its churchly form has from the beginning properly worked, is one in which the distinction of church and world is transcended.

The name for this social whole—Rothe adopted it from Hegel—is the state; not of course simply as a political entity but as the inclusive moral organization of the world. As long as the state has not attained fulfillment, the church exists alongside it; but the goal for Christianity is a world in which the church falls away. As the moral community moves ahead, the exclusively religious community retreats more and more, "until finally, when the religio-ethical community, i.e. the state, has in fact reached its utter universality with the fulfillment of moral development, the exclusively religious community i.e. the church, falls utterly away" (TE², § 415). The whole common life becomes a cultus in a higher sense.

The Reformation, for Rothe, was the fundamental turning point in the history of Christianity away from its churchly form (which found classical shape in Catholicism) toward the secular world. All the dimensions of life were invested directly with Christian significance. And the continuing task of Protestantism is the transformation of Christianity from a churchly to an "ethically-human" form. Thus the confessional-ecclesiastical tendency of the mid-nineteenth century seemed to Rothe the most blatant betrayal of the Reformation. It was plainly heading into a cul-de-sac, a purely cultic conception of community, thus a churchly organization, fellowship, art, and scholarship that were utterly meaningless in the contemporary world. What was needed was not more but less church. The modern world's movement away from the church was not to be understood as a de-Christianization. The historical task for Christianity in the present was to learn to breathe a freer air (free especially from church), and to recognize the working of Christ in "unconscious Christianity," in the profane political and social movements of the modern world in which the moral process of creation and incarnation is being continued. With this, Rothe quite burst the limits of anything that could be called "mediating" theology.

13

Subjectivity as Truth and Untruth:

Søren Kierkegaard

Søren Kierkegaard's immediate influence on his contemporaries, it has been asserted, is not worth discussing.[1] As a comparison with the impact of Kierkegaard on later theology and philosophy, that judgment is doubtless valid. In this sense, Kierkegaard belongs more to the twentieth than to the nineteenth century. But to say only this would be seriously misleading, for Kierkegaard plainly thought in the immediate context of his time, and what he said must be so understood. The central problems of mid-nineteenth-century theology were also his problems. His critique of Christendom was relevant not only to a Hegelianized culture-Christianity, best represented theologically in Denmark by the mediating thinker H. L. Martensen, but also to a Schleiermacherian "eternal covenant" between theology and science (though in other senses Kierkegaard could be called a disciple of Schleiermacher). At some points Kierkegaard was close to the neopietism of the day, particularly in his concentration on the idea of sin. It would be difficult to find a more christocentric thinking than his, even though his idea of contemporaneity with Christ did not speak to the historical problem as it had been posed by Strauss and others. In his protest against modernity and his call for disengagement Kierkegaard shared emphases with the Oxford Movement and with the confessionalists (including the Roman versions). And in his turn to "subjectivity" Kierkegaard was the paradigm of a main tendency of the century as a whole.[2]

---

1. Emanuel Hirsch, *Geschichte* 5 : 444. Among the many Kierkegaard interpreters, Hirsch remains one of the most valuable. See also his *Kierkegaardstudien*, 2 vols. (Gütersloh, 1930–33).

2. To select and organize aspects of Kierkegaard's thought from the standpoint of the mid-19th-century theological scene is of course to give a one-sided interpretation. In other ways, he quite escapes the dominant tendencies of the time and belongs to no century.

The problem is similar to that of the relation of Kierkegaard's literature to his own

Furthermore, in spite of the twentieth century's concentration on the pseudonymous literature of the years 1843–47, it is not incorrect that Kierkegaard was first known abroad (and made his main initial impression in Scandinavia) through the final attack on "Christendom" (i.e. the twenty-one articles in *The Fatherland* from December 1854 to May 1855 and the ten numbers of the *Instant* from May until October 1855, the month before his death). The open attack on the religious establishment was not a diversion or an addendum or a new departure, nor was it a mere consequence of his own tendency toward a more ascetic viewpoint and life. The attack was rather a proper culmination which made clear the meaning of Kierkegaard's whole life work. The change was essentially in the mode of communication from indirect to a new kind of directness, called forth by Professor Martensen's eulogy of Bishop Mynster as a "genuine witness to the truth," a claim which so patently confused the categories that Kierkegaard could no longer refrain from crying aloud (though he did hold back publication from February until

---

life story, in particular his relation to his father, his engagement to Regine, the attack that he invited from the *Corsair*, etc. His whole work is at once bound up with his life story and free from it. While it is true that the broken engagement loosed the springs of his creativity and that the early works (*Either/Or, Repetition,* and *Fear and Trembling,* all published in 1843) can be said to have been written for Regine, it is also true that the project begun in those works can stand quite independently of the details of that relationship or of the psychological dynamics of Kierkegaard's decision that marriage was impossible for him or of his peculiar view of women.

In any case, this chapter is intended as no more than an interpretation of some central themes of Kierkegaard's thought from a perspective that will be at least no more distorting than those that would focus simply on the dynamics of subjectivity or the elements of so-called *Existenzphilosophie.* The Kierkegaard literature is enormous and continues to grow. The standard Danish editions include the *Samlede Vaerker,* 15 vols., 2d ed. (Copenhagen, 1920–36); the *Papirer,* 20 vols., 2d ed. (Copenhagen, 1909–48); and the *Breve,* 2 vols. (Copenhagen, 1953–54). All the principal publications have now been translated into English, along with selections from the *Journals* and *Papers.* For an excellent selected bibliography up to 1962, compiled by Lee M. Capel, with a list of the English translations and well-chosen secondary materials in English, German, French, and Scandinavian languages, see appendix 5 of Walter Lowrie's biography, *Kierkegaard,* 2 vols. (New York, 1962). There is a massive Kierkegaard bibliography edited by J. Himmelstrup, *Søren Kierkegaard, International bibliografi* (Copenhagen, 1962). See also Lowrie's *Short Life of Kierkegaard* (Princeton, 1942); the larger life contains a great deal of citation from the literature which was not translated at the time of original publication (1938). The most useful introductions in English remain those of David F. Swenson, *Something about Kierkegaard,* 2d ed. (Minneapolis, 1945); and Reidar Thomte, *Kierkegaard's Philosophy of Religion* (Princeton, 1948). See also T. H. Croxall, *Kierkegaard Commentary* (New York, 1956); and H. A. Johnson and Niels Thulstrup, eds., *A Kierkegaard Critique* (New York, 1962).

December 1854, after Martensen had been elected bishop and the subscription for a memorial for Mynster was completed). But what Kierkegaard now said openly was often drawn from earlier entries in his journals, and the same conception of Christianity had been quite plainly set forth in the *Works of Love* (1847), *Sickness unto Death* (1849), *Training in Christianity* (1850), and *For Self-Examination* (1851).

Beginning in his earliest writings, Kierkegaard was the critic of contemporary Christendom, seeking to expose its unchristian character in order that it might be possible for an individual to become a Christian. This is not, of course, to assume that Kierkegaard had at the outset a grand scheme for the whole of his works. Nor is it to deny that Kierkegaard became more and more critical of the Establishment and more convinced of the necessity of outward suffering and persecution.

Thus we may legitimately extend to Kierkegaard's entire production, from *Either/Or* to the *Attack,* the interpretation that he himself offered for the works through 1847 in *The Point of View for My Work as an Author.*[3] There Kierkegaard insisted that while "in a certain sense it was not at all my original intention to become a religious author," but rather "to evacuate as hastily as possible the poetical—and then to go out to a country parish," nonetheless "the religious is present from the beginning" and the whole work is to be construed from that point of view (pp. 86, 12, 22 ff.). There was a deliberate and necessary duplicity, represented clearly (to one who could have seen) by paralleling from the start the "aesthetic" writings, issued over pseudonyms, with *Edifying Discourses* issued over Kierkegaard's own name. The problem was simply to destroy the "monstrous illusion" of "Christendom," that is, the supposition of people living in a so-called Christian country that they could call themselves Christians "as a matter of course":

> People who perhaps never once enter a church, never think about God, never mention his name except in oaths! People upon whom it has never dawned that they might have any obligation to God, people who either regard it as a maximum to be guiltless of trans-

3. The *Point of View* was completed in July 1848 but published posthumously (trans. Walter Lowrie, 1939). See also Kierkegaard's statements about his works in the *Concluding Unscientific Postscript,* trans. David F. Swenson and Walter Lowrie (Princeton, 1944), pp. 225 ff., "A Glance at a Contemporary Effort in Danish Literature"; and 551 ff., "First and Last Declaration."

gressing the criminal law, or do not count even this quite necessary!
Yet all these people, even those who assert that no God exists, are all
of them Christians, call themselves Christians, are recognized as
Christians by the State, are buried as Christians by the Church, are
certified as Christians for eternity.[4]

Thus the difficulty of communicating what it means to *become* a
Christian was doubly compounded: how to invite people to become
Christians who already suppose that they are Christians. The initial
attack on this problem was the indirect one of the "aesthetic literature" and the depiction of the "stages," on the grounds that the illusion of Christendom could not be destroyed by frontal assault but
only from within, by becoming an aesthetic author and exposing
Christendom's essentially aesthetic character and thus its fraudu-
lence. Finally, however, the attack was to be open.

CHRISTIANITY VERSUS CHRISTENDOM

This is the shocking thing, that the situation is if possible made
twice as difficult for Christianity as it was when it came into the
world, because now it is confronted, not by pagans and Jews, whose
whole resentment must be aroused, but by *Christians* whom the
clerical gang of swindlers has been made to believe that they are
Christians, and that Christianity is set to the melody of a drinking
song, only still merrier than such a song, which after all is constantly
accompanied by the sad reflection that it is soon over and "in a
hundred years is all forgotten"; whereas the merry Christian drinking
song, according to the assurance of the priests, "lasts an eternity." [5]

Christendom has done away with Christianity, without being quite
aware of it. The consequence is that, if anything is to be done, one
must try again to introduce Christianity into Christendom.[6]

It is a constant theme of the *Attack* that "the Christianity of the New
Testament simply does not exist" in the "common Christianity" or
"official Christianity" of mid-nineteenth-century Denmark. This
Kierkegaard calls his one thesis, comparable to Luther's Ninety-five
Theses. Official Christianity cannot be justified as a mild or accom-
modating form of true Christianity, for there are not two kinds of
Christianity but only one. Christendom—with its thousand clerical
livings, its priestly egoism that seeks many Christians both for

4. *Point of View*, pp. 22–23.
5. *Attack on Christendom*, trans. Walter Lowrie (Princeton, 1968), pp. 142–43 (from
The Instant, no. 4).
6. *Training in Christianity*, trans. Walter Lowrie (Princeton, 1952), p. 39.

pecuniary advantage and for power, its comedy and nonsense of infant baptism and confirmation, its supposition that the authority and validity of Christianity is (like that of the state) proportional to number, its utter worldliness, such that a Bishop Mynster could be called a "witness to the truth" (whereas a witness to the truth "is a man whose life from first to last is unacquainted with everything which is called enjoyment"), such that even the threat of eternal punishment and the hope of eternal blessedness are used not to transform men but to bring about what they already are, to induce them to live as they would most like to live—this Christendom is utter hypocrisy, it is a mockery of God, a betrayal, and open apostasy.[7]

The norm for this judgment upon Christendom was Kierkegaard's understanding of New Testament Christianity. If it is essential to recognize that the one great concern of Kierkegaard was to communicate what it means to become a Christian, it is equally important to see that he meant to draw his definition of being a Christian purely and simply from the New Testament, especially from Christ's utterances in the synoptic Gospels (more than from Paul; and Kierkegaard was able to say that even the apostle was guilty of weakening the gospel by placing a value on numbers of converts). The frequently abstract and formal description of what being a Christian means that characterized the early literature has thus to be viewed in relation to the quite concrete picture given in the later works. It was *Christ's* judgment about official Christianity that Kierkegaard wanted to utter, and from the standpoint of *His* demands and judgment and the evident experience of the earliest community of his followers, Kierkegaard proposed to show the antithesis of "Christendom." Christianity can exist only in contrast; it is by definition against the world. When all are "Christians," therefore, Christianity does not exist. The Christian must suffer hate and persecution—and on this point, Kierkegaard obviously moved in his last years toward the demand for an open and public kind of suffering. Being a Christian is "what most of all is repugnant to the natural man, is an offense to him," because Christianity wants to change everything.[8]

7. See *Attack*, pp. 32–33, 7, and passim.
8. See *Attack*, pp. 115 ff., 150, 164, and passim. Kierkegaard did not himself claim to have attained true Christianity: "Therefore neither do I call myself yet a Christian, I am still far behind. But one advantage I have over all official Christianity (which moreover is bound by an oath upon the New Testament), is that I report truly what Christianity is, and so do not take the liberty of altering what Christianity is, and I report truly how I am related to what Christianity is, and so do not take part in altering what Christianity is in order to win millions of Christians" (*Attack*, p. 189).

Kierkegaard's positive description of Christian existence, set forth especially in *Training in Christianity,* can be summarized in three themes related as concentric circles. First, beginning with the outward or the consequence, the Christian life means heterogeneity to the world, the heterogeneity which is suffering and conflict with the world, a crucifixion in contrast to the worldly success of Christendom, an opposition between God's idea and man's idea of what life ought to be.

Second, Christianity is a life of suffering because it is a life of discipleship in which Christ is the pattern. To become a Christian is to take Christ as the model and to accept the requirement of unconditional obedience (which even the apostles began to relax). Here in part Kierkegaard was explicitly offering a corrective for the time. The Middle Ages had falsely emphasized Christ as the pattern, encouraging a "works righteousness"; thus Luther rightly protested on behalf of an understanding of Christ as a gift appropriated simply in faith. But now faith had become distorted, made a screen behind which to hide the most unchristian life—and had become faith in a right object of belief. A new and unequivocal demand for obedience and conformity to Christ was needed. But for Kierkegaard to say (here or elsewhere) that he was proposing a "corrective" was not at all to say that he was uttering only a qualified or exaggerated truth. Rather, the real dialectic had to be maintained. The Christ who offends is the one who invites. He who commands is he who supports. Christ is both the pattern and the atoner: when the striving one sinks under the burden of the pattern, the atoner raises him up again; but in the same moment he is again the pattern so that he may be kept striving. Christ is both imitated and worshipped. The tension is not surpassed, as in pietism, which made the experience of forgiveness equal to being rid of sin and the attaining of peace with God. Rather, sin and justification, despair and consolation, offence and overcoming the offence, are held together in tension—thus Kierkegaard's favorite figure of the believer's being suspended over seventy thousand fathoms of water.

Third, then, being a Christian may be described as contemporaneity with Christ—a theme worked out especially in the *Fragments,* the *Postscript,* and *Training in Christianity.* Contemporaneity was not for Kierkegaard primarily a historical problem but first and last a question of actual encounter with the concrete figure of Jesus Christ, with the actual severity and grace of this God-man, who precisely in humiliation invites men to come hither and who can only be believed and obeyed. Further, the "Offence" of the God-man is not in the first instance the intellectual problem of the conjunction of eternity and time. The antithesis of those categories, to be sure, is ingredient in the paradox, but the importance of that sort of paradox is actually derivative from the historical form of the Redeemer. The offence properly is that this poor, lowly man, this actual man, should give it out or imply that he is God and should be the Inviter, the appearance of divine compassion.[9] Here is a conception entirely different from the purely human idea of what is man's wretchedness and what form compassion should take. The offence of the God-man is not in relation to a doctrine but in relation to the actual lowliness of this man, or rather the lowliness of God in this man (who is thus an actually human Christ in contrast to all the fantastic Christ-figures of theology).[10] Contemporaneity with Christ means being confronted with this concretely humble one, who is not within but is wholly objective; who meets, challenges, invites, and requires decision, and to whose presence eighteen hundred years is irrelevant.

The distinctiveness of Kierkegaard's thought, however, does not lie in the contrast he drew between New Testament Christianity and Christendom. Often his complaints parallel those of radical Christian groups or sects of the past—though Kierkegaard was not at all tempted to the formation of special purified religious communities. He sought rather simply to speak to the "individual" to whom many of his writings were explicitly addressed. Further, there is in the repetitiveness of the *Attack* and the later journals a bitter note suggestive of morbidity, masochism, and near-messianic self-understanding. What was distinctive with Kierkegaard, and far more interesting, was the subtlety of the attack as pressed indirectly in the earlier writings and the development of the idea of truth as subjectivity.

For two major reasons, the communication attempted in the pseudonymous literature from *Either/Or* through the *Postscript* had to be indirect. First, Kierkegaard sought an "existential com-

---

9. Cf. the picture of Jesus in *Training in Christianity*, pp. 26 ff., 40–65, 105–06.

10. Cf. *Training in Christianity*, pp. 108–09: "Christianity is not a doctrine. All the talk about offence in relation to Christianity as a doctrine is a misunderstanding, it is a device to mitigate the shock of offence at the scandal—as, for example, when one speaks of the offence of the doctrine of the God-Man and the doctrine of Atonement. No, the offence is related either to Christ or to the fact of being oneself a Christian."

One would like to know to what extent, if at all, Kierkegaard was familiar with the development of kenotic Christologies in Germany in the 1840s.

munication," that is, a communication of a mode of existing rather than a doctrine. Second, as we have noted, the dominant presuppositions and confusions of the age which led men to believe that they were already Christians were indeed such as to make Christianity impossible. It had, therefore, to be exploded from within. This indirect attack, or propaedeutic, had itself two forms: the idea of the stages, showing the way from the aesthetic to the religious, and the critique of Hegel's logic and epistemology in order to allow a kind of thinking that would at least make Christianity possible.

AWAY FROM THE AESTHETIC!

In the doctrine of the "stages"—or, better, the spheres of existence, each of which is to be seen as both a way of life and a view of life—Kierkegaard begins to transform the question of the relation between Christianity and the natural or the rational (the question that had dominated the Enlightenment) into the question of the relation of the Christian to the human. The decisive question is not what Christianity means for a view of the world but what it means for the self. The stages are adumbrated especially in *Either/Or* (1843), *Fear and Trembling* (1843), and *Stages on Life's Way* (1845).

The point of departure was necessarily the distinction between the aesthetic and the ethical (*Either/Or*), for the aesthetic was the presupposition and principle of the present age. It was to be depicted wholly from within, allowed to speak for itself.[11] Through the self-presentation of the aesthetic style of life and its consequences, the reader might be able to recognize himself in his own situation. Nowhere, of course, were the elements of the aesthetic life, or the comparisons with other life styles, analytically set out by Kierkegaard. Rather, each author and character was a distinct exemplification; hence all summary descriptions are distortions and do violence to the variety and richness of characterization as well as to the mode of communication. Yet certain themes constantly recur. The aesthetic life is defined as immediacy in relation to the external. Its

11. Thus the pseudonymous nature of this writing is of critical importance. The authors are Kierkegaard's creations but they speak their own views. Though Kierkegaard took great pains for a time to give out the impression that his own life was that of an aesthete and an idler (see *Point of View*, pp. 45 ff.), he also emphasized the distinction by the simultaneous publication of *Discourses* under his own name. By thus hiding himself, Kierkegaard hoped to engage the reader not as one professing to be a Christian and speaking from outside his reader's world, but rather by finding the reader where he was.

fundamental determination is from the finite and the accidental. Its world is one of fortune and misfortune, success and failure as outwardly determined. Love—which is supremely illustrative of the contrast between the aesthetic and the ethical—is for the aesthetic life-view a succession of first loves: it is one of the occasions, it is part of an experiment, it is uncertain, it requires outward qualifications and a series of finite justifications, it is secretive, an affair between only two persons. Engagement is for the aesthete more beautiful than marriage, marriage has its goal in personal enjoyment and is a matter of continual avoidance of disappointment, boredom is the great evil —and so on. The consequence of the aesthetic mode of existence is melancholy and despair.

The decisive distinction between the ethical and the aesthetic is suggested not only by the great differences in the style of their presentations—the aesthete is flowery and colorful, the ethical man by comparison is turgid and plain, appearing less profound and eloquent—but more vividly by their being placed in the separate volumes of *Either/Or*. Between the volumes intervenes the choice, which cannot be put in the book. The transition is not a movement in thought but a movement in the self, a resolution, a decision—and the way out of the aesthetic is thus the willing of despair.[12] The meaning of life centers in a choice. It is more a matter of choosing deeply, with energy, than of choosing "rightly," for the crucial decision is to live under the determinants of good and evil, rather than to decide between particular goods and evils. Kierkegaard had no interest in denying the objectivity of values, but for the sake of the fundamental distinction, it was sufficient to assume that the particular right or the good will easily enough emerge with a sufficient degree of choice; whereas without the primary acceptance of the "ought" and the universality of the obligation, any discussion of particular goods is pointless. The Kantian dimension of Kierkegaard's idea of the universality of the ethical is evident.

The choice of the ethical, that is, of the self in relation to the universally or eternally valid, is precisely the choice of the self. It is the movement from outward to inward determination, it is the act of freedom, the realization of potentiality. It is thus the emergence of the self, the actualization of spirit, the self's giving birth to itself by finding itself in its eternal validity. Thus the ethical is that whereby a man becomes what he becomes, whereas the aesthetic is

12. *Either/Or*, trans. Walter Lowrie (Garden City, N.Y., 1959), 2 : 212 ff.

that whereby a man is what he is. Concretely, the ethical man's duty and task emerges where he is. His duty is his "calling" with respect to whatever his talent may be. His talent is accidental but in no way determinative for the ethical. The ethical is the demand that one be all he can be; thus each person can do just as much that is essential as any other. Friendship and marriage become the natural examples of the ethical life: here are constancy, inward determination and qualification, openness, choice of reality and thought in relation to it rather than to a poetized ideality.[13]

In *Fear and Trembling*, the most beautiful of the literary productions, a third sphere of life is added, the religious. The contrast is drawn between the knight of faith and the knight of infinite resignation. Abraham, in the story of the sacrifices of Isaac, is the representative of Christian faith. He is described, however, from the viewpoint of one who has not gone beyond the level of infinite resignation, that is, of the ethical, and who therefore has no categories by which Abraham can be made intelligible. Just as the aesthete cannot give an adequate theoretical rendering of his own position because his immediacy is below the level of the universal, so Abraham, who is above the level of the universal, cannot be understood by one at the ethical level. His hope remains simply paradoxical. The commandment of God to sacrifice Isaac comes to Abraham as something absolutely particular, in opposition to the universally valid ethical demand. Thus the ethical, for the man of faith, becomes the temptation, the good which keeps him from doing God's will. The consequence of this is the "teleological suspension" of the ethical—not its abolition, but a paradoxical expression of the particularity of the individual's absolute relation to this particular God. The command no longer has the universal validity of the self's own consciousness but is external.

Similarly, the knight of faith returns and holds fast to the finite (Abraham's hope for the return of Isaac). The farthest movement within the ethical is that of infinite resignation, the giving up of all finite goods (thus the tragic hero is the model). One can think his way through to this point. But the knight of faith, having made the move of infinite resignation, comes back and lives in and with the finite and temporal, though only by means of a relationship with God that cannot be comprehended on the level of understanding,

13. On the ethical, see "Equilibrium" in *Either/Or*, vol. 2, and "Various Observations about Marriage" in *Stages on Life's Way*.

that is, on the level of the universal and ethical, or the ordinary consciousness. The knight of faith thus looks outwardly more like an aesthete or a Philistine, but he is inwardly qualified by a double movement of spirit, through infinite resignation to faith. The sphere of the (Christianly) religious is thus characterized especially by the particularity of the God-relationship and the return to the finite.[14]

The number of the spheres of existence was not the decisive aspect for Kierkegaard, and he does not always speak of three or the same three. One may with equal validity identify three spheres above the aesthetic: the ethical, the spiritually religious which is not yet Christian (religiousness A in the *Postscript*), and the spiritually religious which is defined as Christian (religiousness B). One may also think of the ethico-religious as a continuum including the ethical and religiousness A. Much more important is the relationship of the spheres. On the one hand, it is possible to speak of the lower as included in the higher. The aesthetic is not abolished but dethroned in the ethical. The aesthetic provides the raw material of every man's life, its absoluteness is excluded in the ethical but it is left in its relativity. The individual does not become another nature. That is, the aesthetic and immediate is relegated to a subordinate position, it is purified and transformed and becomes a contributing element in the ethical formation of personality. The religious, similarly, is not the abolition of the ethical (Kierkegaard does not even speak of dethronement here) but its fulfillment. The ethical is the absolute, the category of eternity and universality, and it remains the task for every individual. The ethical is an expression for the God-relationship, so that Kierkegaard can speak of the ethico-religious, especially in the *Postscript,* where immanent religiousness (religiousness A) is still within the determinants of the ethical. Christian existence, further, takes into itself the unconditionality of the ethical and the depth of religious suffering and guilt which are characteristic of the pathos of religiousness A. Religiousness B possesses the pathos of A and also the peculiar pathos of discrimination, of particularity (see pp. 310–13 below).

14. Drawing on a half-concealed summary statement in the "Panegyric upon Abraham" in *Fear and Trembling* (Princeton, 1941), pp. 19–20, one may compare the stages in a four-fold way: in relation to what men expect, to what men love, to what men strive for, and to the means of apprehension. The aesthete expects the possible, the ethical man the eternal, and the religious man the impossible. Love, similarly, is of the self, of others, and of God. Man strives to overcome the world, with himself or to master himself, and with God. The aesthete apprehends by the senses, the ethical man by the understanding, and the religious man by faith.

But the stages are not continuous with each other either in thought or in life. The ethical is marked by a transition from immediacy to the universal, and faith by a return to the individual. These are transitions only by choice, venture, decision, determination of the self. Despair is called the transition to the ethical. Since the aesthetic, with its immediate determination, always leads to melancholy and thence to despair, all men are "objectively" in despair. But the move to the ethical requires a willing to despair, a choosing of despair by despairing, whereby one breaks through to the ethical. In a related way, the movement to faith—whether from infinite resignation to faith (as in *Fear and Trembling*) or from immanent religiousness to Christian faith (as in the *Postscript*)—requires the "leap" par excellence. It is a life-transition that requires divine assistance, an absolute choice and venture.

The purpose of the distinctions was not, for Kierkegaard, to lay out a curriculum vitae or a necessary succession of temporal movements for each life. The "three" stages are better understood as constituents of a life which can come to faith; the aesthetic is always there, and faith can exist only "beyond" the ethical decision.[15] Most important was to show up the illusion of Christendom by enabling men to see that their lives were in fact not Christianly qualified but essentially aesthetic or at most ethical, and to make absolutely clear that no one starts in faith (as opposed to Hegel's idea of faith as immediacy) but proceeds to faith only by movements of freedom, choice, decision, resolution. To make these things clear does not produce Christianity, but it at least helps to make plain what becoming a Christian means.

Away from the System: Thought and Existence

The program of the *Philosophical Fragments* (1844) and its much longer "sequel" the *Concluding Unscientific Postscript* (1846) was also directed to the question of what it means to become a Christian. In the "asthetic works" the movement was away from the aesthetic to Christianity, in the *Fragments* and the *Postscript* it was away from the system, from speculation as exemplified in the Hegelian system, in order to become a Christian. Yet this was not another program but the same one, for it was precisely the system that supported the illusion, and in both lines of development Kierkegaard was dealing

15. Kierkegaard's suggestion that woman can move directly from the aesthetic to the religious is probably to be seen as a function of his peculiar attitude toward woman generally.

with the problem of the nature of thinking and existing. Thus the *Postscript,* which was apparently really intended as a conclusion, only presented more directly the problem of becoming a Christian, and at the end of it Kierkegaard avowed his authorship of the pseudonymous literature.

The attack on Hegel's view of Christianity, however, was also indirect, taking the form of a critique of Hegel's understanding of truth. Kierkegaard judged that it was Hegel's view of truth that committed him to his view of Christianity, hence that was the essential place to combat him. Kierkegaard's counterview of thought and truth was to be at least commensurate with Christianity. It did not make Christianity true or necessary, but only possible (though at some points Kierkegaard's view of truth, even of logic, seems necessitated by his idea of Christianity). Hegel's view of truth, however, made Christianity in the New Testament sense impossible. The attack on Hegel was two-pronged: on the one hand, it was a critique of Hegel's epistemology and logic; on the other hand, it took the form of the counterposing of subjective to objective truth.

First, then, against any suggestion that Kierkegaard was an irrationalist, it must be insisted that he was a logical realist. There was for him a logical order, which is not arbitrary but is the way one must think if he thinks rightly. Logic is not knowledge. Knowledge involves an existence claim, whereas logic deals with possibles; it is "empty" and does not change with the content of knowledge. But logic is the necessary instrument of knowing. With respect to the nature of logic, Kierkegaard was content with the ancients, especially the Eleatics: there is one logic, valid and always the same, whose highest principle is tautology, and whose characteristic relation is implication, providing necessary conclusions in which nothing is contained that was not in the premises. Here A never equals not-A. The Eleatics (i.e. Parmenides) made the mistake of transferring thought to existence, thus concluding that nothing comes into being but everything simply is. That is a true statement for logic, but not for existence. The error was not in the logic but in making the criteria of logic the criteria of reality, which involves becoming.[16]

It was a fundamental error of Hegel that he too identified thought and being and he abandoned valid logic, abolishing the principle of contradiction and introducing "becoming" into logic. For the latter step Kierkegaard had only scorn: "Hegel's unparalleled discovery,

16. Cf. *The Concept of Dread* (Princeton, 1944), p. 12.

the subject of so unparalleled an admiration, namely, the introduction of movement into logic, is a sheer confusion of logical science." In logic, the only "movement" is that of logical implication, and a logical system is possible, relating distinct concepts and possibilities. Becoming, or transition, however, "cannot be anything but a witty conceit in logic. It belongs in the sphere of historical freedom." [17]

The issue here was one of the greatest practical import, for the Hegelian confusion of the categories (including especially the concepts of time and eternity, God and man, good and evil) was exactly what was expressed in the "present age," with its lack of critical and absolute significance for the categories of good and evil, its awful leveling, and its abolition of the principle of contradiction. Christianity requires "conceptual and terminological definiteness and firmness," it requires a qualitative dialectic that recognizes real qualitative distinctions, in contrast to the "quantitative dialectic" in which everything merges into everything else through a more and less.[18]

Knowledge, for Kierkegaard, involves a claim upon existence, a uniting of concept and thing through an act. Existence is never given *in* thought, for it is not an essence or a logical implicate but brute factual being, in which there is never a more or less (so Kierkegaard can say that "a fly, when it exists, has as much being as God; . . . factual existence is wholly indifferent to any and all variations in essence").[19] Existence cannot be got out of the understanding; there is no logical movement from the possible to the actual—hence the absurdity of the ontological argument for God, and indeed of all the arguments, which never pull existence out at the end unless it has been put in at the beginning.

The reason existence cannot be got out of thought is, again, that existence means freedom, becoming, the transition from the possible to the actual; and this transition is precisely what cannot be contained in logic. Thus a system of existence is impossible for us. Therefore "historical knowledge"—knowledge of what comes into being—always involves uncertainty. There can be certainty in the realm of logic, but never about that which becomes.[20]

17. *Postscript*, p. 99; *Concept of Dread*, p. 74; cf. pp. 73 ff.

18. See *Authority and Revelation* (Princeton, 1955), pp. 165 and passim.

19. *Philosophical Fragments*, trans. David F. Swenson (Princeton, 1944), pp. 32–33.

20. The approximation process applies not only to the collecting of evidence about the historically past (cf. *Postscript*, pp. 24 ff.) but also to all assertions about existence. Thus "historical knowledge," especially in the *Fragments*, can refer to knowledge of any existent.

Historical knowledge therefore involves a leap, a believing of existence then a reasoning about it. Existence can be called a paradox, that is, something which thought cannot think, and all knowledge can be said to involve a first level of faith, which is like belief in God and the existence of Christ, though it is not yet faith in the eminent sense, for this can be directed only toward the absolute paradox.[21]

In a qualitative dialectic, further, eternal truth remains utterly independent of "historical" proof. The endurance of eighteen hundred years has nothing to do with the proof of eternal truth, which is from first to last equally true, in its last instant not more than in its first. Contrary to the Hegelian view, eternal truth does not "unfold" in time; that idea is sheer confusion of time and eternity and it supports the popular illusions. "It is important above all that there be fixed an unshakable qualitative difference between *the historical element in Christianity* (the paradox that the eternal came into existence once in time) and *the history of* Christianity, the history of its followers, etc." [22] For one's eternal happiness to be based on a moment in time is in no sense to make that happiness more certain through the passage of time. There can be no immanent historical proofs for this movement of the self, and indeed the task is not to make Christianity "plausible" by such proofs but to make it implausible. "The fact that the eternal once came into existence in time is not a something which has to be tested in time, not something which *men are to test,* but is the paradox by which *men are to be tested.*" [23]

Away from the System: Truth Is Subjectivity

The second prong of the attack on Hegel's idea of truth (and that of the age and of the Enlightenment and of philosophy generally) was the distinction between objective and subjective truth, developed especially in the *Postscript.* Here Kierkegaard brought to sharpest expression, though in a way quite his own, a dominant motif in the

21. For the preceding discussion, see *Fragments,* pp. 31 ff., 60 ff.

22. *Authority and Revelation,* trans. Walter Lowrie (Princeton, 1955), p. 58. This work (the "book on Adler") is important on the point and belongs with the treatment of contemporaneousness in the *Fragments* (pp. 78–93) and the discussions in the *Postscript* (pp. 45–47 and 86 ff.). In the latter, Kierkegaard found Lessing useful; even the historical element in Christianity was like the eternal truth that could not be proved by accidental truths of history.

23. *Authority and Revelation,* p. 58.

theology of the whole nineteenth century: the turn to the religious subject—the subject's stance, his point of view, his "interest," his willing and choosing—as the point from which theological reflection has to begin.[24]

By "objective truth" Kierkegaard meant truth as the quality of a proposition, its character of correspondence to reality. To this, Kierkegaard was not at all indifferent. Objective truth is important not only at the level of natural science and ordinary existence, it is also essential in stating correctly what Christianity is—and that Kierkegaard certainly thought it possible to do (see *Fragments; Postscript*, especially pp. 330 ff.; *Authority and Revelation;* and *Training in Christianity*). But the definition of Christianity does not give its existence. The crucial truth here is not objective but subjective, since the problem is that of *becoming* a Christian. That is, it is possible to know what Christianity is without being a Christian; but it is not possible to know what it is to *be* a Christian without being one. And the Christian must know what Christianity is and be able to say it, so far as he is a Christian. In relation to a doctrine, "understanding" is the maximum attainment, and direct communication of the truth is possible. But "in relation to an existential communication"—that is, of what it is to *be* a Christian—"existing in it is the maximum of attainment, and understanding it is merely an evasion of the task." [25]

With respect to the problem of becoming a Christian, then, truth *is* subjectivity, a quality of the existing individual, of the thinking person rather than of the thought. That is why Hegel was so comical: he left out the thinking subject whose *act* is necessary to get the supposedly presuppositionless system going at all. And that is why Hegel and the present age were so disastrously in error: they had left the subject for the "objective" and thereby made the subject accidental and existence something indifferent. Ethically and religiously speaking, this direction must be exactly reversed. Truth is the appropriation of subjectivity, it is a mode of existence, of the subject's relation to the truth.

> When the question of truth is raised in an objective manner, reflection is directed objectively to the truth, as an object to which the knower is related. Reflection is not focused on the relationship,

---

24. See above, pp. 59–61. Here Kierkegaard moved especially in the tradition of Luther and Pascal, and in the 19th century he belongs above all with Coleridge and William James.

25. *Postscript*, p. 332; cf. p. 339.

however, but upon the question of whether it is the truth to which
the knower is related. If only the object to which he is related is the
truth, the subject is accounted to be in the truth. When the question
of the truth is raised subjectively, reflection is directed subjectively
to the nature of the individual's relationship; if only the mode of
this relationship is in the truth, the individual is in the truth even
if he should happen to be thus related to what is not true. [*Postscript,* p. 178]

For the subjective thinker, then, thinking is always by this existing
individual. It refers to an either/or, not a both/and. It is the
thinking of the whole man who is deciding, with the will at the
highest point of tension. As in the ethical question it is a matter of
choosing to relate oneself to good and evil, so in the God-relationship
one must decide to believe or not to believe. The God-relationship
cannot merely be kept dangling, waiting for a proof, for the question
is not of "objective certainty" or even of coherence, but "Am I in
the truth?" Not, "Does God exist?" but, "Am I in relation to God?"
The question is always of truth for the self. And subjectivity is a
matter of passion, of the appropriation of inwardness in passionate
relation to the truth. The mode of the relation rather than the object is crucial for religion, the how rather than the what.

The ideal of truth as subjectivity is infinite passion, the infinite
concern for one's eternal happiness. The greater the passion the
less the concern for objectivity. An infinite passion toward a false
object (an idol) is a higher truth than a relative passion toward an
"objective truth" (the true God). "The highest truth attainable for
an existing individual" is "an objective uncertainty held fast in an
appropriation-process of the most passionate inwardness" (*Postscript,*
p. 182). And this definition of truth is also "an equivalent expression for faith." Although Kierkegaard did not hold this definition to
be adequate for the specifically Christian faith, it nonetheless makes
clear in part why Kierkegaard could bypass the historical problem
as it had been posed by Strauss (even though Kierkegaard had been
directed to Lessing's formulations by reading Strauss's *Glaubenslehre*). In one sense Kierkegaard simply did not really accept the
historical question, since he had no doubts about the reliability of
the gospel tradition and judged Strauss's criticism to be godlessness;
but he could on the other hand insist that neither radically negative
conclusions about the gospel reports nor full substantiation of them
as historical records could have any bearing on the act of faith. Com-

plete proof of the reliability of the Bible could not bring faith one step nearer to actualization, nor could negative criticism abolish Christianity or damage faith—for faith is not a matter of objective truth-judgment about Christ but a mode of relationship to Christ, the contemporaneity which is passionate inwardness (*Postscript,* pp. 25 ff., 86 ff.).

Within the sphere of ethical or immanent religiousness (religiousness A), Kierkegaard further develops the truth of subjectivity in the three-fold expression of existential pathos (*Postscript,* pp. 347 ff.). The *initial* expression is the "absolute direction toward the absolute *telos*" and a "relative relation to relative ends." Everything in existence, that is, must be brought into conformity with this highest good, eternal happiness. If there is anything one is not willing to give up for the sake of his eternal happiness, the relationship is not there. The absolute distinction here does not mean indifference to the finite, as in monasticism, but rather relativization of the finite in which one remains. An absolute telos exists for the individual only when he yields it an absolute devotion.

The *essential* expression of existential pathos is suffering, which is not here a matter of misfortune accidental to existence (as in an aesthetic mode of existence), but derives essentially from the togetherness in existence of the absoluteness of the religious relation and the particularities of life. This is a suffering of pure inwardness, different from the voluntarily assumed outward suffering of the Christian life as described in Kierkegaard's later works, though not inconsistent with that. It comes from the required transformation of the self, its dying away from all natural roots in the immediate, to an absolute relation to God. It comes also from the fact that the religious individual is separated from his eternal happiness, which cannot be laid hold of in time. And the "deepest thinkable" suffering of true religiosity derives from standing related to God in an absolutely decisive manner and yet being unable to find any decisive *external* (i.e. finite) expression for the relation (see *Postscript,* pp. 493–94).

The *decisive* expression of existential pathos is guilt, the consciousness of the inability to meet the absolute demand because a bad beginning has already been made and guilt is present at every point. It is total guilt because it is in relation to God and an eternal happiness (i.e. a qualitative rather than a quantitative determination). Consciousness of guilt is the decisive expression because it is the deepest plunge into existence, a kind of absolute subjectivity, the most concrete expression of existence because the self is unqualifiedly at the center of the problem. Yet even this disruption of the God-relationship is supported by a consciousness of God. It still lies on the continuum of God-relationship within the religion of immanence and is thus the farthest the self can go in the expression of its subjectivity, the deepest self-definition.

SUBJECTIVITY AS UNTRUTH

Christian religiousness, for Kierkegaard, required a still further movement, a leap or breach comparable only to the transition from the aesthetic to the ethical, but now a movement which the self cannot give to itself. It is a return to the objective.[26] For Christianity the object of passionate inwardness is by no means a matter of indifference. While the mode of relationship is not that of "objective truth," there is only one object to which Christian subjectivity may be directed, namely, the God-man. Further, while this relationship is not to a doctrine, but to that Person, it is plain that Kierkegaard was committed to a quite definite understanding of the God-man and to a broad range of items of Christian orthodoxy. He was, quite simply, a theological conservative. While he had no interest in argument about two-natures Christology, for example, he had no thought of amending the Chalcedonian Christology. His insistence on terminological clarity and definiteness and on a qualitative dialectic meant, moreover, a rigorous maintenance of the antithetical nature of the relation between the concepts of God and man, eternity and time.[27]

Christianity comes into existence when the object of infinite passion is the absolute paradox of the God-man and Christ becomes the pattern. The God-relationship is no longer found within oneself, as in immanent religiousness, but in relation to something outside oneself. Even though in religiousness A one's concern is for the

26. These aspects of Christian faith are depicted particularly in the figure of Abraham in *Fear and Trembling,* in the situation of the learner in *Philosophical Fragments,* and in religiousness B in the *Postscript.* See also, of course, *Sickness unto Death, Training in Christianity,* and *Authority and Revelation.*

27. *Authority and Revelation* is especially useful for understanding this side of Kierkegaard. It also makes clear Kierkegaard's unquestioning acceptance of a propositional view of revelation and his commitment to an idea of revelation and authority in which the authority of the disclosure has nothing to do with the content that is revealed but only with the source of the revelation.

eternal, still at that level God arises out of the passionate relationship. God thus comes into being for the ethical.

This object is a reality which is paradoxical in itself, the reality of God become man, eternity in time. Thereby the subjectivity of the existing individual becomes doubly paradoxical (paradox, again, meaning that which thought cannot think, which may include the alogical as well as the contradictory). A first level of paradox (the Socratic paradox, or the paradox of merely immanent religiousness) comes into being whenever the eternal truth is posited or related to an existing individual. That paradox is not in the character of the eternal truth itself, but in its "objective uncertainty" and by virtue of the relation to it of an individual in time. But when the truth to which the individual is thus passionately related is not only objectively uncertain but is in itself a paradox (i.e. the eternal in time, God become man), then the relationship is doubly paradoxical, or "absolutely paradoxical," and one may properly speak of the "absurd." "Instead of the objective uncertainty, there is here a certainty, namely, that objectively it is absurd. . . . The absurd is . . . that God has come into being, has been born, has grown up, and so forth, . . . and this absurdity, held fast in the passion of inwardness, is faith." [28]

But precisely at this point subjectivity as truth has reached a still higher level. "Existence has stamped itself upon the existing individual a second time."

> Since the paradox is not in the first instance itself paradoxical (but only in its relationship to the existing individual), it does not repel with a sufficient intensive inwardness. For without risk there is no faith, and the greater the risk the greater the faith; the more objective security the less inwardness (for inwardness is precisely subjectivity), and the less objective security the more profound the possible inwardness. When the paradox is paradoxical in itself, it repels the individual by virtue of its absurdity, and the corresponding passion of inwardness is faith. [*Postscript,* pp. 186, 188]

Christian faith, therefore, involves both a return to the objective and an intensification of subjectivity because of the nature of the object. It seems almost that Kierkegaard was arguing for the emergence of the internally paradoxical, the God-man, as the only possible object for the final development of inwardness. Each degree of subjectivity has correlation with the greatness of the object, and

28. *Postscript,* p. 188; cf. pp. 186 ff.

the appropriate object emerges for each degree of inwardness. The
"subjectivity" of the aesthetic stage is related to the finite world in
such a way that the subject is immediately determined by the external. With ethical or ethico-religious subjectivity emerges the relation to the eternal (both as the moral law and as God the eternal).
But that cannot be the highest inwardness, for the eternal essential
truth is not in itself a paradox. Hence the development of subjectivity finally requires the qualification of the doubly paradoxical,
of the individual in time being related to the eternal in time. At
any rate, in his definition of what it is, subjectively, to become a
Christian, Kierkegaard was unequivocal about the object for that
inwardness:

> The decision lies in the subject. The appropriation is the paradox-
> ical inwardness which is specifically different from all other inward-
> ness. The thing of being a Christian is not determined by the *what*
> of Christianity but by the *how* of the Christian. This *how* can only
> correspond with one thing, the absolute paradox. . . . *To believe*
> is specifically different from all other appropriation and inwardness.
> Faith is the objective uncertainty due to the repulsion of the absurd
> held fast by the passion of inwardness, which in this instance is in-
> tensified to the utmost degree. [*Postscript,* p. 540]

Yet it must be emphasized that the absolute paradox, for Kierkegaard, was not in the first instance a doctrine, a merely rational contradiction and in that sense absurd and an offence. The idea of the
God-man did for him involve such a contradiction, from the standpoint of the understanding, because the concepts are quite opposed.
But the reasons for affirming this rational antithesis also, and primarily, include its correspondence to the real offence, the declaration that man is in error and that for Christianity *subjectivity is
untruth.*

To say that subjectivity is untruth means essentially, for Christianity, that man does not possess truth within himself, by virtue
of his inwardness. The attainment of this truth is not a matter of
self-realization. Man is given his truth by God. Translated into
epistemological language in the *Fragments,* this is to say that the
learner does not come to the truth by recollection of what he already knows (the Socratic doctrine, in which the teacher is merely
an occasion for the learner's knowing), but rather the learner is given
both the truth and the capacity for apprehending the truth and is
thus entirely dependent on the teacher (that is, the Savior). In theo-

logical language, as developed especially in *The Concept of Dread,* the *Postscript,* and *Sickness unto Death,* the discontinuity is expressed by saying that sin has intervened and faith is a gift from God. The consciousness of the self as a sinner is a *sine qua non* of Christianity.

Here again it is crucial to set Kierkegaard in the context of nineteenth-century theology. He was impressed by Kant's doctrine of radical evil, though not uncritically so. He was close to Julius Müller (of whom he thought highly) and the neopietists in judging sin to be the stumbling point for all the idealist versions of Christianity—though his psychological analysis of the origin of sin (in *The Concept of Dread* and *Sickness unto Death*) was quite different, and far richer, than Müller's. And in his account, Kierkegaard stood quite in the tradition of both Schleiermacher and Hegel in freeing the idea of original sin from a mere historical association with a first human being and in establishing its universal ingredience in human existence.

Sin is to be sharply distinguished from the "guilt" which was the decisive expression of existential pathos in religiousness A. The individual can acquire the latter for himself, but not the consciousness of sin, which is a new medium for existence. Sin has to be disclosed to him. The knowledge of it is a breach in his consciousness. It is a measure he cannot give to himself. Sin is despair *before God,* before the Christian God. More precisely, "sin is, after having been informed by a revelation from God what sin is, then before God in despair not to will to be oneself, or before God in despair to will to be oneself." Thus it is by the concept of sin that Christianity "distinguishes itself qualitatively and most decisively from paganism. . . . Neither paganism nor the natural man knows what sin is." [29]

The offence of Christianity is therefore not simply or essentially an affair of the intellect; it is the offence of the self's being given a new measure before and by God (sin is of course not comprehensible by the understanding, for it is a qualitative leap, a movement of freedom, such that sin must be said to posit itself—see *The Concept of Dread*). Sin means an alteration of the subject's existence; by coming into life he has become other than he was, thus a new crea-

---

29. *Sickness unto Death,* trans. Walter Lowrie (New York, 1954), pp. 227, 220. Note that the revelation of sin is in this discussion quite distinct from the disclosure of grace (cf. pp. 244 ff.). It seems that one can know the true God as the judge of sin without knowing Christ and the forgiveness of sins.

tion is needed. This is the "offence to the human heart" (*Fragments*, p. 86) which is the real obstacle to becoming a Christian. "The exister must have lost continuity with himself, must have become another (not different from himself within himself), and then, by receiving the condition from the Deity, he must have become a new creature. The contradiction is that this thing of becoming a Christian begins with the miracle of creation, and that this occurs to one who already is created" (*Postscript,* p. 510).

And so we return to the concrete figure of the God-man in the New Testament, the inviter and the pattern. The "Halt now" is imposed simply by the one who in humiliation says "Come hither." The response is either offence and continuation in the despair which is sin, or the faith in which one is suspended over seventy thousand fathoms. Those were finally the only options, as Kierkegaard saw it. The historical problem could be set aside as a question of "objective" truth irrelevant to the decision which is religious faith. And the doubt about the possibility of theology with which most of the rest of the century was struggling was something into which Kierkegaard did not enter at all. The religious judgment was for him of an entirely different order.

Yet this is not to say that Kierkegaard stood outside the nineteenth-century problem setting for theology. Whether historical and metaphysical doubts and questions were real problems or only misunderstandings of the nature of religious truth was to continue to lie at the deepest level of theological concern in the nineteenth century and in the twentieth as well. Kierkegaard did not first pose these problems, and his own formulations were more influential in the twentieth century than in his day; but in his stand he brought to clearest expression one of the major ways in which theology in the nineteenth century was seeking to resolve its difficulties and overcome its embarrassment.

Index

Absolute religion: Christianity in Hegel, 99–100

Absolute Spirit: function of in Hegel, 93–94

Addison, Joseph, 49; on nature, 33

Ahlstrom, Sydney E., 10, 11

Allen, Ethan, 129*n*

American Revolution, 3, 15, 108, 127

Ames, William, 23

Annet, Peter: and radical deism, 38–39

Anthropomorphism: and Coleridge, 120; and Feuerbach, 175

Apologetics: for Schleiermacher, 70

Aquinas, Thomas, 144

Arminianism, 128, 154; Edwards on, 26; and Calvinism, 108–09

Arndt, Johann: and pietism, 23

Arnold, Matthew, 142; on Christianity, 188; on religion and culture, 188–89; on religion and morality, 189

Arnold, Thomas: and the Broad Church, 186; on religion, 186–87

Astruc, Jean: on literary styles in Genesis, 41

Atonement, doctrine of: in Hofmann, 225

Augsburg Confession, 200

Authority, principle of: in Lutheran confessionalism, 197–98

Barnes, Albert: on Darwinism, 204*n*

Barth, Karl, 8, 15, 17, 18, 170, 177; on pietism, 28; on Kant, 47

Bauer, Bruno, 7, 88, 142, 143

Baumgarten, Michael, 36

Baur, Ferdinand Christian, 60*n*, 105, 141, 142, 145, 148, 151, 152, 161, 168, 170, 198, 231, 233, 235, 265; and historical theology, 155–60; on the historical Jesus, 155–59; divergence from Schleiermacher, 156; on faith, 157; divergence from Hegel, 157–58; on Christianity, 158; on rationalism, 159; on supernaturalism, 159; on historical methodology, 159–60

Bayle, Pierre, 54; on religious toleration, 32

Beck, Johann Tobias, 11*n*, 143, 193, 218; and confessionalism, 198; on *Innere Mission*, 198; on biblical truth, 199; on the Kingdom of God, 199–200

Beecher, Lyman, 129, 144, 200

Bellamy, Joseph, 128

Bengal, J. A., 24

Bentham, Jeremy, 3, 110, 136, 137, 191; on utilitarian ethics, 111–12

Bible, and history: in the Enlightenment, 40–41

Bible, and inspiration: in Coleridge, 124–26; in Hengstenberg, 195–96; in Hodge, 203; in Hofmann, 221–22; in Rothe, 288–89

Bible, authority of, 5; in the Enlightenment, 40–41; and morality, 59; in Schleiermacher, 85; in Channing, 133; in Hodge, 201; in Harless, 220; in Erlangen theology, 222; in Hofmann, 222. *See also* biblical criticism

Bible societies, 110

Biblical criticism: and Coleridge, 123–26; and Strauss, 147–48; and *Essays and Reviews*, 168–69; and the Oxford Movement, 209; and kenoticism, 233; and Maurice, 256; and Dorner, 276; and Kierkegaard, 308–09

Biblical realism. *See* Beck, J. T.

Biedermann, Alois Emanuel, 105; and the Swiss Union, 160; influence of Strauss, 161; influence of Hegel, 161–62; influence of Schleiermacher, 162; on religious language, 162–64; on Christology, 164–67

Blumhart, Johann Christoph, 11*n*

Böhler, Peter: influence on Wesley, 24

Broad Church: movement in England, 142; and *Essays and Reviews*, 167; meaning of, 186*n;* and Maurice, 242, 246

Brownson, Orestes A., 180*n*, 183, 228

Buckham, John W., 10*n*

Bultmann, Rudolf, 85

Bushnell, Horace, 3, 13, 21, 109, 112, 127*n*, 144, 146, 189 228, 242; and the question of Christ, 6; and natural religion, 36;

Bushnell, Horace (*continued*)
  on religious language, 60, 259–60; and
  Taylor, 136; on Christian comprehensiveness, 258–59; on dogmatism, 261; on
  rationalism, 261; and experiential theology, 262–63; on moral agency, 263–65;
  and Christology, 265–68; on redemption, 265; on subjective–objective Christianity, 267–68

Calvin, John, 60, 78
Calvinism: and revivalism, 26; and Ar-
  minianism, 108–09; in America, 128, 130
Cambridge Platonists, 21, 35, 38, 112
Cambridge Triumvirate, 13, 124, 242
Campbell, George, 133
Campbell, Macleod, 248n
Canz, Israel Gottlieb, 36
Carlyle, Thomas, 112, 184, 186; on reli-
  gion, 187–88; on the Victorian age, 187
Carpov, Jakob, 36
Catholic Emancipation Act (1829): effect
  on Coleridge, 121
Catholicism: Schleiermacher's view of,
  68. *See also* Roman Catholicism
Chalmers, Thomas: and evangelicals in
  Scotland, 191–92
Channing, William Ellery, 3, 5, 127, 179,
  183, 226; and liberal Christianity, 131–
  32; and reason, 132; on Unitarianism,
  132–33; on biblical authority, 133; on
  dignity of man, 134–35; on sin, 135; and
  Emerson, 136; on supernaturalism, 137
Channing, William Henry, 180n
Chartist movement, 3
Christian Socialism, 4, 6, 145, 183; and
  Maurice, 250–51
Christology: problem of, 6; in Schleier-
  macher, 83–85; in Hegel, 104–05; focus
  of Protestant theology, 145–46; in Baur,
  155–59; in Biedermann, 164–67; in
  Feuerbach, 176; in Emerson, 180; in
  Liddon, 205–07; and Mercersburg the-
  ology, 230; and kenoticism, 233–40; in
  Maurice, 247–53; in Bushnell, 265–68; in
  Dorner, 280–82; and Rothe, 289n; in
  Kierkegaard, 310–11
Church and state: question of, 193. *See
  also* Church of England; Lutheran con-
  fessionalism

Church history: for Baur, 155–57, 159–60;
  and Mercersburg theology, 230–31
Church of England: and evangelicalism,
  109; and rationalism, 109; and supernaturalism, 110; Coleridge's view of, 123;
  Maurice's view of, 251–52. *See also* Oxford Movement
Civil War, American, 141
Clarke, James Freeman, 180n
Clarke, Samuel, 36
Clough, Arthur Hugh, 186n
Coleridge, Samuel Taylor, 3, 5, 13, 16, 21,
  59, 108, 110, 127, 136, 137, 142, 144, 167,
  187, 191, 262; on Kant, 48; and romanticism, 52; on faith and reason, 60, 114n,
  115–20; opposition to Bentham and Paley, 112; influence of Wordsworth, 113;
  and Schleiermacher, 113, 115; rejection
  of religious rationalism, 114–15; and
  evangelicalism, 115; on imagination, 117;
  on the moral conscience and religion,
  117–19; on original sin, 118; on anthropomorphism, 120; and deism, 120;
  on supernaturalism, 120; on the personeity of God, 121; on national
  churches, 121–23; on Christianity, 122–
  23; on the Church of England, 123; on
  inerrancy and biblical truth, 124–26;
  and Newman, 216; and Maurice, 243,
  244
Collegia pietatis, 23; and religious fellowship, 28–29
Collins, Anthony, 36; and religious controversies, 31; and radical deism, 38
Comte, Auguste, 170, 183, 247; on humanistic religion, 183–84; on sociology, 184
Confessionalism, 61, 145; and theology, 19;
  and German Lutheranism, 143, 194–98;
  and Calvinism, 143; and Oxford Movement, 143; and American Lutheranism,
  200–01; and Princeton theology, 201;
  and Liddon, 204–05; and Erlangen theology, 219, 225–26; and kenoticism, 233;
  and mediation theology, 270; and Rothe,
  283–84, 291; and Kierkegaard, 292. *See
  also* Hodge, Charles; Hengstenberg,
  Ernst; Thomasius, Gottfried
Conservatism: and theology, 20; and revivalism, 191–93. *See also* confessionalism
Cousin, Victor, 262

Creation, doctrine of: in Hegel, 101-02
Creed, J. M., 13

Darwin, Charles, 4, 169, 170
Darwinism: and Hodge, 202–03; and Rothe, 287–88
Deism, 79, 109; and Edwards, 26; and religious toleration, 32; radical aspects of, 38–39; and original sin, 40; and Coleridge, 120
Demythologizing theology: in Schleiermacher and Hegel, 61–62
Denominationalism, 190; and Hodge, 201–02. See also confessionalism; sectarianism
Diderot, Denis, 39
Dilthey, Wilhelm Christian Ludwig, 85, 160
Discipleship: Kierkegaard on, 297
Diversity, principle of: in romanticism, 54–55
Dogmatism: and rationalism, 31; Bushnell on, 261
Dorner, Isaak August, 14, 16, 21, 105, 142, 144, 145, 146, 228, 231, 265; and subjectivism, 60; influence of Schleiermacher and Hegel, 274–76; on faith, 275–77; on biblical criticism, 276; and kenoticism, 278; on immutability of God, 278–79; on the Trinity, 279; on progressive Incarnation, 280–82
Dwight, Timothy, 129

Ecclesiology: and theology, 145; and confessionalism, 196–97; and Mercersburg theology, 231
Ecumenism, 190; and Mercersburg theology, 228–33; and Maurice, 246–47
Edwards, Jonathan, 13, 52, 128, 262; influence on Wesley, 24–26; and deism, 26; and Transcendentalism, 26; and evangelicalism, 26; influence of Locke, 26; on emotions, 28
Eichhorn, Johann G., 41, 124
Elliot-Binns, L. E., 10n
Emerson, Ralph Waldo, 3, 6, 7, 13, 52, 127, 133, 134, 142, 170, 183, 228; and romanticism, 52; and Channing, 136; and Feuerbach, 177–78; on transcendence, 178; on nature, 178; on the American man, 178–79; on sin, 179; on Eastern religions, 180; and Unitarianism,

180, 182; on religion, 180–81; on Jesus Christ, 181; and Parker, 183
Enlightenment, 3, 12, 61, 148; and internationalism, 15; and reason, 31–32; and Hegel, 88–89
Erasmus, Desiderius, 41
Erlangen theology, 8, 14, 19, 144, 194, 207, 227; and subjectivism, 60; and confessionalism, 219; theological principles of, 223; and mediation theology, 270
Ernesti, J. A., 37
Erskine, Thomas, 211
Essays and Reviews, 123, 186n, 209; and biblical criticism, 168–69; and Maurice, 256
Eucharist, doctrine of: in Mercersburg theology, 231–32. See also Sacraments
Eudaemonism, 91; and Bentham, 112
Evangelicalism: in America, 26; and Puritanism, 26; and Coleridge, 115; and Oxford Movement, 211–12; and Mercersburg theology, 228–29; and Maurice, 248, 252. See also revivalism
Evans, Marian, 167
Existentialism: and religion, 59–60
Experimental theology: in Bushnell, 262–63

Feuerbach, Ludwig, 3, 7, 88, 106, 142, 143, 145, 154, 161, 162, 163; and materialism, 170; and Hegel, 170, 171–72; and atheism, 171; and empiricism, 171–72; and theological anthropology, 171–72, 175; on religion, 173–75; on imagination, 174; on Christianity, 175–76; protest against theology, 176; on man, 176–77; and Emerson, 177–78
Fichte, I. H., 142
Fichte, J. G., 64, 69; and romanticism, 52; influence on Hegel, 90; on philosophy and religion, 91, 92
Finney, Charles G., 144; and revivalism, 129n, 192
Formalism: opposed by romanticism, 52
Forsyth, P. T., 112
Foster, F. H., 10n
Fourier, Charles, 183
Franco-Prussian War of 1871, 4
Frank, Franz Hermann Reinhold von, 9n, 218
Frank, Gustav, 8

Franke, August Hermann, 26; and pietism, 23

Franklin, Benjamin, 52

Frederick III, 24

French Revolution, 1n, 3, 15, 108, 191

Freud, Sigmund, 171

Froude, Richard Hurrell, 209, 210

Fundamentalism, 201, 206n

Furness, William H., 180n

German Protestant Union, 283

German theology: historical prejudice for, 9

Gess, Wolfgang Friedrich: and kenoticism, 234

Gibbs, Josiah W., 127n, 260n

Godet, Frédéric, 234

Godwin, William, 113

Goethe, Johann Wolfgang, 3, 54

Goodwin, C. W., 168

Görres, Johann Joseph: and romanticism, 52

Gospel of John: Strauss on, 151

Grace, doctrine of: in Schleiermacher, 83; in Maurice, 249–50

Great Awakening of 1740: in America, 15, 128; and pietism, 23, 26

Greek religion: in Hegel, 97–98

Groot, Petrus Hofstede de, 273

Grotius, Hugo, 41

Half-Way Covenant, 26

Hamilton, William, 254

Hampden, Renn Dickson: on religion and dogma, 211

Handy, Robert T., 11n

Hare, Julius, 16, 112, 186n, 187, 244

Harless, Adolf von, 218; and Erlangen theology, 219–21; conversion experience of, 219–20; on authority of the Bible, 220; on the church, 220–21

Harms, Claus, 194

Haroutunian, Joseph, 10n

Harrison, Frederic, 167

Hartley, David, 113

Hase, Karl A., 148

Hegel, Georg Wilhelm Friedrich, 3, 5, 59, 64, 84n, 108, 119, 142, 143, 144, 147, 150, 151, 154, 155, 156, 159, 163, 168, 277, 313; and German culture, 15; and romanticism, 52, 88–89; demythologizing

theology, 61–62; as philosopher and Christian, 86–87; and idealism, 88; relation to Enlightenment, 88–89; and dialectic, 89–90; on logic, 89–91; on Absolute Spirit, 91; on philosophy and religion, 91–92; on Christianity, 92, 99–103; on positive religion, 92, 93; on reconciliation, 92–93, 103; on religious consciousness, 94–95; on worship, 96; on the history of religions, 96–103; on natural religion, 96–97; on the religions of spiritual individuality, 97–99; on Absolute religion, 99–100; on the Reformation, 100; on the Trinity, 100–01; on creation, 101–02; on alienation and original sin, 102; on the incarnation, 103; and pantheism, 104; Christology of, 104–05; legacy of, 104–07; validation and theological statements, 105–07; contrast with Schleiermacher, 106–07; and Baur, 157–58; influence on Biedermann, 161–62; and Feuerbach, 170, 171–72; and mediation theology, 269–70; Müller's critique of, 272; influence on Dorner, 274; and Rothe, 286n, 290; Kierkegaard's critique of, 303–07

Heidegger, Martin, 85

Hengstenberg, Ernst W., 143, 199, 219, 222; and Lutheran confessionalism, 194–98; and biblical inspiration, 195–96; and authority in the church, 197–98

Herbert of Cherbury, 12; and natural religion, 35

Herder, Johann Gottfried, 52, 108; and pietism, 30; on history and the Bible, 41; on history and religion, 54; on Scripture, 54

Hermeneutics, 85. See also biblical criticism

Hermann, Wilhelm, 144, 218

Hirsch, Emanuel, 11, 12, 14, 145

Historical method: in Baur, 159–60

Historical theology: in Schleiermacher, 70; in Strauss, 152–54; in Baur, 155–60

Hobart, John Henry, 200n

Hobbs, Thomas, 33, 35; and the Bible, 40

Hedge, Frederic H., 180n

Hodge, Charles, 3, 228; and confessionalism, 201; on authority of the Bible, 201; on denominationalism, 201–02; and Princeton theology, 201–04; on the Bible and science, 202; on Darwinism, 202–03;

and Scottish philosophy, 202; and Taylorism, 202; and orthodox Calvinism, 202–04; and biblical inspiration, 203; on the task of theology, 203–04

Hofmann, Johannes C. K., 3, 83, 218, 219; on the historicity of Scripture, 221; on salvation history, 221–23; on the authority of the Bible, 222; on task of theology, 223–24; on the atonement, 225; influence on Luther research, 225

Hopkins, Samuel, 128, 133

Hort, F. J. A., 124

Houghton, Walter E., 10n

Humanistic religion: in Comte, 183–84

Hume, David, 12, 33, 34, 59, 110, 114, 131, 132, 168, 171; on miracles, 39, 42–43; on natural religion, 43; epistemology, 43; on history of religions, 43–44; on morals, 44–45

Hutcheson, Francis, 131

Huxley, T. H., 169

Idealism, 108; collapse of, 3; reaction against, 87–88; breakdown in Germany, 141; and Feuerbach, 170. *See also* Hegel; Schleiermacher

Immanentism, 134; rejected by Schleiermacher, 80; in Strauss, 154

Incarnation: Hegel on, 103; Dorner on, 280–82. *See also* Christology, kenoticism

Incarnation theology: and the Oxford Movement, 212

Individualism: and pietism, 28; and romanticism, 52–53

Innere Mission movement, 145, 192–93, 270

Inspiration. *See* Bible

Irving, Edmund, 112

Jacobi, F. H., 112

Jacobism, 129

James, William, 60, 119

Jamison, A. Leland, 11n

Jerusalem, J. F. W., 37; and religious experience, 38

Jewish religion: in Hegel, 97–98

Jowett, Benjamin, 167, 186n; on the Bible, 168–69; on Maurice, 241

Justification: Newman on, 214

Kähler, Martin, 8, 18, 144, 190, 218

Kahnis, K. F. August, 194

Kant, Immanuel, 5, 21, 33, 49, 52, 59, 62, 77, 108, 112, 114, 116n, 119, 128, 150, 153, 162; and pietism, 30; and Enlightenment, 32, 45; and religious toleration, 32; on morality and religion, 34, 46, 47; critique of reason, 45; on the arguments for God's existence, 45–46, on natural theology, 46; on radical evil, 47; on Jesus, 47; theology after him, 47–48; and Coleridge, 117–18; and Kierkegaard, 313

Kattenbusch, Ferdinand, 9

Keble, John, 209, 210; on doctrinal tradition, 213

Kenoticism, 194; in Germany, 146, 233; and Biedermann, 165; collapse of, 239–40; and Dorner, 278. *See also* Thomasius, Gottfried

Kierkegaard, Søren, 3, 7, 9, 13, 88, 105, 143, 144, 145, 170, 198, 272; God-man paradox, 6; and subjectivism, 61; and nineteenth-century theology, 292, 313; on New Testament Christianity, 296, 298; on discipleship, 297; on the heterogeneity of Christianity, 297; on contemporaneity with Christ, 297–98; the aesthetic and the ethical, 299–301; the three stages of existence, 299–303; the religious sphere, 301–02; critique of Hegel, 303–07; and irrationalism, 304; on historical knowledge, 305–06; on objective truth, 307–08; on truth as subjectivity, 307–14; on biblical criticism, 308–09; on Christology, 310–11; on the paradox of faith, 311–12; on original sin, 313–14

Kingsley, Charles, 186n, 250

Kirchentag of 1848, 192n

Kliefoth, Theodor, 143, 194, 195, 197

Kohlbrügge, F. H., 11n, 194n

Kottwitz, Baron von, 24, 192, 218n

Krafft, Johann, 192

Krauth, Charles Philip, 200

Krauth, Charles Porterfield, 200, 218

Kulturprotestantismus, 7, 62

Labadie, Jean de, 23

Lamennais, Félicité de, 13

Lange, Friedrich Albert, 142

Leger, Johann, 23

Leibniz, G. W., 40

Lessing, Gotthold Ephraim, 13, 54, 108, 124, 168, 306n, 308; on religious tolera-

Lessing, Gotthold Ephraim (*continued*)
tion, 32; on the historicity of the Bible,
41; on natural religion, 49–50; transition
from the Enlightenment, 49–51; on the
historicity of religion, 50–51; attack on
biblicism, 51; beginnings of romanticism, 52

Lewes, G. H., 184

Liberal Catholicism, 19; and Maurice, 242

Liberalism, 190; and the Oxford Movement, 210–11

Liberal theology, 18, 20; and Schleiermacher, 85; and Maurice, 242; and
Bushnell, 259, 263n

Lichtenberger, F. A., 9

Liddon, Henry Parry, 169, 193; and confessionalism, 204–05; on Christology,
205–07

Liebner, Karl T. A., 142, 273

Lightfoot, J. B., 124, 169

Livingston, James C., 12

Locke, John, 12, 49, 131; influence on
Edwards, 26; and rational religion, 30–
31; and natural religion, 35–36

Loetscher, Lefferts A., 11n

Löhe, Wilhelm, 143, 194, 197

Lücke, Friedrich, 63, 142, 269n

Ludlow, J. M., 250

Luther, Martin, 60, 78, 196, 273n, 295, 297;
1817 revival of, 15; Feuerbach on, 176n.
See also Erlangen theology

Lutheran confessionalism, 193, 230; in
Germany, 194–98; and biblical inspiration, 195–96; on the church, 196–97; in
America, 200–01; and the Oxford Movement, 207–08

Lux Mundi, 13, 19, 204

McCosh, James: on Darwinism, 204n

McGiffert, A. C., 13–14

Mackintosh, Hugh Ross, 9

Mansel, H. L.: debate with Maurice, 253–
55

Marheineke, Philipp Konrad, 101n, 142

Martensen, H. L., 8, 142, 273, 292, 293

Martineau, James, 112, 254; on Maurice,
241

Marx, Karl, 88, 170, 176

Materialism, 141, 187; and Feuerbach, 170

Maurice, Frederick Denison, 3, 21, 124,
144, 145, 146, 186n, 187, 228, 282; and
the question of Christ, 6; and subjectivism, 60; disciple of Coleridge, 112,
243, 244; and the Broad Church, 242,
246; and theological systems, 242–43;
and Platonism, 244; on sectarianism,
244–45; and the Oxford Movement,
245–46, 252; on the nature of truth, 245,
246; and Christology, 247–53; and evangelicalism, 248, 252; on grace and sin,
249–50; on the Trinity, 249; and Christian Socialism, 250–51; on the Church
of England, 251–53; on the sacraments,
252; and *Essays and Reviews*, 256; on
revelation in the Bible, 255–57; and
biblical criticism, 257

Melanchthon, Philip, 196

Menken, Gottfried, 11n, 24, 25, 198n, 218n

Mercersburg theology, 144, 145, 194, 207;
and romanticism, 52; and ecumenism,
228–33. *See also* Schaff, Philip; Nevin,
John W.

Methodism: in England, 109. *See also*
Wesley, John

Michaelis, J. D., 37

Middle Ages, 61, 297

Mildert, Van, 123n

Mill, John Stuart, 142, 183, 184; on Bentham and Coleridge, 110; on Christianity, 185; on utilitarian religion, 185–86

Ministry: in Lutheran confessionalism,
197

Miracles, 36, 50n; Enlightenment questioning of, 39; Hume on, 42; meaning
of in Schleiermacher, 79n

Möhler, Johann Adam, 228, 270

Moore, E. C., 12

Moralism: and religion, 29; and the Enlightenment, 34

Moravian pietism, 27

Moravians: and religious fellowship, 28;
emphasis on Jesus, 29

Mosheim, Johann Lorentz von, 36

Müller, Adam: and romanticism, 52

Müller, Julius, 24, 144, 218, 219, 269n;
theology of mediation, 271–72; critique
of Schleiermacher and Hegel, 272; and
Kierkegaard, 313

Myth, 61, 62; Strauss's conception of, 148–
49; for Rothe, 289.

National history: and theology, 9–16

Naturalism, 141; and Schleiermacher, 79

Natural religion: and rationalism, 34;

Christianity and, 34–39; and Locke, 35–36; destruction of by Hume and Kant, 42–48; in Lessing 49–50; Hegel and, 96–97

Nature: Enlightenment view of, 33–34; for Emerson, 178

Neander, August, 196, 218n, 230

Neologen, 51; and natural religion, 37; and original sin, 40; Lessing's criticism of, 50

Neopietism, 192, 218; of Menken, 25; in Germany, 144; and Erlangen theology, 218; and mediation theology, 271–72; and Kierkegaard, 292. *See also* pietism

Nevin, John Williamson, 16; and Mercersburg theology, 227–28; on sectarianism, 229; on Christology, 230, on history of the church, 230–31; on Eucharist, 231

New Haven theology. *See* Taylor, Nathaniel William

Newman, John Henry, 143, 145, 186, 210, 212, 230; and romanticism, 52; and the illative sense, 61, 217; on German Protestantism, 208; spiritual and intellectual character of, 209; on liberalism, 210; on apostolic succession, 213; the *via media,* 213–15; on justification, 214; on scripture and tradition, 214; *Tract 90,* 214n; on religious assent, 215–17; and Coleridge, 216

Newton, Isaac, 35

Nicene Creed, 205

Nitzsch, Carl Immanuel, 59, 142, 146, 269n; and the beginning of mediation theology, 270–71

Norton, Andrews, 132n

Novalis: and romanticism, 52; on feeling, 53

Oberlin theology, 144

Objectivism: and Lutheran confessionalism, 194–98; and Beck, 198–99; and Kierkegaard, 307–08

Olshausen, Hermann, 24

Original sin: Wesley and Whitefield on, 27; and rationalism, 34; question in Enlightenment thought, 39–40; Schleiermacher on, 82–83; Hegel on, 102; Coleridge on, 118; Taylor on, 130–31; Emerson on, 179; in Erlangen theology, 218–19; Tholuck on, 218–19; Maurice on,

249–50; Bushnell on, 263–65; Rothe on, 287–88; Kierkegaard on, 313–14

Orthodoxy: and evangelicalism, 25. *See also* confessionalism

Oxford Movement, 13, 14, 15, 19, 143, 145, 194, 204, 227; revival of theology in England, 3, 6; and romanticism, 52; and Lutheran confessionalism, 197n; and reform, 208, 210; and biblical criticism, 209; reaction to Temporalities Bill (1833), 210; and liberalism, 210–11; and evangelicalism, 211–12; and incarnational theology, 212; and supernaturalism, 212–13; on dogmatic tradition, 213; and Maurice, 245–46, 252

Paine, Thomas, 129n

Paley, William, 36, 109n, 110, 114, 133, 137; on natural religion, 33–34; Coleridge on, 110–11

Palmer, Elihu, 129n

Pantheism, 79; relation to Schleiermacher, 80–81; and Hegel, 104; rejected by Coleridge, 120–21; and Strauss, 154; and Dorner, 277

Parker, Theodore, 133, 142, 179, 180n; on Christianity, 182–83; and Emerson, 183; and social reform, 183; and Transcendentalism, 183

Pascal, Blaise, 35, 39, 60, 119

Pattison, Mark, 169; on Coleridge, 113

Peace of Westphalia (1648), 193

Pfleiderer, Otto, 11, 18, 21

Philippi, F. A., 194, 195

Philosophical theology: in Schleiermacher, 70

Pietism, 22, 59, 60, 69, 108–09; eighteenth-century German, 15; influence on theology, 21; meaning of, 22–23; and the Moravian brotherhood, 24; at the University of Halle, 24; in Württemberg, 24; relation to evangelicalism, 24–25; expression of theological mood, 26–27; and religious fellowship, 28; and individualism, 28; and morality, 29; emphasis on Jesus, 29–30; influence on Ritschl, 30; influence on Schleiermacher, 30; and modern culture, 190–91. *See also* neopietism

Pius IX, 143, 190

Platonic method: and Maurice, 244

Plenitude: principle of, in romanticism, 54–55

Pluralism, religious, 193

Polemics: Schleiermacher on, 70

Pope, Alexander: on nature, 33

Positive religion: Lessing on, 51; Schleiermacher on, 67–68; Hegel on, 92

Powell, Baden, 168

Practical theology: Schleiermacher on, 70; and evangelicalism, 110

Priestly, Joseph, 113

Princeton theology, 3, 143, 193. *See also* Hodge, Charles

Protestantism: Schleiermacher on, 68; and Hegel, 87; and Mercersburg theology, 232–33

Puritanism: and pietism, 23

Pusey, Edward Bouverie, 208; and Oxford Movement, 209, 210

Puseyism: and Mercersburg theology, 228

Rationalism, 22, 108, 153, 187, 190n, 192; and Edwards, 26; Hegel's critique of, 88; and Coleridge, 119; and Baur, 159; and Schaff, 229; Bushnell's critique of, 261. *See also* Enlightenment; natural religion

Reardon, Bernard M. G., 11, 13

Reconciliation: doctrine of, in Hegel, 103

Reformation, 145, 153; Hegel on, 100; Mercersburg theology on, 232–33; Rothe on, 290–91

Reform Bill of 1832, 108, 193

Reformed confessionalism, 194n

Reid, Thomas, 131

Reimarus, Hermann, 49, 50, 51, 124; on natural religion, 38; on miracles, 39; on historicity of the Bible, 41

Reinhold, F., 59n

Religious controversies: and rationalism, 31

Religious toleration: and the Enlightenment, 32

Repristination, 59n, 61–62; and Lutheran confessionalism, 195

Revelation, 5, 59; and natural religion, 36–38; Lessing on, 51; Herder on, 54; nineteenth-century reinterpretation of, 60–62; Schleiermacher on, 66–68; Hegel on, 94, 99; Coleridge on, 126; Taylor and Channing on, 136–37; Beck on, 199;

Maurice on, 253–57; Bushnell on, 261–62; Rothe on, 288–89. *See also* biblical criticism

Revivalism, 59, 108–09; influence on theology, 21; in America, 128–29, 144, 192; in Germany, 144, 192–93; and conservatism, 191–93; Mercersburg theology on, 229–30

Revolutions of 1848, 141, 190n, 283

Ripley, George, 180n

Ritschl, Albrecht, 3, 4, 7, 13, 144, 196, 218, 225, 239, 273n, 282; and pietism, 30; school of, 48; on religious knowledge, 60

Roman Catholicism, 143, 190, 193; and Mercersburg theology, 232–33. *See also* Catholicism

Roman Catholic theology: in the nineteenth century, 1n

Roman religion: Hegel on, 98–99

Romanticism, 22, 69, 108; and literature, 3; and Edwards, 26; and Schleiermacher, 55; and Hegel, 88–89; and Emerson, 178; and Oxford Movement, 207n

Rose, Hugh James, 208

Rothe, Richard, 7, 142, 144, 145, 218, 269n; and pietism, 24; originality in theology, 282–83; influence of Schleiermacher, 283; and German Protestant Union, 283; and confessionalism, 283–84; and evolution, 287–88; on sin, 287–88; on revelation, 288–89; and Christology, 289n; on religious knowledge, 289–90; on the church as moral community, 290–91; on the Reformation, 290–91

Rousseau, Jean Jacques, 8, 135; on original sin, 40; place in eighteenth-century scene, 48–49; and romanticism, 52; on emotions, 53

Rückert, Johann Michael Friedrich, 219

Sabatier, Auguste, 13

Sack, A. F. W., 37

Sack, K. H., 272

Sacraments: and Lutheran confessionalism, 197; and Oxford Movement, 213; place in church (Maurice), 252

Salvation history: Hofmann and Erlangen theology on, 221–23

Sartorius, Ernst Wilhelm Christian, 59n, 234

Schaeder, Erich, 9n

Schaff, Philip, 16; and Mercersburg theology, 227–28; on rationalism and sectarianism, 229; on church history, 230–31

Schelling, Friedrich, 88, 108, 112, 119, 120, 148; and romanticism, 52; on philosophy and religion, 91, 92

Schenkel, Daniel, 166, 273

Schiller, Friedrich, 52; on plenitude and diversity, 54–55

Schlegel, Friedrich, 52

Schleiermacher, Friedrich Daniel Ernst, 5, 21, 26, 59, 87, 91, 100, 104, 108, 119, 120, 124, 127n, 137, 142, 144, 146, 148, 150, 151, 152, 154, 155, 160, 166, 168, 170, 173, 211, 219, 230, 279; beginning of theological era, 1–2; christocentric principle of, 6, 83–85; and German culture, 15; and pietism, 24, 30, 62; on original sin and grace, 27, 76, 82–83; enlargement of Kant, 48; on individualism, 52–53; on diversity, 55; on religious self-consciousness, 60, 62, 72; on demythologizing theology, 61–62; on theological assertions, 62; on culture theology, 62–63; on feeling, 62–67; on role of the church, 67–68; on the object of religion, 67; on religion and history, 67; on the philosophy of religion, 69–70; on historical, philosophical, and practical theology, 70; on other religions, 71; on ecclesiology, 71; on dogmatics, 72; definition of Christianity, 73; scheme for the *Glaubenslehre*, 74–75; on God, 76–79; on redemption, 77, 83; on miracles, 79n; on naturalism and supernaturalism, 79; and pantheism, 80–81; historicity of the church, 84; authority of Scripture, 85; the theologian, 86; contrast with Hegel, 106–07; and Coleridge, 113; and Baur, 156; and Biedermann, 162; and mediation theology, 269–70; Müller's critique of, 272; influence on Dorner, 274–76; and Rothe, 283; and Kierkegaard, 313

Schmidt, Martin, 9

Schmucker, Samuel S., 200

Schweitzer, Albert, 38

Schweizer, Alexander, 146, 160; and mediation theology, 271

Science: and theology, 31; and nature, 33

Scottish philosophy, 128, 135, 144; influence on Taylor, 131; influence on Hodge, 202

Sectarianism: and Mercersburg theology, 229; Maurice on, 244–45

Secularization: and the Enlightenment, 34

Semler, J. S., 13, 24, 37, 41, 148

Simon, Richard: on authority of the Bible, 40–41

Slavery, 110, 145, 193, 228; Parker on, 183

Smith, H. Shelton, 11

Smith, James W., 11n

Social Gospel, 19; ethical emphasis of, 7

Social reform: and Methodism, 109; and Transcendentalism, 183

Socinianism, 153

Sociology: Comte on, 184

Solovyov, Vladimir, 13

Somervell, D. C., 10n

Spalding, J. J., 37

Spencer, Herbert, 254

Spener, Philipp Jakob: and pietism, 23; on interiorization of truth, 27; on sanctification, 29

Spinoza, Baruch, 54, 80, 81, 104, 120; on historicity of Bible, 41

Stahl, Friedrich Julius, 194, 197

Stanley, A. P., 167, 186n

Stephan, Horst, 9

Sterling, John, 112

Stewart, Dugald, 131

Storr, G. C., 59n

Storr, V. F., 10n

Strauss, David Friedrich, 3, 6, 7, 88, 105, 141, 142, 145, 146, 155, 156, 161, 166, 167, 170, 171, 183, 233, 235, 265, 308; and biblical criticism, 147–48; and myth, 148–49; on the historical Jesus, 150–51; on Gospel of John, 151; on authority of Scripture, 152; on doctrinal development, 152–54; on historical theology, 152–54; and immanentism, 154; influence on Biedermann, 161

Stuart, Moses, 127n

Sturm und Drang: and romanticism, 52

Subjectivism, 60; and Schleiermacher, 77

Supernaturalism, 59n, 108, 141–42, 148; Schleiermacher on, 79; rejected by Cole-

Supernaturalism (*continued*)
ridge, 120; and Channing, 137; and Taylor, 137; Baur on, 159; and the Oxford Movement, 212–13
Swiss Union: and Biedermann, 160

Taylor, Nathaniel William, 3, 142, 144, 200; and revivalism, 26, 130–31; and New Haven theology, 127; on original sin, 130–31, 136; and the Scottish philosophy, 131; on the sovereignty of God, 131, 135; on moral agency, 133–34; and Bushnell, 136; and supernaturalism, 137; and Hodge, 202
Temporalities Bill (1833), 209–10
Tennyson, Alfred Lord, 186n
Tertullian, 144
Theodicy: question of, in Enlightenment, 39–40
Theological schools: history of, 18–20
Tholuck, Friedrich August, 11n, 24, 144, 196, 218; on sin and regeneration, 218–19
Thomasius, Gottfried, 3, 218, 219, 265; Erlangen confessionalism, 225–26; on dogmatics, 226–27, on kenoticism, 235–40
Throne and altar: in Lutheran confessionalism, 197–98
Tieck, Ludwig, 52
Tillich, Paul, 4, 9
Tillotson, John: on religious moralism, 34; on natural religion, 37
Tindal, Matthew: on religious moralism, 34; on natural religion, 37
Toland, John: on natural religion, 36–37
Tract 90, 214n
Tractarian movement, 186, 193. See also Oxford Movement
Transcendentalism, 3, 142, 146; on Jesus Christ, 6; Edwards and, 26; and romanticism, 52; Channing and, 133; in America, 180n; and Parker, 183; and social reform, 183
Trinity, doctrine of: in Schleiermacher, 72; in Hegel, 100–01; in Thomasius, 239; in Maurice, 249; in Bushnell, 265; in Dorner, 276, 279
Troeltsch, Ernst, 160, 282
Tulloch, John, 10n

Twesten, August D. C., 142; and mediation theology, 271

Ullmann, Karl, 142, 146, 269n; and mediation theology, 270–71
Ultramontanism, 214
Umbreit, F. W. K., 142
Unitarianism, 109, 146; on Christ, 6; in America, 127; Channing on, 132–35; Emerson on, 180, 182
Utilitarianism, 184; and rationalism, 34; Paley and Bentham on, 111

Via media: Newman and, 213–15
Victorian age, 3; and skepticism, 184–85, 191; and progress, 184–85; Carlyle on, 187; time of transition, 190–91
Vilmar, August, 11n, 194, 196, 197, 218
Vinet, Alexander, 273
Voltaire, François Marie Arouet de: on religious toleration, 32; on miracles, 39; on original sin, 40

Wackenroder, W. H., 52
Walther, C. F. W., 200
Ward, William George, 214
Ware, Henry, 132n, 134
Webb, C. C. J., 10n
Weisse, C. H., 142
Wesley, Charles, 27
Wesley, John, 8, 52; his revival, 15; and pietism, 23; on internationalization of truth, 25; on original sin, 27; on sanctification, 29
Westcott, B. F., 167, 169
Westminster Confession, 201
Wette, W. M. L., de, 148, 150, 183; and Kant, 48
Whateley, Richard, 186n
Whitefield, George, 8; and evangelicalism, 26; on original sin, 27; on preaching, 27–28
Wichern, J. H.: and *Innere Mission*, 192–93
Wilberforce, Robert Isaac, 208, 209, 210, 228, 230
Wilberforce, William: and pietism, 30; and Anglican evangelicals, 109
Willey, Basil, 10n, 18, 113

Williams, Daniel D., 10*n*

Williams, Roland, 168

Wolff, Christian, 37, 49, 54; on natural religion, 35–36

Woolston, Thomas: and radical deism, 38

Wordsworth, William, 53

World War I: end of theological era, 1–2

Worship: Hegel on, 96

Zinzendorf, Graf: and Moravian brotherhood, 24; and pietism, 27

THE BROSS FOUNDATION

In 1879, William Bross of Chicago established at Lake Forest College the Bross Foundation, the income from the fund to be used to stimulate the production of the best books or treatises "on the connection, relation and mutual bearing on any practical science, or the history of our race, or the facts in any department of knowledge, with and upon the Christian Religion." From time to time until his death in 1890, Mr. Bross made contributions to the fund, which was to serve as a memorial to his son, Nathaniel, who died in 1856.

To achieve his aim, Mr. Bross provided that competitions should be conducted every decade, the winning manuscript to be published by the Foundation. He also asked that the Trustees of the Bross Foundation purchase suitable manuscripts which it would then publish. Volumes 18, 19, and 20 are in the latter category.

Other volumes in the Bross Library include the first one, *Evidences of Christianity* by Mark Hopkins, published in 1880, *The Sources of Religious Insight* by Josiah Royce in 1911, *The Reasonableness of Christianity* by Douglas Clyde MacIntosh in 1927, *Modern Poetry and the Christian Tradition* by Amos N. Wilder in 1952, *Language and Faith: Studies in Sign, Symbol, and Meaning* by John A. Hutchison in 1963, *The Experience of Nothingness* by Michael Novak in 1970, *The Power to Be Human* by Charles C. West in 1971, and *The Event of the Qur'ān* by Kenneth Cragg also in 1971.

This work, which is designated as Volume 21, is the winner of the 1970 decennial competition.